OLD JERSEY HOUSES
II

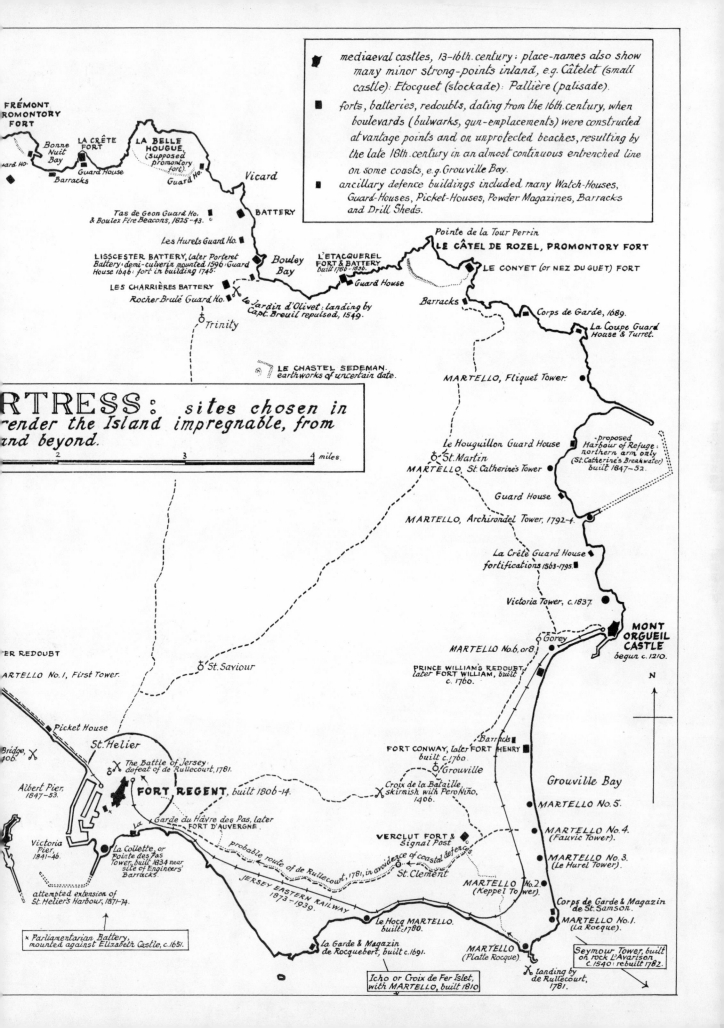

FRÉMONT PROMONTORY FORT

Bonne Nuit Bay
LA CRÊTE FORT
LA BELLE HOUGUE (supposed promontory fort)

Guard House
Barracks

Vicard

mediaeval castles, 13-16th. century: place-names also show many minor strong-points inland, e.g. Câtelet (small castle): Etocquet (stockade): Pallière (palisade).

forts, batteries, redoubts, dating from the 16th. century, when boulevards (bulwarks, gun-emplacements) were constructed at vantage points and on unprotected beaches, resulting by the late 18th. century in an almost continuous entrenched line on some coasts, e.g. Grouville Bay.

ancillary defence buildings included many Watch-Houses, Guard-Houses, Picket-Houses, Powder Magazines, Barracks and Drill Sheds.

Tas de Geon Guard Ho. & Boulex Fire Beacons, 1825-43.
Les Hurets Guard Ho.
LISSCESTER BATTERY, later Porteret Battery: demi-culverin mounted 1596: Guard House 1846: fort in building 1745.
LES CHARRIÈRES BATTERY
Rocher Brulé Guard Ho.
BATTERY
Bouley Bay
L'ETACQUEREL FORT & BATTERY built 1788-1836.
Guard House
Le Jardin d'Olivet: landing by Capt. Breuil repulsed, 1549.
Trinity

Pointe de la Tour Perrin
LE CÂTEL DE ROZEL, PROMONTORY FORT
LE CONYET (or NEZ DU GUET) FORT
Barracks
Corps de Garde, 1689.
La Coupe Guard House & Turret.

LE CHASTEL SEDEMAN. earthworks of uncertain date.

MARTELLO, Fliquet Tower.

RTRESS: *sites chosen in render the Island impregnable, from nd beyond.*

2   3   4 miles

Le Houguillon Guard House
St. Martin
MARTELLO, St. Catherine's Tower.

proposed Harbour of Refuge: northern arm only (St. Catherine's Breakwater) built 1847-52.

Guard House
MARTELLO, Archirondel Tower, 1792-4.
La Crête Guard House fortifications 1563-1795.
Victoria Tower, c.1837.

MONT ORGUEIL CASTLE begun c.1210.

N

ER REDOUBT
ARTELLO No.1, First Tower.
St. Saviour

Gorey
MARTELLO No.6, or 8.
PRINCE WILLIAM'S REDOUBT, later FORT WILLIAM, built c.1760.

Picket House
St. Helier
Bridge, 406.
The Battle of Jersey: defeat of de Rullecourt, 1781.
Albert Pier, 1847-53.
FORT REGENT, built 1806-14.
La Garde du Hâvre des Pas, later FORT D'AUVERGNE.
Victoria Pier, 1841-46.
La Collette, or Pointe des Pas Tower, built 1834 near site of Engineers' Barracks.
attempted extension of St. Helier's Harbour, 1871-74.

x Parliamentarian Battery, mounted against Elizabeth Castle, c.1651.

Probable route of de Rullecourt, 1781, in avoidance of coastal defences
JERSEY EASTERN RAILWAY 1873-1939.

Le Hocq MARTELLO. built 1780.
La Garde & Magazin de Rocquebert, built c.1691.

Icho or Croix de Fer Islet, with MARTELLO, built 1810

Barracks
FORT CONWAY, later FORT HENRY, built c.1760.
Grouville
Croix de la Bataille: skirmish with Pero Niño, 1406.
VERCLUT FORT & Signal Post
St. Clement

Grouville Bay

MARTELLO No.5.
MARTELLO No.4. (Fauvic Tower).
MARTELLO No.3. (Le Hurel Tower).
MARTELLO No.2. (Keppel Tower).
Corps de Garde & Magazin de St. Samson.
MARTELLO No.1. (La Rocque).

MARTELLO (Platte Rocque).

MARTELLO (Platte Rocque).
x landing by de Rullecourt, 1781.

Seymour Tower, built on rock L'Avarison c.1540: rebuilt 1782.

a. La Hougue (P)

b. Initialled stone at Lowlands (P)

OLD JERSEY HOUSES

and
THOSE WHO LIVED IN THEM

Volume II
from 1700 onwards

by
JOAN STEVENS

Drawings by
CHARLES STEVENS

PHILLIMORE

1977

Published by
PHILLIMORE & CO. LTD.
London and Chichester

Head Office: Shopwyke Hall,
Chichester, Sussex, England

ISBN 0 85033 269 9

*Like its predecessor, this volume is dedicated
to you who live in these Jersey houses, without whose
co-operation my work, which has been a joy, would have
been impossible.*

Printed in Great Britain by
UNWIN BROTHERS LTD.
at The Gresham Press, Old Woking, Surrey

CONTENTS

LIST OF ILLUSTRATIONS
Photographs

(The initial letter after the name of a house denotes the parish in which it is situated)

Drawings

FOREWORD

by

SIR ROBERT MARETT, K.C. M. G., O. B. E.

HAVING BEEN ONE of the original sponsors of the first volume of *Old Jersey Houses*—I was far away in Peru when Joan Stevens wrote to me about the book, but knowing her so well I never had any doubt about its success—I am honoured to be asked to write the foreword to the long-awaited second volume of this invaluable work.

The first volume dealt with the period 1500 to 1700, when, as Lord Coutanche pointed out in his foreword, most of our ancestors were still leading the life of simple yeoman farmers. In the period covered by this second volume two important tendencies combined to change quite drastically both the character of the Island and its architecture. In the first place Jersey became progressively more wealthy through the development of a flourishing shipping industry, with the balance of power shifting away from the land-owning Seigneurs to the merchants. Secondly, and equally important, the Island increasingly looked to England rather than to France for inspiration and supplies, partly because of the constant wars between England and France, but also for religious and commercial reasons. As the Island became more anglicised, so also did the architecture and furnishing of its houses, without, however, losing their distinctive Jersey character.

In the first part of this volume there is a series of fascinating chapters on the way of life of the islanders, based on painstaking research by the author among the papers of a number of Jersey families, including, I am glad to say, those of my own La Haule branch of the Marett family. A single sentence in a diary can convey a wealth of information about the times in which the writer lived; for example an entry in his diary shows my ancestor Edouard Marett (1691-1758) in the depth of despair because one of his ships had been seized in France; his son Philippe (1744-1826) records that on a single day he paraded with the Militia in the morning, made hay in the afternoon and in the evening enjoyed himself at the quadrille.

From a wide cross-section of such family records Joan Stevens makes our ancestors come alive —solid down-to-earth folk, who either farmed their own land, or as merchants and sailors, reaped the harvest of the sea. Those who remained in the Island, whatever their occupation, were always ready to give honorary service to the Militia, to the parish and to the States. And on top of all these activities the records make it clear that these tough old ancestors of ours still managed to lead a gay social life.

In the second part of the book the author examines the rich architectural heritage that our property-loving ancestors have bequeathed for the enjoyment of future generations. The history and architectural features of many Jersey houses, large and small, are described in meticulous detail, and accompanied by the most beautiful drawings by Charles Stevens, and photographs, most of which were produced by members of the gifted Stevens family. With so many old houses being pulled down, or converted almost beyond recognition, the book provides an invaluable record of the past, and it will increase in value as the years go by.

I have no hesitation in saying that the two volumes of *Old Jersey Houses* should have a place in the library of everybody who cares about Jersey and its heritage.

Mon Plaisir,   ROBERT MARETT
La Haule

PREFACE

TWELVE YEARS have elapsed since Volume I of *Old Jersey Houses* appeared. This was an attempt to record the houses built in Jersey before 1700, and the life of those who lived in them, and to show both to ourselves and to the outside world that we had something of which we could be proud, to tell the owners of these houses what they had in their possession, and to record all information that had been found at that time, lest some should perish without record.

In 1676 John Bunyan wrote ". . . some said John print it, others said not so. Some said 'It might do good', others said no. Now I was in a strait and did not see which was the best thing to be done by me. At last I thought, since you are thus divided, I will print it, and so the case decided". The would-be author of 1976 is in a similar dilemma and has come to the same decision.

There is both good and bad news to report since Volume I appeared. The book had more success than one ever dared to hope, and it does seem to have encouraged owners to value what they hold; but some houses have suffered and there are those which have been over-restored, and so have lost their simple vernacular character, whilst too many others have been demolished in the name of progress.

The style of local architecture changed very suddenly around 1700 and this book will try to describe the transition, how and why it occurred and what effect it had. The lives of those who lived in these houses will be shown from the evidence of contemporary documents. Jersey families are rich in manuscript material, and it is from these collections, rather than from published works, that the facts and impressions offered to you in these pages have been taken. Precise references are not given in the entries quoted; so many have come from private collections that are not accessible to the public, that this would be pointless, and in any case owners might not wish such information to be given. But you have my assurance that every fact quoted has been drawn from a genuine local document.

This rich harvest of information would not have been available without the co-operation and generous trust of the owners of the documents. The collections are many but the largest to be drawn upon are those of St. Ouen's Manor, La Haule Manor, La Hague Manor, Le Couteur of Belle Vue, le Fief de Meleches, Le Colombier Manor, Colonel A. G. de Carteret, Mr. G. E. de Carteret, and my own, the Collas documents. Those from La Hague Manor and Bell Vue have been generously given to La Société Jersiaise by Miss M. E. Le Cornu and the Sumner family respectively, and some others quoted are also in the Museum library.

Direct quotations are given in their original spelling, and usually in French. In general these have not been translated, unless there are unusual words which might be unfamiliar to the average reader. In Volume I all quotations were translated, but when we enter the 18th century the French is, for the most part, readily understandable, though the spelling may be somewhat erratic.

In Volume I an attempt was made to mention every house known to me which exhibited characteristics dating before 1700. For the later period such complete coverage would be quite impractical. Therefore it has been necessary to take a cross-section of houses with historical interest or architectural merit, and some 264 are included. If your house is not here, the omission is in the interest of preventing this book from running into several volumes.

The condition of a house is described as it was when examined, which is not necessarily how it is now. It would be quite impossible to check every house again just before going to print, and even if one did achieve this, there would be considerable change before publication, so fast and so drastic are some alterations. But the situation as described may often be the only evidence about a house before its conversion or reconstruction. It is relevant to mention that in the opinion of the *Architect's Journal* for December 1975 a building under threat of demolition should be considered innocent until proved guilty, and the onus should be on the potential destroyer to prove why his action is necessary.

With regard to printed works, an exception has been made in quoting from some of the early guide books, in particular that of J. Stead, as his is perhaps the earliest of a long line of guide books which poured from the printing presses during the 19th century, and therefore the most rewarding for this particular study.

Two maps have been particularly helpful, the so-called Richmond map (1795) and Godfray's map (1849), the first giving all roads and fields, but no names, and the second giving no field boundaries, but showing the name of the proprietor of every house, except in the towns where even Hugh Godfray's fine copper engraving could not cope. House names, in this book, are followed by the initial of the parish; these are self explanatory, with Mt. for St. Martin and My. for St. Mary. The reference '. . . on Godfray' for each house described gives therefore, the name of the proprietor (or, rarely, the tenant) on Godfray's map.

As always, one is deeply indebted to the writers of the past, to the mass of information in the publications of la Société Jersiaise, and to early maps. Without these one would be lost, and one cannot over-estimate the help that one draws from them, and none more so than the writings of the Reverend and Mrs. Messervy.

I am grateful to Professor Nieboer for permission to reproduce the following photographs which he was so kind as to take especially for me:

> I, II b and c, IVa, XVIIIa, XXa, XXIIIa, XXXIIc.

For other photographs I am grateful to the following friends:

> Lady McKie for XVa, XIXa, XVIIIb, XXVc, XXVIIIa, XXXIa.
> Mr. M. L. Stevens for III.
> Mr. D. Bishop for XXIV.
> Mr. R. Querée for XXVa and XXIXd, and for the trouble he has taken in processing hundreds of my photographs.
> Miss S. Sandall for the trouble she has taken with Xa and c, XVb, XXd, XXIa, XXVIb, XXIXa, XXXIc, XXXIIb.
> Mr. R. Long for colour print Ib.

All the remaining photographs were taken by my son Philip, or myself.

I am grateful for co-operation, guidance and sympathy from all my dear friends at the Museum, particularly those on the Archives, History and Publications Committees; I would also mention Miss J. Arthur for many happy hours of work done together, to Mr. P. Bisson for help in tracing past owners of properties, to Mr. S. W. Bisson for help in many historical matters, to Mr. R. Long for help and guidance as Editor, and to Mrs. M. Long, to Mrs. B. de Veulle, Mrs. W. Macready and Mr. G. Drew for their patience in attending to my frequent requests, and to Mr. J. Renault to access to the Registry. There are many others who have helped me, and been willing to discuss my work with me, amongst them Mr. F. de L. Bois, Mr. R. Cox, Mr. H. Coutanche, Mr. G. Croad, Mrs. F. Le Sueur, Mr. R. Mayne, Mr. I. Monins, Mr. B. Pipon, Mr. A. Podger, Mr. J. Taylor and Mrs. D. Wallbridge, as well as the many others who have been willing to give information about their families and their properties.

But most of all I thank my family for their forbearance with my endless talk about Jersey houses and their problems; my son John who drew me some ground plans and gave architectural advice, my daughter Collette who can always give advice about horses, my son Philip who took so much trouble with photography, and drew my attention to some apposite quotations from both sides of the Channel, and my son Richard for his records and drawings of the threshing house at Avranches. But above all I thank my husband, Charles, for giving all his spare time for about two years making drawings, and for being my constant mentor and guide, for proof reading and help with indexing and cataloguing initialled stones.

To them all I am indeed grateful, and not least to my old friend Sir Robert Marett for consenting to write the foreword.

La Grange,
St. Mary, Jersey, 1977

PLATE I TOWNSCAPES

a. Gloucester Terrace, *c* 1835

b. Hemery Row, *c* 1800

PLATE II REGENCY ST HELIER

a. Almorah Crescent, *c* 1840

b. Havre des Pas

c. Detail of ironwork

Part One

THE BACKGROUND

"... these curiosities would be quite forgott did not such idle fellowes
as I am putt them downe."

JOHN AUBREY (1626–1697)

CHAPTER ONE

THE AFTERMATH

*"Nothing would give so just an idea of an age as genuine
letters; nay, history waits for its last seal from them."*

—HORACE WALPOLE (1717-97)

IT WAS NATURAL, and indeed it was a hope expressed in Volume I, that more information on older houses would be forthcoming as a result of the earlier survey.

This has now come about, and for two reasons. Apart from another decade of research, one cause is that discoveries have since been made about houses not then examined, or unsuspected of being of early date. Another cause is the vast amount of reconstruction, as well as demolition, that we have seen in recent years, which has uncovered hidden treasures in the way of fireplaces, windows, window frames, and in one case, a bénitier. So these additional houses, or in some cases, additional information about some already described, is now offered, in spite of the fact that it may belie the title of "houses built after 1700." To omit them for this technicality would, it is felt, be a pity, so they are included at the risk of a criticism of inconsistency. One cannot, as a wise one-time President of the Island Development Committee once said, be both reasonable and consistent at the same time.

It was stated in Volume I that the local style of architecture changed drastically and very suddenly around 1700, and nothing discovered since then has altered that verdict. Exceptions? Yes, of course there are exceptions, as there always will be in human affairs. But for the most part, from 1700, we in Jersey ceased to make round arches, the glory of our local architecture, and turned to straight-topped, unchamfered doorways and windows; the latter gradually increased in size as glass became available to a larger section of the community, and wooden staircases replaced the stone tourelles. Decoration in granite, except for some heraldic devices, disappeared and the stonemason's art was confined to the ubiquitous marriage stones.

So, having rejected the architectural style of the 17th century, with what did later builders replace it? The new fashion was a symmetrically-balanced granite house of Georgian proportions. It is often said that all Jersey houses are exactly alike, and so there is no point in describing more than one example. The same criticism is sometimes levelled at the Gothic cathedrals of France, and it is the task of this book to prove that the former taunt is no more justified than the latter.

Admittedly the basic design does not vary very much, until the late Georgian and Victorian

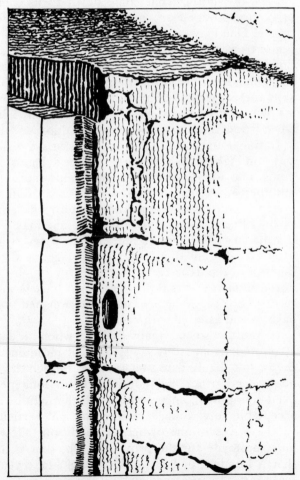

*socket for bar to door; Le Bel, St. Ouen:
(a house lately destroyed by fire).*

1

de Carteret stone, formerly in base of wall of a shop north of St. John's Church.

2

fashions introduced styles into Jersey which are in no way vernacular, that is to say, typically regional. These styles will, however, be included and illustrated insofar as they are a part of the local scene, but they are a manifestation of changing conditions and, above all, a shift from France to England for inspiration and for supplies. There were four main reasons for this: one was continuous war between England and France (though this was nothing new); another was the gradual improvement in communications, accelerated by the introduction of steamships, the first one being seen in Jersey waters in 1823; then Jersey was entirely Anglican or nonconformist, and Catholicism was deeply feared, and so Jersey families who wished to send their sons away for schooling or university, greatly preferred to send them to a Protestant environment. Perhaps most of all, it was shipping which brought about the change; this was to Canada mainly, but our ships also traded through English ports. So one might say that patriotism, religion and commerce all combined to bend our interests to the north rather than to the south.

As the work of the stonemason became, not less skilful, but certainly less ornate, the work of the carpenter increased in quality. There may have been good woodwork in our 17th century houses, but nothing has come down to us comparable with the Tudor workmanship of England, or contemporary work in Normandy or Brittany, and such fragments as have survived are very simple. One may cite a door to a 1686 arch from La Fosse (T), and a shutter attached to a window frame from Ville à l'Evêque (T), of comparable age. The Governor's and Bailiff's chairs in the Royal Court must be early, though there is no documentary evidence concerning them.

Perhaps the megalithic tradition for using vast blocks of granite for lintels and steps may have kept the carpenter at bay, but he certainly came into his own, and showed such skill as we can only admire, when wooden staircases became the fahion.

Dating houses, and items in them, is a risky business, and one takes one's courage in one's hands in so doing. Our wealth of dated stones helps enormously, but they must be interpreted with care. If all other evidence confirms the announcement on a date stone, such as Beechfield (T), for example, one may accept it at its face value. On the other hand a dated stone so often recalls an alteration, a marriage, a date of inheritance, purchase, an anniversary, or any of a dozen human events the owner might have wished to record. So the evidence must be weighed in the balance and assessed with care.

It must also be realised that when a date is attributed to an item, say a style of moulding, it is the *earliest* likely date that is given, though the form might, and often did, continue for a long period, overlapping with a new fashion, which might be more acceptable to a younger generation, and particularly to the wives of the owners. In addition, allowance must be made for the provincial gap, that is to say that a London, or Paris, fashion might take years to reach a distant province, and all the more so to reach a remote island with conservative tastes. As time went on, and there was more communication with England,

a 16th century window at Badier.

3

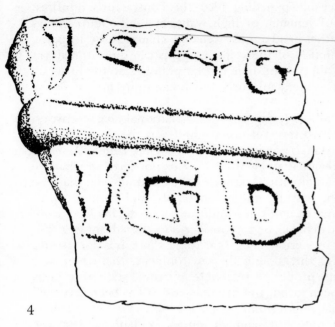

gable-stone of Jean Grandin, at Mont Pellier, (T).

4

and easier travelling facilities, this gap doubtless narrowed, and probably by the mid-Victorian era, fashions reached us almost as soon as they arrived in any provincial town the size of St. Helier. The latest news from the metropolis would have been spread by the members of each regiment arriving for garrison duty, too.

The absence of information about architects working in the Island is rather puzzling, especially as fine and quite sophisticated work was being done by about 1800. We know that Richard Bentley (1708-82) of Strawberry Hill fame, visited Jersey when financial embarrassment drove him from England, and that he drew a design for the "Cohue or Town House in St. Helier, Jersey 1753", and that Horace Walpole thought it had been accepted by the States. Examination of the Court House actually built between 1764-68 in later engravings, and in Copley's painting of "The Death of Major Peirson" (1781) suggests that Bentley's design was not used, though it may have formed a basis for the eventual building.

It seems as though we must have had a series of gifted builders, who worked, perhaps, through some of the many pattern books that were available to guide the amateur. But as such designs often only gave an elevation and plan, they must indeed have been skilful craftsmen who constructed our buildings from them. One such was Amice Norman, who was commissioned by the States to prepare a plan and model for the new prison, which was being contemplated in 1809, though the actual architect was Capt. Prott, R.E. Norman was described as "Maître charpentier", and a man who could be responsible for such a building as the prison must have built many others, and one is bound to wonder which they were. Evidence is not forthcoming, and one can only guess, but his name comes to mind when one is examining some of the superior houses build in the first half of the century.

He died at his home in Hilgrove Lane in 1834 at the age of 63, and so was born in 1771. In June 1834 *Le Constitutionel* says that his death left a void in society, and that he was one of the best architects which the Island had produced.

Later, Philippe de la Mare (1818-89) became the best-known local builder, constructing, apart from some houses, La Collette Martello Tower (1824), the "B" block at the Prison (1838), and the Masonic Temple in Stopford Road. The Victoria and Albert Piers, the former costing £280,000 and the latter £549,000, were built by another Philippe de la Mare, born 1823.*

So much building and alteration has taken place in Jersey since the last war, and even more so in the last few years, a decade of demolition and bonfires. This is not the first generation to destroy the monuments of the past, but the difference is the pace. It is now possible to demolish a house in days, or lay low a district in weeks. Since Volume I of this work was prepared, a distressing number of local buildings have gone, and many others altered out of recognition. This survey has been a decade in preparation, and it may be that some details, and even the houses, have disappeared before publication, but one can only describe the *status quo* when an examination was made.

It is a pity that some alterations that make a house more pleasant for the inmates so spoil its outer appearance. In this category one may mention huge dormers, looking like packing cases dropped on the roof by a giant plane, large sightless plate glass windows (immediately veiled by curtains or venetian blinds) replacing the warm and friendly twelve-pane sash, and large glass-sectioned front doors in place of the solid security of a six-panelled wooden door. For fear of

---

*Elisabeth de la Mare Tate, her ancestry and descendants.

insect or fungus damage large areas of irreplaceable panelling feed the contractor's bonfires. Luxuriant gardens are hidden behind palisades of fencing, or high walls, making country lanes into tunnels, but no longer leafy tunnels. On the other hand a most welcome change is the stripping of deadening plaster, revealing the granite construction of the walls, and this can quite transform the appearance of a house. It would be nice if the old type of lime mortar pointing, so unobtrusive, could be employed again, instead of the modern cement mixture, which can quite dominate the visual impression of a façade.

It is serious when a country, be it never so small, as Jersey is, loses its national characteristics. Regional feeling is so vital, for what does it profit to travel if every country is the same? If you live in New York, you go to India to see the Taj Mahal, not skyscrapers. A society called "Maisons Paysannes de France" is struggling to maintain regional styles there. Let us not jettison what we have, and let us remember that it is not only the architectural façade of the buildings that matters; it is that combined with a feeling for proportion, texture, colour, materials, and harmony with the landscape. Naturally one should not be dogmatic, and one would not want to live in a community in which freeholders were not free, and it behoves us to consider also the advantages that have come to Jersey during this most prosperous period. For one thing there is a far greater awareness of historical value, and of the dangers threatening the environment, than there was twenty years ago. Also there is no doubt that some properties that were in a sorry state of neglect, and had very little hope of being repaired, have been saved, and in some cases it has been very well done. It is my opinion (and I must accept personal responsibility for all these views) that the best restorations have been where there was just, but only just, enough money available, so that the structure had been repaired, and the house made comfortable, but its essential character has been preserved. If a castle is desired, a castle should be bought, and not a modest farmhouse. When "The Treatment" is given to a humble homestead, it loses its own character, gains nothing, and becomes rather ridiculous with "folie de grandeur". A censorious posterity will perhaps try to re-create what we are in danger of throwing away. Let us not risk their indictment.

In the following chapters the various aspects of Island life will be examined. Perhaps it would be true to say that Jerseymen became more in touch with the outside world, largely through trade and a post-war euphoria after Waterloo, which permitted men to build houses such as their fathers would never have considered. Power passed from the old feudal families to the successful "commercants", the nouveaux riches being only too ready to buy up the ancient fiefs, and benefit therefrom.

So through these pages the shift of emphasis will be seen, producing the unique character of the Channel Islaands, a territory adjacent to France, and speaking a tongue derived from Normandy, its people as proud of their Norman ancestry as they are of their allegiance to the British Crown.

By drawing on manuscript information, previously unpublished, it is hoped that a full picture of 18th- and early 19th-century life may be shown, in a manner more direct and more human than any official or legal evidence could furnish.

So let us take heart, and recall what a very famous visitor said in 1883: Renoir recorded that ". . . we arrived at Jersey (whose) remarkable scenery stretched out and dazzled us . . ." Would that he had recorded his impressions for posterity.

CHAPTER TWO

RELIGION

"Monsieur Pierre Seale a donné ce livre pour la chappelle qui doit etre bastie a St. Aubin moyennant la grace de dieu qui nous implorons ardement."

August 14, 1723. Account book for St. Aubin's chapel

THE OLD ORDER had changed and given place to the new, but religion continued to be a dominant and dominating factor in the life of the ordinary household.

The Reformation, reaching Jersey in a violent form in 1547, had swept away all traces of Catholicism, and Protestantism was accepted universally and with remarkable docility, the form adopted in Jersey being Calvinistic. This was not surprising for Jersey was French speaking, and among the Huguenot refugees who fled to the Island from the fierce anti-Protestant régime in France were French ministers who stepped automatically into the vacant Rectorships of Jersey parishes. Meanwhile the Island authorities saw a danger in this lack of potential Rectors, and scholarships to universities were established by the Crown and others to ensure that Jerseymen should be available for these posts in future.

It was not until 1774 that Methodism arrived in the Island, through the work of Pierre Le Sueur, a Jerseyman who had earlier emigrated to Newfoundland. He established Methodist preaching, mostly in private houses, but also at La Chapelle de Notre Dame des Pas, a mediaeval chapel which he bought in 1782. No. 15 Old Street was the home of Brackenbury, a bi-lingual Methodist preacher sent to Jersey in 1783, and it was there that John Wesley stayed, and preached, in 1787, during a visit of several days. Meeting with acute hostility to begin with, Methodism slowly gained support, and became a strong factor in local affairs, and over the period 1790–1873 there were 29 non-conformist chapels built.

The bewildering changes in religion which succeeded the Reformation were summed up thus by the Rev. Edouard Durell: ". . . Church of England under Edward VI, Catholic under Mary, Calvinistic under Elizabeth and the greater part of James I, Church of England under Charles I, Calvinistic again under Cromwell's usurpation. From the Restoration in 1660 and for nearly 150 subsequent years the Island has strictly conformed to the Church of England, but at the present time, in 1837, it contains a mixture of episcopalians and dissenters". At that time, he said, there were no foreign Protestant ministers holding Rectorships.* Stead, in 1809, observed that although the majority of islanders were Anglicans, there were also Calvinists and Arminians (i.e., anti-Calvinistic nonconformists).

The attitude to foreigners, as distinct from religious refugees, is well summed up by Daniel Messervy when he reports on the petition to the King from the townsmen in 1769, the last item of which says: "Que il ne sera point permis aux Etrangers de s'établir dans cette isle au prejudice des Habitants, excepté aux Protestants Refugiez pour cause de Religion qui sont permits et encouragez dans toutes les Domaines de Sa Majesté."†

A schedule of bye-laws dated 1715 gives strict instructions for the observance of Sunday. No one might remain in the cemetery after the bell had ceased to ring, and all persons found in a tavern after Divine Service, or drunk anywhere on a Sunday, were fined. No one was to carry burdens on a Sunday or utter blasphemous words at any time, and publicans were not permitted

---

*Falle's *History*, ed. 1837, Durell's notes, p. 440.   †Journal de Daniel Messervy, p. 87.

to sell liquor during Divine Service. Taverners had to keep at least two good beds for strangers, and they were not to permit drunkenness or blasphemy in their taverns, nor any fighting, nor keep children or servants against the wishes of their parents or employers, nor permit the poor to drink more than they could afford, and finally, no wine was to be sold that had not been tasted by the Bailiff or his Lieutenant. They probably did a brisk trade when the congregation emerged from a service to collect their horses stabled at the inn.

Dominant religion may have been, but decorous it was not. Naturally, as in all circumstances, it is the noisy minority which claims public attention, but even this liberal generation can still feel a sense of shock at some of the recorded instances of bad behaviour. For instance, in 1789, the Rector of St. Lawrence, the Reverend Amice Bisson, was accused on the day of an election for Centeniers and Constables, of behaving in a way derogatory to his character and his cloth. He had neglected to hold services, leaving this to a stranger, while he disported himself in the public house (cabaret) and had even been into the church with drunken persons, and immediately after the election "il a jetté des Huzzas" in the cemetery and assisted in chairing his chosen candidate around it. In 1739 the service in St. Clement's church was interrupted by loud talk and a quarrel between Jeanne Collas, wife of Helier Dumaresq, and Louis Bureau, and as a result they were banned from entering the church for three months. Such cases of interruption often occur, and one alleged cause was women wearing patens, a kind of overshoe with metal on the sole, which was forbidden in 1799; however, Marie Balleine, wife of Thomas Pipon continued to wear them, and most particularly on 25 May 1800, when she and her daughter came in during the reading of the second lesson, "blessant par là la décence et le bon ordre qui doivent regner en audience de la parole de Dieu."

In 1744 Elizabeth Robert caused a scandal by being drunk in church and in court. She was condemned to do penance in St. Mary's Church, by kneeling, admitting her sin and the scandal she had caused, after which she was re-admitted into the peace of the church.

Paillardise, that is the birth of an illegitimate child, was severely punished. Plees mentions that, to his surprise, bastards became legitimate by law in Jersey, if the parents married subsequently and acknowledged the child, and provided that neither party had been married at the time of the birth. In a case in 1784 witnesses were called and the girl, Jeanne Gruchy named Jean Le Brocq "pour etre son accomplice." The couple were condemned to admit their sin and the scandal they had caused, and Le Brocq was ordered to pay costs. Jeanne had to pray for forgiveness publicly, in the church, and then remain on her knees during the singing of Psalm 51, after which she was re-admitted into the peace of the church. Another couple, in 1789, came before the ecclesiastical court to ask pardon for "L'anticipation de la bénédiction de leur marriage", and they were pardoned.

The allocation of church pews caused endless trouble. In 1704 Jean Le Couteur (great great grandfather of Sir John) had the use of a certain pew in St. John's Church, but it blocked the way by which Josué Ahier went to his pew. The quarrel dragged on and in 1707 Le Couteur was excommunicated for continual contempt of court and refusal to accept the court's decisions, and this was announced at all the parish churches. This meant that he could not receive the sacrament, and all persons except his servants were ordered not to meet him or do business with him for fear of contamination. Prayers were even offered by the parish for his repentance, as they considered he stood sorely in need of their intercession. In 1708 he, with the Crown Officers, actioned all the Rectors for having published the excommunication, and all were fined, paying about £50 tournois, the money to be paid half to the Queen, a quarter to the poor and a quarter to Le Couteur, a small reward for four years of victimisation.

Church pews were identified with a particular house rather than with its occupant. For instance in 1778 the Churchwardens of St. Peter sold to Pierre Le Brocq for £10 tournois a pew, "the fourth in the Grande Chapelle to the north . . . according to the 1760 plan of pews", and Le Brocq and his heirs had possession of the pew so long as they owned their "present" house (perhaps La Fontaine). In 1787 when Pierre Patriarche exchanged a house in Mulcaster Street for Jeanne Thérèse Pradié's in New Street, the church pew changed hands at the same time. In 1801 the pew of Jean Anley in St. Peter's Church was sold to Jean de Carteret for £300 tournois including the "deniers à Dieu", that is earnest money or a deposit. In 1872 Colonel Le Cornu of La Hague recorded that he had paid £32 10s. for a pew which had been attached to La Hague for 200 years, as proved by a document of 1673 in his possession. But he admitted that the prevailing rule was that when a property changed hands by sale the pew was included, half of its value going to the Trésor and half to the former proprietor.

The church could be a firm disciplinarian when it chose. In 1759 Nicholas Anthoine, having committed an unspecified fault, contrary to Canon 52 of the Ecclesiastical Discipline, was condemned to major excommunication (a sacris et societate fidelium). The Viscount was authorised to make him prisoner, forcibly if he resisted. It is interesting to find excommunication being used at such late dates, but suspicion of anything reminiscent of popery continued, and this remained the ultimate sanction. In 1761 Jean Pipon "a literate person of Jersey" was appointed a notary and his affirmation included a declaration against popery. A certain James Bisson, living in St. Aubin in 1865 prayed to be "preserved from all idols, especially greenhouses", a startling request explained by the fact that the family was engaged in glasshouse culture and may have attended to it when they should have been in church.

Not that church attendance was unpopular, for the average parishioner valued it as a social occasion and excuse for a chance of a gossip. For many of the poor it was the only respite from work and the only opportunity for wearing a best suit or dress. It gave young people a chance to meet others of their own age, and perhaps the only chance of meeting those of the opposite sex who were not members of the family. Marriage among cousins was as much the rule as the exception, partly as parents liked to keep money and property in the family, and partly because her cousin might be the only man a girl met who was not her father or her brother, and one whom, being a member of the family, she could get to know without restraint. All this led to marriages within parishes, and up to about 1800, one can make a fair guess in which parish to search for details of a certain family, so localised were they. It has been found, however, that couples often got married away from their home parish, and it has been suggested that this was in order to avoid the "horse play" associated with weddings in country districts.

Rectors were not always popular, but we have an instance, in 1813, when the Constable of St. Peter, Jean Pipon, wrote to the Lieutenant Governor on behalf of the Reverend Mr. Ricard, who had applied to be made Chaplain to the troops at the recently erected St. Peter's Barracks. Pipon admitted that Ricard ". . . may not have adopted those respectful terms due to Your Excellency . . ." but the parishioners ardently recommended him. The outcome was not recorded but General Don's reply promised to submit the request to the Chaplain General.

Tithes or Dîmes (that is a tenth part) were due to the Church or the King, payable on both the produce of the land and the increase of farm animals. There were Great and Little Tithes, payable on arable and recently cultivated land respectively, the Great Tithes usually being due to the Crown and the Small Tithes to the Rector. But the rules governing payment, being largely traditional and unwritten, led to endless disputes in which the person paying was in genuine doubt which crops were liable and to whom the money should be paid. St. Peter's Church documents show that as early as 1598 there were 169 households owing tithes in that parish. In 1707 several Rectors were worried over the tithes due on hemp and flax which had been claimed by the Crown when the land grew corn, and so the Court decided on a judgment of Solomon, that is to say an equal division,* but the trouble arose again in 1714. In 1806 a total of 4,390 sheaves of various sorts of grain, plus 107 of peas, beans and vetch, was collected in St. Peter, and the same totals were given in 1863. In 1815 the accounts of Abraham Gibaut included £9 tournois paid to the Rector, the Reverend George du Heaume, for his "dîmes de pommes" as well as sums to the Receiver General for "dîmes de grain". In 1837 Durell noted that the Great tithes were divided, three quarters going to the King, an eighth to the Rectors and an eighth to the Dean. The Rectors used to rely on the Novales, newly cultivated land, but Durell remarks that ". . . never very considerable, they have become still more trifling since the planting of orchards and the raising of other produce has occasioned a decrease in tillage". Fields, and there are many, called Le Clos des Levées, had apple trees planted in the surrounding banks, and these were tithe free as the bank was considered to be uncultivated land.

---

*B.S.J., 1876, p. 105.

It may sometimes seem as if the Rectors were rapacious in collecting their tithes and other dues, but it must be remembered that they had no fixed stipend, and were dependant on any dues, in money or in kind, which they could collect. Whilst having but little substance, they were expected to be educated and learned, wise counsellors and devoted teachers of the young, as well as representing their flocks in the States assembly. Is it surprising that they were intent on collecting the tenth part of the apple crop, or receiving one piglet out of a litter of ten?

The parish churches held, and still hold, small accounts known as le Trésor and la Charité, which derive in part from ancient charitable bequests, given in the form of wheat rentes. The Trésor is intended for the repair and maintenance of the Parish church and rectory, and la Charité for the relief of the poor.

In 1758 steps were taken regarding the instruction of the young in the catechism. It was ordained that there would be Divine Service morning and evening, every Sunday, in every church, and parishioners were reminded that public instruction of the young was of the greatest importance. The Rectors were "assiduously to observe the rubriques given in the 15th Canon of the Ecclesiastical Constitution, wherein it was laid down that the Rectors, after public prayers, should explain some passage in Holy Writ in the morning and in the afternoon, and take the points of the catechism".

For centuries the only churches in the island were the 12 parish churches, the chapel of ease at St. Aubin being the only place of worship to be built in addition, until the mid-Victorian burst of church building. St. Aubin's chapel was erected at the expense of the founders, mostly merchants, who petitioned the Bishop of Winchester in 1716, pointing out the distance that some inhabitants had to travel to attend St. Brelade's church, and the difficulty of the journey owing to the lack of roads. It was over 30 years before services were actually held there, but it lasted for 130 years, though it was then condemned as unsafe and replaced by the present Victorian Gothic church. There were 27 original founders, and conditions were laid down about the services in 1749, by when some of the original founders were dead and others had inherited the position. A sum of £25 sterling was allocated for the Vicar, through the Rector (of St. Brelade), the exchange at that time being £14 tournois to £1 sterling. This enterprise was an excellent example of self-help, and the founders and other well-wishers all gave what they could, from silver cups and alms boxes, now very valuable, to planks of wood and tiles, rope for the bell, and cartage of material brought from town or from Wayné (Ouaisné).*

A funeral was a matter for great ceremony to our ancestors, and governed by stiff protocol. Invitations to attend were sent out, gloves and other mourning materials were supplied to the mourners, and a huge feast was prepared to follow the service. In 1854 an account was paid for a Gibaut funeral, including "deux jours a prier l'enterrement, £6", meaning the delivery of invitations to attend. In 1747 Edouard de Ste Croix supplied 60lbs. of beef and two sheep for the funeral of Jean Dumaresq of Les Augrès. In 1750 Henry Jacobson supplied for the funeral of Captain Snow 4 black laces at 3s. per yard, 3 ells of silk at 4/10, 3 yards of cloth for the church, 8 pairs of women's and 6 pairs of men's gloves, for a total of £21 tournois. In 1763 payments were made by Edouard Gibaut "pour lenteremen de son defund pere" and Jean Pinel, a butcher, provided 136lbs. of beef, and other supplies were tobacco, snuff, tea, pepper, ginger, candles and wine. In addition there were 23 verges of shroud material, 29 pairs of men's white gloves, 5 pairs of men's black gloves, 12 pairs of women's black gloves, 2 pairs of children's black gloves, 4 pairs of women's white gloves. The coffin cost £7 13s., £1 10s. was paid to the Rector for his prayers, 10s. to the Lecteur, 11s. to the gravedigger, with a drink, and £20 given to the poor, all doubtless in livres tournois. In 1774 Edouard Gibaut died, and his funeral expenses included 5 cabots of wheat, a barrel of cider, 42lbs. of beef, a payment to the gravedigger for making "la fosse", and again an amount for gloves. When François Journeaux's grandmother died in 1802 the actual burial expenses were £16, but £27 was paid for wine. In 1832 Abraham Gibaut left directions for 8 of the 12 cabots of wheat supplied to be given to the poor.

With the very intricate relationships carrying an obligation to attend many funerals, they became rather a frequent occurrence, and in February 1837 Philippe Marett attended four in one week.

Acting as a pall bearer was also important and regarded as a sacred duty. In 1819 Philippe Marett's uncle de Gruchy died and he said ". . . my poor uncle was conducted by Dan and I (as)

*St. Aubin's chapel account book.

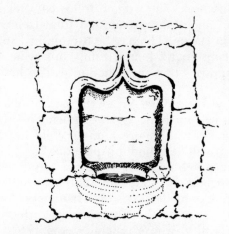

FIVE MORE BÉNITIERS
(PISCINAE OR STOUPS)
recorded since the
publication of Volume I,

bringing the total to 24.

St. Mary's Church, (My).
(when uncovered in 1976).
21 × 16 ins.
(cf. Drawing no. 47. Vol. I).

Oaklands, (L).
36 × 26 ins.

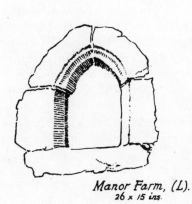

Manor Farm, (L).
26 × 15 ins.

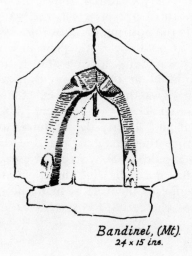

Bandinel, (Mt).
24 × 15 ins.

St. Simon's Church, (H).
32 × 23 ins.

5

mourners, 6 bearers and a number of his acquaintances. The women followed after in four gigs."
In 1811 David Crassard, who was presumably an undertaker, requested Jurat Hemery and others
to be pall bearers at the funeral of Monsieur de la Hague, Thomas Le Breton. In 1864 Sir John Le
Couteur acted as a pall bearer at the funeral of his friend James Robin, but as he was 74 at the
time and was also very short in stature, one supposes that the function was to be in attendance
on the coffin, not actually to carry it.

It need not be thought that Jersey funerals were unusual in all the pomp and circumstance
which accompanied them; indeed they were quite outshone by the funeral of a Jerseyman in
London in 1712, that of Philippe de Carteret, aged only 17, a posthumous child and the last of the
direct line of de Carterets of St. Ouen. The full text will be found in Appendix 2.

Jean Simon, who has left a most informative notebook, was clearly a carpenter and also an
undertaker. He often asked his son-in-law in England to send him tools and materials, such as
"winscut" (wainscotting) saws, tenon saws, plane blades, scissors, hammers, and "ecusons"
(surrounds for locks). He mentions several coffins, using the English word, which he supplied.
One was for François de Carteret, Constable of Trinity, whose funeral was in 1761, when he also
supplied tallow and resin for it. One for Jeanne de Carteret, including two handles for the coffin,
3½ verges of serge, 2 aunes of cloth, and notices and figures (probably for the inscription). In 1766
he supplied the coffin for Françoise de St. Paul, wife of Charles de Carteret of Trinity.

Mourning visits, like visits of congratulation after a marriage or a birth, were de rigueur, but
they do not seem to have been very consoling. In 1794 Philippe de Vaumorel, serving at Fort
Mulgrave near Toulon, was reported killed and his sister Elizabeth was in despair until news came
that he was in fact alive. Her uncle Peter, wrote, ". . . during all that space of time, till last Sunday,
when we received the joyful news of his being alive and well, we neither saw nor heard anything
concerning him, but what was more alarming, in all that time your sister received dayly a croud
of mourning visits from all her friends in order to dissuade her from entertaining any vain hope
or flatter herself against all evidence and resign herself to the will of heaven . . . now all the
mourning visits are changed into felicitations". Mementoes were sometimes given in the form of
mourning jewelry, and in her will, Ann Luce, devoted nurse and housekeeper to the Le Couteurs
of Belle Vue bequeathed to her employer "deux louis pour acheter une bague en mémoire
de moi".

In 1789 the *Gazette de l'Ile,* reporting a death, says that as the lady was a Methodist, according
to their custom she was buried fully dressed, even to her slippers, which, it was claimed somewhat
facetiously, were essential for the long walk she would be taking from this world to the next.
Like the Duke of Plaza-Toro, our ancestors enjoyed an enterrement.

Occasionally a bénitier, which could have been a piscina or a holy water stoup, is found in the
course of alterations to a house, as in the case of Bandinel q.v. In 1976 when plaster was being
stripped off the inner face of the south wall in St. Mary's Church, the outline of such an object
could be seen. When the recess was emptied of in-fill it became clear, for two reasons, that this
was a holy water stoup; firstly it was situated beside the position of a now blocked south door, and
secondly it had a shallow depression in the base to hold the water. The base stone would have
projected and has been cut back when plastering was done, leaving only half the basin intact.
It is likely, though not proven, that this was first done at the Reformation, making its present
discovery extremely important. Its outline, with ogival head, is an exact counterpart of the
surviving piscina in the church, minus the decorative head of the latter. Also an aumbry was
uncovered, to the left of the altar. Its chamfered and slightly ogival lintel, so similar to some
early domestic windows, offers the possibility that they may be dated earlier than one had
previously thought. Additional clusters of rope moulding above the piscina were also found
under the plaster. These items are in the part of the church bearing the apparently contemporary
date of 1342, and this seems a logical date to ascribe to them. How many more such objects lie
beneath the plaster in our parish churches, covered by the zeal of reformers?

CHAPTER THREE

THE FEUDAL TRADITION

". . . et doivent les tenants audit Seigneur . . . une chartée suffisante a quattre beste du moins de vraic taillé . . . la tournaison d'une vergée de terre . . . par an . . . une journée de charette . . . une journée de travail d'un homme de bras . . . pour faire le travail nécessaire à la reparation rebastiment et entretien du manoir . . . aussi le colombier et moulins de ladite Seigneurie . . . de vuider les ecluses et refaire les chaussées . . . apprester les foins et le rendre prest a charier . . ."

Part of the duties owed on a certain field by a tenant to a Seigneur in 1722.

THE WHOLE ISLAND was divided into holdings named fiefs, whose existence may pre-date the parishes. The boundaries, where they can be established, usually, but not always, follow parish boundaries, though both tend to take a natural division, such as a stream, when possible.

Far the biggest fief holder, and in fact the only one in origin, was the sovereign, and he parcelled out land to abbeys, or to individuals, at his pleasure. These seigneurs, in their turn, passed land to others, creating sub-fiefs, and so the word degenerated, and in some of the Extentes one is forced to the conclusion that the word might indicate only a holding, a "tenement".

There are 15 main fiefs which owe Suite de Cour, that is the duty, or privilege of appearing at the Assise d'Héritage; this number includes the five fiefs nobles, and those which the Crown confiscated at the Reformation or before (some of which were reallocated by subsequent Kings), and some others. Over 80 others are recorded by name, and their location is known, though not generally their precise boundaries.

It is perhaps well to stress that the Seigneur did not own the freehold of his fief, but he owned certain rights over it, varying greatly from one fief to another; it follows therefore that he held rights over those who lived on his fief. This is not the place to go into the very complex history of our manifold fiefs, but only to record how the system affected the lives of the Jerseymen in the period we are studying.

Many feudal records have survived, but the earliest so far examined by me started in 1606. There are two types of record, the accounts of the Chefs Plaids, that is the minutes of the sittings of a particular court, and the Livres des Aveux, that is declarations by tenants of the land they held on the fief in question.

Over the years the atmosphere changed in these records, and one has the impression that in the 17th century the seigneurial court sat, not only in the interests of the Seigneur, but equally in those of his tenants. They could bring to their Chefs Plaids all their troubles and obtain a fair hearing and substantial justice. Whereas some of the fines may sound harsh to us, the patience of the court is noticeable, and a judgment is sometimes repeated and repeated over the years with the miscreant refusing—or omitting—to pay his fine. The subject for complaint may also seem trivial to us, but people were very poor and their worldly possessions so precious that the loss of a hoe, the trampling of a crop by a neighbour's pig, or the breaking of a piece of timber, were really serious matters. As the 18th century progresses one can trace a decline in the interests of the tenants and an increase in those of the Seigneur. Gradually the Aveux take up most of the space in the books, the Seigneur being intent on any activity on which he could collect dues or labour, as witness the heading of this chapter. Most particularly did he wish to know the names of those who had died without heirs and on whose property he could claim the income for a year and a day, the lists being careful to record every such death, and including the deaths of those

13

living, and dying elsewhere but who might own land on the fief. By the middle of the 19th century, though such lists were still compiled, they were far less complete, many tenants being marked as having failed to "faire comparence", indicating that they no longer bothered to comply with regulations they considered outdated or unreasonable. At the same time fiefs had begun to change hands like to many stocks and shares, and the only interest a purchaser had in a fief he bought seems to have been the amount of income he could extract from it. The mediaeval notion that the Seigneur would protect his people was quite démodé. In recent times the Seigneur has been shorn of most of his perquisites, the last to go being the année de jouissance payments, in 1966.

The oath administered to the Greffier of the Fief ès Cras in 1770 shows the spirit in which the work of the court was intended to be approached, and is worthy of quotation in full: "Vous jurez et prometterez par la foi et serment que vous devez à Dieu, que bien et fidèlement vous exercerez la charge de Greffier de la Cour et Seigneurie ès Cras, que vous enregîterez fidellement les sentences de la cour dudit fief sellon qu'elles vous seront pronouncées par la bouche du Sénéchal, vous garderez et fairez garder le Droit du Seigneur et celui des Tenans, et fairez generalement tous les Devoirs attachez à ladite charge". The oath for the Prévôt was in similar vein. The Fief ès Cras was a small dependency of the larger Fief of Meleches, situated in the Sion district.

It was the duty of the Prévôt to collect dues owing to the Seigneur, from which he derived his own profit, in the shape of a commission, and if the Seigneur failed to hold his court the Prévôt was out of pocket. A "cri de coeur" from a Prévôt in this position, written in 1806, reads:—

Monsieur.
Je vous prie d'excuser de ma faiblesse et de mon yniorance a vous represent le tort que vous me faite en ne tenant pas vos cour comme vous me lavies promint il y a un an desja passé et je vous prie de me faire droit comme ils dépent de vous et de tous autre seigneur de fief de donner des régistre a tous leurs prévôt pour qu'il puisse lever les ferme et autre droits seignieuriot que prévôt sont obliges de lever et dans payer les deniers a leur seigneur soit qu'il les aits receu ou non, comme ont été ceux dauparavant moy, car il est bien dure a un prévôt de payer de largent a sont seigneur et qui ne luis donne pas le moyen de pouvoir le recevoir la ou il est seu. Je n'écriré pas davantage Monsr. je demeure votre tres hüble serviteurs et attendant votre response Elie Lesbirel, Prévôt de deux de vos cour. (Spelling as in the original.)

Unlike Guernsey we did not have special places for the Court sittings. They usually took place at the house of one of the tenants, occasionally they were "dans la maison", the weather probably being the deciding factor. Sometimes they were held at the site of some controversy which was to be discussed. One most interesting entry in the rolls of the little Fief of St. Clair, at the top of Mont Cochon, records that in 1753 Philippe de Ste Croix fs. Philippe fs. Abraham "a fourny une table pour le tenue de cette cour suivant qu'il est obligé pour ses heritages". There is a field called Le Champ de la Table, 2½ vergées, in the Ruelle de St. Clair, which obviously refers to this duty.

When one Seigneur owned several fiefs, as he often did, the sittings might take place on the same day, though each one had to be held on its own land, however small its extent. In 1846, for example, the court of ès Hastains, situated at the top of Mont Félard, was held at 10 o'clock, and that of St. Clair at 11 o'clock on the same day, 29 May; one hopes that George Brown, the miller at the Moulin à Sucre in Waterworks Valley, had a good horse, as he had to appear at both courts, one on either side of the valley.

The frequency of court sittings varied enormously, and as time went on tended to become more rare and more erratic. For instance, in the case of La Hague, starting in 1748 (in one particular record book) the court sat twice a year, and then once, and then alternate years, and finally there were gaps with no sitting at all between 1784-92 and again 1828-51.

Let us look at a cross-section of cases considered in some seigneurial courts.

Many are the cases of "verp brisé". This means that an animal had strayed, been collected and put in the verp (that is the cattle pound of the fief) by the messier and that subsequently the owner had removed his animals without paying the necessary fine. In 1703 the court of Noirmont passed sentence on Jean Le Couteur for shooting game on the fief, this being the prerogative of the Seigneur. An appeal to the Royal Court upheld the sentence, and further fined him for "folappell". In 1722 a tenant of St. Ouen's fief complained of the dues she owed to the Seigneur, then the absentee Lord John Carteret, who had inherited a much encumbered estate. She was Georgette

Herival, wife of Philippe Vibert, who owed on some of her land dues similar to those quoted at the head of this chapter. One surprising item, in the circumstances, is that the Seigneur himself was responsible for the "brasse de l'encloteure", which probably meant a fathom of the sluice of the mill, or the section nearest to the mill building.* In 1767 the court of Avranches was held in Philippe Vaudin's house, and he was accused of planting apple trees and making new banks and enclosures on "terre campartière" (that is land on which the Seigneur could exact dues). He was ordered to uproot the saplings and demolish the banks, while Jeanne Pinel, widow of Noé Vaudin, was punished for not having cultivated her terre campartière. In 1793 the co-Seigneur of St. Ouen, Daniel Messervy, complained that Susanne Belin had found a barrel of butter washed up on the shore of his fief, and kept it; Susanne was ordered to return the butter in the same condition in which she found it, on pain of a fine of 60 sous. One rather hopes that all the little Belins had already enjoyed butter for their tea.

Dues owing to seigneurs were in kind as well as in labour, and varied enormously, often reflecting the geographical situation of the land. For instance one tenant on the fief de la Fosse owed "cendres de vraic" (ash of burnt seaweed) and this was still being paid in 1868. Some of the tenants of Samarès, in 1754, owed salt, an important item of produce from the low-lying areas which used to be flooded by the sea; another owed a pot (half gallon) of Gascon wine when the court was held at her house; another owed "un racle et un comble", perhaps a staff for levelling off grain and the measure itself. Such items had to be transported wherever the Seigneur desired, usually to his manor, and we find in 1801 that poultry dues were paid off in wheat rente to the then Seigneur of La Hague, Thomas Le Breton fs. Thomas. Previously the tenant, Jacques Payn fs. Jacques fs. Jean fs. Jacques had had to take 30 hens, 2 geese and 2 capons to the manor, being given a day's notice, which notice must be served to Payn's house; however the Seigneur could not demand more than two couples (of birds) at a time. One can see a glimmer of consideration here.

If dues were not paid the Seigneur could take what seem to us rather severe measures, and in 1798 the Seigneur of Vingt Livres was able to seize the goods of Abraham Le Gresley who owed him rente; two years later his granddaughter Anne, through her tuteur, was fined for fief brisé (disobedience to court order) the Seigneur being permitted to apply to the Royal Court to imprison her guardian. In 1806 he had permission to escheat her goods for payment of the rente, so the family had managed to delay the day of judgment for eight years.

When the Fief de Lecq was sold by Jean de Carteret to Raulin Le Vesconte in 1749, the dues on it were 31½ sols, 7 quarters, 7½ sixtonniers wheat, 1½ cabots oats, seven day's work for one man, 1 day's work with a cart to transport sheaves of grain, 23 hens and 64 hens' eggs. This fief also had, as had La Fosse and some others, a vraic officer, "pour la conservation et le partage des vraics au Havre de la Grève de Lecq". It is rare, though not unknown, to find a stipulation that eggs due must be hens' eggs, but the importance of vraic, and its fair division, was of universal interest at all times, and can scarcely be comprehended in these days of "bag farming", and the ease with which fertilisers can be obtained.

The feudal system continued in Jersey long after it had disappeared in England, and may be said to have outlived its usefulness, having become so far divorced from its original function of reciprocal advantage to Seigneur and tenant.

---

*Extente 1607, p. 16, 1668, p. 99.

CHAPTER FOUR

DEFENCE AND POLITICS

*". . . our debonaire Prince and other ministers of state are constantly consider-
ing our safety. When we are in danger they send warships to surround our
island and a numerous militia watches our safety, and I think it most unlikely
that they will really undertake an attack."*

Jean Simon, to his daughter in England. 1761.

IN SPITE OF the confidence evidently felt within the Island about defence, in 1799, the very
year in which the Prince of Nassau did attempt to invade Jersey, Horace Walpole was writing to
the Countess of Aylesbury, referring to Marshal Conway, our then Lieutenant Governor. He said:
"You do not know that I have had my terrors for Mr. Conway, but at present they are out of
the question from the insignificance of his island . . . a large garrison would be to tempt the
French thither, were it to be to distress this country, and, what is worse, encourage Mr. Conway
to make an impracticable defence".

To a small island defence must always be of paramount concern, and all the more so to one
which was British territory, but so close to the coasts of England's old adversary, France. Throughout her history this small island has been regarded with covetous eyes by potential invaders, who
wanted it for anchorage, shelter, trade or settlement. The last of the many occasions when France
tried to gain possession of Jersey (and the other islands in the group would soon have followed)
was in 1781, when the Battle of Jersey took place in the Royal Square, then the place du Marché,
on 6 January. The short duration of the engagement and the small number of casualties should
not blind one to the potential danger of such an invasion, had it been successful. Every local
history gives prominence to it, and it was surely the most stirring event of the century. The news
quickly reached other countries, and expatriates. A certain William Le Marchant of Guernsey

6

wrote, at 8 a.m. on 8 January to Abraham
Poingdestre at Bonne Nuit that he had just heard
of the defeat of the enemy, and rejoiced in it,
but thought that the Master of the boat bringing the news had been so dilatory that he had
not recompensed him. Dr. Daniel Dumaresq
(1712-1805) wrote to his sister, Madame de
Carteret of Vinchelez de Bas in February 1781:
". . . I only knew of your danger by vague
rumour which gave me the greatest anxiety . . .
the next morning I heard that the enemy troops
had been dispersed and had been totally
defeated and ruined". He hoped that due respect
would always be paid to the memory of Major
Peirson, and suggested that the Mont ès Pendus
(Westmount) should be re-named Le Mont
Peirson. What a pity his suggestion was not
adopted.

The Jersey militia was a force which no
intending intruder could ignore. As its function
was purely defensive no militiaman was bound

*a gun-emplacement at L'Etacquerel Fort and
Battery, built 1786-1836.*

16

PLATE III COMPARATIVE MAPS PART OF ST MARTIN

a. Duke of Richmond's survey, 1795

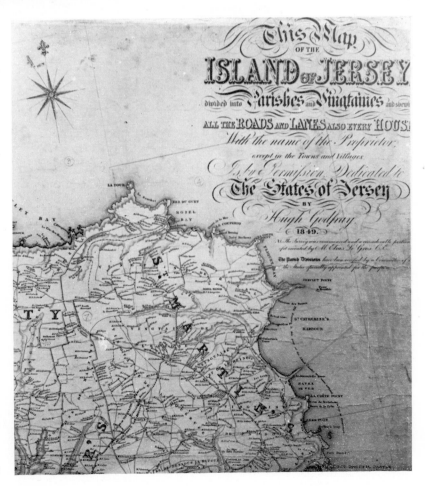

b. Hugh Godfray's map, 1849

PLATE IV MILITARIA

a. Grève de Lecq Barracks, built *c* 1815. Before restoration

b. A militia review at Bel Royal, *c* 1860 by E. de la Taste

to serve outside his own island, except for the personal protection of the sovereign. Within Jersey the militia maintained a high standard of guard and sentry duty. Militia activities entered into the life of every family, as men between 16 and 60 had to serve. Accounts of their effectiveness and discipline vary considerably, but in general they have a proud record. Although service was voluntary, in the sense of being unpaid, instructors and equipment were supplied by England. Militia drill for boys was instituted by General Le Couteur, and in 1811 he wrote a memorandum saying that short carbines were being supplied for the smallest and weakest boys, and long ones for the stoutest and strongest boys, and strict detailed instructions were given for the care of these weapons. In 1800 the fines for non-attendance on parade were raised. Coast-guard duty occurred about once in 16–18 nights, and Stead noted ten signal posts with fire beacons.

SEYMOUR TOWER, in 1925.
built 1782

7

The very existence of the militia and its known efficiency may partly account for the fact that the Island never suffered from press-gangs, as all able-bodied men were already serving their country; indeed a one-time Governor was able to emphasise this very point and win his argument. Lieut. James de Carteret was in Jersey in 1783 (procuring men for His Majesty's fleet), and he disbursed some £25, presumably sterling, to this end. He enlisted four men, one volunteer, one straggler, one deserter and one "prest". Items of expenditure which appear repeatedly in his account are: "Horse hire to St. Aubin after seaman 4/6"; "apprehending a seaman who had secreted himself £2"; "Lodging room for one week £1.4."; "Beat of drum and fife playing during the week 10/-"; "Midshipman's one month's wages 13/9"; "boat hire to carry one man on board of the True Briton in the Road 15/-". It would seem rather a costly enterprise to raise only four recruits.

Our coasts, particularly the south, are ringed with defensive towers, built to resist invasion during the Napoleonic Wars. They fell into two groups, though all go under the inaccurate name of Martello, applied to them as early as 1809 by Stead. The later examples, dating from about

MARTELLO TOWERS

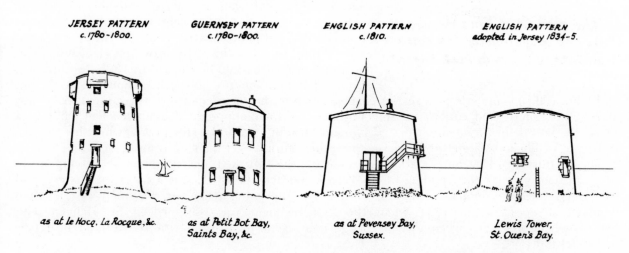

JERSEY PATTERN
c. 1780–1800.

GUERNSEY PATTERN
c. 1780–1800.

ENGLISH PATTERN
c. 1810.

ENGLISH PATTERN
adopted in Jersey 1834–5.

as at le Hocq, La Rocque, &c.

as at Petit Bot Bay, Saints Bay, &c.

as at Pevensey Bay, Sussex.

Lewis Tower, St. Ouen's Bay.

8

1804 (e.g., Portelet) are Martello towers, similar to those built at the same period on the Kent and Sussex coasts, round and squat like a child's sandcastle. The earlier examples are taller, tapering and more elegant, built in granite with machiolations, and these were started in 1779, a total of 32 being contemplated, 22 of which had been completed by 1794.* The design used differs from any other towers, even those in Guernsey and the name of the architect has yet to be found, but he is likely to have been a Royal Engineer officer stationed here. In 1838 Inglis thought that they "added to the picturesque aspect of the shore, but little, I suspect, to the security of the island". Until 1800 or so they were designated by a number, such as "No. 4 dans la Baie de Grouville". The only one to retain its number now is the first tower west of St. Helier, which gave its name to the village of First Tower.

We have always imported granite from Chausey for important building works, and in 1744 we are told in *La Surprise de Jersey*: 400 stone masons brought over granite which was used for port and defence works.

the cipher of King George III
on the keystone of the main
entrance arch to Fort Regent.

9

General Don (1756-1832, Lieutenant Governor 1806-1809 and 1810-1814) was indefatigable in improving our defences, and from 1806 onwards made a network of main roads to enable troops to move swiftly from one place to another, though he was criticised for aiding the enemy to be more mobile at the same time. The army often assisted in road-making operations, as in 1811, when a sergeant with 12 men of the Royal Irish Regiment were stationed at La Hague under instructions from the Constable, and arrangements were made for straw, fuel and bread to be supplied to them.

The strength of the militia has naturally varied from time to time, but in 1869 Sir John Le Couteur, as ardent a militiaman as his father, drew up a memorandum assessing it at 5,325 men, divided into four regiments.

Originally the militia were provided with muskets by the inhabitants, according to their financial ability, assessed on the rateable value of their property. In 1774 the States laid down that those who paid 20 quarters rate must provide one musket, 50 quarters 3 muskets, and 100 quarters 4 muskets. This provision of arms appears again and again in partages of inheritance. The eldest son, who had to accept this duty as the new householder, obtained extra land in the partage to compensate him for this. The provision of a horse was an alternative that could be chosen. In 1805, for instance, Edouard Remon inherited his father's house in St. Aubin, with the well, a founder's pew in the chapel, and for the maintenance of three muskets he was allocated a vallette and côtil. The same was the case for Philippe de Veulle, who had part of La Pièce du Havard for the maintenance of two muskets; this was in Le Hocq Lane, where his parents, Aaron de Veulle and Marguerite Le Neveu, have their initials over their front door.

The production of accommodation and food for the British troops stationed here, temporarily or permanently, until the building of St. Peter's Barracks in 1811, was a cause for anxiety, and sometimes for the commandeering of houses. Yet the good behaviour of the troops is often commented upon, as in 1831 when the 31st regiment was stationed in St. Helier.† This had also been the case when the very large contingent of Russian troops wintered in Jersey in 1799/1800.‡

---

*B.S.J. 1971, p. 289.   †Actes des Etats 1744, p. 78.   ‡B.S.J. 1914; p. 416, 1968, p. 327; 1974, p. 258.

"Service des Prisonniers" was a due owing on certain properties (not on the owners as such) of conducting accused persons from the prison at Mont Orgueil to town for their trials. After the establishment of a goal in town, this duty must have become much less onerous, and in any case it applied only to certain houses in St. Martin, fewer in Grouville and still fewer in St. Saviour. The duty is mentioned in a de Quetteville document of 1779 and repeated in 1788. Owners of these houses had a halberd, originally an offensive weapon no doubt, but latterly a symbol of office, and it is regrettable, and surprising, that so few of these halberds have survived. There was one at St. Martin's House until recent years, when it appears to have been stolen.

rain-water tank, Grève de Lecq Barracks. 10

"Le Voyage à Guernsey" was likewise owed by certain house owners in St. Clement, who had, to quote one case in 1740, to "fournir la moitié d'un homme au voyage de Guernesey", and for this Bernaby Godfray was allocated an extra 26 perch of land in the family partage. Presumably neighbours shared the duty, or took alternate calls, hence the half man; this arrangement was designed to cover emergencies when urgent news needed to be taken to Guernsey by boat. Although by then it must have become an anachronism, it was quoted in 1896 when Philippe de Ste Croix bought a house near La Rocque from Thomas Journeaux; in 1902 the house was sold to James Joslin Dupré, and this service was repeated, as indeed it still was in 1924. Like the Service des Prisonniers, it was attached to the property, not to the owner as such.

From time to time subscriptions were raised for patriotic causes, some of them rather unexpected. In 1803, 15 contributors in St. Peter promised money in the event of attack on the Island, and for the relief of those who distinguished themselves or were wounded in action, or the dependants of those killed. This fund was to be administered by a committee of 13, plus a President, and one wonders who was the lone contributor who had no seat on the committee. The amount promised was £2,781 tournois, and the date lay between the Peace of Amiens in 1802, and the second war of 1805-1815, indicating a well-founded lack of trust in the peace by the inhabitants of St. Peter. In 1809 the inhabitants of the Vingtaine du Douet in St. Peter subscribed £159 tournois for ". . . le soulagement de nos compatriots actuellement prisonniers de Guere en France". It is not meant to suggest that the parish of St. Peter, and still more the Vingtaine du Douet, were more patriotic or generous than other parishes or vingtaines, but it merely happens that proof of their actions has survived on paper. Then in 1857 there was the Indian Mutiny Sufferers Relief Fund, which raised £62 13s., with £10 from the Governor and £5 from his wife; the Treasurer was Robert Pipon Marett, who would have had a personal interest as his brother, Peter Daniel Marett was in India at the time. The scheme does not seem to have met with a particularly generous response.

The first official census was taken in 1821, when the population was 29,000 (to the nearest thousand). Stead had estimated it at 25,000 a decade earlier; de la Croix's estimate in about 1850, 23,000, is quite at variance with the official figures. All the figures are somewhere in the region of a third of the present-day population. In the intervening years it increased until 1851, when it was 57,000, and it did not again reach that figure until 1951. Before these official census returns, we had General Don's lists, made specifically to discover the number of men of military age, though all inhabitants were included. Plees, writing in 1817, gave a total of 23,000 (a far lower figure than the official number), stating that 10,000 were men or boys, and 13,000 women or girls. From manuscript sources one can glean further evidence if one is fortunate. In 1718 a list appeared for the parish of St. Saviour, giving a total of 114 households; with an average of five persons to a house that would give a population of 720 for the parish (as compared with 11,000 in the 1971 census). In 1774 a rate list for St. Peter showed 236 householders who owed rates, which amounted to 1,462 quarters of wheat rente, and provided 250 muskets; on an average of five to a household again this would suggest a parish population of 1,280 persons, vastly greater than that of St. Saviour some fifty years earlier. In 1788 a simple manuscript census appeared, unfortunately omitting St. Peter. For the 11 parishes it totalled 19,214 persons, and if we add the 1,280 in St. Peter in 1774, the total would be 20,494. Compared with the 1971 census the great increases are in town, St. Saviour, St. Clement and St. Brelade; the increase in St. Mary is small, and Trinity has actually dropped, which is hard to credit.

In about 1800 Pierre Mauger produced a curious memorandum assessing the numbers of houses as 987 in the western parishes, 1,044 in the northern, and 1,010 in the eastern (which included St. Helier, always the thickest population). This gives a total of 3,014 houses, fairly evenly distributed, with the least in St. Mary and St. Clement, and the most in St. Helier and Trinity. An undated memorandum, probably about 1800, which will be referred to later, suggests a population at that time of 28,000, with 12,000 acres under wheat and 1,000 men employed exclusively on that crop.

a cabin built astride the St. Helier–Trinity boundary: a landowner's ruse to establish voting rights in both parishes.

11

In 1831 Sir John Le Couteur, then Constable of St. Brelade, assessed his parish as follows: 307 houses inhabited by 432 families: 128 families employed in agriculture, and 191 families otherwise employed: total of persons 2,069, with more females than males, as always.

The ugly face of party politics began to show itself in about 1770, when those of the Conservative element were called Charlots after their leader Charles Lemprière, and by about 1800 they adopted the laurel as their symbol. The Liberal thought was led by Sir John Dumaresq; they were first called the Jeannots, and later the Magots, cheese mites, a sobriquet adopted in defiance (like those of the "Contemptible Little Army" or "The Desert Rats" of Tobruk), and their symbol was the rose. These parties dominated political, commercial and social life to a deplorable degree. Inglis wrote that he was amazed that a people of such fiercely independent character could be so subjugated to bitter philosophies. The feelings this spirit engendered are well portrayed in Hilda Balleine's book *Rose and Laurel,* written early in this century.

One had heard that even families were rent in twain by their political thought, but the Royal Commissioners of 1846, surprisingly, found that parishes adhered to one or the other of the parties. In their opinion St. Ouen, Trinity, Grouville and St. Clement were predominantly Laurel, the Rose claiming St. Mary, St. John, St. Peter, St. Lawrence, St. Helier, St. Martin, and St. Saviour, with St. Brelade neutral. This suggests a change from the original allocation, with Sir John Dumaresq in St. Peter for the Rose and Charles Lemprière in St. Martin for the Laurel. Newspapers supported their favourite party, the Rose (Jeannots) claiming *La Gazette de l'Ile, Le Chronique* and *L'Impartial,* and the Laurel (Charlots) *Le Constitutionel* and *Le Soleil.* Many house names still testify to adherence to one or the other political party, and such names should be retained, as recording a piece of history, albeit a facet we are glad is in the past, and that Jersey is now free of party politics.

Are the truly enormous laurel bushes at Les Prés Manor, in Grouville, indicative of conservative sympathies? It has been suggested that houses even had their woodwork painted green or pink, according to the owners' political views. If this is so, and it is not at all improbable, houses with a tradition of green paint, or where old green paint can be traced, should have laurel bushes in their gardens, and those with the typical "Jersey pink" (not often seen nowadays) should have ancient rose bushes and no laurels. Recent plantings should, naturally, be ignored.

CHAPTER FIVE

THE FRUITS OF THE EARTH

L'île est féconde; elle a deux villes et douze paroisses; elle est couverte de maisons de campagnes et de troupeaux. La vent de l'Océan, qui semble démentir sa rudesse, donne à Jersey du miel exquis, de la crème d'une douceur extraordinaire et du beurre d'un jaune foncé, qui sent la violette.

R. de Chateaubriand 1793.

IN 1838 INGLIS thought the state of agriculture was backward, and attributed this mainly to the minute division of property amongst heirs. This view is put forward by most writers, and although largely true, documents show that as well as getting the field nearest the house in his *préciput* the eldest son frequently bought back from his brothers their share of the inheritance; sisters often had to be content with rentes, but if they did inherit land, and were married, they also often preferred to sell this back to the eldest brother. It was never questioned that the eldest son would want the property and would farm the land.

Farmers did, and do, work hard, but some were able to have varied days. Philippe Marett of La Haule, for example, recorded in his diary for 4 June 1821, "Went under arms at 3 o'clock. Made hay. Finished making the lucerne, and in the evening went to the Quadrille". Again in 1858, his son recorded on 1 January, "Called at Government House and several other calls. Sowed wheat in the Clos de la Fosse". Sir John Le Couteur's diaries follow the same pattern, a varied programme of militia duties, parochial, States and farming activities, gardening, fishing, taking part in building operations, being an attentive father, and leading a gay social life.

Let us consider the crops that were grown, the animals raised and the implements used for the work.

By far the most important crop, probably since neolithic times, and until this century, was corn, primarily wheat, but also oats, barley and rye. It was virtually currency and payments, sales and rentes were assessed on the value of wheat at the time. In 1709 the States recorded that the Island had enjoyed such an abundant crop of grain that the inhabitants were not in danger of a bread shortage as other countries were, but they felt it expedient to forbid the export of bread, grain or vegetables. In the 1769 Petition to the King it was stated that the Island could only produce enough grain to supply the inhabitants' needs for six to eight months, even in the best years, and that good land was far better employed producing grain rather than orchards; further it was requested that it should be permissible to import apples, as otherwise in a poor year people were forced to drink bad beer, to the prejudice of their health.* A century later Victor Hugo, quoting Charassin, an agronomist, said that if France was cultivated like Jersey it could feed seven millions.†

In August 1858 Philippe Marett still spoke of "cutting the wheat" (that is with scythes) and a few days later he took 427lbs. wheat to the windmill for grinding. He did not say which windmill, but one must assume that it was a dry year and that the water flow was insufficient to turn the wheel of the water mill, as he would surely have taken it to the Moulin d'Egoutte Pluie otherwise. Sir John Le Couteur worked for years to improve local wheat, and he displayed 104 varieties from his own ground at the Great Exhibition in 1853, and wrote a book on its culture which gained him the Fellowship of the Royal Society. In 1837 Durell would have preferred us to grow cider

---

*Journal de Daniel Messervy, p. 84.   †L'Archipel de la Manche. Hugo.

apples and other fruits, and considered the soil more appropriate for that than for corn, but in time of war—so frequent—corn was the life saver. A document of about 1801, in the La Hague collection, gives an assessment of population, and the production of wheat, with an estimated cost of raising it at £150 tournois per vergée; it states that 12,000 were then cultivated, producing 25 cabots per vergée, and this the writer thought represented 312,000 days' work on this crop alone, as one vergée took 26 man days. Continuing to urge the expansion of agriculture, the writer ended: "L'interêt de la ville et celui de la campagne est le même; il ne peut être séparé; si la campagne fleurit, la ville fleurit aussi". Wise words from nearly two hundred years ago.

In the 18th century the next most important crop was apples for cider, the main beverage of the inhabitants. As early as 1733 Marie Lemprière received 30 cabots of rente on a house in apples, and this she refused to accept unless it was measured by the recently-established apple measure, but she lost her point. Every farm had its cider press, crusher and equipment, and making the year's supply of cider for the family and the labourers was part of the Jersey way of life. There was even a Cyder Society, which invited Jean Pipon of La Hague to dinner at La Motte House on Thursday, 20 March of an unspecified year, and on 1 October 1834 Philippe Marett wrote, "Tenth day making cider".

The quantity and quality of the cider varied enormously. In 1735 Pierre de Ste Croix wrote to Thomas Bandinel in Southton (sic) to say that he had consigned by Captain Luce two barrels of cider which he hoped would be satisfactory, but that the cider that year was poor (méchant). Stead said that 35,000 hogsheads were made annually and 5,000 exported, while Plees, a decade later, estimated that 24,000 hogsheads were made annually, of which 1800 were exported: a hogshead is 48 gallons. At the time of the Richmond map (1795) over 20 per cent. of arable land was under orchard, or 15 per cent. of the whole Island. Quayle in 1815, considered that a quarter of all arable land was under apples, particularly in the eastern parishes.*

The apple trees were raised by grafting which is most carefully described by the

*B.S.J. 1951, p. 332; 1952, p. 439.

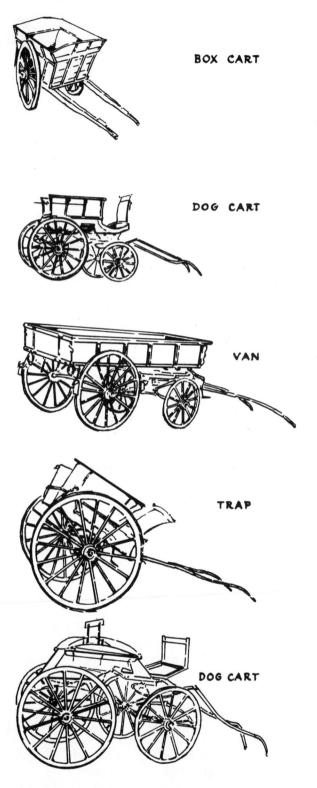

BOX CART

DOG CART

VAN

TRAP

DOG CART

HORSE-DRAWN VEHICLES
SURVIVING IN JERSEY.
forerunners of the car, lorry and tractor.   12

Reverend François Le Couteur;* it was he who suggested a means of stopping the crushing wheel from slipping over the fruit without breaking it. He illustrates a simple mechanism of gears which would force the crusher down on the pulp, but no trace of this ingenious contraption can now be found at his home, Les Pré Manor, Grouville.† Patches of land called Le Clos or Jardin, des Greffes refer to the raising of young stock, as does a Pepinière, and Le Jardin, being the actual orchard, is among the most common of field names. As early as 1739 the States had forbidden the importation of apples or cider into the Island.‡

Opinions differ on the quality of our cider, but in 1856 a French Agricultural Society saw fit to come and examine our cider-making methods, and they extolled the quality of the produce of Mainland, Bel Royal,** owned by Moise Gibaut. Those two great agriculturists, Sir John Le Couteur and Colonel C. P. Le Cornu both gave close attention to cider making,†† and the former, through his wife's water colours, has left us beautiful illustrations of the apples and pears in cultivation. Her album of painting shows 87 varieties of apples and 165 of pears, and until the Second War pears were so plentiful and so excellent that they were constantly sent as presents to England. In September 1834 it is recorded that Philippe Marett sold 100lbs. of Chaumontel pears for 15s.

A bill paid in 1835 shows us the current prices for beverages: 6 bottles of sherry, 12s. 6d.; brandy 1s. 6d. a bottle; rum, 1s.; 6 dozen porter, 4s.; 6 dozen ale, 3s. 6d. In 1762 Jean Simon of St. John sent his son Edouard in London a present of a dozen bottles of French wine, Château Margat, in a hamper, by Captain Lys's boat. There is a bunch of extremely interesting letters exchanged between Edouard Marett of La Haule and Jean Martel of brandy fame, in the course of which Marett ordered brandy and red and white bordeaux, but complained that the Grande Borderie wines were not liked (méprisable), being subject to yellowing. Included in the order, on one occasion, were 1½ tons of syrup and a loaf of sugar: the syrup was molasses and the loaf is sometimes described as a "mannequin". One bill was paid in Spanish gold pieces. In 1820 Philippe Marett gave his recipe for blackcurrant brandy, as 1 pot gin, 1 pot brandy, 8lbs. currants and some "syrop pinks". "Good", he said, "by February 1821", and it sounds fairly potent. Gin was usually referred to as geneva, and brandy appeared in a variety of spellings, such as "dodevi" and "odedue". Sure it is that Jerseymen did not go short of good drinks, and commentators such as Inglis and Durell remark on the great quantity of spirits consumed. Vines were grown fairly profusely, but it seems as if little or no wine was made.

Parsnips were widely cultivated and used both for human consumption and as an animal foodstuff, and Clos de Panais occurs in field names. Potato cultivation for export is comparatively recent, but Sir John Le Couteur's wife included some potatoes in her water colours; one page is entitled "Seedling potatoes of 1832 raised from the one apple (sic) by J.L.C.", and another "Philip's red potato given to me by Mr. Isaac Gosset in 1822, grown at Belle Vue 25 October 1833, weighed 1lb. 7ozs. (Jersey measure)". He said it was "A capital sort" in 1855. On 28 January 1864 Philippe Marett recorded, "Finished planting potatoes in the top field, about 6 perch of flukes". This is a highly important entry as it is generally agreed that the Royal Jersey Fluke was introduced by Hugh de la Haye in 1880, but clearly fluke was a name already in use. In 1803 potatoes were planted at Belle Vue on 28 March; the ground was ploughed by two horses, 11″ deep, the tubers being put 7–8″ deep in alternate furrows.

Oxen were still used when Plees was writing, but were gradually displaced by horses, which he says were small, strong and hardy. It is said that local animals were crossed with Russian horses left behind when the troops left in 1800. Stead says they were small and hardy, resembling the smaller Suffolk horses, but he considered that they were worked at too young an age. Large numbers of horses also came with every regiment stationed in the Island. In 1819 Philippe Marett was making his horse stable, cobbling it with stones he collected from St. Ouen, in six cartloads, with the help of two men and four carts. In 1836 he paid £16 10s. for a mare: in 1831 Abraham Gibaut paid Philippe Fleury £8 10s. (probably tournois) for a years' shoeing for his horse.

---

*Aperçu sur le cidre. Rev. F. Le Couteur.   †op. cit., p. 105.   ‡Actes des Etats, 1739, p. 53.
**B.S.J. 1970, p. 164.   ††Bulletin de l'Assembliée d'Jèrriais, 1954, No. 9.

All the local writers remark on the Jersey sheep, and their ownership was established by marking their ears, "Merches du bercail", a custom which seems repugnant to us, as the animals' ears were sadly maimed to make these distinguishing marks; for instance the Prévôt of the Fief de Vingt Livres in 1806, confiscated a grey ewe and her lamb, and her mark was "the right ear cut off at the end, a hole in it and a knife mark on it". One hopes that Quayle's account of the treatment of animals, particularly horses and sheep, was exaggerated or based on exceptional cases. The six-horned sheep, considered to be a local peculiarity, is shown in Sullivan's well-known picture of the Market Place (Royal Square) dated 1738.

Plees says the sheep were diminutive and mostly black, and were kept mainly in the northern parishes, and on open land such as Noirmont and fief communes, and Stead remarks on the excellence of the meat. In 1818 Philippe Marett went to Lessay Fair, where he bought a horse and 12 sheep, which he had trouble in bringing home; he says, "Took the sheep at the Douane and with two men to drive them with a great deal of trouble, having been thrown by Pierre in the Duet de Creance. Wet to the knee we came on board at 2 in the morning; the tide came under about 5, we therefore set sail, wind north east, and in three hours were at the Old Castle, having experienced a very rough passage and without proper persons to direct the vessel". In 1832 Sir John Le Couteur wrote to a supplier at Smithfield to enquire the price of one ram and 24 ewes, but was told that it "would be almost impossible to procure you a good black ram; a good white one would cost £6 and the ewes £4 each".

Many States' acts regulated the importation of wool, the weaving of which was a most important form of employment, and recognised as such in 1709. Another act recognised irregularity in the distribution of import licences in 1744, and again in 1748, when workers were left without wool, the Island not providing anything like the quantity needed by those occupied in knitting. Some merchants approached François Marett of Avranches, Receiver General, in 1748, complaining that they were not getting their due share of the import licences; he replied that he had orders from the Governor, Lord Cobham, not to change the situation, but they protested vigorously that they had a quantity of wool ready to be shipped from Southampton. In 1788 the States sent Sir John Dumaresq, as their Deputy, to go to England to plead the Island's cause, in order to preserve for the inhabitants the privilege of importing English wool, and to show that a cessation of this trade would bring ruin to the Island; they all owed Dumaresq one guinea per day above his travelling expenses, this amount to be recovered from the parishes out of their rates. Dr. Richard Valpy estimated 4,000 tods of wool were imported annually to be made into stockings, gloves and other garments, for export largely to Portugal. A tod was about 28lbs.

Among all the farm animals the cow was, and is, pre-eminent. The breed has been protected since 1789, since when no live bovine has been imported. (There were some exceptions during the German Occupation.) This alone did not produce the best animals until Sir John Le Couteur recognised the importance of selective breeding. Before him, no one had thought that the choice of the sire was as important as that of the dam. His work was continued by Colonel C. P. Le Cornu, who instituted the Herd Book. It was during this period that the export of cattle started, destined to become one of Jersey's premier trades. There were some unexpected episodes, such as the case of Major P. D. Marett who, in 1827, was supplying friends in England with cows, and one unfortunate animal calved on the way from Southampton to London, and the calf had to be brought to Sloane Street, the destination, in a cart, which suggests that the poor cow was expected to walk. She was then tethered in Hyde Park, and recovered from her journey. An undated early 19th-century book on navigation, by a certain Jean Touzel, gave instructions to use carbolic acid and common tar for foot and mouth disease. The perennial in-calf difficulties are reflected in General Le Couteur's farm diary, but in 1819 he recorded that his black cow was giving over five pots (2½ gallons) of milk daily, yielding 6lbs. butter per week. The butter fat percentage is more impressive than the milk yield in this entry. Black or "mulberry" cows were fairly common at that period, but are very rare now.

Hay was grown on a large scale, with rye grass, lucerne and clover. In 1834 Philippe Marett mowed his hay on 30 May and on 5 June brought in "five thousand", that is bundles. Lucerne was much favoured, particularly in dry weather.

When the land was let instructions were always laid down about manuring, what trees and hedges could be cut, and above all the rotation of crops. For Le Clos de Bisson (B. 849) in 1843 the programme was:

1st year.—Manured for potatoes, parsnips, or white carrots.
2nd year.—Treat with ash, lime or soot for cereals.
3rd year.—Clover and rye grass.
4th year.—Grass.

All the manure collected on the farm was to be used thereon and none sold. In 1826 Le Clos Rose in St. Brelade was let for five years,

porch-pillars, demoted to the rank of field gate-posts, on the south side of field T.125b, and east side of T.1257.

13

and clover was to be sown in the last year of the tenancy. A curious provision appeared in 1814 when Abraham Gibaut let an eight-vergée field to Jean Le Boutillier; it reads, "if peace occurs the lease should be broken with six months warning". In 1837, however, when Philippe Le Cornu let La Villaise du Sud (O.1063) to Rachel Le Masurier for £6 sterling annually it was stated that this would be raised to £6 10s. if war broke out.

In 1790 François Messervy complained that people crossed his field, Le Clos du Bailly, broke his gates and knocked down his banks. He was permitted to put up a notice in St. Helier and adjoining parishes, forbidding trespass on his land "in the usual place", meaning the parish notice board at the church. In 1751 Elie Gibaut was permitted to publish a notice that no one could make a path across his fields in St. Lawrence, on the Royal Fief, cut down his banks or destroy his hedges. Another tenant, Philippe de Ste Croix, neglected to plant grafted stock to replace apple trees on land he rented from Abraham Gibaut in 1773. In 1780 Edouard Gibaut let Les Clos du Mailler to Edouard Luce, who was obliged to follow the rotation and supply 6lbs. "graine de traiflaitte" (clover seed) par vergée dans du Renoulyn la dernière année dudil baille" (this presumably meaning "renouveler"). Another lease, in 1807, allowed Philippe Barbier a right of way over Philippe Syvret's field at Val de la Mare to go and get his hay (aller querier son foin) at the appropriate season, and to take and fetch (requerer) his animals.

Fields were enclosed by walls or banks. The earliest document so far found referring to a field as a clos is in the Cartulaire (p. 60) when it appears as "clausum" in 1215. From the 14th century it appears in the French form, an instance in 1366 having been found in Guernsey, Le Clos de Tehit in the Catel parish, and from about 1400 it comes into more general use. Poingdestre, in 1680, tells us how field banks were topped with hawthorn hedges, the forerunner of the modern electric fence, and rather more effective. The entrances to fields were closed by simple gates, or just a cross-bar inserted into stone gateposts. These changed over the years, from large rough pieces of granite, sometimes re-used menhirs (such as field P. 689), to squared columns of dressed stone, and finally to quite elaborate entrance pillars. The actual gates to houses also evolved from

Cyclopean masonry, in a field wall off La Route du Nord. (J).

SOME FARM BELLS

bell canopy, Les Côtils, (T).

bell turret, Le Marais, (My).

bell gable, La Fontaine, (My).

bell gable, Morel Farm, (L).

1

the simple to the ornate, each good in its own style. A local design which is becoming rare has a semi-circular bar holding in place rounded uprights within a framework. (Plate V.)

No farm buildings of any great age have survived, and it seems likely that outhouses were roughly constructed and of an impermanent nature until the 19th century, when well-to-do farmers started to construct stables and hay-lofts. When the potato became an important crop, there was the further need for warm, frost-free storage for the seed. Among the best examples of substantial farm buildings are those at The Oaks (P), dated 1837, and those at Melbourne House (J), and Manor Farm (O); many others seem to have been built from the middle of the 19th century onwards.

Pigs were kept automatically on every farm, and in about 1820 General Le Couteur was fattening his pigs exclusively on boiled potatoes and acorns, with occasional greens, parsnips and carrots: it was thought that the parsnips gave a "peculiar delicacy" to the pork.

Pig sties have received little attention, but the farmer was at pains to accommodate his pigs well. The most usual style is a lean-to, with slate or tile roof, often three sections in a row. They were constructed with the inner room for sleeping, roofed over, and an open enclosed space for the pig to exercise and bask in, with a door, usually wood, but occasionally iron, and an aperture through which the pig swill was tipped into a trough inside. These troughs are usually simple granite bowls, square, round or semi-circular, but on occasion older and more venerable bowls have been found in use for this utilitarian purpose. The granite setts, about a foot square, with which the courtyard of the sty was paved, are much in demand for garden paths nowadays, and pig-keeping on a small scale has so much disappeared from the economy that comparatively few of these sties have survived, and those which have no longer serve their original purpose.

A most interesting variant of the pig sty has been noticed. This follows the standard pattern, except for the roof which is hipped and covered in rough cement, made of sea sand and quarry gravel. Inside the ceiling the "room" is domed with granite slabs, most beautifully fitted. Of those so far noticed two are in St. Ouen, two in St. Mary and five in St. John. This close geographical distribution suggests one particular mason who created and perfected this style; how one wishes one knew who he was, and even more so, when he was at work. The only pig sty (of the usual type) recorded with a date is that at La Grange (My), with 1834. It seems impossible to discover the date of the domed sties, but the middle of the 19th century is likely. One may wonder if the domed stone roof on La Crête Fort in Bonne Buit Bay, dated 1835, is indicative, and it seems not impossible that these domed sties could be of this period. They range in quality from the simple one-sty version at London House in the Mourier Valley, to the superb and very large piggery at Le Douet (J). The properties where they have (so far) been noted are:

    St. Ouen.—Merrivale, Le Coin; and Les Ormes, Grantez.
    St. Mary.—London House (1842); and Falaise House (1842).
    St. John.—Rosedale (near Melbourne House); Highcliff (Becquet ès Chats) (demolished); Le Douet (Hautes
        Croix) (1875); Le Vivier (Mont Mado) (1745); Maple Grove (Mont Mado) (demolished).
      (The dates refer to the houses and may be quite irrelevant to the pig sties.)

No instance has been found suggesting a thatched roof for a pig sty, which is surprising as it would be so much warmer, and warmth is essential to the well-being of a pig. There is one instance of arrangements for keeping the pigs warm, at L'Hermitage J, q.v., and it has also been noticed that sties are often built up against a wash-house, but that may have been more for convenience in carrying the swill, cooked on the wash-house fire.

Various erections, on or near farms, such as lavoirs (douets à laver), fontaines, abreuvoirs and lime kilns all had simple effective uses. The kiln, fourné à caux, was for burning lime for building purposes, and as a fertiliser and insecticide spray. Shells were imported, being brought in as ballast from England, but oysters used to be so common in Jersey, as well as limpets and ormers, that doubtless their shells were as much in demand in order to produce lime to sweeten the soil. It seems that the shells and fuel were piled in alternate layers, the kiln being filled from the upper level, a fire kindled and the resulting ash collected from below, the kiln being built into a hillside. A very fine example is being restored at Augrès (now the Jersey Wildlife Preservation Trust). It consists of a burning kiln, a storage shed and a slaking pit, so that either hydrated or carbonate of lime could be obtained. Quayle, writing in 1813, says that the lime was then imported from Normandy in time of peace, but that "20 years have elapsed since it was first burnt in the Island, and no more than 12 since its

16

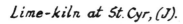

Lime-kiln at St. Cyr, (J).

first application to agriculture". In 1801, he says, Plymouth limestone was imported and converted into lime in the brick kilns, but the price being high "this will prevent its general use".

The best known of the existing lavoirs is that at St. Cyr (J) erected in its present form in 1811. There are many others, smaller and simpler, and a beautiful example is Le Douet Fleury (q.v. under La Cornetterie) in St. Martin, so secluded that few know of its existence.

When a lavoir (often incorporating an abreuvoir for watering animals) was erected it often happened that a contract was drawn up, the contracting parties agreeing to share equally in all expenses and to observe certain rules. For example in 1846,* ten shareholders living near and to the east of St. Martin's Church, built one at La Fontaine de Gallie, a field then belonging to Philippe Vardon fs. Louis, and described as "qui fut au Reverend Bulkeley Bandinel". This is Mt. 380, later reunited with the Bandinel Farm lands. Any person wishing to wash his linen there had to give 48 hours notice to Vardon; none might wash very dirty garments, nor dry his linen on the said field, on pain of losing his rights to the said "lavoir et abreuvoir". The syllabic initials of the shareholders are incised on a stone at the back of the abreuvoir; they include CP for Chapelle, the Methodist Chapel in the Rue du Belin. The contract for one attached to Les Grandes Rues, Faldouet, built in 1835,† was very similar and it served 13 proprietors in the vicinity. Another on Bouley Bay hill, served some of the tenants of the fief de l'Abbesse de Caen, and here the initials of those having the right to use it are on the trough; it is dated 1834 and bears seven sets of initials. The remote position

Fontaine and Lavoir at La Fortunée, (T).

*Livre 191, folio 46.
†Livre 163, folio 83.

on the steep hill side is surprising until one studies Richmond's map, and sees that the road then passed right beside it. Even so, it is some distance (over a quarter of a mile) from the homes of those who could use it, and who can be identified with reasonable certainty on Godfray's map as living north of Les Croix, and near La Hurette.

One system of washing was resuscitated during the Occupation when soap was unobtainable. Clothes were put in layers, interspersed with a good quantity of wood ash, in a wooden trough, and hot water was poured on, and then left to soak This was found to be very effective, and was as was done in "temps passé". This may constitute a link between the cold-water washing in the brook and the boiling made possible when coppers were introduced, probably around 1850. In fact the appearance of the wash-house copper must have been hailed as a major labour-saving device, enabling the housewife not only to wash her linen in hot water for the first time, but also to do so on her own premises.

Hunting and shooting in Jersey have been mainly restricted to the ubiquitous rabbit. Nonetheless hunting rights were jealously guarded by all seigneurs, including the King, and no man dared hunt, trap or shoot without permission. The meat eaten was mostly mutton, but also veal and beef, and one notices, with a sigh of envy perhaps, the size of the joints ordered, often 15 or 20lbs.

Moles, first complained of by Poingdestre in 1680, continued to be a great nuisance to farmers, and efforts to control them, largely ineffective, often appeared in the Actes des Etats, when rewards were paid for each mole caught. A curious comment was made by Jean Mauger in 1761 when he said in a letter to a relative that there had been so little warmth that no lizards had been seen, but that he would try to send some by the next boat. He does not make it clear whether the skin or the creature is to be sent. They were, said Stead, ". . . the most beautiful lizards in the world . . . glittering like emeralds studded with gold".

The farm implements used in the past would seem to us heavy and unwieldy. In 1772 in the Court Rolls of the small fief of Lecq there was an argument between Gideon Le Gresley and Philippe de la Perrelle who jointly owned a plough and a harrow (herche à dents de fer) and this is an important entry. The borrowing, non-return and damaging of ploughs often appears in seigneurial records and a plough was often a man's most valuable asset. A brand new plough, from Le Brun in St. Mary, was recorded as costing £4 5s. in 1851. A wide variety of implements, still in existence, and some still in use, is illustrated on page 30. The various farm carts and carriages in use at different periods are of the greatest interest and could constitute a study in their own right. Though the elegant local horse van* came into prominence with the growing importance of the potato trade, around 1870, a contractor named Pierre Omont advertised that he had for sale oak, elm and ash wood, "propre pour faire des charrettes" in 1853.† His initials POM, may be seen on the parish stone (illustrated on Plate VIId) in 1838 when he was the contractor in charge of work at Rozel.

Fishing used to be far more a part of life than it now is, and on 12 August 1834 Philippe Marett "drew the net" in St. Brelade's Bay and caught 250 mackerel, certainly a good catch. Stead noted 21 kinds of locally-caught fish in the market. Cod came from Newfoundland or Gaspé in great quantities and a diary entry in September 1820 records that "The Charlotte arrived this day bringing news of the Esther having sailed with 1339 quarters of codfish". In 1738 a payment of 30s. due by Captain Edouard Vibert to Edouard Marett was made in fish. In 1772 one Richard Bermingham wrote to Captain Daniel Messervy of the schooner Molly, at Santander, from St. Sebastian, advising him of a hold up in the fish trade and "stagnation" so that he knew not where to store the cargoes that were expected; on the other hand in 1777 François Journeaux received a letter from his mother-in-law's brother Mathieu Shoemans to say that in Bordeaux cod was selling well, with great profit, but that this was not the case with salt salmon.

Vraic and its collection were immensely important and controlled by law. Vraic ash was sometimes paid as a seigneurial due, and many inhabitants in the parishes bordering St. Ouen's Bay had "une place à sécher du vraic" on the sand dunes. Vraic officers were appointed both by the fiefs and the parish authorities, and in 1801 the Constable of St. Brelade appointed four for

SOME JERSEY FARM IMPLEMENTS,

PAST AND PRESENT.

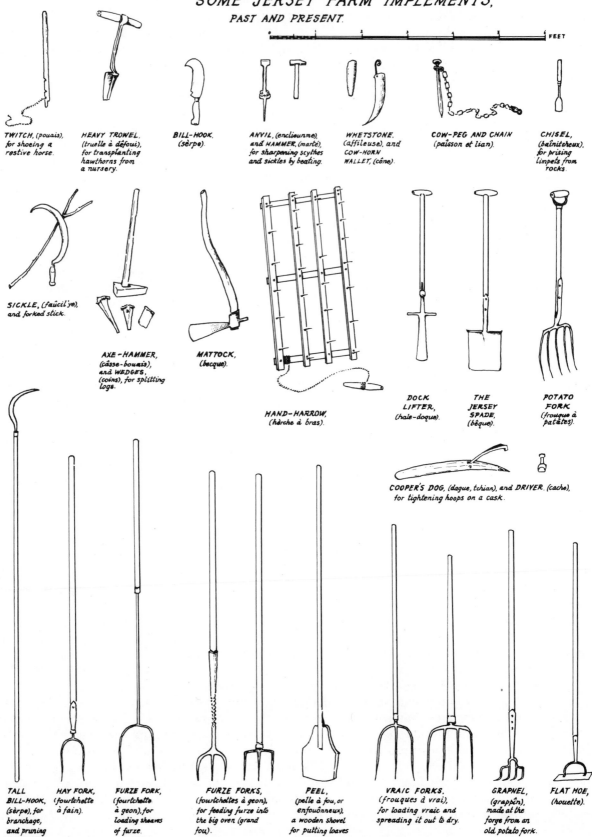

TWITCH, (pouais), for shoeing a restive horse.

HEAVY TROWEL, (truelle à défoui), for transplanting hawthorns from a nursery.

BILL-HOOK, (sèrpe).

ANVIL, (enclieunme), and HAMMER, (marté), for sharpening scythes and sickles by beating.

WHETSTONE, (affileuse), and COW-HORN WALLET, (cône).

COW-PEG AND CHAIN (paisson et lian).

CHISEL, (bainitcheux), for prising limpets from rocks.

SICKLE, (faûcil'ye), and forked stick.

AXE-HAMMER, (câsse-bouais), and WEDGES, (coins), for splitting logs.

MATTOCK, (becque).

HAND-HARROW, (hèrche à bras).

DOCK LIFTER, (hale-doque).

THE JERSEY SPADE, (bêque).

POTATO FORK (frouque à patates).

COOPER'S DOG, (dague, tchian), and DRIVER, (cache), for tightening hoops on a cask.

TALL BILL-HOOK, (sèrpe), for branchage, and pruning in the fields.

HAY FORK, (fourtchette à fain).

FURZE FORK, (fourtchette à geon), for loading sheaves of furze.

FURZE FORKS, (fourtcheltes à geon), for feeding furze into the big oven (grand fou).

PEEL, (pelle à fou, or enfouônneux), a wooden shovel for putting loaves in the oven.

VRAIC FORKS, (frouques à vrai), for loading vraic and spreading it out to dry.

GRAPNEL, (grappên), made at the forge from an old potato fork.

FLAT HOE, (houette).

the area of La Pulente alone. Sir John Le Couteur recorded seeing 250 carts and 17 boats in one day, collecting vraic, probably at La Pulente. How fortunate that Jersey's great artist, Edmund Blampied, so often chose for his paintings and drawings, a scene of vraic being collected by horse and cart, in the traditional manner.

Slight as the evidence is, there are clues about gardens from the earliest times. Vinchelez de Haut had a Jardin de la Minauderie (a strolling garden or plaisaunce) in the early 19th century, and probably far earlier. But what of the humbler homes? In England the cottage garden was a feature of village life, visible to friends, neighbours and passers-by, on foot or mounted, no longer noticed by occupants of the streams of cars and coaches thundering past to-day with noise and fumes. Neither cottage nor village are really germane to the Jersey landscape, the pattern being more of large or small farms, and scattered rather than grouped.

After about 1820 there is a great deal of horticultural information available, but we are at a loss to find details about 18th-century gardens. One partage dated 1730, mentions a Jardin des Fleurs at Les aix (P.).

Local houses were often built with one or other gable end abutting on a road; occasionally the north wall did the same but never the front (except in towns naturally). The small, enclosed front patch, usually rectangular but sometimes triangular, is so frequently met with, in houses of all sizes and dates, that it must be safe to assume that this was a traditional plan. It often had (and has) a circular or rectangular patch of grass, with the centre piece of pampas grass, yucca or palm: later in the century the monkey puzzle (introduced into the British Isles in 1795) appeared in many a front garden, and simple topiary is seen in some Victorian photographs. It is noticeable that Jersey people speak of their flower beds as borders, perhaps a relic of the surround to the grass patch, enclosed within a low wall. Typical examples of this type of front garden are at La Caroline (O), The Elms (My), Ville ès Philippes (G), Terrebonne (G), Slate Farm (C), La Profonde Rue (T).

Documents describing property suggest that vegetables were grown in a Jardin à Potage, Jardin aux Herbes, or Jardin Muré, often situated to the side or at the back of the house. Cider apple grafts were raised in the Jardin des Greffes, the apple trees being in the Jardin des Pommiers. The word Jardin causes some confusion in this particular context, as it was used for any orchard.

Flowers and perhaps soft fruits tended to be grown in the front patch, sometimes nonchalantly mixed. One wonders what varieties were grown, and whether for pleasure, for culinary and medicinal purposes, or for sale in the market place on Saturdays; probably all three, according to the status of the owners.

It seems that all sorts of vegetables were grown, with the accent on beans, cabbages and parsnips, and of course the tall Jersey cabbage or Long Jack. All fruits flourished and were grown in far more variety than nowdays, particularly apples and pears, often trained against walls. All early guide books speak in enthusiastic terms of the quality and flavour of the fruit grown. There were, too, figs, grapes and melons, and all the usual stone and soft fruits. The nurseryman Langellier stocked 500 varieties of pear in 1838. Where the sewage works now are Mr. E. Nicolle established a vineyard at his house, Bellozanne, favourably commented upon by the Horticultural Committee in 1838. Medlars and walnuts were grown, and loquats, oranges and strawberry vines were tried. Part of this success may perhaps be attributed to bee keeping. In 1756 we know that Thomas Le Maistre of St. Saviour collected his honey three times,* and Jersey honey was famed for its flavour. And in 1809 Stead said, "There were formerly a great many apiaries in the Island; before the introduction of cider the principal drink of the inhabitants being mead".†

The flowers grown were very much the same as those found in English gardens, with pinks (border carnations) dominating in early summer. There were also lilac, lily of the valley, fuchsia, old-fashioned roses and many types of geranium. Arum lilies grew in pots or in the ground round the houses, as did Jersey lilies, the amaryllis belladonna or Les Belles Dames toutes nues, the date of whose introduction to the Island has not yet been established. The dahlia was not introduced until 1820, when Sir John Le Couteur planted it at Le Bocage, and it soon showed itself to be particularly well suited to Jersey. At that time he was also planting magnolias and many other

---

*B.S.J. 1967, p. 245.   †Stead, p. 82.

rare species, partly as a result of his friendship with Professor La Gasca of Madrid, then living in the Island, and also Mr. Curtis of La Chaire (q.v.).* The camellia (introduced into the British Isles in 1739) thrives in Jersey and many houses built from about 1820 onwards have such ancient camellia bushes that one may infer that they are contemporary with the house. Some examples of this are Noirmont Manor (B) (1830); Mon Plaisir (B) (1820); Midvale Road Houses (H) (*c.* 1835); Mainland (L) (*c.* 1845); L'Espine, Millbrook (*c.* 1830). Langellier in 1850 had 30,000 camellia stock. Householders were buying plants and bulbs from nurseries in England and France, witness the diaries of Sir John Le Couteur and Philippe Marett of La Haule. The mimosa may also have been introduced at this period, and was quickly found to be well suited to our conditions.

The early records of the R.J.A. & H.S., started in 1834, mention their exhibitions of geraniums, ixias and cacti as being particularly good. In that first year the spring flower prizes were awarded for geraniums, pinks, roses, heartsease (pansy) and greenhouse bulbs: for fruit, prizes were given for grapes, pineapples and strawberries: and for vegetables, potatoes, asparagus, cauliflower, cabbage and peas. One of the judges was Professor La Gasca. At the autumn show of that year dahlias and asters were added to the list, melons, peaches, pears, cherries and red currants to the fruit, and onions, celery, marrow, tomatoes, shallots, carrots, parsnips, turnips, beet, parsley, mushrooms and kidney beans to the vegetables.

By 1839 the scope of the Society had greatly broadened and there was a very large range of dahlias exhibited; prizes, some given by the States, were offered to "cottagers" for dahlias, marigolds, chrysanthemums, mixed bunches, apples, pears, outdoor grapes and currants. It was noted that cottage gardens were inspected and showed "great improvement in neatness and cleanliness in their dwellings which are the fruits of industry and good management".

By the time of the Channel Islands Exhibition in 1871 the scope of the exhibits had been further enlarged, and zonal pelargoniums had almost ousted all other flowers, probably a matter of fashion; there were also hothouse plants, begonias, ferns and coleus. The "cottagers" prizes then included roses, mixed bouquets and many vegetables.

François Guillaume Collas, of St. Martin's House, used to record the components of a nosegay he picked every Christmas Day. In 1837 he was able to gather laurestina, chrysanthemum, primrose, auricula, cystus, jonquil, French marigold, hydrangea, snowberry tree, anemone, heartsease, strawberry blossom, fuchsia, coronilla, sweet william, christmas rose, pyrus japonica, red and white roses, and another japonica. In 1839 "a sprig of heliotrope" was added.

The many guide books of the 19th century all speak of flowers and gardens, and Stead mentions the superior flavour of the locally-grown fruit, particularly the Chaumontelle pear. Quayle, a few years later, mentions the high quality of the vegetables. Plees says that "private gardens yield every natural luxury that the climate can produce . . . the peach apricot is remarkable for its size and beauty, melons are in profusion . . . strawberries have been noticed for superiority of flavour . . . the immediate environs of the town are crowded with small private gardens, from many of which the market is supplied". Inglis, a little later remarks on the "pretty peeps" one gets into gardens, and says, "It is seldom that one sees a house or cottage, not absolutely in a street, unaccompanied by less or more garden . . . a fine bloom of beautiful flowers is generally seen . . . all kinds of myrtles grow luxuriantly . . . the hydrangea is seen at almost every other cottage door, measuring perhaps from eight to twelve feet in circumference, and four or five feet in height. The verbena, or lemon plant, is also common . . . Spanish chestnut and evergreen oak are more often seen than in England". Inglis also remarks on the prevalence of blue hydrangeas, in particular at La Hougue Bie. de la Croix, in about 1860, says ". . . on dirait une forêt d'arbres frutiers . . . avec les habitations charmantes, tapissées de pierres et de vignes vierges, une foule de délicieux 'cottages' tenus avec la plus exquise propreté, entourés d'arbustes et de fleurs . . .". (It seems to be a forest of fruit trees . . . with charming dwellings covered with ivy and vines, a mass of delicious little cottages, kept so beautifully clean and surrounded with shrubs and flowers.)

In the period when farms had an enclosed courtyard, often entered through the large round arch, this formed the actual farmyard. When the fashion changed, around 1700, it looks as if the

* *Victorian Voices*, p. 64, 242.

farmyard moved from the front to the back of the house, and this may have given the incentive to plant a "front garden", so that the rectangular front patch which we have been considering seems to have replaced the farmyard, and to have followed it in size and shape.

So all the records we have, sparse as they are before 1800, offer a picture of great luxuriance and fertility, with vegetables, fruit and flowers being grown in abundance by rich and poor alike, whether for pleasure or for profit, or for both. The markets were clearly well stocked, as they are now, but in those days all the produce for sale would be home grown. All diaries speak of sending fruit to relatives in England, Jerseymen being persuaded at all times that the produce of their Island is superior to that grown anywhere else.

It should not be thought that the Jerseyman neglected the planting of trees, and diarists tell us of much activity in this respect. For instance in 1820 Philippe Marett purchased for 10s. 8d., from Mr. Le Maistre, 12 laurestinas, 12 bay, 12 scotch fir, 12 silver fir, 12 Portugal laurel (P. Lusitanica) and two plane trees, as well as two others whose names cannot be deciphered. But in 1821 he "knocked down seven elm trees that were along the new road about the place intended to build the slip". In 1835 he was selling sycamore wood at 1s. 2d. per foot, and in 1847 289ft. of oak for 2s. 2d. per foot, one oak being 32½ft. long. He also planted evergreen oak (ilex) acorns in his côtils. In a boundary dispute between George Badier and Abraham Gibaut of St. Lawrence in 1832 the types of trees mentioned were oak, elm and willow. In 1862 the contents of the garden at Claremont, Mont Millais, were valued at £54 0s. 6d. by Saunders, the nurseryman, and this may be seen to indicate a well stocked garden when compared with the purchases made for the same garden by Miss Robin, the tenant, in 1877.

There can be no doubt that the face of Jersey in our memories, in books and in pictures, is predominantly rural, and that until the present century every family's life was directly or indirectly connected with farming. The parson, the Seigneur, the Jurat and the Constable, all farmed, and this was not "Piccadilly farming" but real participation on the part of the "Patron" as we have seen in the cases of men like Marett and Le Couteur. They were actively concerned with milking the cows (even leaving advice on how to control a kicking cow during milking); they took part in carting the hay and the vraic. Theirs was an active, varied and healthy life, which kept the Island largely self-supporting, and preserved the environment, a word which has acquired a well-nigh holy status in this decade, now that its quality and sometimes its very existence are in mortal danger.

CHAPTER SIX

SHIPPING AND SHOPPING

"My nephew Richard Valpy had the misfortune to be taken last week in François Le Boutillier's boat, bound for Guernsey, by a corsair from Carteret, and sent there for ransom."

Jean Simon, c. 1760. (translated)

THE WEALTHIEST ERA Jersey ever knew was based on the cod, "la morue". Even allowing for the decline in the value of money, surely at no other period have so many native Jerseymen been rich. This is so well recognised that any large or superior house is referred to, often loosely, as a Cod House, a Maison de Terreneuve. (This does not mean, as some people think, that it was built by a Mr. Cod.) It does mean, however, that it was built by fortunes derived from the cod fishing industry. This trade with Newfoundland and the Gaspé coast was established by the end of the 16th century, but its heyday was in the 19th. Young Jerseymen took to the sea in the spring, returning in the autumn to help their fathers and wives with the autumn cultivation, and during that time they had fished in the rich Newfoundland banks, taking their salted cod to the South Americas or the Mediterranean countries, and bringing home with them rich treasures, notably the mahogany, which swiftly replaced native oak and elm for fashionable furniture. Each year the first ship back from Newfoundland had the right to tie up at La Boué du Roi, the King's Buoy. This spot was immediately east of the Janvrin pier at St. Aubin (built in 1818) and remained drier than any other mooring.*

Linked with the fishing industry was that of ship building, and St. Aubin's Bay and the Gorey coast were ringed with ship-building yards where sturdy, but graceful vessels were created by craftsmen, to the sound of hammer beat and song, and the smell of rope and tar and wood, men living for and near the sea, and familiar with every changing mood of the weather and every vagary of the fierce tides which ebb and flow round our coasts. There are many records of individual ships, and lists of the names in the Almanacs of the times. In 1834, on 5 November Philippe Marett recorded, "The Glenarm was launched from St. Aubin's Fort, the very first vessel built there." Fortunately there still exist some very early photographs of these ship-building yards, faded as many of them are. Le Vesconte's yard alone, in 1864, had eight vessels on the stocks, totalling over 4,000 tons: the largest vessel built was the *Rescue*, 1,187 tons. By about 1870 the industry had all but disappeared, and the ship-building yards but were but a memory of the past.†

Let us see what contemporary records have to tell us about shipping in general, a subject on which the La Haule papers offer much original information. Privateers were said to be ". . . well manned and appointed, and have proved a great annoyance to the trade of the enemy and a

a ship's mast, in service as a roof beam, in Commercial St., St. Helier.

19

*Information from the late Lord Coutanche.
†See *Jersey through the Lens*; B.S.J. 1962, p. 229; Jèrri Jadis, by George d'la Forge; Balleine, Bailiwick of Jersey, p. 19.

enemy and a benefit to the public as well as to their individual proprietors". So spake the contemporary voice of Stead. Letters of marque, permitting a form of legalised piracy, were obtained by many shipowners, and these enabled a merchant vessel to act as a naval one, attack the King's enemies, and bring in the captured vessel as a prize. In 1693 the barque *Ann of Jersey,* previously called the *Mary,* with Gyles Le Paumelle as Master, 25 tons, was owned by six Jerseymen who had to be "His Majesty's naturall borne subjects . . .", and she was a captured prize. The oldest recorded letter of marque is dated 1692 and was granted to Jean Maugier.

It is only to be expected that smuggling prospered equally, but naturally it is never mentioned in surviving documents, and so all information about it is hearsay. The proximity of the French coast, and the large number of vessels at sea, made it highly profitable, and well-nigh irresistible. Tobacco, spirits, lead, pepper and many other commodities found their way ashore without attracting customs dues. In 1701 a boat sailing to Normandy had packages of money on board and these were seized; the money, the boat and its equipment were confiscated and the Master and two seamen put in prison for three months. The owner, Jacques Hue, had been warned not to put contraband on board, and so was made to compensate Averty, the Master. In 1717 Edouard Marett recorded, in despair, that his ship had been confiscated at Rouan (*sic*) coming from Spain, and that consequently he was reduced to beggary. Another local vessel was the *Venus* of which Richard de Carteret (unidentified) owned a tenth part in 1774, paying his share of charges, materials, insurance and fitting out the vessel for "ye Bay of Honduras", the cost being £5,971 livres tournois. Another was the *Young Phoenix,* built in 1802/3, three masted, carvel built with a square stern, extreme length 83ft., extreme width 22ft., 182 tons. She was granted a charter as a privateer, and was owned by the Janvrin brothers. In 1805 she was described as being "armed and equipped for war, having commissions of reprisal against the enemies of His Majesty", and was then about to start for Newfoundland with a cargo of coal. The chance of earning prize money made it easier to recruit crews for vessels such as these.

Ships' Masters sometimes had trouble with their crews. In 1721 Jean Mauger was Commandant of the brigantine *Jean de Jersey* homeward bound; when their ship was in peril the crew disobeyed orders in a tumultous way, endeavouring to ferment a revolt, and Mauger asked that they should be charged and deprived of their share of the cargo of cod, as well as their wine and wages.

Ships were often owned by syndicates, and in 1721 the Master of *L'Accident,* Samuel Perrand having died, his one-eighth share had to be sold at St. Aubin, and the money used to pay arrears of salary due to him and the crew, and food for the boy employed to guard the ship. In 1727 Edouard Marett was tuteur to a child who had inherited three-sixteenth of two vessels, *La Bonne Industrie* and *Le Jean,* both engaged in the Newfoundland trade. With all this maritime prosperity it is not surprising to find that Victor Hugo considered Jersey to be the seventh port in the British Isles.

Children were taken on the trans-Atlantic voyages as apprentices, and one, Eleazer Dolbel, sailed in 1715, with Captain Jean Mauger as Master, in the *Bonne Espérance,* belonging to Captain Edouard Le Brun. The vessel was to go to New England for three years, the apprentice was to receive food and clothing, and a new suit of clothes at the end of his service "as is customary", and in return Dolbel promised to serve faithfully, and not to absent himself by day or night. One is glad to know that it was also stipulated that he was to be treated humanely. In another instance the apprentice was a girl, Marie Esnouf, aged 19, and she was engaged to serve whatever employer the Captain, William Bushell, could find for her, for four years. At the end of that time, having served faithfully, Marie was to receive a new dress for Sundays. Another case was that of Philippe Le Gros, aged seven, who was hired on similar terms for fourteen years. Soon afterwards, in 1723, the States ordained that no foreigners or their agents might take from the Island children who were in the charge of the parishes, or who were begging. If such people wished to take children away they had to obtain official permission. Sad indeed was the fate of pauper children.

A hazard that these sea-faring adventures attracted was the ever-present possibility of being captured and being held for ransom. In 1700 the States were arranging for payment to be made for the relief and ransom of islanders held by the King of Morocco, and in 1760 Jean Simon reported that a boat from St. John's had been taken by a corsair from Carteret, the required ransom soon being paid. When his own nephew was captured, as quoted at the heading to this chapter, the ransom asked was only £400, livres tournois presumably, and again this was soon paid.

It is perhaps surprising to find vessels being insured as early as 1738, when Abraham Malzard instructed Jean Seale to insure his share of the vessel *Pipon Galley* for £100 at 1½ per cent. for the journey to Terreneuve. It was stated that insurance was at that rate for Portugal or Italy, but more expensive for Spain, because of the fear of war.

In 1751 an interesting deed was drawn up between Madeleine and Elizabeth Dauvergne, and the widower of their sister Anne, Philippe Robin, referring to themselves as "mestiers de marchandise". All their goods were divided, half to Robin and a quarter each to his sisters-in-law. They decided to continue to live together in Robin's house, which had come to him through his wife, and to share in the educational expenses of his children. The youngest of the three sons, Charles, became famous as the founder of Charles Robin and Co., the greatest of the Newfoundland fishing firms, and the eldest son, Philippe, was the ancestor of the family now living in the Island. The house in question may have been that now called St. Magloire, where Charles died in 1824.

Harbour facilities were minimal until 1846, when the Victoria Pier was built, to be followed by the Albert Pier in 1853. Before that passengers and commercial activities had to be content with the tiny Havre des Anglais and Havre des Français, constructed between 1700–20.

Treacherous rocks menace our shores and many are the wrecks which have occurred. Various writers have tried to set down and describe safe passages of approach, and one was Jean Maugier (*sic*) who, in about 1719, copied a list of rocks and sailing instructions from some seventy years earlier. An example of his directions is: "Hubot. Il faut amener ou avoir la Rousse p(ar) la maison Jeremie Grandin et St. Sauv(eur) et au lis du Chateaux an rouge Galle". Clearly the pilot needed to be a Jerseyman, and to know

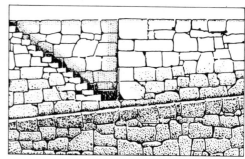

FEATS OF MASONRY, seen in harbour wall, stair and slipway, at St. Helier (above) and St. Aubin (below).   20

where people lived, to understand these instructions. To take but one example of a wreck, there is a tombstone at All Saints Church, commemorating the loss of the cutter *Fanny* on 7 January 1825, with Anne Querinot and her little daughter Fanny Ellie, aged eight; the poor widower, Elie, was left with five other children.

Until 1823 no steamship had been seen in Jersey waters, and their advent was a tremendous step forward into the new century and a wonderful time saver. In the days of sail it could easily take two days to reach Portsmouth or Weymouth, as Sir John Dumasesq found on the many trips he made to England on States' business. When Stead first came to the Island in 1809 he embarked in the *Rover,* Captain Quirk, saying it was ". . . remarkably clean and commodious . . . No packet employed by the Post Office between Weymouth and Jersey has ever been lost or taken". The *Rover* was built in 1789, 67 tons, 53ft. long, armed with carriage guns and small arms. She and the *Royal Charlotte* were the first of the Post Office cutters.* In 1809 the fare to Weymouth was 27s. or £1 by a trading vessel, and in 1837 when Ann Marett went to England her fare to Southampton was 15s.

Within the Island travel was naturally by foot or by horse, Plees mentioning that there were few closed carriages. In 1795 Sir John Dumaresq had caused quite a sensation by importing the first post-chaise to be seen in Jersey, which cost him £75, probably sterling in this case. In about

---

*Mailships of the Channel Islands, R. Mayne, p. 5.

1820 Sir John Le Couteur bought a phaeton in London, painted "drab colour" and in 1821 Philippe Marett paid 21 guineas for a second-hand gig. In the 1860s Sidney Nicolle described picnic parties, with young people going to visit beauty spots in wagonnettes and various styles of carriage, and the most searched-after seat was the dickey, with a chosen girl friend, coming home by moonlight and invisible to the chaperone accompanying the party. The poorer people travelled by farm van, on horseback or on foot, and the longest journey most of them undertook was the weekly visit to town to take in produce to sell in the market. In some cases travel was easier by boat than by road, as in 1818 when Philippe Marett "went to town at 4 in Dan'l J's* boat; we had a pleasant sail along the shore and came in at Mr Durell at about ½8".

In Jersey, as in all countries in those days, the roads were narrow and uneven, dusty in summer and muddy in winter. As early as 1824 Le Couteur introduced "Macadam's system" into the western parishes, but this would only have referred to a few main roads, although St. Peter's Valley, he records, was "newly macadamised" by 1830. The cost for this work was 12s. per perch at 8ft. wide. Many arguments occur in records concerning the widening or straightening of roads, and owners sometimes improved their own properties by giving land to widen, or alter, a public road. Philippe Le Feuvre in 1847 failed to do this, as it was claimed that he only wanted personal advantage at public expense. In 1811 Jean Pipon, Seigneur de la Hague, *causa uxoris,* succeeded in having Le Mont du Chêne closed ("aboli") as it ran through his property and this was agreed to on condition that he made le Mont du Presbytère (just to the south of his property) into a public road, surfacing and graduating it and making it 14ft. wide, all at his own expense. A document of 1799 is relevant, giving the names of the men, 12 in Coin Varin and 14 in Le Douet, who did corvée on the Ruelle du Presbytère in July of that year. Some parishioners in the Coin Varin objected, saying that Le Mont du Chêne was a much more direct route for them when going to church or to St. Ouen's Bay for vraic; they had slight, but only very slight, justification for saying this. However, the change was made and Le Mont du Chêne became a private drive which has fallen quite out of use at the present time. In 1878 the then Seigneur of St. Ouen, E. C. Malet de Carteret offered the parish land on which the present main road past the Manor lies, in exchange for treating the then existing road as a private drive, and this was accepted. Elm trees were planted to line the new strip, and survived until recent years, but are now being replaced. In 1813 the Govenor offered the help of the troops in making St. Peter's valley road, provided that it would be considered as a main road ("ouvert en grande route").

In 1770 there was a move to abolish "tresnaux sur terre" (sledges) as, Daniel Messervy says, they ruined the roads. One can well imagine that he was right, on dirt roads with no surface.

It is hard to evaluate the cost of items when currency was not only so different, but also changing over the years, and to complicate the issue still further there were different currencies in use in Jersey simultaneously. In general, if sterling is meant in a document written in French, it will say so, and if it is not specified it can be assumed that livres tournois are being quoted; if the document is written in English the money is more likely, but by no means certainly, to be pounds and shillings. In 1834 sterling became the legal currency in Jersey, and the parishioners of St. Mary (rather surprisingly as the parish was conservative in feeling) instructed their Constable to vote in favour of this, and the exchange was then declared to be £1 stg. = £26 tournois. But the old currency continued in use, and a British shilling was worth 13 Jersey pence, and it was not until 1876 that the British currency was fully accepted. The situation was made even more involved by the existence of "Livres selon l'ordre du Roi" of "Livres d'ordre", they being worth somewhat more than tournois. Little wonder that men so constantly challenged claims for payment. One may assume also that some people profited from the inevitable confusion.

In collections of documents there are always many bills, and these make fascinating reading. Some of the items cannot be identified or even read in some cases, and most shops stocked an arbitrary selection of goods. It is hard to compare prices, as in addition to the currency difficulty, quantities vary so widely, and are not always stated. Materials were usually measured by the verge (yard) or aune (ell = 45 ft.).

---

*Daniel Janvrin.

The vanishing village shop: An example (now demolished) at Beaumont.
21

An account with Aaron de Ste Croix, for goods supplied to Captain Snow in 1759, included sugar, wine, black tea (at 4s. lb.), thread, garters, handkerchiefs, Indian chintz, grenadine silk, persian cloth and "camlo", a cheap cotton material. In another account, with the same customer appearing as "Capitaine Cenos", he owed for soap (in blocks), coffee, brandy (odedue), wine, tea black and green, and sugar loaf (sucre en pain). In 1748 M. D. Messervy was on a visit to London and bought a "figured allemade capusheen" for £2 2s., clearly a hooded cape, and perhaps "à la mode", and also a pair of black lace muffetees. In a more practical mood, a few days later, he bought various brushes and mops, a water jug, hand "boules" (? bowls) and ladles, and for a total of 18s. 7d. sterling he bought two dozen wine glasses, 1 quart and two half pint cans, two tea potts, a box, three flower glasses, and had a stopper ground for 6d. In 1799 Mrs. Le Breton of La Hague was in London with her husband, and kept her household accounts in a curious little home-made book; she gives the prices but usually not the quantities, though she does tell us that a turkey was 6d. and tobacco 9d. The purchases are quite normal and the weekly bill is usually about 6s., unless there has been the most costly purchase of all, tea. Oranges are mentioned and currents (*sic*).

James de Carteret (b. 1737), son of Jean of Vinchelez de Haut was in the Navy, and we have a bill that he owed to Sara Le Vesconte, receipted by her in 1769. It includes tea, nails, silk, various materials by the yard, a bonnet, lace, starch, Pontivy (meaning cloth as made in that town), tape and thread. In 1779 James bought mourning garments from Mr. Seaton, totalling £75 2s. 6d. tournois, which included 28 yards of mourning crape (*sic*) for £70. In 1777 he bought from Charles Bishop £202 worth of goods including two stript waistcoats, 2 and three-eighths yards superfine Kersey Bath coating, three-quarters yard glas'd linen, a crimson velvet collar, 2 and a quarter yards ververette, silk garters, buckram canvas, riding trowsers, half a yard blue duffel, silver plated breast buttons, dimity, and "a pair of stays for your lady".

An undated list of clothing for "Master John Carteret" in the same manuscript collection, suggests a school list. He was probably the son of James de Carteret and Ann Le Vesconte, and lived 1770–85. Whatever the purpose, young John had to have "a new blue suit of cloathes, complete, one new Brown coat, one old black coat, one pair of new trowsers, one pair of old blue pantaloons, one new great coat, one stripd yellow waistcoat, one spotted waistcoat, one dozen new Irish shirts, three night cotton shirts, four night caps, six neck handkerchiefs, three black silk do, nine pocket handkerchiefs, seven pairs of cotton stockings, six pairs of woollen do, six balls of worsted and cotton thread, two hats, one new and one old, three pairs of shoes". There is a blank after an item "two pairs of . . .". Dare one suggest under-pants?

A large account was owed by Edouard Gibaut when he came under curatel, including £1 to the Jurats, 13s. for paper and drinks, 6s. for a dinner with the co-guardians, and various enigmatic entries "pour un noguin".

A collection of billheads lent for examination showed J. Wilcox, a linen and wool draper at 23 Beresford Street, in 1862, and he supplied 2 sunshades, calico at 6d. a yard, and sheets at 4s. 9d. per pair. Thomas Messervy in 1869, trading at Simon Place, supplied 11 bushels of small coals for 6s. 1½d., and charged 12s. 10d. for 15 bushels of coals delivered weekly. Pierre Guillaume at 24 New Street, supplied a copper (capeur de laverie) for 17s. 6d. less 7s. deducted for the old one.

There is no end to the fascination of these accounts, bills paid by our ancestors for the necessities of life, some being just like our own purchases, such as tea, sugar, soap, shoes and farm implements. But some items we cannot even identify, like 16 vogamachez for £16, perhaps Locofoco matches, then quite a new invention. Another puzzle is a "chirème", and some of the textiles had intriguing names and one would dearly like to see these materials.

The export of knitted goods was, both in quantity and quality, so considerable that one is delighted to find contemporary records. In 1741 Jean Mauger reported "Jean Le Gros hath shipped on the Jane of Jersey, of which he is Master, to Dartmouth 120 trees grown in the island, one hogshead of cider for John Seale, produced on the said Seal's own estate, and five bales containing 145 dozen worsted stockings, 15 knitted waistcoats, 4 pairs of knitted breeches, 11 knitted caps, 2 dozen knitted gloves, all manufactured here, and to be free of customs according to Royal grant given at Castle Elizabeth". Jean Simon, the carpenter-undertaker, as well as an export merchant, mentions sending by Captain Lys in the *Esther* in 1759, a consignment of stockings, with 30 dozen balls of wool, and wrapping to cover the stockings. His full list, untranslated, is:

```
 6 paires a cot es sous le talon
 2 doz a careaux au bout du pie
 1 doz a costes a l'ourlet
 1 doz a costes sous le pie
 2 doz a costes derriere le talon
 1 doz a costes a la jartiere
 6 paires en plein sous le talon
 3 doz do au col du pie
16 doz do a la jartiere
 3 doz Femme au bout du pie
 5 doz Femme a l'ourlet          Total 44 doz.
```

In 1760 he sent 67 dozen pairs of stockings on 10 March and 20 dozen on 31 May. Further consignments were said to be "portes a laver" or "a laver Samedy", and some were red and some blue. In 1761 he had an enquiry about silk stockings. In 1776 Mathieu Shoemans, an agent in Bordeaux, wrote asking his brother-in-law, Jacques Pradié Desarnauds, in Jersey to send him two pairs of wool stockings "brochés" (with embroidered clox perhaps?) not too big, as he had thin legs. A further letter referred to stockings "a cotte en trois fils", presumably in three-ply wool.

We may sympathise with the writer of a poem of 1725, found in a secret drawer of a locally-made desk; the secrets it contained were "frozen" from that time, as no papers found in it had dates after then, until it was opened in the 1960s. The poem laments the fate of those who travelled away from their homeland in search of commercial profit, and suggests that the cod fishing fortunes were gained at the expense of much toil and labour.

Chanson Nouvelle des Terreneuviers. 1725.

Braves garcons des Isles qui voullez naviguet,
nallez pas terreneuve pour vos jours abregé
il n'y a que la peine sants jamais nul plaisir,
toujours de sur les ondes au danger d'en mourir.

Et puis quand onne arrive dans ce mechant pays
l'onne se mait amorfondre dans des peaux de brebis
tout le monde resemble a se que vous voyez
en France sur les tiatres pour la farce jouir.

C'est un pays de Diable ou il n'y croit jamais rien
sans les navires des Isles nous y mourirons de faim
si non quullque vistualles qui nous sont apportez
par les navieres des Islaes pour nous fair subsister.

Retournons en nos Isles cest un heureux sejour
allons voir nos maitresses et leur fair lamour
Leur contant le mistaire quon nous a fait souffrir
pendant qu'ils sont a terre a bien leur rejouir.

(Spelling and punctuation as in the original, which
comprises ten verses. The poem appears to have
been written by three different hands.)

So Jersey took steps to alleviate the hardships suffered.

The Chamber of Commerce was founded in 1768, the first in the English-speaking world. It is interesting to note that the title is a straight translation of our Chambre de Commerce. It was founded by a group of merchants who wished to establish better understanding and safeguards for their interests, and each member contributed to a fund according to the amount of shipping which he owned, or on the same par if he were not a ship owner. Most of this money was used to relieve distress amongst seamen and their dependants. On one occasion at least, in November 1786, they sent out a relief ship, of which the Master asked no wages, to meet the vessels returning from Newfoundland; they had been so much delayed by contrary winds that they were thought to be seriously short of provisions.

PLATE V FARM BUILDINGS AND LAVOIRS

a. The Oaks (P), 1837

b. The Oaks (P), detail of stable floor

c. Lavoir at Slate Farm (C) (note wall daisies, or Mexican fleabane)

d. Water trough at lavoir on Bouley Bay Hill (T), 1834

PLATE VI GATES

a. La Pompe (My)

b. Vale Farm (P)

c. Mon Plaisir (L)

d. Ville au Veslet (L)

PLATE VII GATE POSTS AND PARISH STONES

a. A field in St Clement's parish

b. St Ouen's Manor, 1885

6
1838
Thomas Gallichan Connetable
George Larbalestier
Jean Dorey
Philippe Le Masurier
(Comité des Chemins)
Philippe de Gruchy, Vingtenier.
Pierre Omont Contractor

c. In Rosel Bay, 1838

d. A Clos des Pauvres, 1881

PLATE VIII LOCALLY MADE FURNITURE

b. A fruit wood chair.
Country type

c. An oak chest, *c* 1720. Original drawer handles
were metal, peardrop pattern

a. Long case clock by Louis Poignand, *c* 1780

CHAPTER SEVEN

FAMILY LIFE

"Ah, j'nouos accouôsinnons, car touos les Jèrriais sont couôsîns".

Dictionnaire Jersiais-Français, p. 5.

THE MOST ATTRACTIVE of all documents, for the social historian, are personal and family letters, and of all these the most endearing are those of young children.

In 1734 Marguerite Dumaresq, aged about ten, wrote from England to her uncle Edouard Marett of La Haule, and her letter is given in the original with a translation, insofar as it is possible to interpret it.

Mon cher oncle de la Haull,

Jeresuets lavots le 26 de Mars e le deux guines par Monsieus Jant Dumaresq carivets luntiets osour a London. Jevous suets infineetsmant aublieste des bonts ont que vous de mous e sivouple de panser en mous e de ne melesser pamanque de rients, siouple et de ma nvoest de largant pour a seter un Epinette ac plutos siauples de manvoets de labaties e dutes eu robe dinteentsne siauples par Madamant Dumaresq e de crier Mousieur de Gruchie de lie crier si jenets cunnantne a de meurets a lecoul ilya siex moust que je suiet jenet pont que siet monst a idemeurets a lecoul gisuets forbient siuouples de remetes de largant paseque nousavonts un bale se mous de Mey pasque jorets besont de bient de souts, vous giets panser siauples e de remet de largant pour que je de seque besont. mecomplimant a ma tant e a me cousient siouple. Je met pont doutre sout a vous marsets me siuouple de me crier avoplito je finiet a votre treuentble servante e a fessonet nesse Juque a la mort.

Marguerite Dumaresq.

My dear Uncle de la Haull,

I received yours of 26 March and the two guineas by Monsieur Jean Dumaresq which arrived Monday evening in London. I am infinitely obliged for the goodness you have shown me, and please to think of me and not to leave me lacking in anything, please send me money to buy a spinet as soon as possible please send me (?) labaties and some tea and a (?) dimity gown please by Madame Dumaresq and to write to Monsieur de Gruchy to write to her that I have but one year to stay at school, it is six months that I am here and I have only six months to stay here at school, I am very happy here, please send some money because we are having a ball this month of May because I shall need much money, you will think of this please and send money because I need it. My compliments to my aunt and my cousins please. I have nothing more to tell you but please write to me as soon as possible I end your very humble servant and affectionate niece until death.

Marguerite Dumaresq.

Marguerite was his ward, orphan child of his sister Marguerite. He replied to her letter, saying that he had difficulty in sending her tea, as he could not find anyone to take it. He said he had sent her more money, but begged her to be economical (mesnagère), money being hard to come by (difficile à attrapper). The main point about this letter is that it shows that the child was sent to boarding school before she could write French properly, let alone English. The school was kept by a Mrs. Jane Pym of Queen Street, Bristol.

Another little girl, Sophia, aged 9, wrote to her father, Pierre Daniel Marett, then at Madras, in 1816, saying "I have a great wish, dear Papa, to learn music; will you have the goodness to allow me to begin soon . . . my next letter will, I trust, dear Papa, be better written than this; I hope you will excuse it, being my first attempt". It is in fact very well written. Gordon Le Couteur, at the age of six, wrote to his elder brother, aged 11, at school in England, saying "I long for next summer that you may come. I love you dearly". Gordon died at the age of 16, probably from tuberculosis.

In about 1700 Elizabeth La Cloche wrote from London to her sister, Mrs. Peter Marett, saying that she was so sorry to hear that the children had smallpox and hoped that it would not prove mortal. She then said that Madame (Mrs. Durand, née Jeanne de la Cloche) asked "la faveur de luis pretes le cors de nostre cales et de luis enevuos pas le ates (?) le prochans retour". She continued begging the Maretts not to refuse "Ma Dame". The only explanation of this enigmatic request is that it was the horn of the family coach, but one wonders why it was so important.

A group of letters from Jourdain Gibaut to his father Abraham culminate with one from Cronstadt, dated 30 July 1822, including the extraordinary announcement, "Mon cher père Je vous prie quand vous ecrives des laitre ne faite pas mansion de nom de Gibaut parce que Je change monnon comme je vous e marque ayparavan . . . Je suis sus poin de me marier a une fille de Newyork une desparente de nos armateur el est agee de 15 ans et demi . . . Sil est possible je vas faire le malade pour ne pas aler au Indes sest un paiye que je nume pas baucou et les voyages sont trop long . . . Je demeure votre Fils jusque a mor LGB Richard Burr".

(My dear Father. I beg that when you write letters (to me) you will make no mention of the name Gibaut as I have changed my name as I already indicated to you. I am on the point of marrying a New York girl, related to one of our privateers; she is 15½ years old . . . If possible I intend to feign illness so as not to go to India. It is a country that I do not like much and the voyages are so long. I remain your son until death. JGB.) When he wrote to his brother Abraham in 1835 he was the father of five children.

Mothers' letters to their absent children have a timeless quality, and are always tinged with anxiety, and a longing for news, and for the return home of the child, whatever his age. They all contain admonitions about behaviour, care of health and economy, and give any local news which the mother hopes will be of interest, plus such philosophic musings as, "never be ashamed to acknowledge you have changed your way of thinking . . . for a wise man is always in a progressive state of improvement, but fools never change and end where they began", this being offered to John Le Couteur, then a cadet at Marlow, by his mother.

Mrs. Pipon of La Hague wrote in 1811, with similar sentiments but in a less educated manner, to her son at school with the famous Dr. Lemprière at Exeter. It seems that her daughters were also at boarding school, as she wrote to her husband, "I am surprised at your long stay at Weymouth . . . it is not possible for you to think of going (to Mr. de Lisle) this winter as the girls must not miss one day of their school . . . I hope you have considered the great expenses that attend being so long in England I am very short of money having to pay a great deal and not received much".

Not all wives wrote so plaintively. Mary Ann Marett wrote to her husband in 1821, addressing him as "my dearest husband" but surprisingly signing herself "Yours sincerely". She speaks of her great longing for his return and goes on to give him detailed news of the family, of her care of his mare, and of the fowls and the garden and of "our little darling boy" who ". . . is as good and quiet as ever". This baby was a future Bailiff.

Schooling in England was not all bliss, and in 1779 Thomas Le Breton (b. 1763) wrote to his uncle to say that he could no longer bear to stay at his school, and indeed conditions at that period were unduly severe.

Bad news had often to be sent overseas, or to the Island from elsewhere, as when Jean Le Gresley (1777–1868) heard of the death of his son Philippe, aged 23, in 1846, and this occurred ". . . sur le passage dans la premiere nuit de ma sorties a une demi heure apres minui ces la perte de Philip votre fils qui m'a causé bien de la peine et du chagrin il alait pour serrer le flying gib avec le second contre maitre et il a disparu sans en avoir aucune connaissance". (On the first night of our passage, at half past midnight, we lost Philip your son which has caused me great grief and sorrow. He went to tie the flying jib with the junior second mate and he disappeared without us knowing anything about it.) This boy's parents lived at Hampton Villa (L), where there is a datestone 18 ILGL. SBP 48. Their son Jean married Emilie Hamptonne and the house must derive its name from this union.

In 1867 Mary Ann Gibaut was writing to her half-brother Edouard, in English, her spelling being as irregular as the French of her uncles. Poor girl, she had probably had no education at all, but one wonders why she wrote in English which must have been less familiar to her than French. Stead, some time earlier, remarked that ". . . few of the rising generation cannot both read and write in the English and French languages" and also that many private schoolmasters were French emigrés.

Most letters, after pious expressions of hope regarding the health of the recipients, and all their relatives, complain of not having received letters. Parents, particularly, bemoan the scarcity of letters from their children and this is hardly surprising when the silence is sometimes measured in years. Some letters are extremely cheerful, like one written by Lt. John Collas from the schooner *Netley*, to his brother Philippe at St. Martin's House. He relates that ". . . I had the misfortune of being left behind in Scotland, the ship sailing by express while the Purser and I were dining with some friends in Edinburgh". He goes on to extol the friendliness and hospitality of the Scots.

When the father of a child died a tuteur was appointed, with a committee of electeurs, the mother often being chosen as tutrice. There is every indication that these guardians chose relatives, who fulfilled their obligations most conscientiously in the interests of the child or children. Their zeal was sometimes rewarded by "un diner pour les electeurs". Such a dinner, costing £12 tournois, was provided for the guardians of the children of Jean Sauvage of St. Mary, and 7s. 6d. was also paid for delivering notices to the said electeurs, some of whom may have lived far away, and had to undertake a day's journey to attend. The family home was in field My. 898, where all that now remains is a well-head.

Mortality among children was tragically high, and one's feelings go out over the years to the mothers who bore so many and lost so many. To take an isolated example, the newspaper *La Gazette de Jersey* in May 1788 mentions the prevalence of whooping cough, saying it was sometimes fatal in children, and also "putrid fever". Margaret Harliston's romantic family of 21 in the 15th century is matched by that of Jeanne Dumaresq, who married Philippe Le Geyt in 1701 and had 21 children between 1702-28, eleven of whom died in childhood. Anne Tapin who married François Marett at the age of 22, had nine children in 13 years, one stillborn, two dying at birth and two dying young, while she herself died at the birth of her last child, when she was only 38. My own great grandmother, Laura Pipon, who married Reverend William Braithwaite, had 15 children, all but one of whom survived childhood, but this was exceptional.

St. Mannelier and St. Anastase were the only schools in the Island for many years. In the 19th century many sprang up in every district and there was a multiplicity of Dame's schools, combining the duties of a modern nursery school and primary school. For such a small and remote community education was taken very seriously from an early period. In 1713 Edouard Marett arranged to pay for his sister Douce to stay on longer in England as she "cannot yet be parfait in the Inglishe take". In 1729 he was writing to Mr. Kingman, Master of the Free School in Southampton, to whom he sent his relative George Marett, asking that the boy be sent to "the writing and arithmetic schools" and undertaking the fees, with board. At the same time he advised young George to buy chamois breeches as they would outwear three pairs of "trap", and urged him to get them big enough, and to be thinking of his future career. Poor Edouard, whose letter books contain so many references to poverty and anxiety about his income, seems to have taken on the responsibility for educating other children as well as his own.

In 1768 Elie Le Maistre and Jeanne Dumaresq his wife, of St. Ouen's Manor, went so far as to send a Remonstrance to the Royal Court, saying that they could not afford the education of the "tendres fruits de leur union" according to the condition which their birth assigned to them in society, complaining of the refusal of Elie Le Maistre senior to assist in maintaining his seven grandchildren, of whom only one of the sons lived to have children himself.

Local parents tended to send their sons either to Winchester College, or to Jersey schoolmasters in England, such as Dr. John Lemprière or Dr. Richard Valpy. In 1772 young Jean de Carteret was sent by his grandmother to her brother, the famous Dr. Daniel Dumaresq (1712-1805) who sent the boy to school with a Mr. Topham at Yeatminster in Somerset, the holidays being spent with his great-uncle. Rather surprisingly the boy said he had already had dancing lessons in Jersey, but his great-uncle considered his French to be bad, and constantly refers to his bad English pronunciation, his laziness and bad behaviour. Perhaps a case of youth and crabbèd age, but clearly they were not congenial to one another.

In 1804 Dr. Lemprière was reporting on a certain George Balleine, saying ". . . his progress is slow; you will judge of it by his pronunciation of the English language which is very defective . . . if he intends to take up a parish in Jersey . . . it is by no means necessary for him to be at the expense of an Oxford education . . .". Balleine did, in fact, go to Oxford, witness a letter of 1809 from W. Jackson, a saddler of St. Aldates, saying he cannot get payment from Balleine for £7 10s. for a saddle.

In 1834 Mary Ann Le Gallais (later Mrs. Le Quesne) wrote to her parents from school asking for a winter dress, coat and woollen stockings. She had been taken to see the British Museum and spoke of a terrific fire which reduced the Houses of Parliament to ruins, Westminster Hall having been miraculously saved. In 1858 Philippe Marett took his daughter Letitia to school in Paris, though this was somewhat unusual for religious and political reasons.

It sounds as if the "Grand Tour" was not unknown, as in 1772 Daniel Messervy went to see Monsieur d'Avranches (Philippe Marett 1744-91) who had just returned from an absence of 2½ years having been to Paris, Dunkirque, Nancy, Geneva, Leghorn, Rome, Venice and Naples.

A paper on schools, prepared by the Select Committee on the Education of the Poor, shown to me by the late Mr. Ahier, is undated, but must fall between 1819-22 to judge by the names of the Rectors quoted; it assesses the educational facilities in each parish, and briefly they are as follows:

Grouville	No endowments. A day school and a Sunday school taking 50 and 70 children respectively. The poor have the right to send their children to St. Mannelier and to the parish school.
St. Brelade	Population 1,650. Six day schools catering for 168 children, and others for girls who are taught sewing. A Lancastrian school much needed for the poor.
St. Clement	A parish day school for 40 children and a Sunday school for 60. The poor have the right to send their children there or to St. Mannelier.
St. Helier	Population 7,000. A national school for the infant poor taking 274 children, many of them clothed annually, supported by voluntary subscription. Forty day schools paid by the parents, taking 700 children. All the poorer classes have means of education.
St. John	Population 1,800. A Sunday school supported by 12 inhabitants, taking 91 children, and taught by Dr. Bell's plan. Many of the poor have no means of education but the Sunday school and "are very desirous of receiving further instruction".
St. Lawrence	Four schools. A Sunday school for boys and one for girls, supported by the parish, taking 70-80 children, taught on Dr. Bell's plan. The poor are provided for.
St. Martin	Population 1,800. A school for 12 children, the Master receiving 6/3 a year from the Don Baudains. Also a day school with 70 children, and 13 Dame's schools with an average of 14 children. A Sunday school of 115 children with books supplied by the S.P.C.K. The poor are amply provided for by the liberality of the parish.
St. Mary	Population 300. A day school partly supported by the parish, a Sunday school with 24 boys and 16 girls, instructed on Dr. Bell's system by the Rector's family and a young lady.
St. Ouen	Population 1,450. A great number of schools. The poor possess sufficient means of education. The S.P.C.K. and the Female Auxiliary Bible Society, under Mrs. Le Couteur, distribute bibles and religious tracts to the poor.
St. Peter	Population 1,450. A free Grammar school for the youth of six parishes. The Master's salary is £30 a year and he instructs 30-50 boys. There are also two fee-paying schools and a Sunday school taking 70-80 children. Some of the poor are without means of education.
St. Saviour	Population 1,500. A free Grammar school founded by Henry VII, where French and Latin are taught, takes 15 or 16, and a few boarders from England who come to learn French. The Master's salary is about £100 a year including a house and some corn rentes. There is also a writing school and several Dame's schools and a Sunday school supported by a number of gentlemen in the parish. The Minister of St. Saviour has heard most unfavourable reports on St. Anastase's School (v. St. Peter) which are to be investigated by the States.
Trinity	Population 2,400. A school kept by the clerk of the parish for nearly 200 years at a stipend of 4/- per year, taking 65 children. Another school taking 50 children and a Sunday school supported by voluntary contributions taking 100 children, but the poor are without sufficient means of education.

One notes a surprising variety in the arrangements between the parishes, but in general a high standard of availability of schooling. The Bell and Lancaster systems mentioned represent Joseph Lancaster (1778-1839) and Andrew Bell (1753-1832), both pioneers in education. The former's system was based on the elder children teaching the younger, the "Monitorial" scheme, and the latter's the "Madras" scheme based on mutual teaching among the children. It is recorded that Lancaster's punishments were very severe, including manacling children, and hanging them suspended in baskets from the ceiling. For a time the two men worked together but later they became estranged.

When a ward came of age he was "approuvé en âge" at 20 years, if his guardians considered this wise, as in the case of Jean, son of the late Martin Messervy and the late Marie Machone, who in

1702 was considered by his electeurs to be of sufficient discretion to conduct his own affairs. Such declarations appear quite frequently in collections of family papers.

Guardians naturally had to give consent for the marriage of their under-age wards. In 1700 Abraham Poingdestre asked for consent to marry Marie Messervy; he had spoken to the girl's mother, and Marie herself said that she had promised to marry Abraham, but wanted her guardian's permission; this they saw no reason to refuse as she was 19. In another case, in 1755 Edouard Gibaut promised to give Maîtresse Elizabeth de Ste Croix £60 (monnaie d'ordre) "par promesse de marriage".

The protection and care of parents has always been a strong tradition in the Jersey way of life. The widow was sure of her third, that is a minimum of a third of her husband's estate, and this meant also a third of the house for her lifetime, and a few examples of this may be quoted. In 1730 when Jean Simon sold Vale Farm Cottage in St. Peter to Jean de Carteret, the latter had to promise to provide dower apartments for his own mother. As Simon and his wife retained the usufruct of the eastern part of this very small house, everyone concerned must have been somewhat cramped. In a partage of 1731, the mother, Elizabeth Payn, née Nicolle, retained "l'usage sa vie durante" of part of the family house. Sara Le Bastard, widow of Jean Messervy, had many conditions imposed upon her; she was allotted "l'estre de bas"* (a small room) and the cellar below, a door in the former leading to the farmyard being made at the joint expense of herself and her son. She also had to maintain the barn roof, the "estre" and the stable; she was permitted to use the barn to thresh her corn, and to carry firewood through the barn, to use the cider press, though only for the crushing of apples, and to use the oven, but only for bread. She had a right to a third of the firewood growing on La Valette du Saut Geffroi, but had to contribute a third of the cost of maintaining a musket (this for militia duty). She was allowed a third of the apples in the year of the partage, but had to pay 26 sous 8 deniers for a third of the cost of a new roof to the house. Does one see the eternal mother-in-law problem here? In 1803 Susanne Alexandre, widow of Hugh Dupont, living at Vieux Ménage, St. Saviour, was given the usufruct of the room west of the new end of the house, and a third of the loft "sur l'etable appele le douaire". In this case the widow was permitted to bake her bread in the kitchen oven. In 1736 Jean Payn sold his property in St. Peter to his son, but retained for his lifetime the use of the bake-house, press-house, vegetable garden and the barn for threshing his grain in season; the son had to maintain his father, keep the bake-house well roofed, and replace with good grafts any apple trees which died.

Not infrequently a man would sell his house on condition that he was to be cared for during his lifetime. In 1728 Jean Touzel gave all his property to Jean Ahier and his wife Marthe Touzel, probably Jean's daughter, in exchange for food, lodging, washing his clothing and giving care in sickness. These conditions are often followed by an injunction to have the old people decently buried according to their "état et condition". In 1840 Philippe Luce promised to pay a life pension of 5s. weekly (ancien cours de France, that is livres tournois) to his father, so long as the latter did not remarry ("ne convolera pas en secondes noces") indicating that as a lonely widower he would anyway have to pay someone to cook and launder for him.

In 1851 Arthur Sohier sold his house to his mother, on condition that she lodged, laundered and fed him for his life and paid him a life pension of 10s. stg. a week, a most curious arrangement. Naturally one does not know the special, very human, conditions which prevailed in each of these cases.

The poor have also been well cared for in Jersey, and wills, from mediaeval times, show innumerable bequests for their assistance. Sometimes land was bequeathed to bring in an income for the poor, as in 1747, when half Le Clos de L'Hermitte and Le Clos de la Montagne (P.373a and 383) on the Fief des Vingt Livres, was sold to the parish for the benefit of the poor, the owner retaining the right to use the abreuvoir, as stated in a previous contract of 1735, it says. The vendor, Thomas Binet, lived in the house now called Fontis (q.v.). In 1782 a land contract mentions a Maison des Pauvres as adjoining certain property in St. Helier, somewhere near the church. Another kind of Alms House, called Les Places de St. Pierre, near that church, was mentioned in a similar land

---

*Dictionnaire Jersiais Français, p. 13.

contract in 1795; this land was sold the next year by the Constable to Edouard Nicolle; the evidence for this is that the description of the land in question mentions ". . . the south west corner of La Maison des Pauvres".

There is a fascination in studying the doctor's bills which appear among collections of family documents. For example, in 1746 Dr. Forbes attended John Dumaresq of St. Clement, and charged him for a vomit, a purging powder, bleeding, blistering, and eight doses of Peruvian bark for 2s., which suggests quinine, perhaps for malaria, or some similar fever. Dr. de Vaumorel's bill to Madame de Samarès in 1759 includes "a cephalic powder" and also an item of 15s. for "dressing and curing her leg". The next year Jean Simon reported that he was "parfaitement retably du mal des jambes par le moyen du Doct. Vaumorell". The Actes des Etats for 1773 records that Dr. de Vaumorel had agreed to attend the poor at the hospital without fees, charging only for his medicines. In 1797 Dr. Seelle attended Mr. Marett of Avranches for a "maladie inflamatoire des yeux", and signed himself with enigmatic letters which Professor Bergel has interpreted for me as meaning Surgeon and Doctor of Durham Infirmary, Master of the Medical Professional Order, this being approximately the equivalent of a modern M.S. of the R.C.S.

In a writing desk, mentioned elsewhere, there was found a printed advertisement from a Dr. Richard Smith, dating from before 1745, when the Royal College of Surgeons was founded—an endeavour to control the activities of quack doctors. This advertises scurvy grass (*cochlearia danica*), which was a very ancient cure for scurvy, and became a fashionable drink, though it had a bitter taste and was later superseded by lime and watercress. Scurvy grass, which grew near sea coasts, would have been a valuable medicine to a sea-faring community, and a species of it still grows in Jersey, thriving in stony field banks or walls. Like the lime and cress it clearly contained Vitamin C.*

Gout was almost endemic, mainly amongst men, though Mrs. (General) Le Couteur suffered from it considerably in her later years. In 1734 Philippe Marett, writing from Boston to his brother in Jersey, said, "I have had gout since October, and still have difficulty in writing, having much pain in my arms and right hand. God has given us another girl on September 19th last named Esther". In 1743 James Pipon (1700-66) of Noirmont wrote to his lawyer, Pierre Mauger, saying he could not go to town because of a condition of his foot which prevented him from putting on socks or shoes. Gout was frequently mentioned by Daniel Messervy in his diary; in 1769 he reported that Mr. Le Hardy was prevented by gout from attending a militia review of the East Regiment, of which he was Colonel; in 1770 Monsieur de la Haule was said to be "souvent incommodé de la goute" and in the same year poor Mr. Patriarche is referred to as Le Diable Boiteux, as he suffered from gout.

A simple recipe has survived for a syrup to nourish and fortify pneumonia sufferers. It was made of leaves of Pas d'ane (winter heliotrope), fig leaves and sugar, and was to be taken with fresh warm milk from 1 May onwards.

The only reference to a dentist so far found in family papers is a terse entry in Philippe Marett's diary for 1834 when he says, "Had one of my teeth drawn by Wilcox 2/6". Veterinary surgeons were referred to as "the horse doctor" by the same writer when he sold a lame cow for £1 5s., and in 1840 he paid the sum of 8s. 8d. to "Monsieur Godfray the horse doctor".

Of all illnesses perhaps consumption was the most prevalent and the most feared, and Victor Hugo referred to "les poitrines délicates d'albion" and gave the view that the Vallée des Vaux was particularly bad for this illness. Inevitably there were also epidemics of plague, diphtheria and cholera, the last being particularly bad in 1832† and 1849. This was directly traced to contamination of the water supplies from drains, and was therefore far worse in the town than in the country parishes.

Let us round off this chapter on family affairs by considering the choice of Christian names for children, a problem faced by every parent in every age. The chart shown in Appendix 2 gives the names chosen for an eastern parish, St. Martin, and a western parish, St. Peter, for three decades, 1700-10, 1750-60, and 1800-1810. It will be noticed that there is far more variety in the

---

*Information from the late Mr. A. C. Halliwell, M.R.C.S.   †B.S.J. 1966, p. 146.

later years, especially for girls. In fact at the beginning of the 18th century there were only 16 names, at most, in use for girls, the early ones like Philipine, Cardine, Lucasse, Mauricette and Peronnelle having gone quite out of fashion. There is no doubt that the most popular girls' names were Marie and Elizabeth, followed by Jeanne, Anne and Susanne. For the boys there is more variety between parishes, but Jean and Philippe win every time, the next most popular being François, Edouard and Nicolas. Many biblical names appear, such as Abraham, Aaron, Elie and Josué, and as time goes on the choice widens. We seem to have lost Amice, Hélier and Clément, though they may well become popular again. Before the 19th century it was rare to give a child two Christian names, the only examples at earlier dates being Esther Jeanne Le Montais in 1677, Louise Elizabeth Rouillé in 1703 and Esther Jeanne Horman in 1757, amongst those so far recorded by me. A date stone of 1823 on the dower wing at La Vallette, St. John, represents Sophie Elizabeth Rondel. After 1800 English forms appear, and one may find both Jean and John, Guillaume and William, as well as the baptisms of children of French emigrés, with characteristic names. It was quite usual for parents to use a name more than once; if a child died the next son would be given the same name, particularly if he was being called after his grandfather. Occasionally the name occurs twice among the children, when one supposes the elder child was so sickly when the next one was born, that he was not expected to live, but in fact did so. With a combination of the small number of names in use, and the very large families, it must have been quite a puzzle to choose a name for the younger children. A custom which was very prevalent was to add the mother's maiden name to that of her sons. Later in the 19th century some unexpected names, particularly for boys, appeared, amongst the most popular being Hedley, Winter, Snowdon, Clifford, and Garnet. These seem unusual choices, and the reasons for Nelson and Wesley (and later Winston) are easier to understand.

CHAPTER EIGHT

PERSONALIA

". . . a ma fille Marguerite de la Closche tous mes habits et linge avec le baheur ou mon nom est dessus . . . a ma fille Elizabeth de la Closche mon lict sur lequel je couche avec ses tentes deux couvertures deux paires de Drap de lict et deux paires d'anties . . ."

Will of Marguerite de la Cloche, née de Carteret. 1704.
(B.S.J. 1934, p. 319.)

THE BEST INDICATION we have of the contents of our ancestors' houses is contained in inventories and wills. They show a greatly improved standard of comfort in the 18th century, with the kind of elegant furniture which is so much prized now. Doubtless there are elements which we would find unacceptable, most of all perhaps the lack of washing facilities. No form of bedroom washstand, recognisable as such, appears before about 1800. Carpets were very rare and window curtains appeared for the first time (in inventories studied so far) in 1763. When "rideaux" are mentioned they are usually the bed-hangings, and these were considered as being an integral part of the bed, as were the sheets, covers, pillow slips and bolsters.* The bed was immensely important and was the main item of furniture to be listed, from an instance in 1523 when Thomas Gosselin (grandfather of Nicollas Gosselin, one of the original tenants of Sark) left various items to his daughter Katherine, including a bed with its coverings and drapings (caputtegnum cum nodatura), up to more modern times. The colour of the bed-hangings, red, blue, green, yellow, or flowered, was always specified.

In some wills the testator had very little to leave: Mathieu de Ste Croix for example left £10 tournois each to the poor of St. Helier and St. Lawrence, £3 each to his two brothers, and the residue to his four sisters in recognition of the "amitié" they had always shown him, and he exhorted them to look after their mother Esther Le Gallais. In 1737 Nicolas Remon (1666–1739) left £4 tournois to the poor of St. Lawrence, and small legacies, some only 1s., to his relatives; he lived at La Qualité, St. Lawrence. The will of Mary Bartlett, dated 1740, left £10 sterling to a cousin Jean Mauger, and this was equated to £213 tournois, so that legacies of a few pounds tournois cannot have been very significant, even at that period, but this is an indication of how very poor many people were. In 1750 Nicolas Gibaut bequeathed a cow to his sister Sara, and she was to choose the one she preferred, as well as 1 quarter wheat rente, 1 quarter of lard and 50 bundles of fern. Sara's daughter, however, got a silver cup, probably far less useful to her than her mother's cow. The will of George Collingwood, Lieutenant Governor left, among other legacies, ". . . to my grand nephew Henry Collingwood, now at school with Mr. Mattinglye . . . all my English estates". He commented that Henry was ". . . an ingenious boy . . . far in his Latten and French which at his age is very commendable", a commendation which could fairly extend to his teacher Mr. Mattingley, Regent of St. Mannelier from 1732-61. Collingwood was Lieutenant Governor from 1753-56, so this will of 1760, in which he desired to be buried in St. Helier, suggests that he stayed on in Jersey.

The wills of Thomas Denton and of his widow, dated 1790, contained mainly monetary bequests, to the poor of all parishes, to St. Aubin's Hospital £1,500 stg., and small legacies to their many

---

*B.S.J. 1972, p. 361.

relatives, but one niece inherited "four pictures, one of Jacques Denton and three others"; another niece, Elizabeth Marett, widow of Jean Le Couteur, was left a gold watch and two pictures, "one of my husband one of me". The former is presumably the painting of Thomas Denton which, in a sorry state of repair, is at St. Aubin's Hospital still. In 1704 Elizabeth de Vaumorel (1760–95), a daughter of the Dr. de Vaumorel mentioned elsewhere, made her will, much of which is in the customary style, including a bequest of £100 tournois to the poor of St. Helier. She left £50 to her servant Elizabeth Noel, and everything else to her two brothers Jean and Philippe, and should her brothers predecease her she left her whole estate to her cousins Constance Charlotte Hardy and Jane Hardy, daughters of Colonel Hardy; the only exception was her pictures, family portraits, which were bequeathed to her cousin Thomas Carteret Hardy. In the event her brother Jean inherited them and they remain in the Island. Again, mourning rings are mentioned, to be bought out of £10 stg. allocated for that purpose. One of her executors was François Kerby, perhaps the local silversmith. It is interesting to note that the name was quoted as Hardy, without Le at this date. After her death most of her silver was "found hid in the oven in the kitchen" of her house in Hue Street. After her death her administrators let her house to Joseph Marie Gringnard, Seigneur de Champsavoy, for as long as he wished, or until he could return home

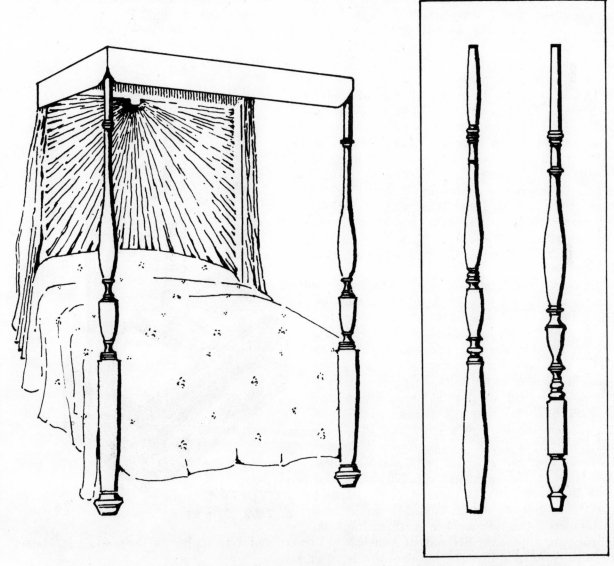

a four-poster, locally made in mahogany; with two alternative models of bed-post; from Le Marinel, (J).

22

safely, the rent being 60 louis d'or per year. One gains the impression that many French refugees lived in that western part of the town.

In 1801 all that Elie Trachy, living near Six Rues in St. Lawrence, had he left to his sister and niece, only small sums of money being mentioned. In 1802 Debora Dumaresq (1744–1802), daughter of Jean de St. Clement, left £100 tournois to the poor widows of the parish, to be distributed to them a month after her decease. She bequeathed a bed and its hangings to her niece, and these were described as being of red flowered Indian material with a hand embroidered chintz coverlet, six pairs of sheets and two good blankets. Another niece, Debora Anne Bisson (1795–1849) inherited a similar bed with one white dimity cover. Someone

23 *pitchers and bowls in local use, 18–20th. century.*
    from the collection of Mr. B.J. Le Brocq.

called James Watts had "une petite mogue d'argent marqué D.D.". A Miss Nugent of Valognes inherited all her money, invested at 3 per cent.

The surviving part of the will of Philippe Dumaresq, R.N., mentions silver only, including 2 tablespoons and 3 teaspoons "which he had with him on board of ship". It is a most comprehensive list and includes 49 tablespoons, 27 teaspoons, with but four forks "one very old, 1706". One notices on every occasion when silver is mentioned how many spoons there were, and how few forks, even as late as 1819, as in this case. This is reflected in present-day sales where Jersey silver forks are extremely rare.

The will of Marie Journeaux, widow of Amice Balleine (in 1811), bequeaths "my tobacco box" to a niece. At the end of her bequest of money and objects to various relatives comes a direction for five mourning rings for relatives to be paid for out of her personal estate "as a mark of friendship and esteem". An undated list of goods belonging to a Jeanne Balleine, under care of a curateur, listed some clothes, including many handkerchiefs and some house linen, with an item of 29 hand towels and a quantity of silver, mentioning a spoon "à poisson", that is rat-tailed.

Partage is the local word used to indicate the sharing of an estate after a death, usually by the children and widow of the deceased. In 1764 Philippe Mallet fils Jean got his share of a plough, a cart, an oak chest, an armchair stuffed with straw, two cows, one young bull, a mare and one old pig. Out of his total inheritance of £435 tournois he had to pay £110 to his mother and £114 to his sister. A partage of 1779 in the de Quetteville family gave land to all the children, but it underlines that "droit d'aînesse" carried obligations as well as privileges. The eldest son Jean, got the main house (unidentified, but probably near Croix ès Gaudins in St. Martin) and land, but he owed "pour le service des prisonniers", the maintenance of three muskets,

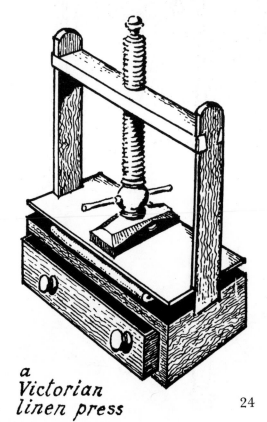

a Victorian linen press   24

wheat rente due to the Seigneur of Anneville et Everart, and some barley for the poor of St. Martin, to be distributed at the main house of the deceased.

Partages could easily lead to litigation, especially in wealthy families, and never more so than when the main line of the de Carterets failed and the Fiefs of St. Ouen and Rosel were in question.

In 1715 the three younger heiresses Anne Corbet, de la Rivière Messervy and Elizabeth Bandinel, expressed the view that it was unnecessary for the eldest claimant to take the case to the Privy Council "as their Lordships have made their opinion clear". The main bone of contention was whether a seigneurie was divisible when the heirs were females, which they said was so, "though the law of Jersey has never been written and is in the heads of the Jurats". Speaking in a frivolous vein, the appellants made mock of the defendant who spoke of the right of the Seigneur of Rosel to ride into the sea to meet the sovereign, telling him (the husband of the heiress) to "ride his Bucephalus back into the stable until such time as it is known that His Majesty is about to visit the island". In the event Anne Corbet obtained Rosel, buying out her co-heiresses. The failure of the de Carteret male line certainly is a case of what the Americans call "daughtering out".

Occasionally parents made a pre-partage, as did Martin Messervy in 1707; he said that he was getting old and wished to divide his property among his three children, so that they should remain in concord after his death, and so he allocated to them all his lands and rentes in St. Martin.

With the wealth brought back over the Atlantic came a change in furniture fashions, not only because of the financial resources, but also because of the South American mahogany with which the ships returned. Before this trade became so flourishing, local furniture was made of oak or pine, sometimes chestnut or elm, and occasionally beech or sycamore. Floor boards, stair treads and partitions between rooms can be found made of elm or chestnut. But new horizons had opened up. The "acajou" became the fashionable wood, and in inventories one notices the mahogany appearing in the best rooms, with oak and pine relegated to kitchen and secondary bedrooms. Walnut and exotic woods do not often feature. The standard of craftsmanship was high, and definite types of furniture are recognisable as being locally made, though it is rare to find a maker's name on a piece. The most typically Jersey items are the presses; one style is a two-doored wardrobe, each door usually having three fielded panels; a variant has a two-doored top section, with oval inset panels, exquisitely made sliding shelves, and drawers in the lower section, and this style often carried the fashionable pediment on top. Yet another style found is the tallboys, often with reeded chamfers at the corners. Handles have often been replaced, particularly where the drawers are heavy, as they certainly are in the oak pieces. The feet on which a chest stands are sometimes a later addition, as the original bases suffered from standing on damp, often earth, floors. The cases for "grandfather" clocks (the mechanism being imported) were locally made, as were many chairs of Chippendale style, and other far simpler chairs, often of apple or pear wood. And there were the elegant occasional tables, generally known as gueridons, and doubtless the bedposts were also locally made, the so-called four-poster bed usually having plain posts at the head and lathe-turned posts at the foot. Early examples are slender and delicate, but gradually become more sturdy and heavy as Victorian solidarity and confidence replaced Georgian and Regency lightheartedness. The half-tester, known in Jersey as an Albert bed, came into fashion in the middle of the 19th century, and in this case the curtained canopy extended only over the pillow area. The height of late-19th-century skill can be seen in the Victorian bedroom at the local museum.

No doubt a good deal of furniture was imported, mainly from England, but also from France. In 1743 Pierre Mauger received a letter saying that the ship *William,* Captain Coutanche, had on board his table, labelled P.M. In 1787 when François Journeaux sold his house in St. Helier he retained the right to keep for his own profit the railings, mirrors, corner cubords (*sic*), tables, dresser etc., and all other furniture even if attached by lime, nails or pegs. Philippe Marett in 1821 mentioned a dressing case, made for £168 tournois. Inglis (1838) said that furniture was cheap in Jersey, particularly that which was locally made, and this he attributed to the absence of duty on imported timber, and Durell (1847) mentioned that in the country the parlours and kitchens were fitted up neatly, and even with luxury, and he also remarked on their cleanliness.

One of the most interesting items to be found in Jersey houses is the baheur, generally considered to be a bridal chest, and a surprising number of them have survived considering the size of the Island. They are wooden chests, covered with leather, often referred to as "cuir de Russie", meaning leather scented with birch bark. This is reflected in an inventory of Thomas Rondel, dated 1811, which mentions "un baheur de Roussi". On the front and lid they were studded with elaborate and intricate designs in brass-headed nails, and the motif frequently incorporates the tulip. In some

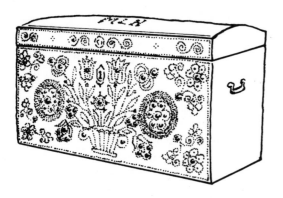
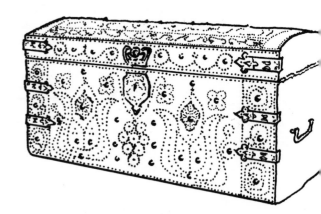

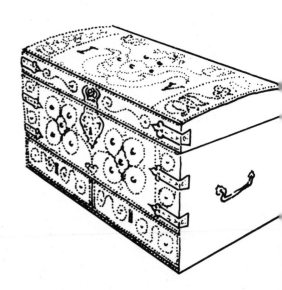

The **BAHEUR**. *Examples of a leather-covered trunk ornamented with brass nails, in vogue in Jersey c. 1680-1760.*

25

cases one feels that the initials, when present, have been added to a chest bought from stock, and in others they, and sometimes a date as well, are integral with the design. If one is fortunate the date and the initials of the first owner appear on the lid; if one is even more lucky the marbled original lining paper has survived, and in a very few cases the maker's trade card is still inside the lid, which is often rounded. The key escutcheon is usually in the form of a crown (though this does not indicate a gift from Charles II as is sometimes claimed), and there are strong brass corner plates. Originally designed as travelling trunks, these chests became pieces of furniture, and clearly too precious to be humped around on coaches or in ships, and in Jersey there would be little need for travel once the bride had made the journey to her new home. Herein lies the reason, one must suppose, for their survival in such good condition.

A number of examples are still in the possession of Jersey families, but bear no identifying dates or initials. Two were sold (one of them for £10) as lots Nos. 251 and 268 among the effects of Elise Osmont, daughter of Eugéne Osmont of Caen and Sophia de Carteret of Trinity, at her sale at Mont â l'Abbé Manor in 1932. In the inventory of effects of Elizabeth de Vaumorel, made in 1795, there is mention of a large leather trunk marked I D C, which could be a baheur, and might have come from her great-grandmother, Jeanne de Carteret. "Un petit baheur marqué E L G" appeared in the list of possessions of Edouard Gibaut fs. Elie in 1768. The word baheur could however refer to any trunk, and these may not all be the superior type of chest we are considering.

Of the four makers whose trade cards have survived Edward Smith and John Selby, both of the "Dover Castle, ye corner of St Nicholas Lane and Cannon Street", used a simple design of card. It seems likely that the latter is Jonathan Selby, admitted to servitude (apprenticeship) in 1723, whose father was a "hozyer" named John. Of the other two recorded locally, and who favoured a more rococo style of card, Richard Lucas, of the same address as Selby and Smith, is recorded in 1763 in Mortimer's *London Directory,* though we have an example of his card in a chest dated 1755; the other, John Clements appears in the directory in 1763 and 1774-89, operating from "St Pauls next Cheapside". It is curious that this particular item of equipment for the home should always have been ordered from England, never from France, and apparently never made in Jersey. Examples noticed in Brittany appear to be 17th century rather than 18th, the leather is darker in colour than our examples and the key escutcheon is not in the form of a crown. The chart in Appendix 4 will show that the heyday for baheurs in Jersey was about 1750. One may notice that both Clement(s) and Lucas are names long established in Jersey, and one wonders if this is coincidence, or if local families bought from their compatriots. It is sad that one cannot identify more of the original owners, and that so many have passed through the sale rooms, so that their origin and identity are soon lost. Happy are those families who have managed to preserve these objects, which combine historial interest, utility and beauty.*

Jersey silver is now widely known and appreciated both for its quality and its rarity value. By the period we are now considering the French Huguenot silversmiths had become integrated into Island life and they formed an important and prosperous part of the commercial community. Silver items appear in inventories even when the rest of the contents suggest a fairly humble household. The most common objects are, of course, spoons, but we find a wide variety of others.

In 1704 Anne Seale, wife of François de Carteret, and secondly of Philippe Pipon, had a great deal of silver, including 4 bowls, 13 spoons, 7 forks, 4 salt cellars, 2 tankards, 2 mugs and 2 cups as well as jewelry. In 1757 the inventory of the effects of Philippe de Ste Croix included several silver spoons and cups, mostly initialled. In 1763 Thomas Pipon fs. Thomas, living at Elliston House, St. Aubin, had a quantity of silver, see Appendix 4. In 1835 Jean Bichard, perhaps of Seaview, St. Lawrence, had in silver 7 large spoons, 12 teaspoons, one pair of tongs, one cup and one milk jug. In 1865 at the sale of the effects of Moise Orange, of Les Ruettes, St. John, the silver was mostly spoons, but also included were a thimble marked S D P (Sophie Rachel du Pont), a milk jug and sugar basin, a sifting spoon, a tobacco box, most of the items being initialled. These items, at such periods, would be real silver, and not plate, and much of it doubtless locally made. In

---

*Antique Furniture, L. G. Ramsey and Helen Comstock. English Cottage Furniture, F. Gordon Roe, p. 46, *et seq.*
Information from Mr. J. Warterer of the Museum of Leathercraft, and the Worshipful Company of Cordwainers.

addition, all the lists included considerable amounts of pewter and copper. Amusingly the word kettle is taken over and quoted with an engaging variety of spellings, such as "tea quittll" in 1768, and "tickle en caper" in 1831.

That people valued their property is shown by the early instances of insurance, though fire is the main, if not the only, hazard considered. In 1733 Pierre Mauger paid a 15s. premium for his house (probably Les Fontaines, near Morel Farm, St. Lawrence), its contents, press-house and stables, the said buildings being of stone, covered with thatch, and the sum insured was £150 for the house £80 for the contents and £70 for the outhouses. The amounts quoted must surely be in sterling. In 1834 Philippe Marett insured La Haule Manor for £2,900 for an annual premium of £3 12s. In 1836 Abraham Gibaut paid 9s. for a cover of £200, presumably referring to his house. The principal companies operating were all English based, and included Legal and General, West of England, Sun, Norwich Union, Royal, Unity and Church of England.* About ten examples of their plaques, indicating that a certain house was insured with them have remained, though they do not show up to the casual glance and are often too high to be noticed in the ordinary way.

Wage levels are hard to assess with the various currencies in use, and the lack of details for the work done, in records. In 1833 Edouard Le Maistre was paid £80 stg. for work done at La Hague, the amount having been translated from livres tournois, and the men receiving from 15 to 56 sols tournois per day. In 1835 Philippe Marett paid George Henri £59 tournois for men working for one day. In 1834 he took into his employ one John Counter at 2s. 6d. a week, and to Miss Le Cras, the ironing woman, he paid 12s. "to Easter day next" in February 1835. In 1858 his son paid Sara, the maid-servant £1 14s. for seven months, but presumably she lived in.

You may wonder what language these people were speaking to each other, particularly in Jersey where so many were, and still are, tri-lingual, being fluent in English, French and Jersey-French. There is little doubt that amongst themselves the country people would have spoken Jersey-French, a lineal descendant from Norman French, and farmers would have spoken it to their employees. Chateaubriand remarked ". . . On retrouve à Jersey un echantillon des vieux Normands; on croît entendre parler Guillaume le Bâtard ou l'auteur du Roman de Rou . . .". Jersey-French was not a written language until recent years, and there was considerable variation between districts in the form of words and pronunciation. Standard French, even if with some local terms and idio-syncrasies, was in general use for all official business, and consequently all Royal Court and States records were (and some still are) in standard French; it therefore follows that all legal and official documents in family collections are not in Jersey-French, as so many people assume. An engagingly illogical bi-lingualism has always persisted in Jersey; for instance until after the Second War the minutes of the Société Jersiaise were kept in French (not Jersey-French), though for many years the discussions which they recorded had been in English, and a great deal of English was spoken in the Island from the early 19th century onwards. While cultural and commercial links with France remained strong, French had been the lingua franca, but with the shift of emphasis to England, English gradually took its place. There were several contributory causes for this, as suggested in chapter one; the main one was patriotic, when Napoléon was uppermost in men's minds; secondly, the cod trade and other shipping interests brought Jerseymen into contact with English ports, such as Bristol, Portsmouth and Southampton; thirdly, the advent of steam made the hitherto long and dangerous journey to England comparatively simple; fourthly, some local families preferred their children to be educated in England, mainly for religious reasons, but also so that they could take advantage of the various Oxford scholarships open to them. Then there were many Jerseymen serving in the army and navy, to whom English became their natural tongue, and after Waterloo there was an influx of English emigrés, mainly from the services, hoping to take advantage of our leisurely way of life, lower cost of living and good educational opportunities. They introduced a new element into society, and there was also the influence of the British army regiment garrisoned here. With the founding of Victoria College (1853) English became the educated lauguage, though the Jerseyman continued to be fluent in French and probably

---

*Advertised in *Payne's Armorial*.

Jersey-French too. Perhaps the transition is best illustrated by the diaries of the Maretts of La Haule; Edouard (1691-1758) wrote in French with occasional incursions into indifferent English: his son Philippe (1744-1826) wrote in sometimes faltering English, but nonetheless used it most of the time, and his son Philippe (1798-1866) was completely at ease in English, and his son-in-law, Sir Robert Pipon Marett (1820-84), whilst speaking both the main languages fluently, was amongst the first to commit Jersey-French to writing, composing excellent poems. Sir John Le Couteur and his wife, in about 1820, actually went to live in France for a while to improve their French, which he rightly considered important for a man in local public affairs.

This linguistic change is reflected in house names. Very few houses had names at all until the coming of postal services made them essential, but such early ones as did exist, like Les Aix, Le Ponterrin, La Maison de St. Martin, Le Fleurion, were automatically in French. Then round about 1820 romantic names appeared, with the "picturesque" architecture of the period, and there was an outcrop of Belle Vue, Mon Plaisir, Le Bocage, Bel Air, Beaulieu and such like, but at the same time English names were appearing, and we find The Elms, Highcliff, Mainland, Highlands, Oaklands, Broadlands and so on. Today the emphasis has veered back to the French. The Firs becoming Les Sapins and Elmwood Bois de L'Orme. A very welcome new trend is a desire to perpetuate the name of the field on which a house is built, many of these names being of great antiquity and most worthy of preservation. Political adherence appears in various forms of Laurel House, Les Lauriers, La Rosière, Rose Farm, and so on, and national events are sometimes recorded in such names as Waterloo, Minden, Inkerman, and Malakoff..

A great deal of entertainment took place, at all levels of society, and largely within families, as with so much inter-marriage the number of relatives any family could claim was legion. The poorer people entertained their relatives and neighbours to occasions like black butter making, cider making and threshing sessions, as well as evenings of recounting stories and singing, to the accompaniment of knitting, good food and cider. The richer people entertained their friends and relatives to dinners, and to "drink tea", which was a luxury. Official entertainment is recorded in several instances by Daniel Messervy (pp. 32, 44, 70). On 18 January 1770 Colonel Bentinck gave a ball in "la chambre de sur la Cohue" inviting 139 persons, and the company danced until 4 a.m. to the Regimental band. In May of the same year another ball was given in the same room, in celebration of the King's birthday. On 9 June 1771 Lord Albemarle, the Governor, gave a dinner "dans la chambre sur la Nouvelle Cohue" to the militia officers, and in the evening Lady Albemarle gave a ball. When the Governor arrived on this, his first, visit, in June, he came from Granville on board the sloop *Gautier*; he had his carriage put on board, on the bridge, and there he and his lady slept. On arrival they went to stay with Major Corbet, then the Lieutenant Governor, presumably at La Maison de la Motte, now demolished.

As a postscript to a chapter mainly on the contents of houses I cannot refrain from mentioning home-made red ink, should you require any. An anonymous writer in 1725 left a simple recipe: "Take ground Brazeel 2 oz; boil it in a pint of water to half, strain it then".

CHAPTER NINE

THE ARCHITECTURAL HERITAGE

"If ever I am rich enough to buy a house, it will have to be in St Ouens to get out of the reach of the ever increasing town and population . . . I expect soon to hear that all the beauties of the Island have been spoilt by their confounded improving and building mania."

Letter from P. D. Marett to his mother, 1847.

AS HAS BEEN EXPLAINED in Volume I, the vernacular architecture of Jersey underwent a dramatic change in about 1700.

The previous form had been a small, four-roomed granite cottage with a round arched front door, chamfered and with decorated chamfer stops, a stone tourelle stairway, and small, uneven windows with chamfers and decorated lintels. Inside there were huge hearths with stone lintels, the partitions between rooms were most often in wood, and ground floor rooms had but clay floors. With dramatic suddenness we adopted the Georgian love of symmetry. Away went all the carved embellishments and attractive inequalities, to be replaced by a geometrical façade, with a straight topped unchamfered doorway, and plain identical window apertures. The sturdy granite chimneys continued, modified only when slate replaced thatch, so that thatch stones became redundant, though existing ones have generally remained *in situ,* and in some cases vestigial thatch stones appear on chimneys that never carried a reed roof.

The 18th-century house is in less danger from the restorer or developer than that of former years, its salvation being the size of the windows; the ubiquitous sash window does not need to be enlarged for modern living, though often the attractive twelve-paned version has been replaced by a soulless two-paned variety, out of keeping with the character and proportions of an 18th-century façade. After 1700 stone stairs were replaced by wooden flights, slate or tile gradually replaced thatch for roofs, and fireplaces assumed more moderate proportions as grates and kitchen ranges came into use. Naturally these changes were gradual, and there will always be anomalies in dating.

The 18th century offered us nothing so spectacular, unique, or photogenic as the Jersey round arch of former centuries. A flattened type of rounded arch did return to favour, and is seen mainly in farm buildings. It appears as early as 1837 at The Oaks, St. Peter (q.v.) and reappeared on many farms in the 1870–80 period. Handsome as these arches are, they never regained the perfection of the 17th-century version.

After this somewhat sudden change in style, it is inside the house that one must go for interest and the appreciation of local skill and ingenuity, and it is to the carpenter rather than to the stonemason that one must look. The traditional skill in handling enormous blocks of stone, inherited from our dolmen building ancestors, was still there, and may be seen in the massive construction of harbours, towers and forts, as well as in many domestic buildings and in the initialled stones set into them. But the flourishing shipbuilding trade produced generations of skilled carpenters who gave us not only ships that could brave the Atlantic, but furniture, doors, panelling and staircases that have stood the test of time and remain as a monument to their expertise.

The material for building a house remained exclusively granite. Some builders, or their employers, tried to vary its appearance with patterning in stone, but this novelty was no improvement, the beauty of the Jersey granite lying in its infinite variation in texture, shape and colouring, rivalling the colours of autumn leaves.

SOME INSCRIBED STONES. I.

(NOT DRAWN TO UNIFORM SCALE).

1. *Le Taillis, (Mt). Colas Baudains, 1588.*

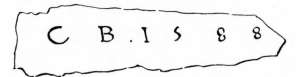

2. *Les Prés, (Mt). 1675.*
Estienne Anthoine m. Marthe Aubin, 1664.

3. *L'Ancienneté, (My). ? Arthur – du Pré, 1659.*

4. *Haut de Tombette, (My).*

5. *Mon Plaisir, (L).*
Raulin Benest – Sara Bailhache.

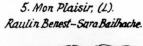

6. *Beechfield, (T). Thomas Le Breton.*

7. *Champ Collin, (S). Timothée Mourant, m. Suzanne Aubin, 1681.*

8. *near Hôtel de France, (H).*

9. *Vieille Maison, St. Aubin.*
Pierre Le Bailly.

10. *La Motte Street, (H).*

11. *La Malzarderie, (J). Jean Dolbel m. Thomassine Remon, 1699.*

SOME INSCRIBED STONES. 2.

(NOT DRAWN TO UNIFORM SCALE).

12. *Maison Le Maistre, St. Aubin. Jean Lemprière — Anne Durell.*

14. *Highcliff, (J). Helier Chevalier — Jeanne Esnouf*

13. *La Sergine, (J).*

15. *near L'Horizon, (B). le Rossignol — ?. 1710.*

16. *Vale Lodge, (P). Jean Simon — ?*

17. *Fontis, (P).*

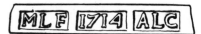

18. *St. Mary's Village. Simon Lemprière — Marie Mauger, (m.1707).*

19. *Hollybank, (Mt). Philippe Fauvel — Elizabeth Bandinel. 1716.*

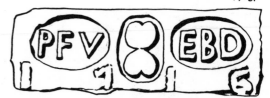

20. *Maison du Buisson, (T). Beniamin Binet of (T) m. Jeanne Le Broc of (O), 1711.*

21. *Oakdale, (S).*

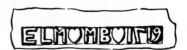

27

SOME INSCRIBED STONES. 3.

(NOT DRAWN TO UNIFORM SCALE).

22. *Les Grès, (B). Thomas Prideaux — ? : Jean Prideaux — Katherine Alexandre.*

TPMNJ7321PKAL

23. *La Feverie, (S). ?Godfray — Valpy.*

J7JGF ♡ FVP3J

24. *Maison du Buisson, (T). Pierre de Gruchy m. Marie Hocquart, 1719.*

PDG·MHC·1733

25.

PH·AC·1737

26. *No.15, Hue Street, (H). Nicolas de Ste.Croix : and Pierre Luce who m. Sara Giffard.*

ND S X PL♡SGF
Ms. 30 ◇ J739

27. *Brampton Farm, (O). Augustin Le Rossignol m. Marguérite Guillet, 1702: their son Pierre.*

ALR 1733 M GL R

28. *Les Ifs, (T). Richard du Feu — Elizabeth Gruchy, 29.Oct.1746. (m.1737).*

R E · 1 7 D4 6 F Ci
29 Mo 8BR

29.

FLB♡IDH·1756

29a. *Le Câtel, (T). Jean de Gruchy m. Jeanne Le Quesne, 1730.*

17·IDG♡IL9·44

30. *No.16, Hill Street, (H). Jean Perrochon.*

I P ❀ 1748

31. *Le Taillis, (Mt). Edouard Payn — Elizabeth Nicolle.*

J7·EP♡ENC·5J

SOME INSCRIBED STONES. 4.

(NOT DRAWN TO UNIFORM SCALE).

32. Les Câteaux, (T). Edouard Journeaux
m. Caterine Bisson, 1740.

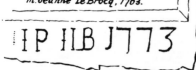

33. Hue Street, (H). ? Le Sueur.

34. Croix au Lion, (P). Jacques Payn
m. Jeanne Le Brocq, 1763.

35. Les Câteaux, (T). Philippe Le Gros, m. Jeanne Joubaire 1751, &
bought Les Câteaux, 1767.

PLG♡JJBJ777

36. Les Montagnes, (L). Jean Langlois, who m. Elizabeth
de Ste. Croix 1745: twin gate-pillars: left-hand pillar, now
a door-lintel, partly conjectural.

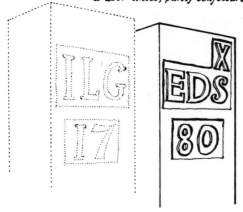

37. L'Abri, (J). Hocquard — Anley.

JJAHC·IAL86

38. Le Ponterrin, (S), in a field wall: Thomas le Hardy.

39. Mainland, (L). Philippe Gibaut — Elizabeth Dean.

PGBWED 1802

41. Coutanche Farm, (T). Charles Coutanche — Jeanne le Bas.

40. south of La Chouquetterie, (Mt), in wall of field Mt.577,
on site of house of J. Gallichan, 1849.

SOME INSCRIBED STONES . 5.

(NOT DRAWN TO UNIFORM SCALE).

42. *Old Farm, (H). Renouf.*

43. *La Sergenté, (Mt). ? Pallot—Perchard.*

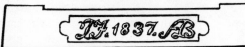

44. *La Vallette, Mourier, (J). Hamon—Malzard.*

18 C· H M 🖤 J·M Z 28

45. *Le Geyt House, Five Oaks, (S). Abraham Le Geyt.*

18 A L.G. 🖤· I E N 32

48. *Le Pavillon, (Mt). Beaugié.*

46. *Les Nièmes, (P). Philippe le Feuvre—Anne Le Bas.*

P.F. 1837. A.B

47. *London House, (J). Edouard Ahier — Esther Dauvergne.*

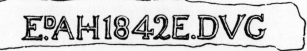

E.D AH 1842 E. DVG

49. *Oakdale, (J). Le Boutillier—Pinel.*

E.G.L.BT.🖤E.PN
1866

49. *La Rigondaine, (G). Jean Graut.*

J.G
1870

30

The only embellishment permitted, once the façade had become stereotyped, was the carved marriage stone inserted, usually over the front door, giving the initials of the man and wife who built, altered or inherited the house in the year stated on the stone, though their marriage could have taken place twenty or more years previously. Within strict limits there is an immense variety in these attractive stones. The rule is that the man's name appears on the left, and his wife's on the right, but even this had one exception (the only one so far found) at Beechfield, Trinity. Very occasionally a son's initials may replace those of a wife, or two generations may be recorded on one stone, and then some examples defy all efforts at detection. On occasion this is because the letters, if incised, and particularly if the background of the stone is rough, are illegible, and sometimes it is that the owner knew exactly what he meant but we lack the wit to comprehend it. In the great majority of stones syllabic initialling is used for the surname, Dumaresq being shown as DMR for example. One or two carved hearts, often intertwined, became part of the established fashion; the earliest example found of this motif is at L'Ancienneté, St. Mary, dated 1659, showing two hearts, raised, and separated. One isolated example earlier has a heart but no accompanying initials, at Oaklands, St. Helier. In 1706 at La Maison Le Maistre, St. Aubin, and in 1715, at Vale Cottage, St. Peter we find one heart; from then on the heart design became almost de rigueur. These stones are of inestimable value to the researcher, though great caution must be exercised in interpreting them. It will be noticed, from the drawings, that J, the commonest of all initials, appears as I, often with a short cross bar, and that N is frequently reversed. The figure 7 sometimes gets reversed too, as can 4, and the shape of the 5 is often an indication as to whether a 16th-century stone is genuine, or a later reproduction. As time went on the lettering became both more intricate and more stereotyped, though obviously home-made examples occur at every date.

Unfortunately no ground plans of any age have so far been found, but two plans reproduced here, showing all the buildings on a property, are of considerable interest. One is entitled Trodez and is dated 1805, and shows the triangle of land on which Morville House now stands, as it then was. The other, drawn by Colonel Le Cornu in 1853, from a sketch dated 1838, is a bird's-eye view of Vinchelez de Haut, and this shows a self-supporting unit almost collegiate or monastic in its completeness.

The ground plan of the local house has remained consistent and its basis is a rectangle containing two living rooms divided by a passage; in early days this led to the tourelle but after the introduction of wooden stairs this passage needed to be slightly wider and became an entrance hall. In the vernacular style the hearths were at the gable end, so that chimneys always appear at the extreme ends of the roof. Sometimes, but rarely, two hearths are superimposed, those on the first floor serving the main bedrooms. A third bedroom, known as "le cabinet", destined for young children, was squeezed in over the entrance passage.

It is interesting to speculate at what date the two-room deep or double-pile plan was introduced; in towns where the site area was very restricted this would have been far earlier than in the country, and in St. Helier and St. Aubin there are double-pile houses from about 1700. In the country one of the earliest examples must be La Haule Manor (1796) though it is possible that The Elms, St. Mary, and Slate Farm, St. Clement, may be as early. It was rare, though not unknown, to enlarge a house by adding a third storey, as at Le Colombier, St. Lawrence, and Le Marais Farm, St. Mary. Only two instances have been noted where the enlargement was made to the south, at Belle Vue and St. Magloire, both in St. Aubin. Far the commonest practice was to add rooms to the north, though east or west additions are not unknown, either single- or double-storeyed. These extensions could envelop a tourelle as at La Sergenté, St. Mary and La Malzarderie, St. John. Where such additions have been made, be it at the back or at either end, this can usually be seen in the stonework; for example an interior wall of unnecessary thickness was an outer wall in origin, and one can often detect an earlier roof level in the masonry at the gable end. As living standards improved, houses became bigger and bigger, the reverse tendency operating at the present time.

One is often asked why there appear to be no really old single-storeyed houses, why none of any age are semi-detached or in terraces, and why there are no farm labourer's cottages.

To take these questions in order, it is true that very few single-storeyed houses exhibiting recognisable 17th-century features have survived, and these few have been altered, as Broadfields

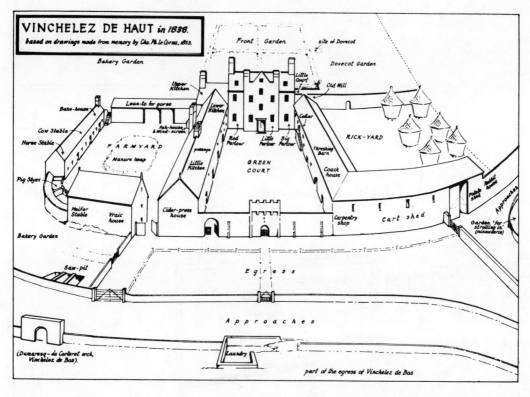

VINCHELEZ DE HAUT in 1838.
based on drawings made from memory by Chas. Ph. le Cornu, 1853.

Bakery Garden

Front Garden — site of Dovecot

Dovecot Garden

Upper Kitchen — Little Court — Old Mill

Bake-house — Lean-to for gorse — Lower Kitchen

Ash-houses & Wind-screen

Cow Stable

Horse Stable

FARMYARD — Manure heap — passage — Red Parlour — Little Parlour — Big Parlour — Cellar — Threshing Barn — RICK-YARD

Pig Styes

Little Kitchen — GREEN COURT — Coach house

Heifer Stable — Vraic house — Cider-press house — Carpentry shop — Cart shed — Potato shed — Rabbit house — Approaches

Bakery Garden

Garden 'for strolling in' (minauderie)

Saw-pit

Egress

(Dunaresq – de Carteret arch, Vinchelez de Bas).

Approaches

Laundry

part of the egress of Vinchelez de Bas

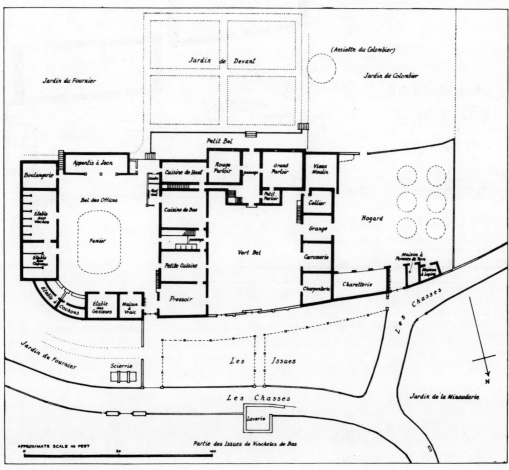

Jardin de Devant

(Assiette du Colombier)

Jardin du Fournier

Jardin du Colombier

Petit Bel

Appentis à Jean — Cuisine de Haut — Rouge Parlour — passage — Grand Parloir — Vieux Moulin

Boulangerie

Bel des Offices — Cndre — Four — Petit Parloir — Collier

Étable aux Vaches — Cuisine de Bas — Grange — Hogard

Fumier — passage — Vert Bel — Carrosserie

Étable aux Chevaux — Petite Cuisine — Charpenterie — Charetterie — Maison à Pommes de Terre — Maison à Lapins

Étable Cochons — Étable aux Génisses — Maison à Vraic — Pressoir — Les Chasses

Jardin du Fournier — Scierrie — Les Issues — Les Chasses

Les Chasses — Laverie — Jardin de la Minauderie

N

Partie des Issues de Vinchelez de Bas

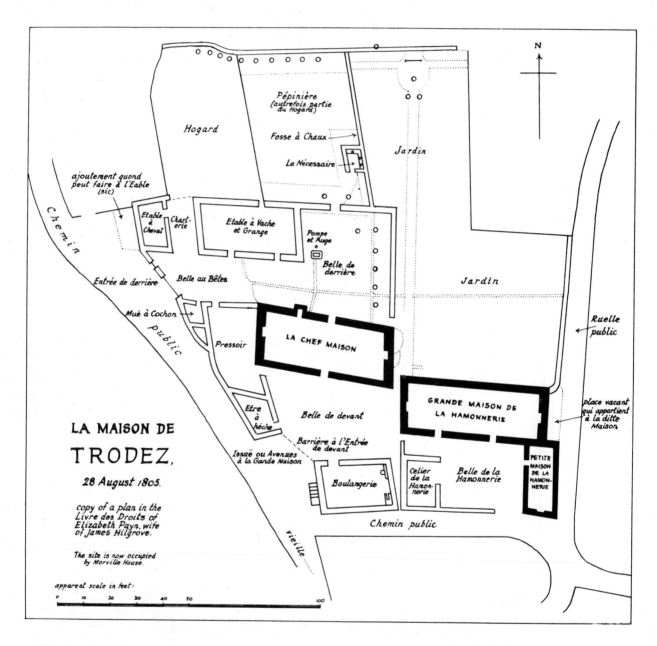

N

Pépinière
(autrefois partie
du Hogard)

Hogard

Fosse à Chaux

Jardin

La Nécessaire

ajoutement quond
peut faire à l'Eable
(sic)

Etable
à
Cheval

Chart-
erie

Etable à Vache
et Grange

Pompe
et Auge

Chemin

Belle de
derrière

Jardin

Entrée de derrière

Belle au Bêtes

public

Muë à Cochon

Ruelle
public

Pressoir

LA CHEF MAISON

GRANDE MAISON DE
LA HAMONNERIE

place vacant
qui appartient
à la ditte
Maison

Belle de devant

Etre
à
péche

Barrière à l'Entrée
de devant

PETITE
MAISON
DE LA
HAMON-
NERIE

Issuë ou Avenues
à la Gande Maison

LA MAISON DE
TRODEZ,

28 August 1805.

copy of a plan in the
Livre des Droits of
Elizabeth Payn, wife
of James Hilgrove.

The site is now occupied
by Morville House.

Boulangerie

Celier
de la
Hamon-
nerie

Belle de la
Hamonnerie

vieille

Chemin public

apparent scale in feet:

0   10   20   30   40   50   100

PLATE IX BAHEURS

a. A typical mid-18th century baheur

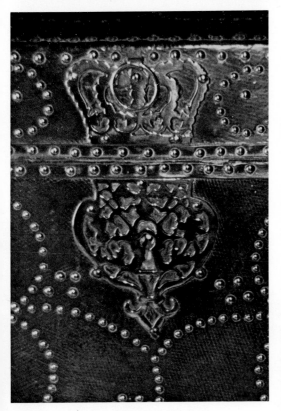

b. Detail of a key escutcheon

c. John Selby's trade card

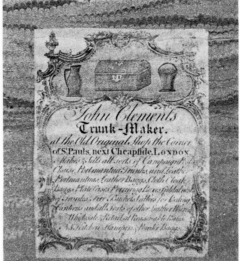

d. John Clements' trade card

PLATE X COTTAGES

a. Le Coin Cottages (B), ? 17th century

b. At La Rocque (G)

c. On Mont de l'Ecole (P)

d. In Gorey village (G), early
19th century

PLATE XI DOORS AND WINDOWS

Mid-18th century doors

a. Potirons de Bas (My)

b. In Hue Street (H)

d. A casement window at The Elms (My)

c. Early sash window, The Hollies (B)

PLATE XII GRATES

a. A Grandin range in
use at La Fosse (T)

c. A Victorian grate inserted in earlier panelling
at La Vignette (S)

b. Typical hob grate, *c* 1780–1820

Cottage, St. Lawrence, or demolished like one seen at Fauvic. Doubtless they existed, but being very small and simple, and built without lime, they have perished. An exception is Le Ménage ès Feuvres, St. Ouen, believed to be at least three hundred years old. Semi-detached houses occur in towns, St. Helier, St. Aubin and Gorey, but in the country there was no need for them, and the Jerseyman has always been a strong individualist. He welcomed the parents living in the dower wing, and "Manman" was doubtless invaluable for looking after the young children while the wife was working in the fields. The Jerseyman also welcomed a family association of houses known by a group name, such as Ville ès Philippes, Grouville, which in origin and object was a kind of co-operative farming venture.

The absence of labourer's cottages is certainly curious and the English "tied cottage" rarely appears in Jersey. It is partly due to family co-operation, as already mentioned, and partly to the smallness of the farming units. It also seems as if farm labourers tended to be bachelors, and in recent times immigrant Breton workers, and these employees were housed in rooms within the farm buildings. It remains to be explained why there is so little variation in size between the smallest and the largest houses, even the manors. This makes Jersey houses particularly adaptable to modern living, where few people now want less than three or more than five bedrooms.

In all but the wealthier houses, flooring was beaten earth on the ground level, one solitary example of a cobbled floor appearing in the old house at Le Bocage, St. Brelade (1751). The first floor rooms presumably always had wooden floors, and in general the wider the floor boards the older is the floor. Swanage paving stones have been imported for a very long time. Indeed Chevalier in 1647 speaks of ". . . sanwouych, ou ils prinderent des pierres piates a pauer les quelles ils apportirent en Jersey q estois pierres propres pour pauer soubs les canons". (Swanage whence they brought flat stones for paving, to Jersey, which were suitable stones for the paving under cannon.) In 1645 he said ". . . chargez le pierre blanche carree pour pauer q.p. toit de sen ouich . . ." (. . . laden with square white stones for paving and for roofing from Swanage). In 1708 the States laid down that Swanidge stone be used for paving the Halle à Blé (Cornmarket). This engaging variation in spelling continued and in 1745 the accounts for the building of St. Aubin's Chapel contain an item "Payé à Mons Charles Amy por 150 pieds de pierre de Soinigdie £60 tournois", with a further 4s. 8d. for carting the said stones from town. Again in 1774 when the States were considering a pork market (marché à lard) they said it was necessary to pave it with "petite pierre de Swanidge qu'on appelle Pitchers de maniere que l'epur de l'edifice puisse s'ecouler convenablement" (small Swanage stones named pitchers, so that the building may be conveniently drained). The market built in 1800 was paved with Swanage stone. These excellent paving stones, durable, easy to keep clean, and pleasant to see, remain in many a hall and kitchen.

The normal roofing material was thatch, which was of course highly inflammable, and by-laws were introduced in 1715 to curtail its use. There are now no thatched houses in Jersey, and slate became the commonest medium, with much use of tile in the town. In 1643 Chevalier, describing the bombing of the town from Elizabeth Castle, reports that the roof of his own house in the Royal Square suffered ". . . enportant laterre et paille de dessus le faist de la maison . . ." suggesting a clay covering over the thatch. By chance we

33

Door-case at N°2, Bond St., St. Helier

know the name of one thatcher, for Daniel Messervy (p. 15) tells us that on 23 November 1769 Michel de la Haye was thatching Estienne Martin's house.

As well as providing a comparatively fireproof covering slate has other advantages. Thatch needs to be renewed fairly frequently, but also it requires a steep pitch to drain the rainwater, and it was soon realised that the slate or tiled roof which replaced it did not call for such an acute angle and that it was therefore possible to brace up the roof timbers, heighten the front wall by a foot or two, and so convert small attics into good bedrooms. An unexpected item, referring to La Haule Manor in 1820, says "uncovered our house for covering it with lead". In 1842 it cost £32 stg. to roof Les Vaux, St. Lawrence; "pour avoir le lief de votre maison" (roof timbers) the bill reads.

The main front door, central in the façade, was sturdily built, usually with six panels, the type of panelling naturally varying with the date; it led into a hall which, like the kitchen, was often paved with the Swanage stones already referred to. Philippe Marett bought from Mr. Westaway 269ft. of Swanage stones in 1837, for his kitchen, at 6d. each.

It is likely that early in the 18th century the windows were mostly casements, but very few examples of these have survived, one instance being an extremely small window lighting the circular wooden stairs at La Vieille Maison, St. Aubin; a few seen but a decade ago have since disappeared, in one case the explanation offered being, "but you see it was so old". La Ville Mars, built in 1765 has casements which, if not contemporary, are certainly very old, particularly those at the back of the house, with their small panes of uneven glass and L-shaped hinges.

The earliest sash windows had only one section opening, and these could date from 1700, when this type appeared at Sausmarez Manor in Guernsey, and may still be seen in one house in St. Aubin, The Hollies. The width of the glazing bars may often proclaim an 18th-century date, and the style of latches, appearance of the glass, and proportions, put many others in that century. In general the smaller and more square the panes, the older the window. Sometimes the style of the sash, taken in conjunction with clear signs of the enlargement of the aperture, is a pointer to the

SOME FAN-LIGHTS IN ST. HELIER

26. New St.

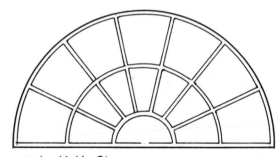

45. La Motte St.

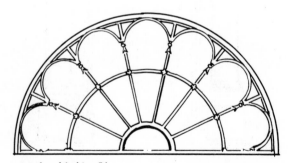

39. La Motte St.

9. Castle St.

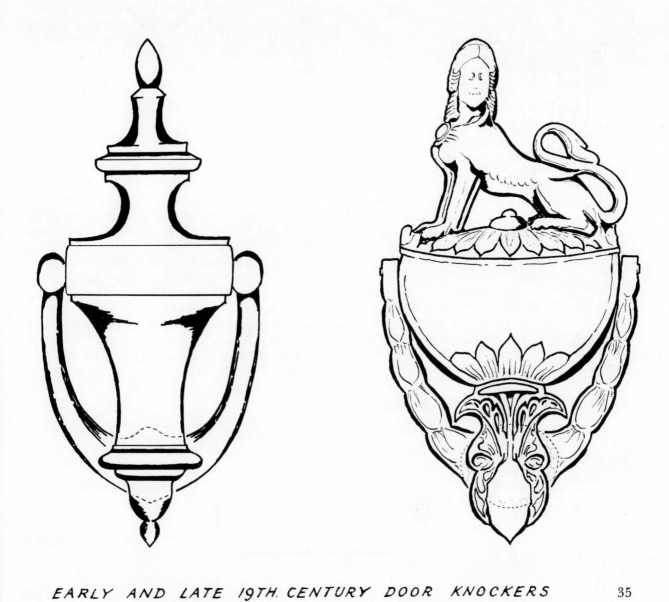

EARLY AND LATE 19TH CENTURY DOOR KNOCKERS   35

0   1   2   3   6   *inches*

age. In 1844 Mr. Morel of Leda House, St. Lawrence, paid Philippe Le Quesne £151 11s. tournois for 433ft. of glass for 15 windows, but unfortunately the number of panes was not stated.

When the sash window became general it was set into a deep embrasure with wooden shutters, and the type of moulding on these matched the rest of the woodwork of the room.

The oldest grates we have are probably not earlier than 1780; before that fire baskets would have been placed in the recess where formerly there were open wood fires, but not one of these seems to have survived, nor have any firebacks that are either locally made or with clear local associations. Various styles of cast-iron hob grate came into fashion, presumably imported, and they in turn were replaced by the round-topped 19th-century grate, with a more generous fire space, for the hob grate allowed but little fuel at a time. These can still be found in the less important rooms, or even attic bedrooms to which they were banished when passing fashion changed the style of grate in the best rooms. That the space round the small hob grate was filled

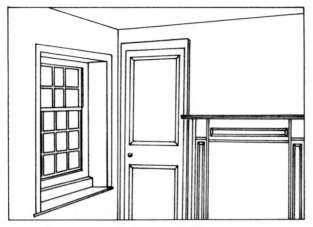

an early type of sash window and a contemporary door at L'Abri, St. John: the mantelpiece is later.

36

with tiles, is clear from a few examples. Such tiles were usually blue and white, depicting biblical scenes and they have been found at Rochebois (B), Le Marinel (J), Les Câteaux and possibly Longueville Farm (S). Kitchen ranges, when they became available, tended to be referred to as an "apparatus". Doors to bread ovens, of which a certain number have survived, bear the names of local suppliers, such as Le Feuvre of Don St.

It is clear that in the second half of the 18th century there was a great deal of pine panelling in Jersey houses. Some of it is still *in situ*, but many rooms have been stripped of it in recent years for fear of dry rot or woodworm. Some of the examples illustrated in this book have already disappeared. Similar, but older panelling in houses in Britanny has escaped the ravages of fungus and insect, and the equally damaging effects of central heating, because it was made of a hardwood, usually chestnut. Wallpaper was rare before about 1800.

Many rooms were lined from floor to ceiling with this woodwork, with its fielded panels and dado rail, doors panelled to match and dado panels lining the wall beside the stairs. The wood was painted in soft colours, white, buff, very pale blue, green or grey, and not only gave a well-knit attractive appearance to the room, but also insulated and warmed it. One is tempted to think that

WINDOW GLAZING BARS

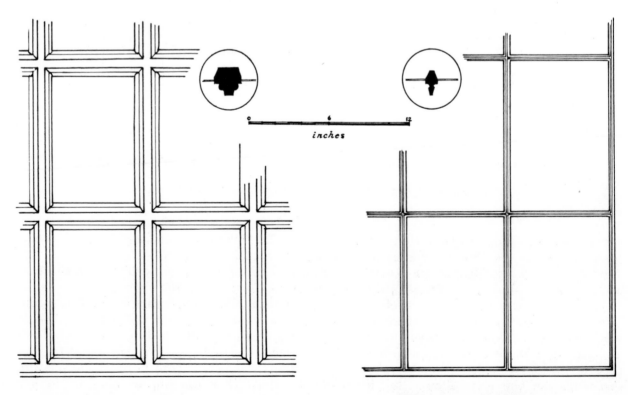

inches

37   *heavy type, before 1800.*   *light type, after 1800.*

IRON FIRE-GRATES, c.1780-1850.

Terrebonne

La Grange

La Sergenté, (Mt.)

Le Marinel

Grève de Lecq Barracks

Le Geyt Farm

Le Geyt Farm

Hue Street, (H). and Le Geyt Farm

La Vignette

38

a window with elaborate architraves, bosses and shutters was never meant to be curtained, although the shutters continued to be provided through the 19th century when curtains, thick heavy velvet or plush, as well as lace, draped every window. The fireplace surrounds were designed as a part of the panelling and had elaborate Georgian mouldings, a narrow moulded mantleshelf and a panel destined to frame a picture above the hearth. Doors could have two, three or more panels, and would have had wooden latches, though elegant brass ones soon replaced these in well-to-do houses, and may still be seen, as at The Elms, St. Mary. The door mouldings went through various styles, bolection, fielded, astragal and reeded, or a curious combination of two of these, indicating a transitional stage from one to the other. Care has to be taken in ascribing dates, as any style can return to popularity or overlap another in chronological sequence, or the owner of a house might have chosen a design which he, or his wife, liked, regardless of fashion.

When ceiling mouldings, cornices and central roses, or at least the moulds in which they were made, could be obtained commercially, they found favour in the Island. The outcrop of houses dated in or near 1820 all exhibit them, this continuing well into the century, and very handsome they are. Surprisingly the lovely Queen Anne decorated ceilings often found in English houses are quite absent in Jersey, though our craftsmen were sufficiently skilled to have produced plasterwork of this kind.

The Jersey staircases are notable and worthy of careful study. The oldest, as we know, are spiral stone stairs, enclosed in a semi-circular or square tower-like projection on the north of the house.

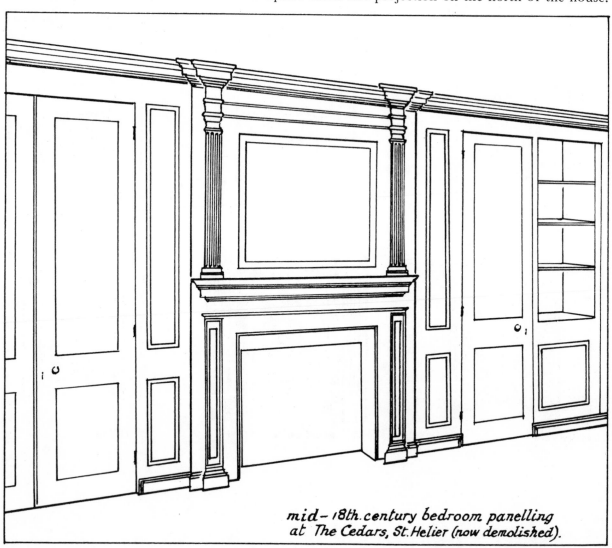

mid–18th. century bedroom panelling
at The Cedars, St. Helier (now demolished).

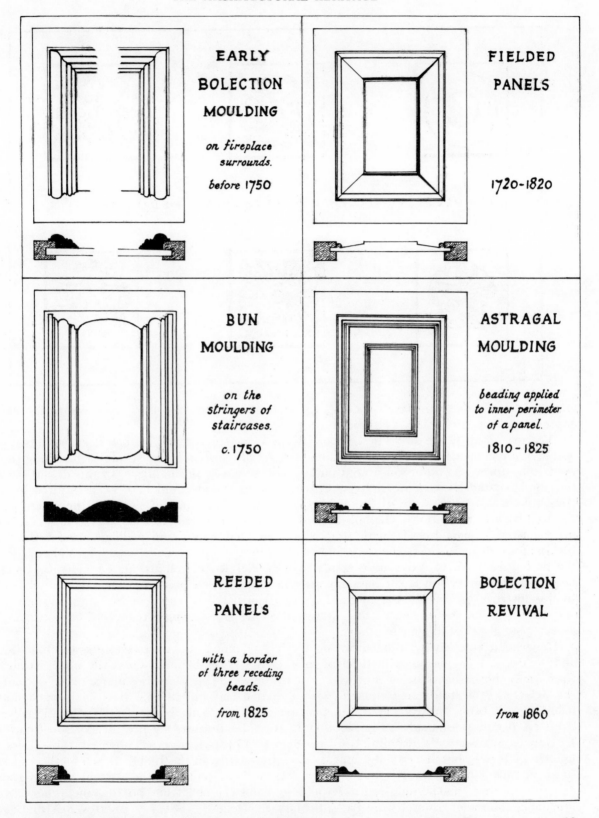

EARLY
BOLECTION
MOULDING

*on fireplace
surrounds.*
before 1750

FIELDED
PANELS

1720-1820

BUN
MOULDING

*on the
stringers of
staircases.*
c.1750

ASTRAGAL
MOULDING

*beading applied
to inner perimeter
of a panel.*
1810-1825

REEDED
PANELS

*with a border
of three receding
beads.*
from 1825

BOLECTION
REVIVAL

from 1860

WOODWORK AS A GUIDE TO DATING

40

0   10   20 *inches*

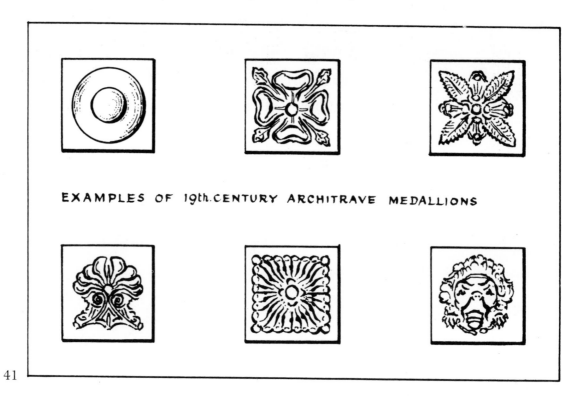

EXAMPLES OF 19th. CENTURY ARCHITRAVE MEDALLIONS

41

Once wood was used in place of stone, the staircases readily fall into three categories, each of approximately a half century's duration.

The first group is the direct descendant of the stone spiral stairs, though it came to be housed within the rectangular ground plan. In some remarkable instances the whole flight, rising three or even four storeys, is borne on a continuous central newel, in one piece. In this design the stairs turn at sharp angles and are rather steep and narrow, and could have been inspired by ships' companionways. In the case of St. Aubin, where they have mainly survived, they were perhaps dictated by cramped sites on the hillside. This style is often made in oak, and has well-constructed urn balusters, square newels, with squared or rounded knobs and pendants, and a flat-topped handrail; a stringer encloses the steps and is often bun-moulded. These examples fall roughly into the period 1680–1720. A variation appeared at 7 Pier Road, a house dated 1751, on its cistern head, where a projection at the back housed the stairs, a leave-over from the older tourelle notion. In this instance the size of the rooms has been sacrificed to over-generous proportions of stairs and landings, and the allowance of a stair-well shows this example to be old-fashioned in some aspects, and ahead of its time in others.

The second category set out to be slightly less cramped but not to waste space in a stair-well and so evolved an ingenious method of making the lower handrail cross the upper stringer, to form an X, both flights being morticed into the newel. This form is square, never circular, and the newel is still sturdy and squared with moulded cap and the handrail flat topped, but the baluster, still often turned and urn-shaped, becomes gradually more slender. Occasionally stick balusters occur, presumably as an economy, as at Le Bocage, St. Brelade; Maison Charles, St. Lawrence; St. Brelade's Hospital; 19 Hue Street (1748). It is not known if this X design is unique to Jersey, but it certainly appears very frequently in the Island. It is a method of saving space in small houses, whilst moving forward from the circular to the straight-flighted stairs. A variation during this period was a serpentine baluster, cut from boards, the other elements remaining the same. Examples are La Ville Mars, St. Helier (1768); Les Ruettes, St. John (1756); 16 Hill Street (1748); Bellozanne Abbey, St. Helier; and La Chasse, St. John. Longueville Farm (1776) has yet another slight variation. As it is so rare it seems likely to have been the brain-child of a particular carpenter. Unfortunately we do not know his name, though he may have inscribed it somewhere on his work, if one knew where to search. This idea of a two-, instead of a three-dimensional urn baluster may be seen in Brittany, and this may have inspired our carpenter with the idea. Another example incorporating various styles is Philippe Falle's library (1757) where the balusters are fully urn-shaped, the stairs curve round to the first and second floor landings, and therefore do not have the X formation, nor a stair-well. This style, with its variants, continued until the end of the 18th century. A transitional type was seen at Elms Farm, St. Mary (1796) with slender-turned balusters and octagonal capped newel. This was the same year as the erection of La Haule Manor, where a far more advanced type was built, showing the older fashion persisting in the country.

The third category appeared at the beginning of the 19th century, when the more ambitious owners ordered flying stairs. Here we find stick, or slender-turned balusters, a rounded mahogany handrail and open steps with the risers often decorated with mahogany appliqué, ingeniously fitted when the steps take an adventurous curve, thus creating a stair-well, and obviating all need for the X intersection. Sometimes one may find the two styles in one house, as at Belle Vue, St. Brelade, where an early staircase to the second floor is outshone by the light elegant sweep of the 1815 model.

The newel of this third category was turned, and usually mahogany, with its termination either turned or vertical (e.g., La Grange, St. Mary) or in a horizontal whorl (e.g., The Museum, 1815); Le Colombier, St. Lawrence; and La Hougue, St. Peter (1822); Beechfield, Trinity (1822); Windsor Crescent. St. Helier (1835); Les Nièmes, St. Peter (1829). Sometimes the handrail was delicately cut in a swan-neck curve at each change in level (e.g., 12 Hue Street). Frequently a small mother-of-pearl or ivory disc was inserted in the top of the newel.

A variant seldom found in Jersey houses is the barley-sugar baluster, so far noticed only at Colomberie House, St. Helier. Nor is the metal baluster often seen, being recorded only at Avranches Manor, St. Lawrence (1819) and the lower flight at the Museum.

By the middle of the 19th century the flying stair was fully established, but its treatment became gradually heavier (e.g., Mainland, St. Lawrence (c. 1840) and St. Martin's House (altered 1868) and examples late in the century are even more substantial (e.g., La Pompe, St. Mary, 1888).

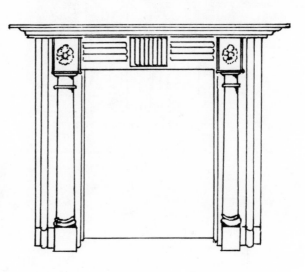

18th. and 19th. century fireplace surrounds, Hue Street, St.Helier.

La Vallette, (J). mantelpiece, c.1820.

42

EVOLUTION OF THE STAIRCASE IN JERSEY HOUSES.

1. The spiral stone stair is abandoned and a wooden substitute built, in a confined space.

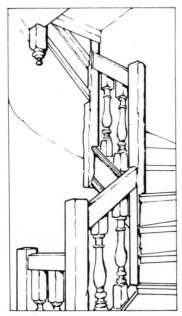

THE HOLLIES, St. Aubin. 1683.

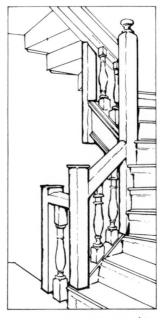

LA VIEILLE MAISON, St. Aubin. 1687.

2. a large square well-staircase occupies most of the available space, resulting in very small rooms.

NO. 7. PIER ROAD, St. Helier. 1751.

43

EVOLUTION OF THE STAIRCASE IN JERSEY HOUSES.

3. for strength, and to save space, the hand-rail intersects with the stringer above, and both are mortised into the newel.

L'ANCIENNETÉ, St. Aubin. c.1750.

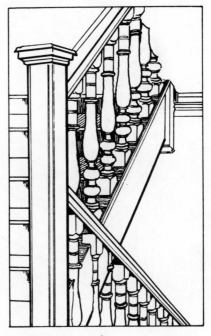

LA VALEUSE. c.1760.

OAK FARM. c.1750.

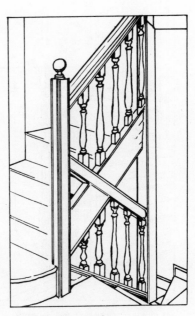

THE CEDARS. c.1780.

44

EVOLUTION OF THE STAIRCASE IN JERSEY HOUSES.

4. to save expense, stick balusters instead of turned balusters are used.

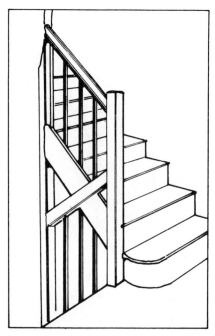

No.19. HUE STREET, St.Helier. 1748.

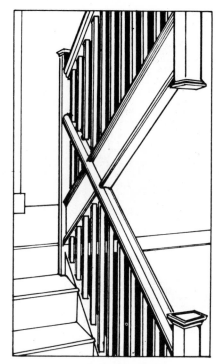

LA MAISON CHARLES. c.1740.

5. another economy: serpentine balusters cut from boards.

No. 16. HILL STREET, St.Helier. 1748.

BELLOZANNE ABBEY. c.1750.

EVOLUTION OF THE STAIRCASE IN JERSEY HOUSES.

6. *circular well with flying stair : no landings : walls niched for statuary : risers decorated with mahogany applique.*

LE COLOMBIER. c. 1820.

HIGHLANDS. c. 1820.

7. *square well : landings : treads no longer enclosed by stringer : round-topped hand-rail.*

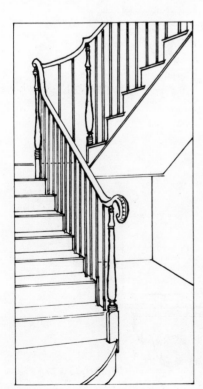

LA GRANGE. 1831.

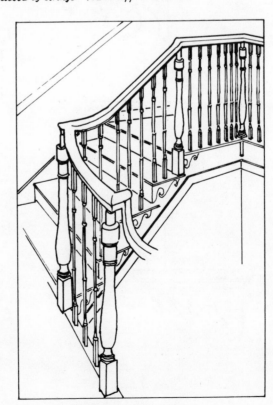

NO. 12. HUE STREET, St. Helier. c. 1860.

46

EXAMPLES OF DECORATED RISERS IN JERSEY STAIRCASES.

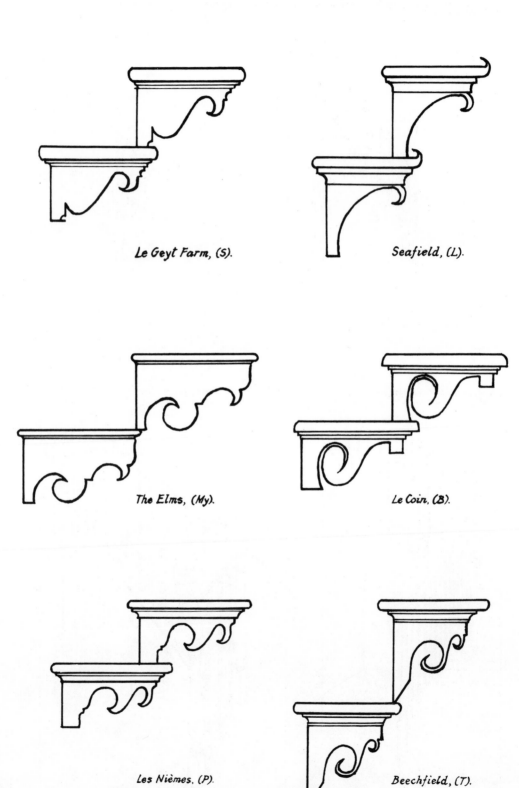

Le Geyt Farm, (S).

Seafield, (L).

The Elms, (My).

Le Coin, (B).

Les Nièmes, (P).

Beechfield, (T).

CISTERN - HEADS

at 7. Pier Road, (H).
initials of Nicolas Fiott
and his wife Ann Dumaresq.

at La Maison Maret, (T).
initials of Charles Marett and
Anne Messervy, 1755: (married 1742).

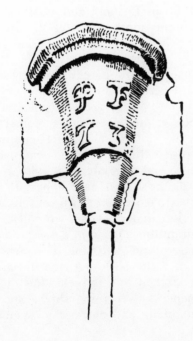

on the Old Library, (H).
initials of Philippe Falle, 1736.

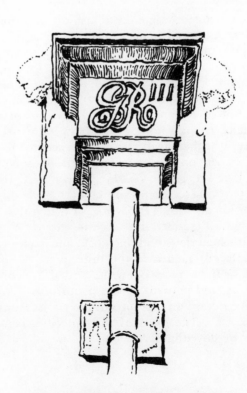

48

on the Picket House, Royal Square.
cipher of King George III.

49 *VILLE AU VESLET, (L): gable-stone 1694 HRM (Remon): marriage-stone 1739 IRM. RPD (Remon-Poingdestre): thatch survives under iron roof.*

The stick baluster came into fashion in about 1780 in England and clearly overlapped with other styles. A turned baluster came later again, becoming more portly as Victorianism advanced through the century, unwittingly returning to the proportions of the Tudors, indignantly rejected by the Georgians.

There is not a great deal of good ironwork in Jersey, and apparently none was made locally. There are, however, some most attractive examples of verandahs on several houses at Havre des Pas, probably of Regency date, and because of their rarity they are of considerable value to us. Cistern heads, though not proof of the date of a house, provide strong circumstantial evidence, particularly if other features are in accord with the embossed date. The appearance of an embossed crown on a rain-water head does NOT prove that the house was ever Government House or that Ralegh or Charles II ever lived there, as one is sometimes told. It is a great pity that so few of these interesting objects have survived; those that have appear to be in perfectly good condition and doing the work for which they were designed some two centuries ago.

Having now described the architecture of the period under review, we will deal in the final chapter with materials, building costs and styles of alteration, noting in passing that a guide book of 1847 (Durell) mentions the orderliness of the farmhouses, advising the tourist to enter one where "he will be received with cordial welcome . . . the parlour fitted up with neat chairs, carpet, tables, and perhaps even a pianoforte . . . the kitchen too, though a less showy apartment, has also its luxury in the profusion of its conveniences. Everything shines and has an air of satisfaction . . . The dress of the family is neat but plain, and betrays no symptoms either of poverty or of slovenliness".

PLATE XIII STAIRCASES

c. New Street, *c* 1750

d. Le Quai des Marchands, *c* 1820

PLATE XIV PORCHES

a. La Vallette (J), possibly 1796

b. Highcliff (J), *c* 1830

c. L'Abri (Mt), late 19th century

d. Melbourne Cottage (J), very late 19th century with older door

PLATE XV DORMERS

a. L'Ancienneté (B), 18th century

b. Rouge Bouillon (H), 18th,
19th and 20th century dormers

c. Gallichans, Royal Square, 19th century house

d. La Mielle (B), typical early 19th
century dormers

PLATE XVI VARIOUS

a. Dower wing at La Vallette (J), 1826

b. Mon Séjour (P), 1734, showing change of roof slope.

c. Forge door at St Martin with clients' brands

d. Insurance plaque at Haut des Buttes (My)

CHAPTER TEN

MAINTENANCE AND ALTERATIONS

"We are plagued with workmen, and the work not going on as fast as we could wish; not so with the money. I am teazed with housekeeping and want of convenience to give dinners."

Mary Le Couteur to her son. 1816.

LET US NOW SEE what our contemporary records can tell us about building construction and maintenance, and the materials used. The by-laws of 1715, although they do not seem to have been obeyed to any marked extent, show that the authorities were primarily interested in buildings as a possible source of fire, and of contamination if the occupants had slovenly habits. They provide that town dwellers must maintain the pavements in front of their houses, and were forbidden to throw anything into the streets, or to keep pigs, goats or geese running free. Owners of houses were to have a barrel in which to put sweepings until the crossing sweeper (boueur) came to empty them of their rubbish, the word used being "frange", from the old French "fruisser", to fragment, hence fringe. Wool combers, washers of stockings, tanners and butchers were forbidden to throw their dirty water into the streams or on to the pavements of St. Helier and St. Aubin, or to throw or permit to be thrown excrement or filth, and the inhabitants had to pay a small fee for the collection of the garbage. In order to prevent fires in the towns of St. Helier and St. Aubin within the ensuing ten years, all houses were to be roofed in tile or slate and all new houses and outbuildings were to be roofed similarly, and it was ordered that within one year all householders were to provide themselves with two good leather buckets as a fire precaution.

Unfortunately few old shops have survived in our town. The last genuine bow window found a home at the Museum when it was ousted from La Motte Street, to give place to a modern shop frontage; now the pendulum has swung and shops are copying the very bow window rejected a couple of decades earlier. There are still two attractive shop fronts in Broad Street, though one has been altered and has had its small panes of glass removed. One which has remained unaltered is Gallichans, the jewellers in Vine Street, which is now recognised as quite a "period piece" and must surely be preserved.

Houses fell into a sorry state of neglect when they were empty, or the occupiers too poor to repair them, and we have many instances of this. In 1753 Pierre Mauger received a letter from Mr. Seale, a client of his in London, regarding a house which he wished to sell, in which he asks Mauger to miss no opportunity to sell both houses and land as "the more it ages the less one wants to have it". There is reason to think that this referred to The Old Court House at St. Aubin.

Part, but alas only part of a building account for La Hague, dated 1757 (four years after a known re-building) has survived, the sum mentioned being £3,486 tournois, but this was only part of the total. The most interesting items are for 1,400 tiles and 100 piles (? bundles) of thatching grass for £90; 12 loads of stone for £6 15s., and £40 to Clement Pinel of Mont Mado (perhaps living at La Valette), this probably for granite. For 128 bushels of English lime £153 12s. was paid, and this is an interesting item, for we have seen that the importation of shells, for burning lime locally, dated from rather later, nearer to 1800. And 358 Dutch tiles cost £24 10s.: were they for fireplace surrounds? On another occasion Pierre Mauger receipted a bill dated 1759, for Capitaine Cenos (Snow) which included carriage on a barrel of lime, as well as 475 bundles of thatching grass; on another occasion £6 5s. 4d. was paid for seven days' work by a carpenter, including "5 quart de cent" (125) of nails, the currency in this case being stated as monnaie d'ordre.

In 1786 the house named Le Clos Luce (in St. Ouen's Bay but in St. Peter's parish) was built and involved a payment for 16lb. beef for the carters transporting the wood and tiles, and for three pots of cider when the beams were up "en montant les poutres". Amounts were paid for 1,600 tiles, 100 bricks, 4lb. paint, linseed oil, straw for faggots, iron work, clay (rouge terre); for carting gravel, for a door frame, thatch for a lean-to shed, and a barrel of lime. £197 was paid to carpenters, £17 to glaziers and £78 to masons.

An account dated 1818 owed by François Marett to N. L. J. Brohier totalled £22,784, presumably tournois. Items included "for six years of his attendance working and superintending the workmen at Montchoix or Bagatelle @ £90 per annum . . . for his servants, horses and cart . . . horse and man or boy constantly sent backwards and forwards in messages to St. Lawrence. For cash to Mr Le Brun for his child's dress and clothes sent for the said child from England". After this charming diversion, we return to the building costs and find a bell for the top of the house, 20 buckets furnished and worn out at the building, 20 wheelbarrows, 30 spades and shovels, a thousand bricks, bars and iron chains worn out at the building and two bath stoves stolen. François' cousin Philippe Marett said in his diary for that year: ". . . took a walk by Bagatelle which is building very fast . . .". In this same year François was also building Avranches Manor. Bagatelle seems to have been an ambitious project, and must have replaced a house on the same site in which Philippe d'Auvergne, Prince and Admiral (1754-1816) lived when in Jersey, and this is probably the Bagatelle in which Thomas Le Breton, Bailiff (1763-1838) also lived.

Another builder's account, dated 1839, contained payments for £26 for 8 days' work, £3 for 50 laths, £1 for 12lb. of hair (for binding mortar) and 1½ cabots of lime.

In 1842 work done at Les Vaux, St. Lawrence, included 2,000 Bridgewater tiles at 8s. per 100, £34 for roofing the house, and 3,050 slates 18in. by 10in. at £4 per 100. Other sums were for nails, spikes, cement at 1d. per lb. and slate nails at 6d. per lb. Labour was paid at between 10d. and 2s. 9d. per day, and the whole of this particular account seems to be in sterling. In the same year £18 tournois was paid to Philippe Le Quesne by Mr. Morel for two hearthstones of 6ft. squared paving, and £48 for 160 lengths of guttering. Two "Italian veined marble chimney pieces" cost £10 and slate backs and hearths 16s. 4d., plus 6s. for fixing two Register stoves. All these items were for Leda House, St. Lawrence.

The sorry condition into which a house could fall, already mentioned, is illustrated by some entries in fief books. In 1721 experts on the fief of Nobretez were called to look at Philippe Le Bosquet's house, which had fallen into the Seigneur's care, on behalf of the former's orphan minor children. Some windows were missing as well as the glass; the back of the house and a third of the front were in ruins and roofless, there were no stairs, the outbuildings were equally ruinous, the trees poor, with ditches, banks and walls in disrepair. It was the same story in 1724 when they examined Pierre Descaudeville's house, fallen to the Seigneur until a legitimate heir could be found. It was said to be roofless and about to fall down, with no woodwork and few windows, hardly any floor boards, all rafters and purlins absent and the thatch ruinous; apart from that, they said cheerfully, the house was serviceable. In 1778 a house in Hue Street, belonging to Nicholas Le Quesne, who was en décret, was no better. Two windows with 23 leaded panes are mentioned, but the whole place was clearly in a sad state of neglect. Vicart Mill was in a bad condition in 1784, with broken tiles in the roof, doors missing, windows broken, and parts of the water mill and horse mill were missing. In 1789 it was much the same for Philippe Hubert's house, in or near the Royal Square, and here leaded window panes are again mentioned. Nathaniel Oppenham's house was found to be dilapidated in 1801 in the fief books of Meleches. By 1804 a similar report speaks of window cords and sashes. Over and over again in fief books, and particularly in the fief of Meleches which was largely in town, we find such melancholy descriptions. Some of the words used are borrowed from the English, such as slab, toplight, chetteur (shutter) and cubort.

Nor was the situation any better where the King's property was concerned, as we see by an order to examine it in 1749, presumably as a prelude to preparing the Extente of that year. The account of the Royal Court building leaves one unsurprised that it was rebuilt fifteen years later.

Even the seats of the Magistrate, Jurats and Rectors needed repair. The situation at the prison, established only some 70 years previously, was even worse. The main door needed repairs to the lock, the sewers were in a very bad state, with no outlet, and the Porter's Lodge was in ruins. The so-called King's House in St. Lawrence (perhaps Le Bordage at Bel Royal, the hangman's house) was likewise in a bad condition. In the case of land all banks, walls, gates and gateposts seem to have been sadly neglected as had the mill in Grouville. One wonders why Crown property was so neglected, and whether the Extente was the cause or the effect of this survey? In an effort to pay for the repairs Lord Cobham, the then Governor, instructed the Receiver General, François Marett, "to take possession of all warrens, meadows, fowles and poultry . . . and all other revenues of His Majesty".

It may be of interest to compare alterations made to two houses, within a space of 30-odd years, both having definite evidence of a 17th-century origin, if not earlier. At La Vallette, St. John, the alteration was in 1796 and at La Grange, St. Mary in 1831. At La Vallette the façade was re-faced so that all apertures are contemporary, but inside most of the woodwork and the stairs suggest a date earlier in the century. A front door was installed, possibly replacing the round arch which is now in a northern addition. The owners of the day put up their marriage stone in 1796, which also records the passing of the property from the Pinel to the Le Masurier family. In 1826 a single-storey dower wing was added, with decorative woodwork inside, which is in good agreement with this date, and the same pattern of woodwork was installed in the west bedroom of the main house. It is not possible to assign a sure date to the front door, of the type with two-thirds opening ordinarily, and a further third to be opened at will. This pattern is repeated in doors in the hall, and is rare for an interior door, otherwise seen only at Potirons de Bas, St. Mary, dated 1757. Over the front door is a very simple porch carried on unfluted Doric columns. At some stage additional space was added by building, or adapting, rooms in the west wing, but no additional rooms were added to the north, so that the main rooms have windows both north and south.

At La Grange in 1831 (the date and the signature of Philippe Vibert were found pencilled behind some shutters) the owners certainly removed a round arch, of which but one fragment has been found. It was replaced by a straight-topped aperture, far wider than that occupied by the round arch, and a sturdy panelled door with heavy contemporary latch and key. It has a rather more elaborate porch with Tuscan pillars, though very simple compared with those seen in town on rather later houses. The windows were enlarged and the chamfered lintels thrown out, to be found over a century later in the garden. The size of the house was almost doubled by the addition to the north of further rooms, on both storeys. A very pleasing staircase was installed, with stick balusters and mahogany newels and handrail. All doors and shutters have reeded moulding, and the architraves are also moulded with, in the case of the best rooms, concentric circled corner bosses. At the same time, or perhaps later, very large farm buildings and a dower wing were added to the west. The gap of a generation between the alterations made to these two houses shows a more ambitious scheme in the latter case, with more attention paid to the interior details than to the outside appearance.

It is surprising when one finds a builder's estimates written out in English, as was the case in 1868 when J. J. Collas altered St. Martin's House. An interesting item is ". . . present kitchen to be converted into drawing room, and all masonry to be raised 12" with stonework 18" thick". The mortar was to be "all lime, with good sharp gravel, and the roof to be tiled". A reference to "the small staircase in the water closet" is hard to understand, but the latter was to have mahogany risers, seat and flap of Honduras wood and a blue basin. Swanage flagstones again appear, to be removed from the passage and laid in the kitchen. A reference to the kitchen chimney piece ". . . with cross bars above with battens and lining . . . such as is what is generally done in a good kitchen" reminds one of the battens for hanging pots and pans above the kitchen fireplace at Le Marinel, St. John (new house, 1870); The Elms, St. Mary; and at the Museum. The front of the house was to be plastered with lime and "La Rock" gravel, finished with fine stucco, and internal plastering was to be lime with gravel and long hair. "Patent lead pipes" brought water from a cistern to the scullery and a soft-water pump was installed. All woodwork was to be knotted and then to receive four coats of paint. The contractors for this work were

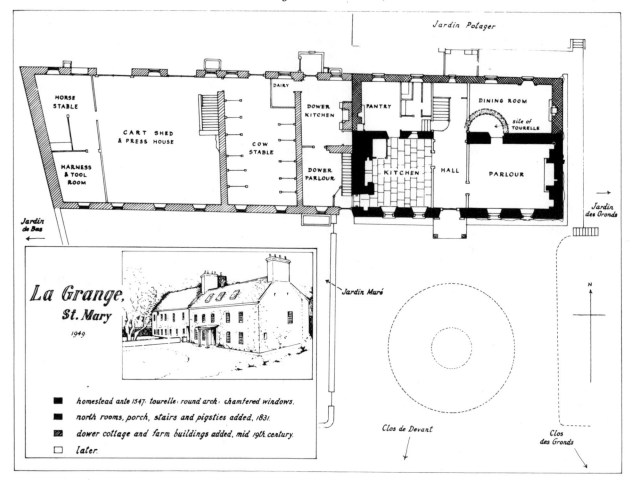

La Grange,
St. Mary
1949

■ homestead ante 1547: tourelle: round arch: chamfered windows.
■ north rooms, porch, stairs and pigsties added, 1831.
▨ dower cottage and farm buildings added, mid 19th century.
□ later.

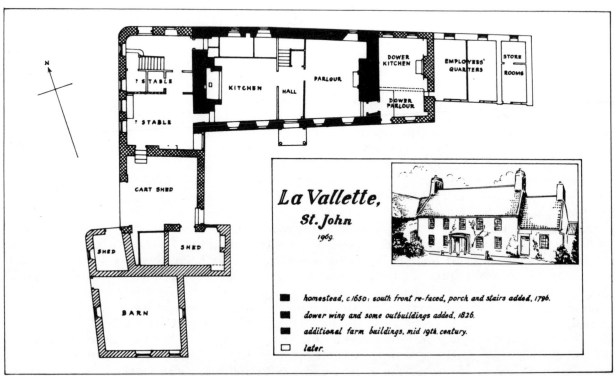

La Vallette,
St. John
1969.

■ homestead, c.1650: south front re-faced, porch and stairs added, 1796.
■ dower wing and some outbuildings added, 1826.
■ additional farm buildings, mid 19th century.
□ later.

TWO WAYS OF ENLARGING AN ANCIENT HOMESTEAD

Fallaize and Tostevin of 32 Dorset Street, and John Laurens of 29 Devonshire Place was the carpenter; the architect was Philippe Le Rossignol (1800–1892) and the total estimate was £370 sterling. The account to George Thom, housepainter, included "marbling" four chimney pieces for 14s., and 1s. for cleaning pictures and frames. An item "lining a beam in the drawing room" for 12s. is winsome, as when this was stripped off recently, to expose the oak beam within, a newspaper of 1868 was found. Thus does each generation destroy the work of the past. As well as the water closet, piping was installed to lay on water from the well to the scullery, which must have been quite an innovation in a country parish.

A rather similar specification was given for La Pompe, St. Mary, built in 1886. The contractors were William Blampied and Alfred Le Sueur, and the witness to the signing of the contract was Mr. Laurens of Millbrook. It is said that Mr. Arthur, the proprietor of the new house in St. Mary, wanted it to be built of granite, as indeed it is, his son, then aged 20, carting all the stone from Mont Mado himself. But his wife wanted the fashionable stucco, and so admired Mr. Laurens' own house at Millbrook (Lansdowne, now called Springland), that her husband bowed to her wishes. Although it is stipulated that the best possible materials should be used in every context, the joints of the chimneys were to be pointed with cow dung. The wood was all to be Baltic red fir, well seasoned, and the floorboards deal. Again mahogany was used in the water closet, with a blue basin, and this must also have been quite an innovation in a country parish. The stairs were red deal, with balusters, newel, nosings, brackets and handrail of mahogany. It was stated that sideboards were to be fitted at each side of the fireplace (hence the name?) in the back parlour, with mahogany cupboards underneath.

The roof slates were described as Bangor Countess. The paving in the hall cost 8s. per yard, exclusive of fixing. The total price for building this large house was £820 sterling.

Houses were rented furnished more often than nowadays, and Philippe Marett seems to have built Mon Plaisir at La Haule, in about 1820, largely in order to lease La Haule Manor, and there are many references in his diaries to these transactions. In 1838 the rent was £3 a week; in 1844 it was £120 a year, and in 1859 it was let to the Earl of Devon for £3 3s. a week. The Rope Walk Cottage (now called West Lodge) was let in 1834 to Richard Satchwell for £11 a year, including the ground appropriately called La Corderie.

The use to which various rooms were put, and what they were named is interesting. There is no doubt that our ancestors needed far more storage space than we, both for food and fuel, and in allotting rooms in our minds this should be remembered. Wood, bracken and vraic all took up more space than coal, and for the winter the larder had to stock salted meat, dried beans and quantities of root vegetables and apples, as well as grain and flour. The first, and indeed the only reference to a dining room was found in the 1763 inventory of Thomas Pipon (1707-63). The assortment of items found in each room in inventories seems rather haphazard to us; in many cases the contents of the main bedroom suggest that the lady of the house entertained her friends to tea there. Further we often find a first-floor drawing room, occupying the same position and purpose as the mediaeval solar in England and elsewhere. In several instances the best and most elaborate fireplace has been found on the first floor in 17th-century houses, like Fernhill, St. Helier; Handois, St. Lawrence; and Mont an Prêtre, St. Helier. It seems likely that the wooden floor boards of the upper room were more conducive to comfort and warmth, and better protection for the feet of cupboards and other furniture. It was truly a "withdrawing" room.

What were the reasons for alterations to houses? Probably very much the same as they are today. There are economic factors, an owner may prosper and gradually be able to enlarge and improve his house, or if he does not prosper, he may sell it to someone else who can afford the alterations. Then there is fashion, and the wife may wish to compete with her relatives and neighbours and to take advantage of new amenities and inventions and labour-saving devices. In such cases it is a matter of petticoat government, usually based on sound common sense. It is often noticeable that a house has undergone a major alteration at approximately one hundred year intervals, and minor adjustments with each succeeding generation, as each new bride has brought her own personality and taste to her new home.

Having completed a general survey, we will now examine some individual houses, and assess their merits and their claim to our attention.

Part Two

THE HOUSES

"These remaines are tanquam Tabulata Naufragy (like fragments of a shipwreck) that after the Revolution of so many Years and Govenments have escaped the Teeth of Time and (which is more dangerous) the Hands of Mistaken Zeale. So that the retriving of these forgotten Things from Oblivion in some sort resembles the Art of a Conjuror, who makes those walke and appeare that have layen in their grave many hundreds of yeares: and to represent as it were to the eie, the places, Customes and Fashions, that were of old Times."

John Aubrey
(1626–1697)

PLATE XVII A WELCOME TO VISIT AN OLD JERSEY HOUSE

PLATE XVIII TOWN AND COUNTRY

a. Royal Crescent (H), *c* 1825.

b. Ty Anna, St. Aubin 1715

PLATE XIX

a. L'Ancienneté (B), *c* 1820

b. Bellozanne Abbey (H)

c. Belvoir, Mont Millais (H), 1825, shortly before demolition

PLATE XX

a. Door at no. 9 Castle Street (H), late 18th century

b. Le Coin (B), *c* 1890

c. La Croix au Lion (P), the gable cross may have come from St Peter's Priory

d. Pig sties at Le Douet (J)

L'ABRI
Opposite Rue des Peupliers (J). (J. Hocquard on Godfray.)

A date stone with IHC IAL and 1786 represents a Hocquard–Anley marriage. The south façade of the house appears to have been re-faced, probably at that date, and in the same manner as La Valette in the same parish. There is, in both cases, rather a rough jointure between the old quoins and the new blocks. Brick chimneys were replaced by granite in 1972. The windows on the south have thin glazing bars and do not seem to have been altered; on the north the windows are much earlier, having sashes with no sash cord, small panes with heavy hand-made glass and heavy glazing bars. These must antedate the 1786 frontage, but indicate that this was always a "double-pile" house, and no interior wall is sufficiently thick ever to have been an exterior wall. There are three granite fireplaces, all the lintels being rather low, and it may be that floor levels have been changed at some period. Some bedroom cupboards are 18th century, but most of the doors are later, and the stairs are not notable.

old pattern of shed or heifer-stable at L'Abri, St. John.

51

In front of the house there is a long stable block, fitted with wooden tethering rings (very rare) and one window has chamfered sides, suggesting an earlier date than the house façade. The roof was slated in about 1940, and an old photograph shows it with tiles in 1906.

There was a remarkable farm building to the south, a crude timber-framed erection, with timber uprights standing on granite boulders and infill of rough stone and clay, open between the top of the wall and the roof, with a clearance of only 5ft. 5in., though the floor level may have been raised over the years. It is said that it was built in about 1900 as a mangold shed for "Uncle Winter Bichard", but its appearance was older than this and it may have been a heifer stable.

See Drawings 29, 36, 51.

L'ABRI
Grand Route de Faldouet (Mt.). (H. Payne on Godfray.)

A standard local house seems to have been built with gables which, though handsome, are not in the vernacular tradition. The trellised porch is a good example of its kind. Over a road-side door is a stone with 1811 H P E G F, for Helier Payne who married Elizabeth Godfray in 1808, and is presumably the same as the proprietor shown on Godfray's map.

See Plate XIV c.

L'AIGUILLON
Rue des Côtils (G). (Noel on Godfray.)

The Appairiement de Grouville suggests that this property belonged to a de Veulle in 1804, but the façade of the house shows a stone with 18 P N M V 05, probably the M. Noel shown on Godfray's map. On an outhouse there is another stone with H M L S R 1712, and a wing at the back of the house has one with 17 E V D M L B 33, and Vardon and Labey are likely names in this parish, though no marriages have been found to substantiate this. Below this last stone there is a window with most curiously carved side jambs, a stylised pot of flowers and moulding, and below this again is the cut portion of a stone with H L P, the last letter being truncated. These carved stones, which have the appearance of antiquity, are unique in the Island. A traditional type arch has been made for the front door, and honourably labelled 1969.

ALBANY HOUSE
Grande Route de St. Laurent (L). (G. Laurens on Godfray.)

Since Volume I was first published, a further stone on the façade of this house has been identified. It is somewhat ornate with LV ♡ RDLC, and on a second line IPV1745. This represents Louis Voisin who married Rachel de la Cour in 1725, and their son Jacob Philippe, born in that year. On closer examination the gable stone proves to be 1644, not 1666 as first thought. The WS represents William Snow, who married Rachel Gibaut, names well known in the parish at that period. The windows have been enlarged at some time, and the roof heightened. The extreme south-west corner, bearing the early gable stone, appears to be older than the rest of the

Voisin-de la Cour stone, Albany House, (L).

52

façade, which was probably rebuilt in 1745.

See Drawing 52.

ALMORAH CRESCENT
Upper King's Cliff (H).

This crescent of ten houses is probably the most distinguished piece of Regency arthitecture in the Channel Islands, though its date of erection is just within Victoria's reign. It has a commanding position above the town and catches every ray of sunshine there is.

Its history is most interesting, both for itself and for the light it sheds on contemporary affairs, and for much of my information I am indebted to Mrs. S. Hillsdon, a resident in the crescent who has taken a great interest in its origins.

The view of St. Helier, by P. H. Rogers (1794-1853) which formed the cover of the Société Jersiaise Centenary Appeal Brochure, was taken from the approximate site of Almorah Crescent. The picture was exhibited at the British Institute in 1833, and at that time the hills above the town were bare of houses, and there were farms in Rouge Bouillon. The northward creep of the town, begun to meet the great demand for superior houses by an influx of English residents after the close of the Napoleonic wars, was extending. At this time a very large area of Mont au Prêtre belonged to George Dumaresq of Ponterrin and his wife Françoise Dumaresq of Les Augrès. Their land was later divided between their two daughters, Jeanne and Françoise. The latter married Thomas Le Hardy (whose initials are on a stone at the foot of St. Saviour's Hill) and they inherited land from Campbell Terrace eastwards to Springfield. The elder daughter had married Mathieu La Cloche, who was Constable of St. Helier 1779-1782, and they inherited the large block of land in Rouge Bouillon and up the hill to King's Cliff. They had two daughters, the younger, Elizabeth, marrying Dr. Edward Thompson Dickson, father of Dr. Jo Dickson, who often features in the Le Couteur diaries. The elder daughter, Jeanne, married Captain Edward Ricard (b. 1756) fs. Charles, of La Robeline, St. Ouen, a brother of the Reverend François Ricard (1751-1823), Rector of St. Peter and St. Ouen, and Dean of Jamaica. Edward Ricard had a son, Charles La Cloche Ricard and several other children, and this Charles was to become a well-known speculative builder, and to lose his money, perhaps through over ambition. He married Dora Louisa, daughter of Dr. H. C. Taylor, the first English child born at Almorah in the Himalayas after it was taken over by the East India Company, hence the name of the Crescent, and the former name of the present Ralegh Avenue. They had two sons who died in childhood, and one daughter, Dora Louisa Ricard.

Her undated letter to the *Evening Post* (perhaps about 1910) has provided more family information. She was their eldest child, born in 1840, and it was in 1838 that Charles Ricard started to exploit his mother's valuable inheritance when he bought his brother's and three sisters' shares of the land. The names as given in Payne's *Armorial* do not quite agree with those in the Public Registry records, nor does his wife's name agree with details in Miss Ricard's letter, and she must have known. The co-heirs were in fact Jean Mathieu, Sophie Julie, Elizabeth Georgiana and Mary Anne Henriette.

In 1844 Charles Ricard was advertising that he had "encore un terrain a disposer sur la terrace de dix maisons qui est en bâtissant au haut de ses terres, et d'où l'on de la plus belle vue de la mer et des environs, qui conviendrait bien à un charpentier, d'autant qu'il est entendu que ceux qui y batissent se donneront de l'ouvrage mutuellement, enfin que la construction se fasse entre eux . . . chaqun fournissant suivant sa branche". In 1845 he was advertising "maisons incomplètes à vendre", built by François Le Brun, of superior materials, and all the descriptions underline that they are respectable and uniform. Some are described as being "sous couverture", which must mean roofed, but not finished. At the same time the States decided to make St. John's Road 28ft. instead of 24ft. wide. Ricard owned so much property in the area that one cannot always be sure to which houses he is referring. One does not know quite how well this novel co-operative effort succeeded, but in 1849 the *Almanac de la Chronique* reported "Les désastreux effects qui produisent l'année dernière la hardiesse ou l'imprévoyance de ces nombreux spéculateurs qui erigeaient maisons après maisons à l'aide du crédit dont ils jouissaient, ne se sont pas reproduits avec la même intensité cette année . . .". It goes on to blame this situation of easy credit, which had led to many bankruptcies, and much hardship to workmen employed in these works, and merchants supplying the materials. This would account for Miss Ricard's remark, "My father, an imprudent man, lost his fortune in Rouge Bouillon grounds, a large portion of which were sold by me". This refers, in fact, to Rouge Bouillon House, formerly on the corner at the foot of St. John's Road.

It is surprising that the ten houses in Almorah Crescent have no outbuildings or stables. They each comprise a basement and four storeys. All the second storey windows have typical hoods over them, and the first floor has a continuous hooded balcony, worthy of the bext Regency architecture. If the interior details are a little disappointing this has been noticed in other houses of the period, where the outside appearance seems to have been the dominant factor in the mind of the designer or owner. In this case it might be a reflection of the sales of incomplete houses, which perhaps took some years to accomplish.

The terrace is an ornament to the town and should be recognised as such.

See Plate IIa.
Payne's *Armorial*, p. 326.
Messervy notebook, No. 51, at Museum.
Public Registry record 169, ff. 161/2 and others.
Almanacs de la Chronique over a long period.

L'ANCIENNETÉ

High Street, St. Aubin (B). (Now called St. Aubin's Hotel.)

An elaborate cistern head on the south façade is dated 1737 with what appear to be the initials T^{P}E. Over the front door (on the north) are the initials IIV for Jean Janvrin fs. Brelade, whose sister Anne married Philippe Marett of La Haule, and their daughter Maria married her first cousin, the next Philippe Marett of La Haule. Another daughter of Brelade's, Elizabeth, married Philippe Hamon, and their date stone with 17PHM EIV76 appears on a house nearby, now called Sables d'Or. There is a stone gutter (cf. Oakwood (My) and Highland, (L)) which is very rare. One is tempted to think that Jean Janvrin re-faced a far older house in about 1820 (his initials and the date 1818 appear on the harbour jetty), and it also seems likely that the enclosed courtyard on the opposite side of the High Street was his shipyard or store, as its entrance pillars are exactly similar to those on the house.

The main room on the High Street level is completely panelled with contemporary woodwork; some of the panels open to disclose cupboards with drop hinges. Jean Janvrin's safe was there until a few years ago, and this must have been the room from which he conducted his prosperous trans-Atlantic business. The stairs, now varnished, are very fine, with urn balusters and typical flat handrail.

See Drawing 44.

Plates XV a, XIX a.

L'ANCIENNETÉ
Grande Route de Ste. Marie (My). (J. Arthur on Godfray.)

There is a most curious stone here, dated 1659, in the portion of the house nearest to the road.

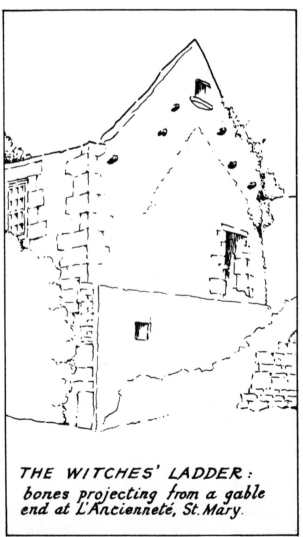

THE WITCHES' LADDER: bones projecting from a gable end at L'Ancienneté, St. Mary.

53

It has the initials F A and N D P suggesting, particularly in this parish, Arthur and du Pré. There are two hearts in the design, and it is the earliest example of this motif. As there are some gaps in the parish registers for St. Mary it has not been possible to identify with certainty the owners of these initials. There was a Nicolas du Pré who had three children baptised between 1661 and 1664, but unfortunately the mother's name was not recorded, as so often happens.

The façade of this house has recently been stripped of its dismal stucco, revealing extremely pleasing honey-coloured granite. What is the dower wing, where the 1659 stone is located, could be the oldest part of the building; its main beam, on the ground floor, is forked where it enters the back wall, a rare but not unknown feature. There are various worked fragments of 17th-century date on the property. There must have been alterations in about 1830, to judge by the stairs and doors, though some of the latter are of earlier pattern. One granite fireplace has a shallow oven in the fireback.

An outbuilding, now demolished, in front of the house had six large animal bones placed at regular intervals parallel with the slope of the gable. It was a curious building, impossible to date, with an irregular façade and few windows. In Guernsey one has heard of witches' steps made of bone inside a chimney, and one can only conclude that these projections, for which no practical purpose can be imagined, were for the use of witches.

See Drawings 26, 53.

L'ARMISTICE
St. Aubin (B).

This is a three-storeyed house, which has many windows blocked in the back and the side walls. Looking at the façade, the part to the left is of later date than the main house. The window apertures are large throughout. The owner recalls that there used to be stairs similar to those at The Hollies (q.v.). None of the old internal décor has survived. On the gable stone is the date 1700 and the initials F K, though the first letter is not sure. This probably represents François Kastel, of the family of William Kastel who was associated, and indeed emigrated to France with, Jean Martel.

ASHLEY COURT
Rue des Chenolles (J). (P. Neel on Godfray.)

This fine house is chiefly known for the excellence of the cider which was made there over the years. The main apples used by the late Mr. Le Brun Le Cornu were La France, Gros Romeril and Vieilles Filles. It is a great pity that the once ubiquitous apple orchards have all but disappeared, and with them the old types of apple which they grew. La France was particularly good as a cooker as well as for cider.

There are two date stones, D A 1725, and 17 D A I A 41. In the past the property has been in the Nicolle family, and also that of P. Neel, Constable of St. John (1870–1909).

AUVERGNE
Augerez (P). (J. Laffoley on Godfray.)

A dated stone has now been seen with M L F 1696. This is likely to be Moyse Le Affolé or Laffoley, a name occurring in seigneurial court rolls in this neighbourhood. It has been suggested that the carved stone in the roadside wall is a chamfer stop, decorated with a building flying a pennant, similar to that at The Elms (My), but other interpretations are possible.

AVRANCHES MANOR
Carrefour Selous (L). (P. Marett on Godfray.)

Such very skilful restoration was done here by a previous owner that it may be well to record what was original and what is reproduction. Some corner bosses to architraves are original, that is to say 1820, and some have been copied. On the north the pediment, architraves and fanlight of the door are new, the actual door having been moved from the south porch. On the south the fanlight and door surround, the porch and its iron railings, are original, but the actual door is new. The cornice of the north part of the hall, created out of a multitude of small rooms, was copied from the south part which, with its pillars, is original. The present dining room was the kitchen, with a flagged floor, and its mahogany doors are original. So are the stairs, with their metal balusters, a type otherwise unknown in Jersey. The fireplaces are contemporary, that is early 19th century, but were imported from Ireland as no good examples survived in the house. The range of garages has been created out of farm buildings, with Ionic columns and facia boards copied from 19th-century shops in St. Helier.

Until recently a remarkable horse-powered threshing house survived in the grounds, being a small two-storey building designed to house a complex mechanism for threshing grain. The wooden parts of the machinery were severely infested with worm and the whole structure had deteriorated beyond repair, but as far as is known it was unique. Photographs and measurements taken before the demolition of this building indicate that sheaves were off-loaded from wagons into the building through the upper bay in the east end. They were then fed to a rotating drum housed in the flooring of the first floor. The drum delivered grain and straw into separate compartments on the ground floor. The grain was shovelled into sacks, raised by hoist to the first floor and carried out through a loading bay, across a plank bridge spanning a distance of only eight feet, into the farm granary. This granary was rat-proofed by a row of projecting stones built into the walls at high level. The straw was ejected through the lower eastern bay to vehicles waiting outside. Rotary movement was imparted to the threshing drum and to the hoist by cogs engaging a heavy

TENTATIVE RECONSTRUCTION OF
THRESHING HOUSE FORMERLY AT AVRANCHES MANOR
copied from drawings by R.L. Stevens.

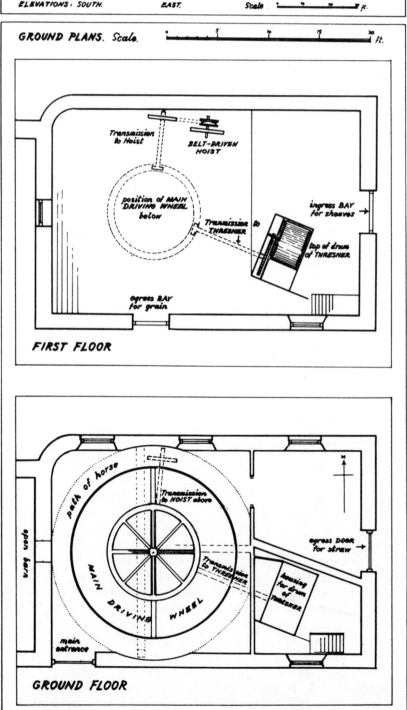

A. *egress bay for grain.*
B. *main entrance.*
C. *stables, with granary above.*
D. *plank bridge.*
E. *ingress bay for sheaves.*
F. *egress door for straw.*

ELEVATIONS: SOUTH.   EAST.

GROUND PLANS. *Scale.*

FIRST FLOOR

GROUND FLOOR

54

THE AVRANCHES THRESHING HOUSE

from photographs by R.L.Stevens.

First Floor, looking east.

55

Ground Floor, looking west.

iron wheel mounted horizontally beneath the ground floor ceiling on a stout timber pinion, from which projected a shaft, similar to those used in cider apple crushers. To this shaft a horse was harnessed, and as it plodded round its orbit the iron wheel drove the threshing drum and the hoist. The hoist consisted of three wooden discs, one mounted near the ground floor ceiling, the other two, belt-driven from the first, on the first floor. That at least is now we interpret the evidence before us of this remarkable piece of ingenuity. But we may be wrong. Other opinions are possible, and invited.

Over the door of a shed for farm implements is a board bearing the following Latin inscription:

> "Omnia quae, multo ante memor, provisa repones
> si te digna manet divini gloria ruris."

These are, in fact, lines 167–168 of Vergil's First Georgic. In the seven lines preceding he has listed the equipment a farmer needs for raising foodstuffs, including the plough and ploughshare, the lumbering wagon, threshing sledges, drags, heavy harrows, inexpensive wicker-work of various kinds, hurdles of arbutus and the winnowing fan. He rounds off the inventory with the above words which mean, in simple terms:

> "All these implements you will have remembered long ago and provided for,
> and you must keep them all at the ready, if the glory of the heavenly country-
> side is to wait on you in a worthwhile fashion."

No better text could have been chosen for a shed for farm equipment. The items differ a little from ours, but the principle is the same. You do not need all these things all the year round, but when they are required they must be there, and accessible. This a further indication (compare IAPDD at Les Pigneaux) that men who composed inscriptions in 19th-century Jersey were often classicists.

See Drawings 54, 55.

BAGATELLE
(S). (F. Godfray on Godfray.)

No trace of Bagatelle remains except the name of the district in which it stood. Nor, it seems, have we any pictorial record of it, nor even of its successor.

The matter is complicated by several changes of ownership over the years. Land in La Vallée Collet, on the fief of La Motte (St. Ouen à St. Sauveur), was sold by Louis Nathaniel Brohier to François Marett, and the latter seems to have built thereon a house which was bought in 1802 by Admiral Philippe d'Auvergne, Prince de Bouillon, through his attorney Thomas Le Breton. It was then described as "appellée le Belvédère et presentement la Bagatelle". It has been suggested that the name Bagatelle is derived from the surname Le Bacotel, but Stead is probably right in attribut- ing it to d'Auvergne's sense of humour. The house seems to have had a third name, Montchoix, for in 1818 Brohier was still trying to get François Marett, heir and nephew of the François above, to pay his account for "superintending the workmen at Montchoix or Bagatelle". When d'Auvergne died in 1816 he was deeply in debt and Thomas Le Breton, by then Lieutenant Bailiff, took the house over for about £2,250, and he died there. In 1809 Stead had given a glowing and eulogistic account of it in the book which he dedicated to d'Auvergne, and in 1847 Durell described it as a "superb mansion". In 1849 its owner on Godfray's map was François Godfray (1807–1868) who had bought it from Thomas Le Breton junior (1791–1857). The site was eventually occupied by the Palace Hotel.

Vandalism, it appears, is no new phenomenon. The Prince had tried opening the grounds of Bagatelle to the public, but, after a short while was forced to discontinue this.

See *A Picture of Jersey*, J. Stead, p. 142.
   The Tragedy of Philippe d'Auvergne, G. R. Balleine, pp. 103, 131.
   B.S.J. 1906, pp. 33, 56, 58; 1914, p. 425.

a. La Haule Manor (B)

b. Melbourne House (J)

a. Les Ruettes (J)

b. Le Douet Fleury (Mt)

BANDINEL
La Chasse ès Demoiselles (Mt).

Recent alterations have uncovered a bénitier, the first to be found for many years, and the first ever in this parish. It is also clear now that there was a stone tourelle, though both the steps and the enclosing tower have disappeared, and the only remaining evidence is the twin stone doorways leading to the becrooms, as at La Tourelle (Mt) and Le Nord (J). A deep recess in the east wall of the main bedroom may have been a powder closet, a few of which have been found.

Doors in two sections, as found here, are not unknown, but these examples are heavy in construction, like the panelling in the eastern ground floor room. This is a far later copy of the Georgian style, found frequently in Jersey, but the reproduction lacks the light touch of the original.

See B.S.J. 1974, p. 289.
Drawing 5.

BEAUVOIR
Les Varines (S). (Capt. Davis on Godfray.)

This is now a luxurious house by any standards, yet when it was built, between 1834-40, it was not apparently considered so. In 1843 Captain Davis, a retired army officer with ten children, bought it and there he and his family lived for nearly thirty years. According to the census of 1851, he had seven employees and a governess. Two of his sons (Nos. 27 and 149 in the College Register) went to Victoria College. The governess made a sketch of the house which is still in the hands of Captain Davis's descendants, showing that it has changed very little.

The land on which it stands was bought in 1834 by Pierre Jean Simon, and by 1840 it was already called Beauvoir. The Davis family sold it to Mr. Deslandes in 1871, and in recent years it has changed hands many times. There are splendid trees in the front garden, notably a turkey oak, very probably contemporary with the house.

BEECH FARM
Rue ès Viberts (P). (J. Vibert on Godfray.)

A marriage stone with P V B △△ I A T 1746 represents Philippe Vibert (1718-1784) and Jeanne Arthur (1719-1788). Over the back door is a stone with 1831 in decorative script, and this probably gives the date when, as so often, the house was enlarged by the addition of rooms to the north. The west gable, on the roadside, has an early chamfered window with a nine-pane fixed sash, and it was probably moved there as being old-fashioned at the time of the 1831 alterations. The four stone fireplaces may not have been meant to have the granite exposed, as they are quite undecorated and have wooden lintels; they could well be contemporary with the 1746 stone.

BEECHFIELD
Mont au Prêtre (T). (J. Emily on Godfray).

If you approach from the east and forget that you are near the main Trinity road, there is an aura of romance about the deserted farmyard with its initialled stones, which have yielded up their secrets and so come to life. One defies explanation. It is used as a door jamb in a small building, perhaps a cendrier, and has been broken on the left where the first two figures of the date would have been. On the right are the figures 36 or perhaps 56, beside a circle containing a raised design shaped like some sort of bat, with four round objects upon it. No arms of any family can be found at all like it.

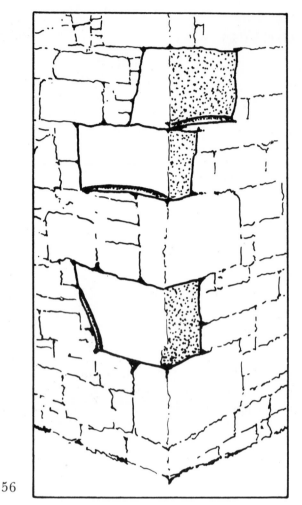

56

three voussoirs of a round arch, incorporated in a later building, at Beechfield, (T).

It is now clear that this was the home of a branch of the Le Breton family from at least 1640 and possibly earlier. The domestic part of the buildings, later demoted into stables, has retained some 17th-century features on the north, but shows three storeys, which is most rare; it can only be explained by the slope of the ground which would have given two levels on the south, now obscured by pig sties. Various chamfered stones, an accolade lintel as a doorstep and fragments suggesting a round arch all speak of the 17th century at least.

There are two stones carved with a shield containing T L B, one dated 1669, the other 1673, clearly the Thomas Le Breton who married in 1678; he later put up an undated lintel with T L B and S P D for himself and his wife Sarah Poingdestre. A delightful lintel, also undated, bears the legend S D G P L B T L B M L B S L B E L B E L B, for Sara de Gruchy (m. 1640), her husband Pierre Le Breton and their children Thomas, Marie, Sara, Elizabeth, and Esther. No other stone like this has been seen, nor any on which the wife's initials precede those of her husband.

We then span the years to a stone inscribed J E M L ♡♡ M M T G 1836. This represents Jean Emily and Marguerite Mattingley, he being a nephew of the last Le Breton owner, Daniel, who died in 1816; their first child Jean was born in 1817. Some years before altering the farm buildings they built themselves the impressive main house to the east, the present Beechfield, with a drive to the west. On the plastered

57

the stone of Sara Le Breton, née de Gruchy, m. 1640, and her five children, at Beechfield, (T).

façade is their stone with J E M L M M T G 1832. The walls are granite under the stucco, as can be seen on the basement on the north.

The front door is approached up a flight of steps and has an imposing pillared porch. Like the Nicolles who built the Museum in Pier Road, Jean Emily made slender brick chimneys instead of the substantial granite stacks to which we are accustomed. He must have been engaged in some profitable business to build himself such a superior house on the farm he had inherited through his mother, Sara Le Breton. The staircase in the house is particularly elegant.

See *Extente* 1668, pp. 21, 69, 71, 72.   *Extente* 1749, p. 54.
    B.S.J. 1906, p. 34.   Drawings 26, 47, 56, 57.

BEECHLEIGH
Les Grupieaux (P). (E. Vibert on Godfray.)

The couple on a date stone with 17 N L B I D C 31 have not been identified, but there is reason to think that the first may be a Le Brun. The initials E L B appear roughly incised on a corner stone, and D L C beside a window.

Here the roof seems to have been raised three times, perhaps at approximately 1650, 1750 and 1850. This can be clearly be seen in the attic, where the early chimney with its thatching stones is evident. The dormers, with barge boards, are a much later addition.

A dado rail up the stairs and in one first-floor room suggest that there may have been 18th-century panelling, but the stairs are later, with the typically local ivory inset in the centre of the newel, stick balusters, mahogany rail and decorated sides to the risers.

BEL AIR
Mont des Vaux (B). (J. Lesbirel on Godfray.)

The exterior does not suggest age, but within, a typical 17th-century house can be discerned. In a bank, pottery, flints and a cannon ball were found.

BELLE VUE
Mont au Roux (B). (Viscount Le Couteur on Godfray.)

This is a most unusual example of additions being made on the front instead of the back, which was customary, and as a result the small 17th-century ground floor rooms are hidden behind the newer structure, which has a third storey as well and a wing to the south.

The first alteration may have been made by Pierre Le Vesconte before 1773, when he sold the house to Philippe Dumaresq (1751-1822), founder of *La Gazette* newspaper. The main staircase, of two flights, must have been inserted then; they are of the style so often found in Jersey in the mid-18th century. One bedroom is completely panelled in the style of that period, and the library on the ground floor was similarly panelled until recently.

In about 1793 John (later General) Le Couteur bought the house from his father-in-law, Jean Dumaresq, who had bought it from his brother Philippe the journalist in 1792. On his retirement in 1816 Le Couteur went to live there, adding the kitchen, and probably the elegant curving staircase from ground to first floor, as well as a cast-iron verandah which at that time would have been most fashionable and advanced for Jersey. The alterations followed a period when the house was leased to tenants, and was used as a barracks in 1799-1800 for the Russian troops then stationed in the Island. This is one of many local houses where the drawing room was on the first floor, and in this case the small room adjacent, known as the boudoir, was the personal sitting room of General Le Couteur's wife, Marie Dumaresq, during her widowhood, when she lived with her son and daughter-in-law.

The earliest ownership of the property traced is that of Jacques Valpy dit Janvrin, whose grandson sold it to Thomas Le Vesconte and Sara Esnouf in 1734; in 1762 they sold it to Philippe Le Vesconte. It passed by sale to Philippe Le Sueur in 1774, but was regained by Le Vesconte by retrait lignager. It remained in the hands of General Le Couteur's descendants until recent years. His son John (later Sir John) (1794-1875) was appointed Vicomte de Jersey in 1842, hence Godfray's entry of "Viscount Le Couteur".

BELLOZANNE ABBEY
Mont à l'Abbé (H). (J. de Gruchy on Godfray.)

This is a misnomer, as there never was such an abbey in Jersey. The name comes from the Fieu de Bellozanne on which the house is situated; this in turn took its name from its parent abbey in the Pays de Bray, north-east of Rouen, a 12th-century foundation. This local fief was granted in 1197 by John, not then King, to the Abbot of Bellozanne. It consisted of 20 librates of land, and remained under the same patronage until the confiscation of the Alien Priories in 1415, when it escheated to the Crown, in whose hands it has since remained.

There are no guiding dates carved on this delightful sheltered house apart from one of 1858 on the garage; but the round arch to the front door is an early example, perhaps as early as 1500. All windows in the façade have been enlarged, and the roof probably raised, but floor and ceiling levels seem to have been retained, and the ceiling beams are good. There is thought to be a niche, now covered over, in one bedroom, and it would be interesting to have it opened up, as it could well be an otherwise unrecorded bénitier.

Panelling at the east end of the east ground floor room is a nice example of mid-18th-century style, though the actual fireplace surround has been altered. The staircase suggests a considerable alteration around 1750; it is an interesting pattern with thin wavy balusters, seen only in a few examples. It seems likely that it replaced a stone staircase which would have been approached through the straight lintel opening opposite the front door. The granite chimneys, one cylindrical and one square, are unexpected, probably the whim of a past owner. There is some good furniture of the 1870 style in the house, and a number of grandfather clocks; among the local names on the clocks may be noted Collinette, Francis Le Feuvre of St. Aubin, and Le Grand of St. Aubin; the Le Grand clock has a large enamel face with floral designs and the name is somewhat obscured.

See Drawing 45.
Plate XIX b.

BEL RESPIRO
Mont au Prêtre (H). (P. Perchard on Godfray.)

A stone fireplace has been found here, and it seems likely that it is contemporary with the front door lintel, which reads 18 P B N ♡ ♡ M H Q 11. It is possible that only the corbels, which are carved and dressed, were intended to be exposed. The lintel is of wood, and near ground level on the left is a recess measuring 19in. by 24in. and only 10in. deep, and it is hard to guess what its purpose was.

BELVOIR
Mont Millais (H).

Standing as it did at the foot of Mont Millais, this house was quite a landmark, with a mountain ash tree flowering in front of the verandah, and jaunty little attic windows in the gables shaped to follow the lines of the roof. It has now been demolished. By a fortunate chance, descendants of the first owner contacted La Société Jersiaise and we have been able to learn more about it.

It was built by David Verner (1780-1826), who settled in Jersey for the sake of his health in about 1820, living for a time at The Cedars (q.v.) and building Belvoir in 1824-1825. Here he lived with his wife Anna née Cole and their ten children, one of whom at least, Frederick Thomas David, was born at Belvoir, in 1825. The property changed hands, and in about 1910 it came into the Germain family. The cement rendering was added between 1880 and 1890, the date being scratched on the stucco.

It is sad that when recently enquiries were received about two old Jersey houses, with requests to identify them, and they turned out to be Belvoir and The Cedars, the reply had to be that both had just been demolished.

See Plate XIX c.

BERRY HOUSE
Val Plaisant (H).

Demolished in 1975, this house took its name from the fact that Charles Ferdinand, Duc de Berry, nephew of Louis XVIII, stayed there from January to April 1814. It must at that time have been quite a new house. The simple frontage, with a Venetian window, led one to expect rather better interior décor than was the case.

Later in the century the house was used as a school by the de la Salle Brothers, being named St. Aloysius' College and continuing its educational functions for many years.

See Plees, pp. 181, 346.

LE BLANC MOULIN
Or Moulin Blanc. Queen's Valley (G).

This farmhouse, its whitened walls and ancillary buildings standing out in contrast to the verdure of Queen's Valley, makes one of the most attractive sights in Jersey. A pair of mills, side by side, once handled grain and malt on this site, and their documented history goes back no less than 750 years. In 1976 a proposal was made to flood the valley, inundating this ancient site among others, and was vigorously opposed by all conservationists and lovers of our countryside. "Save Queen's Valley" stickers were seen on many windscreens. In an enlightened community it should never be necessary to destroy a heritage in order to deal with a temporary shortage of water. There are other methods. Before this book is published, we hope that they will be examined and adopted, and that we as a generation will have the happiness of handing on to posterity a beautiful valley and the old white mill which nestles in it so picturesquely.

In the early middle ages the valley was called Ruaval or Ruequal, and here the King owned two water mills, one near the source of the stream, now called le Moulin de Haut, and the second (which was in fact two mills), now called le Moulin Blanc. Downstream was a third mill, le Moulin de Bas, and a seigneurial mill of the Fieu ès Malets or La Malletière (Les Prés). The revenues of the third mill were granted in 1180 by William the Conqueror to the Abbesse de Caen.

The King's two (actually three) mills upstream are mentioned in writing in 1234 and 1329 as "the water mills of Ruaval". A report of 1328–1331 records that they had just been repaired and that their names then were "the Fauvel mill" and "the middle mill". In the 1331 Extente they are called "the mill of Ruequal" and "le Molyn Maeyn". This word maeyn, also spelt main, means middle. It seems clear that at that time le Moulin de Haut was or had been milled by a Fauvel, and that our Blanc Moulin was regarded as the middle milling station.

The 1528 Extente put us more closely in the picture. By that time the whitewash brush had been called into play and our mill is called "the mylle blanke and the molen Bray". The entry shows that alongside the white mill was a second mill for crushing barley to make beer, the word bray or brée meaning brewer's grains or malt. In the margin the writer of the Extente added the note "the mylne mayne" and crossed it out, which probably means no more than that the name "middle mill" was obsolete, and the names "white mill" and "malt mill" had taken its place.

We next find our mill in 1559, when a new mill-pond for "le Blanc Moulin ès Vaux Mallet" is mentioned. The 1607 Extente confirms, in the entry "the Mault Mill under neath the Brew house and the Whit Mill beneath the said Mault Mill", that on our site there was a malt mill and brewery, and immediately below it downstream the White Mill. In 1668 "le Blanc Moulin" was let for 52 écus per annum, less 12 écus for repairs, a net revenue of 40 écus to the King. In 1749 it was "The Mill (called le Blanc Moulin)". In 1849 Godfray calls it le Moulin de la Reine or Blanc Moulin. It has also been named le Moulin du Roi.

This is the story of Le Blanc Moulin. It is of venerable age and antecendents. As Sir Walter Ralegh wrote of Mont Orgueil Castle in 1600, "it were pitty to cast it down".

See Plate, Colour 4a.

LE BOCAGE
Mont au Roux (B). (J. Le Couteur on Godfray.)

Like Belle Vue (q.v.) this property was purchased by General Le Couteur in 1793 from his father-in-law, Jean Dumaresq. He in turn had purchased the whole from his brother Philippe the previous year, Philippe having brought Le Bocage from Elie Le Bas and Elizabeth Alexandre his wife in 1787. This all refers to the old cottage behind the present Le Bocage, which has a lintel with HLR ♡ ELB 1751 for Helier (or Elie) Le Rossignol and Elizabeth Le Bas, married at St. Ouen in 1745. There is a simple granite fireplace in the east bedroom, without a lintel, this having been replaced by a depressed brick arch. On the ground floor is another fireplace with chamfers and this, appearing to be earlier than 1751, supports the possibility that the north wall of the house is earlier. There are in it several blocked apertures, and one embrasure set at an unusual angle, perhaps in an effort to catch the rays of the setting sun, and a curve in the wall which could be the vestigial remains of a tourelle. The ground floor room is cobbled with perfectly matched sea pebbles, which are rarely found within living rooms. A photograph shows that the roof was still thatched in about 1860.

The newer house in front, when it, too, was thatched, was a perfect example of the "cottage orné". It was built by John (later Sir John) Le Couteur when he married Harriet Janvrin in 1818, and their children were born there. In his diaries he mentions that the builder, Dart, "contracted to build a new cottage for us at 3/3 per perch for stone masonry and 2/6 for 9″ brickwork . . . the house ran up quickly". The imported iron verandah survives. The present slate roof rises higher than the original thatch, doubtless improving the bedrooms but rather altering the intended roofline. Internally it has not been greatly altered, and it is gratifying to feel that a house designed over 150 years ago can be so readily adapted to modern living.

See *Victorian Voices*, J. Stevens, p. 64.

BON AIR

Now called Le Jardin de Remon, Carrefour Selous (L). (P. Gallichan on Godfray.)

The small cottage, on the bend of the road north of the cross roads and in front of Bon Air, has been demolished. It had a stone P G L C C R M 1788, representing Philippe Gallichan (b. 1743), son of Philippe and Madeleine Baudet, and his wife Catherine Remon. It was a simple single-storey building with its chimney placed centrally, and had a bake-oven made of bricks which looked rather modern.

The house behind has a stone over what were the stables with a lintel showing P G C M B D 1756, for Philippe Gallichan and Madeleine Baudet, and another stone has the same initials with the date 1746. This stone, it will be seen, represents the parents of the owners of the front house. The third generation, Philippe Gallichan (b. 1772) and Marie Rondel (m. about 1800), put up their stone P G L C M R D 1810 on the converted house behind. The appearance of this house suggests a re-facing with ashlar blocks, presumably in 1810, and in this it is similar to La Vallette (J), where such work was done 14 years earlier. The stairs and some doors, and a very small sash window on the landing, are of a pattern earlier than 1810, and presumably were not altered at the time of the re-facing. Some protruding pieces of stone in the older house suggest that there may have been a tourelle at some period, and the outline on the Richmond map of 1795 supports this possibility.

BOULIVOT DE BAS

Rue de Boulivot (G). (E. Nicolle on Godfray.)

Over the front door is a stone with 18 ENC 03, and on a shed one with 18 ENC MLB 11. One may interpret this to mean that a Nicolle owner, who was unmarried in 1803 but married by 1811, omitted to add his wife's initials to his earlier stone.

There is a granite fireplace, recently uncovered, in the east ground floor room, with slight decoration on the corbels and a wooden lintel. This has been carefully restored in recent years.

BRAMPTON FARM
Ville au Neveu (O). (P. Le Rossignol on Godfray.)

The house now called Brampton Farm at Ville au Neveu was the home of a branch of the Le Rossignol family from about 1530 when Pierre fs. Guillaume was already established there, and his descendants appear to have remained there until the time of Pierre Philippe (1845-1916) whose son, Peter, emigrated to Canada. Proof of their ownership lies in a most interesting stone with A R L 1733 M G L, for Augustin Le Rossignol (1672-1739) and Marguerite Guillet his wife (1704-1757). The unusual aspect is that at the right-hand end there is a complex monogram which must represent P L R for their son Pierre, the eldest of their six children. Augustin was the son of Augustin (1625-1703) and Catherine Prouings, he being the great grandson of the Pierre of 1530. Marguerite Guillet was the eldest daughter of the Reverend Jean François Guillet, Rector of St. Ouen (1664-1699); coming from Dauphiné he was "naturalisé Jersiais" in 1684. No other stone has been found with initials arranged quite like this. It will be noticed that the couple put up their stone when they had already been married for 30 years, and that Augustin, older than his wife, had but six years to live.

The architect Philip Le Rossignol (1809-1892) was a great-great-grandson of the couple on the stone.

The farm has a good bakehouse and bread oven, and on the wash-house there is a date of 1827.

See Historical Notes on the Le Rossignol family.
B.S.J. 1916, p. 91.
Drawing No. 28.

BRAS DE FER
Rue de la Hauteur (T). (Jurat P. Le Maistre on Godfray.)

This house was completely changed in size and character at an unknown date, perhaps as early as 1780, being given an impressive classical style south front in plaster, rather reminiscent of La Houge Boëte (q.v.). The north side shows exposed granite. The wing at right-angles has been too much altered to hazard a date. In recent alterations some dated window lintels have been brought from elsewhere and inserted. The situation is favoured, and the garden sheltered and luxuriant.

BROADFIELDS
Rue des Chenolles (L). (E. Gibaut on Godfray.)

The middle of the three houses here is now seen to be typical of the date shown in incised letters, 17 I L G R L C 44, for Jean Langlois and Rachel Le Cras, their initials appearing again two years later on a slightly concave stone in the garden wall between this house and its 17th-century neighbour.

Inside there are fielded panel doors, both the two- and the five-panelled varieties, a nicely moulded fireplace surround in one of the bedrooms and a typical mid-18th-century staircase. It is interesting to find these elements in a country area as early as 1744.

BROAD STREET
St. Helier. No. 13. (Now Hambros [Jersey] Ltd.)

The marriage stone preserved in the restored façade reads P M L M C 1762, for Pierre Mallet (1734-1807) and his first wife Marie Chepmell (m. 1758, d. 1763). This is the "chefve maison" inherited by their second son Thomas in 1807. Marie Chepmell had been previously married to a

Thomas Snow (d. 1754), probably a relative of the William Snow who owned a house two doors away in 1782. The banking house which acquired and renovated this property have done so with discrimination, and one could wish that all recent developments in our town had been so carefully effected.

BROAD STREET
St. Helier. No. 31. (Now National and Grindleys Bank.)

Within the building there is a door lintel with a shield carved upon it bearing the initials F D P L, with P G below, flanked by the date 1673. So far all efforts to identify the couple recorded have failed, but the placing of the stone is interesting. If it is still in its original position, it shows the frontage of the house it served, and that in 1673 it had a front garden bordering on the road.

It is almost certainly the earliest surviving date on a domestic building within our fast-changing town.

BROOK FARM
Mont Nicolle (B). (E. Pipon on Godfray.)

A marriage stone which had long been sought has now been found here. It reads H M R A V N 1764, for Henry Marett and Anne Villeneuve. The H M R letters are ligatured and the N is reversed. Their son Jacques (b. 1773) sold the property to his cousin Edouard Pipon in 1800.

The percage of St. Peter passed beside the land of this Henry Marett (d. 1743), and his name appears in contracts of 1704–1708 concerning the placing of boundary stones to mark the limits of the "percage et terres vacantes" then purchased.

BROOKHALL
Rue de Crossbow (T). (P. Gruchy on Godfray.)

Beside a large "maison de Terreneuve" is this small house, its predecessor no doubt, in pleasing coloured granite. It has granite chimneys, the Guernsey pattern of fenestration, and chamfered surrounds to the main door. One small window on the north has surrounds of Caen sandstone, which is most unexpected. There are indications that there may have been a straight exterior stone staircase. The house would seem to be late 17th century in date.

BROOKVALE
Rue du Pont (J). (A. Esnouf on Godfray.)

A carved window lintel here has clearly been removed from some earlier building, and is of interesting and unusual design. The property has been altered at various stages. By the time of the Richmond map of 1795 it already had buildings enclosing a courtyard on three sides. The pointed gables facing west are in no way local in design, but are none the worse for this.

LA BRUYÈRE FARM
Carrefour Selous (L). (E. Le Gros on Godfray.)

From a distance this appears to be no more than a small grey house with stucco and uneven fenestration, but it has features of much interest. It contains a tourelle, the steps of which have been boarded over, and its presence is disclosed by the curve of the roof as seen from the north, similar to that at le Marais or Meadow Court (My). There are two carved gable stones, that on the east having incised lines similar to a Jersey flag, and that on the west having apparently P B I 1605. No identification of these initials has yet been possible as the last letter is uncertain, and could be D, for Badier, or N, for Benest.

LES BURINS
St. Aubin (B).

It has been suggested that the date of this house is 1740, and this is quite feasible. To the south there is a long narrow building, believed to have been a sail loft. It is said that a private slipway ran down to the beach.

The house has been altered at various times. Its simple stairs and most of the doors appear to be original. Many ceiling beams are curved, and those in the attic bedrooms are merely tree trunks cut in half. It is impossible to explain the relation of the stairs to a room on the left of the hall, and to a window across which they cut.

CAMBRAI
Rue de Cambrai (T). (C. Blampied on Godfray.)

This neat little house does not at first suggest great age, but it has in fact a simple tourelle within a square tower, approached by a round arch with hollow chamfer and acorn stops. Under the modern porch on the west section, perhaps a dower wing, is a lintel, roughly chamfered, with a cross carved in the apex of the accolade; the stone is 56in. long and 18in. deep. The house has three chimneys, the centre one having been rebuilt in brick at some period, but retaining its thatch stones. As a central chimney indicates a stone wall to support it, this must have been in origin a more important house than its size suggests.

LA CARREFOUR
Rue Mahier (My). (J. Sauvage on Godfray.)

This is a standard 18th-century house, now much renovated. There are two marriage stones, reading R D G 1723 I A T, and I D G M S V 1820 (Syvret).

LE CARREFOUR
Rue de Brabant (T). (J. Le Boutillier on Godfray.)

Over the front door is a stone I L B T L E D C C 1814, for Le Boutillier; on a shed at the back is another for Messervy, reading A M S V 1897 E P M S V (father and son): and on a doorstep 1819 in fine script. The Messervy inscription has a wide heavy lettering.

An interest here is the fact that this house, Le Carrefour, is on a cross-roads, the next holding being called La Croix. This would substantiate the view that the name Croix did mean the site of a cross, not just a cross-road.

CARREFOUR JENKINS
(L). (C. Jeune on Godfray.)

There are, or were, two little cottages at the cross-roads, and to the casual glance they did not appear exceptional. On investigation, however, the front cottage was found to have a well within its walls; this was approached from the outside, on the north-east corner, and caused a semi-circular bulge in that corner of the living room. The well was said to be very deep, and of excellent quality, and was the sole source of water for both houses.

The back cottage had a typical granite gable stone, inside, in its south-west corner, carved with the date 1664 and the initials W G Q. There was a William Jenkins in the parish in the 17th century; his son William was baptised in 1663, and no other name in the parish register fits the initials and date. The name Jenkins was often written Genkins, and one readily imagine the difficulty of the stonemason confronted with this foreign name and pronounciating its Genniquin. The stone has been incorporated into the garden wall of the new house on the site of the old cottage.

CASTLE STREET
St. Helier

This fine town house was illustrated by E. T. Nicolle in his *The Town of St. Helier,* p. 81, before it had a third storey of full height added. It was then called Elizabeth House, and there were railings in front and a lamp on a bracket over the entrance.

There is a good mahogany staircase, rising to two flights to serve bedrooms and what were mere attics above. In the newel post is a large pottery medallion of Britannia with the date (no longer very clear) 1797; this is a copy of what was known as a Cartwheel twopence, and it seems likely to be the date when the house was built. There is a dining room on the first floor with a built-in sideboard, similar to one at La Haule Manor (1796); it is set in a concave recess. Some of the doors are mahogany; others have been damaged and painted over. One bedroom has a built-in mahogany wardrobe, and it is said that there were others in various rooms. Some of the fireplaces are contemporary.

This was a house belonging to the Néels, a ship-building family, hence the luxury of mahogany. Much of the timber of its construction is reputed to have been shaped for ship-building. What is more likely is that it was fashioned in the shipyard of the owner.

See Drawing 34.
Plate XX a.

LA CÂTEL FARM
Rue du Câtel (T). (T. de Gruchy on Godfray.)

On the east gable is a stone dated 1701. Over the front door is a stone with 18 P C B J B L 83, for Cabot and Billot, so the gable stone is evidence of a far older structure. In a curve of a roadside wall is a vingtaine boundary stone limiting the vingtaines of Rozel (east) and Rondin (west).

LA CAUMINE À MARY BEST
In St. Ouen's Bay

This cottage stands on the foreshore of St. Ouen's Bay, a little south of High Tower and La Louzière. It is sturdily built in granite, the walls rising to form a stone-vaulted roof with a steep gable pitch. It was in origin a powder magazine attached to the redoubt or battery shown there in 1795, which in a map of 1817 is called Middle Battery.

Its isolated position has made it an important landmark for mariners in the past, and it was whitewashed for that purpose, hence the alternative name of White Cottage.

Marie Ann Best, "fille Adam, Anglois, et Marguérite Carrel", was born in 1790. Tradition says that Adam was an English soldier. Mary must have lived in this cottage at one time, but we do not know when or why.

See Plate, Colour 4b.

THE CEDARS
Green Street, St. Helier, previously called La Maison du Mont.

This house fell to the demolition gangs when the Fort Regent tunnel was made. It was probably built around 1750, having typical stairs and panelling of that period and, on the north, early sash windows, which had survived in unimportant positions while the main rooms were given something more up-to-date.

The property had belonged to the Tapins, Maretts and Mallets. The Tapins were a French refugee family, Daniel Tapin marrying Marie Seale. Their son, Pierre Daniel, became Rector of St. Helier and died unmarried, his property passing to his nephew, Philippe Marett. At some period the house passed to the Mallets, who certainly owned it in the early 19th century. It is known that in 1769 Pierre Mallet bought a house "à présent en masures" (in ruins), and the description of it makes it more than likely that he bought the site and ruins of the Marett house, and rebuilt the house we remember. The whole character of the interior woodwork is consistent with such a date, fashions in Jersey being slow to change. The initials of Pierre Mallet's parents appear in Broad Street, above Hambro's Bank (q.v.).

mid-18th. century panelling at The Cedars.

58

See   B.S.J. 1969, p. 63.
      Drawings 39, 44, 58.
      Belvoir (H).

LA CHAIRE
Rozel (Mt). (Mrs. Fothergill on Godfray.)

This property is included in this collection for botanical rather than for architectural reasons.

A note on the Curtis family, associated with the property, may be helpful, as there is some confusion about names. The *Botanical Magazine,* now called *Curtis' Botanical Magazine,* was founded by William Curtis (1746-1799). J. Curtis, who was no relation, was a contributing artist. Samuel Curtis (1799-1860) was first cousin of William, whose daughter he married and it was he who, with his own widowed daughter Mrs. Fothergill, lived at La Chaire. The famous white and pink Magnolia Campbellii cannot have been planted by Curtis, as this species was not introduced into Britain until 1868, though his daughter may have secured a specimen.

The late Mr. A. V. Nicolle, who lived there for some time, left notes on the garden which are most instructive. He tells us that the name La Chaire, meaning a pulpit, referred to a large rock which overhung the hillside and was demolished during the Napoleonic wars so that a battery of 24-pounders could be mounted to command Rozel Bay. Curtis realised that the conglomerate rock would be more readily pierced by tree roots than the denser granite, and in 1840 he chose the site for his home and garden, a favoured and sheltered south-facing situation. He planted sheltering hedges of ilex to east and west, and then built a modest house in 1841, coming to live permanently in Jersey in 1847, and being later joined by his widowed daughter, whose husband Samuel Fothergill had been another famous botanist. He and his daughter are both buried at St. Martin's.

Severe frosts in 1895 destroyed much of his work, and soon afterwards the property was bought by a Mr. Fletcher, who planned the gardens on a more elaborate scale, and built the present house, organising a complex system of irrigation of rain water to all parts of the garden. The Davidia involucrata or Handkerchief Tree, introduced into Britain in 1902, was probably planted by him. In 1932 the property was bought by Mr. Nicolle, whose wife was also a keen gardener, so for over a century this garden was tended with care and expertise.

CHAMBARD
Jambard Lane, Pontac (C). (J. Le Neveu on Godfray.)

Over the front door is 17 D V M ◇ R A M 54 in raised letters, the heart also being in relief. This represents Daniel Venement who married Rachel Amy in 1752. The two main rooms have granite fireplaces, one with two niches, and a recess for fuel storage.

The property must have passed by marriage to the Gaudins, as over the door of a side building is 18 D G D ♡♡ M V M 10. This stands for David Gaudin of St. Martin and Marie Venement, parents of Daniel Gaudin, Constable of St. Clement 1839–1842. Three members of the Le Neveu family were subsequently Constables of the parish; hence the ownership shown on Godfray.

See B.S.J. 1906, p. 18.

CHAMP COLLIN
Near La Hougue Bie (S). (P. Poingdestre on Godfray.)

It is recorded that this house was still thatched in 1911, and that it used to be called La Picoterie. We may however be considering two houses, as the Richmond map confirms the impression of the present owner that an older house stood in the north-east corner of the field to the north.

Over the front door is a stone with 18 P P D ♡♡ I L S 15, repeated over the stable door with one heart only and dated 1806, for Philippe Poingdestre and Isobel Le Sueur. Over the window on the north of an outhouse, to the north of the house, is another stone with 16 T M R S A B 83, all letters being ligatured, and this must surely be for Timothée Mourant, who married Susan Aubin in 1681 and died in 1720. At the time of his death he was described as "Timothée Mourant du Champ Colin". It will be seen, however, from the drawing, that the initials incised do not exactly fit this name.

See Drawing 26.

LES CHAMPS CLAIRS
Rue des Haies (T). (C. Gruchy on Godfray.)

There is a profusion of initialled stones here, all proof of the very long Gruchy tenure of the property; this goes back at least seven generations, and possibly back to the 15th century, if the family re-used the same site to build upon.

In 1774 François Gruchy and Elizabeth Le Bas put up their marriage stone, and again in 1776. In 1814 their son, also Charles, who married Marie Larbalestier in 1810, put up his marriage stone, and again in 1826. In 1817 Charles put his initials, without those of wife, on a gatepost at the end of the long and handsome drive approaching from the south. No south approach existed at the time of the Richmond map, 1795. On the plastered frontage of the house the date 1846 appears, representing no doubt the Charles who was Constable 1864–1868 and Jurat from 1868 until his death in 1900.

This house has departed from the more normal central front door, and has its entrance and fine porch at the left-hand side, as at the Museum.

LES CHARRIÈRES

Bonne Nuit (J). (J. Simon on Godfray.)

There are no date stones to guide one here, but three windows have chamfered accolade lintels, of a style certainly no later than 1650. The wing facing west appears to be about a century later, and contains a very simple granite fireplace, and nice early sash windows with small square panes. There are two somewhat rough outside staircases, and one door has a stone drop-type hinge. The outline shown on Richmond suggests that in 1795 there may have been a tourelle staircase to the main house.

See Drawing 59.

LES CHARRIÈRES

Near Carrefour à Cendre (P). (T. Renouf on Godfray.)

There are two most interesting initialled stones here. One has IHL FLB 1623. No definite identification has been found, but the first letter may be mistaken, as the stone has been uncovered from a layer of plaster. If it is a T, it could stand for Timothy Huelin, whose name appears in the register as father of children born between 1627 and 1633. Another entry seems even more probable: a Nicolas Huelin married a Félice (surname unfortunately not given) who died in 1647.

The second stone also presents problems. It shows IHL CLF IVB 1728. There can be little doubt that the first two sets of letters are the initials of Jean Huelin (b. 1700) who married

59

the granite eye of a pin-and-eye gate-hinge at Les Charrières, (J).

Catherine Le Feuvre in or before 1728, when their first child was born. The I V B could well stand for Jean Vibert, who stood as godfather to their last child and only surviving son, Jean, born in 1731. Godparents were extremely important in the days of early mortality of so many young women, and Jean Vibert may have been a relative or a close friend.

LES CHARRIÈRES DU COIN

(O). (P. Le Feuvre on Godfray.)

Originally coming from Le Moulin de la Mare, the family of Le Feuvre owned this property for almost three centuries, and since 1680 at least, when Pierre Le Feuvre lived there, the first of seven Pierres in direct succession. Their land included some mielles at St. Ouen situated "à l'est de la Grosse Tour", that is to say Kempt Tower. The last Le Feuvre in the direct line, Edouard fs. Edouard fs. Pierre, is said to have absconded to British Columbia for 42 years. It was his daughter who sold the property. The legendary jump of Philippe de Carteret and his horse took place near here, some time between 1461–1468.

LA CHASSE
Rue de l'Etocquet (J). (P. Le Boutillier on Godfray.)

As this façade is cement rendered one cannot see any markings on the stonework, but the unevenness of the fenestration, the almost universal chamfering to the windows, and one decorated lintel, all suggest a 17th-century date. The main entrance door appears to be of later date, perhaps replacing a round arch. This would explain the spacing of the first floor windows, which is such as often accompanies a round arch.

The courtyard is entered through a large, fairly late, round arch. An outhouse contains, on the first floor, a very small fireplace with a mitred lintel, in a room accessible only by an outside flight of steps at the gable end. If this was a dower flat, the access seems a little hard on Grannie.

LA CHASSE
Near the Church (P). (E. Balleine on Godfray.)

This house is probably far older than it appears. There is a date of 1832 on the back façade, perhaps the date of alterations and the addition of a second storey to the north rooms. This is borne out by a water colour painting in the possession of the owner which shows the house thatched and the back rooms only one storey high. The stable is dated 1825. A stone over the stable door, dated 1718, has a string of initials which appear to be E D V M L F L V, but they are very rough and might be read differently. In the avenue is a stone with an incised cross which was found in the meadow; it was clearly in the church at some period, being similar to stones noted at various parish churches.

The ancestor of the present owner was Elie Balleine who, with his wife Marie Falle (b. 1650; m. 1675), bought the property from Sara Balleine in 1681, she being tenant après décret of a Philippe de Carteret. A silver chalice in the family is engraved M F 1696, having no doubt belonged to Marie Falle; but it is far older than this date, and could easily have been taken over from Philippe de Carteret at the time of his décret. It appears to be a design of about 1600, but bears no maker's mark. It is 5½in. high, 4½in. in diameter, and was probably used as a personal communion cup.

Nearby, just south of the church, there is a stream running beside a lane which was a section of the percage path and led past a lavoir known as La Varvotière. A document of 1742 belonging to the owner of La Chasse gives the names of 22 persons who had the right to use this lavoir. It seems likely that it was constructed before 1637 as a copy of a document of that date, in the same ownership, states that during a Visite Royale des Chemins stress was laid on the importance of the Fontaine Bénite and of another fountain lower down on the percage; it was decided that they must be rebuilt for the benefit of the public and for the use of the church. Permission was given for this work to be undertaken by the "voisins et circonvoisins", each one contributing to the cost; at the same time a lavoir was to be built at the lower fountain for the use of the public and the neighbourhood, again at their own cost. A good example of self-help.

See *de la Croix*, III, pp. 365, 395.
    Extente 1668, pp. 96–98.
    Old Channel Islands Silver, R. H. Mayne.
    B. S. J. 1906, p. 218; 1947, p. 319.

LA CHASSE
La Profonde Rue (T). (J. Howard and J. de Gruchy on Godfray.)

This property is referred to in Payne's *Armorial* as being on the five fiefs of Diélament, Gruchetterie, Saval, Petit Rosel and Vanesse. In 1621 Philippe de Gruchy fs. Thomas sold land near La Chasse, on the fief of Gruchetterie and south of le Clos Yées which belonged to a Jean de Gruchy;

Gruchy; one may assume that this is the field now called le Clos de Ziez at La Profonde Rue, another de Gruchy holding. The celebrated Marshal Grouchy, who claimed relationship, visited La Chasse in order to search for the keystone of an arch incised with the family arms (or, fretty azure) which was reputed to have existed; (v. Elms Farm, My).

An inscription over the front door shows an unconventional arrangement with 1 I D G 800. In the farmyard is another with 17 I D L ♡ ♡ I L G 78, for Jean de la Lande who married Jeanne Le Gros in 1772. Another stone shows a shield with E D L above E D G flanked by 17 and 00, with the 7 reversed, for Edouard de la Lande and Esther de Gruchy. Yet another has 18 IDGC JDGC 55, recording the ownership of the eastern portion by Jean de Gruchy, who bought it in 1848. The whole property is now united under one owner.

In the farmyard are several troughs, one in particular being interesting as it has an outlet hole and lifting lug; it is octagonal on the outside, with a diameter of 14in. and interior depth of 3in. A previous owner though it had been used for grinding wheat, with a crusher mounted on an upright fixed in a small shallow depression in the centre; but if so it could only have crushed very small quantities of grain. In the wash-house there is a rough granite fireplace. Two cannon balls, about 4in. in diameter, have been found on the property.

LES CHASSES
Rue des Chasses (J). (C. Le Boutillier on Godfray.)

In the south-west corner of the 18th-century house is a fireplace which is most unusual, in that the granite lintel is concave, as is sometimes found with wooden lintels. It is 7ft. 3in. long and 13in. deep. The beam immediately above it is contemporary, witness the unevenness in height of the stones outside the lintel in order to accommodate the unevenness of the beam.

Within the connecting passage between the old and the newer house is a ground floor chamfered doorway with a cross and acorn as chamfer stops; this would have been on the outside before the main house was built. Within this passage, which is stone roofed, is a niche with a round edged sill and an upright iron bar. This is a mystery. It cannot have been a window as it has six feet of granite wall behind it.

In the attic, right in the eaves, a contract and a pipe were found. The contract, dated 1717, records a purchase of wheat rente by Jean Le Boutillier, confirming that family's ownership from that date at least. It should also serve as an encouragement to owners to hunt for items in the most unexpected places.

See Drawing 60.

18th. century pottery jug found at Les Chasses, (J).

60

CHÂTEAUBRIAND
Faldouet (Mt). (Madame Châteaubriand on Godfray.)

In a commanding position above Anne Port, and looking over to the coast of France, is a standard Jersey farmhouse with this unexpected name. Over the front door is a lintel with 18 F C B 08 incised, and over the door of the dower wing, which may be the older house, is a lintel well carved, with CHB EPL 1751, with initials ligatured, standing for Clement Hubert and Elizabeth Pallot.
The staircase in the main house has nicely-turned newels and decorated risers, and could well be contemporary with the 1808 date stone.

The explanation for all these facts is that Count Armand de Châteaubriand, cousin of the poet François René, came to live in Jersey, from whence he assisted d'Auvergne with La Correspondance, the secret service operating from Mont Orgueil with the Chouan Royalists. In 1795 he married Jeanne Le Brun, daughter of George Le Brun and Marie Hubert, and it seems highly likely that the farm passed through the female line from Hubert to Le Brun and then to Châteaubriand. Armand had two children, Jeanne, who died young, and Fréderic, born in 1803. Armand was arrested and shot in Paris in 1809, and one must assume that his widow (who lived until 1859), put up on the house she had inherited, the initials of her young fatherless son. It is quite possible that the Châteaubriands actually built the 1808 house onto the smaller 1751 cottage, and the mother may have felt it wise to get her son's ownership firmly incised in the house, with her husband engaged in such dangerous work.

See *The Tragedy of Philippe d'Auvergne*, G. R. Balleine, p. 118.
    Payne's *Amorial*, p. 50.
    Jersey Place Names (typescript), p. 165.

LA CHAUMIÈRE
Rue de Haut (L). (Captain Nicholson on Godfray.)

There is here a strong resemblance to Clare House in Kent, built in 1797, and its builder was making quite an innovation in the Jersey pattern of architecture. It is almost certainly the "chaumière at Millbrook", mentioned in the Le Couteur diaries in 1816, where Thomas Dumaresq (1783–1825) lived, and which his widow Sophia Lovelace (d. 1885) sold.

A building to the west, referred to somewhat incongruously as The Chapel, is dated 1895, and has a little cupola with a bell inscribed "Beta 1865". If it is a ship's bell, it is difficult to place, the only locally-registered vessel of that name appearing in 1780. A cider apple crusher has recently been brought to the garden from Les Grandes Rues (Mt). It has on one section the inscription P C R D 1671, which has not yet been interpreted. It is very rare indeed to find an inscription on a cider crusher.

LA CHAUMIÈRE DU CHÊNE
Mont des Vignes (P). (H. Renouf on Godfray.)

Yet another fireplace has been uncovered here, in the western ground floor room, its corbels being decorated with a triangular device. The lintel has succumbed to the ravages of time. There is a recess to the left, and a yet deeper recess within it.

There are indications that there may have been a 17th-century tourelle staircase, and several internal doorways are now seen to have accolade lintels. The present stairs, of the usual pattern, are probably mid-18th century. Partitioned off within the present entrance hall is a small "parloir" with panelling. It has a modern fireplace which shares its chimney with the 1650 bedroom hearth above. This small room feature has also been noticed at Morel Farm (L), and La Tourelle (Mt.).

An interesting inventory of the effects of Clement Le Montais fs. Clement of 1775 has weathered the years, and almost certainly refers to this house.

See *Old Jersey Houses*, J. Stevens, Vol. I, p. 134, and addenda.
    B.S.J. 1972, p. 370.

CHESTNUT FARM
Ouaisné (B). (P. Martin on Godfray.)

On a step in the garden is a stone with — R ◊ M N 1740, but cement masks the first letter. A lintel over the back door has the date 1716 and the wife's initials I L M, but those of the husband cannot be read. The several fireplaces have been much altered, but one in the main sitting room has good chamfer stops. There are some internal chamfered doorways, as seen elsewhere. All the windows in the façade have been enlarged, but some have good chamfering and lintels, and several

a. Queen's Vallet (G)

b. La Caumine à Mary Best (O)

Halkett Place, Morier Lane and Market, St Helier, Jersey, *c* 1846

Royal Square, Jersey. Watercolour by G. S. Shepherd, 1829

have the holes to take iron bars. Clearly a 17th-century house, much altered in the first half of the 18th century.

See *Old Jersey Houses*, J. Stevens, Vol. I, p. 137.

CHESTNUT GROVE
Mont Mado (J). (P. Bichard on Godfray.)

In what was the cowshed when this was a farm, but now being converted, is a stone with I D B T R M 1701 (date unsure) for Jean Dolbel, who married Thomassine Remon in 1699 at St. Saviours.

See *Old Jersey Houses*, J. Stevens, Vol. I, p. 137 and addenda.

CHÂTEAU DES ROCHES
St. Brelade's Bay. (N. Le Rossignol on Godfray.)

Within the grounds of this large house there stood until very recently a charming little cottage, now demolished. Over the doorway was the inscription N L R ♡ E G D 1710, the heart being larger than usual and the N reversed. The right-hand gable stone had the initials I L R or possibly N L R. There were four fireplaces, the corbels having light incised decoration, and it is surprising that a house of such modest size carried four hearths. There was a circular wooden staircase in the accepted tourelle position, but when examined the timbers were too rotten to dare to mount them. The Richmond map of 1795 shows a building standing at right-angles to the cottage, and very little else in the vicinity.

CHINA QUARRY FARM
Ville ès Gazeaux (L). (J. Nicolle on Godfray.)

This is a house with a fine position and outlook, and some interesting carved stones. On the façade is I N C E L S 1819, for Jean Nicolle and Elizabeth Le Sueur, 1819 being almost certainly the date when the house was built. Over a stable door to the east is 17 M P D 15, and over a window nearby R R N, for Michel Poingdestre and Rachel Renouf, married 1692. On a newer stable building to the west is 18 J N C ♡ ♡ A L G 69, for Jean Nicolle and Jeanne Le Grand.

This property remained in the Nicolle family until the time of Jean Nicolle (b. 1860, fs. Jean above), who married Emma Jane Prouings. The Vatchers then bought it in order to work the china clay in the district.

LA CHOUQUETTERIE
Rue de Bouillon (Mt). (J. Godfray on Godfray.)

This house takes its name, as is so often the case, from the family who lived there. The Chouquets were French refugees who are recorded in the Island since 1701.

The main house is plastered in "pierre perdue" and the window apertures are surrounded in brick. A wing at right-angles has, over a window which was formerly a door, I P L A P C 1797. The only marriage found to fit these initials is that of Jean Pallot who married Anne Picot in 1798, and one must assume that they had their stone carved just before their marriage.

The house looks down a slope to a meadow (field Mt. 577) where there is a reversed stone in a wall with P G L C 1807. The Richmond map shows two buildings at this spot, and Godfray gives J. Gallichan as the proprietor. There are too many Gallichans in this parish to be sure which one this is. Three Philippes died in the parish in 1824, 1826 and 1837.

See Drawing 29.

CLAIRFIELD
Maufant (S). (G. Ahier on Godfray.)

A stone here on an outhouse has 17 A F   MN 15; it seems likely that it is not in its original position but that in fact it gives a date associated with the house. Far later, perhaps in the mid-19th century, the front door was widened, the windows were enlarged with brick and a thatched roof replaced. The 18th-century fireplaces have suffered considerably.

In the north wall two window apertures were found with oak window frames and vertical bars, which antedate any glazed casements. This type of window is not common, having usually been replaced or destroyed over the years, but about a dozen have been found recently in the course of alterations to various houses. In the case of Clairfield they could well be evidence of a house a century or more earlier than the 1715 stone, on the same site.

LE COIN
La Haule (B). (J. de Lisle on Godfray.)

The door lintel here, with B IV E D L 1762, represents Brelade Janvrin, a wealthy shipowner, who married Elizabeth de Lecq. Their granddaughter married Frederick de Lisle, to which family it then passed; and their daughter Ann married Philippe Marett of La Haule. The appearance of the house is in good accord with the date of 1672, and the projecting stones on the chimneys show that it was once thatched, but Tobias Young's picture, painted in about 1815, shows that the thatch had by then been removed.

In the room to the right of the front door, beside the fireplace, an unusual incised design was found during alterations. Its maximum width is 2½in. and maximum height 6½in. It may be a masonic mark, but in view of the shipping interests of the families associated with the house it is more likely to be a merchant's mark. There is reason to think that the present stairs may be later than 1762; the sides of the treads, with mahogany appliqué on pine, and the stick balusters, are of late-18th-century style; and there is a mysterious door, now blocked, leading to the big upper room, which is not consistent with the planning of the stairs.

It is very probable that the big first floor room was the drawing room, and this accords with the details of a story told of Elizabeth Janvrin, daughter of the house, and her Russian admirer. It was not at all uncommon to have a first-floor drawing room. A back bedroom has woodwork which could well be 1762, but the more important rooms have been brought up-to-date at some period of decoration.

The property has changed hands many times since Brelade Janvrin built it. In 1812 it passed to Elizabeth Jeanne Valpy dit Janvrin (the older

mason's mark, (6½ x 3¾ ins.), possibly representing a coastal alarm beacon, at Le Coin, (B).

form of the name), daughter of François who had inherited it ca. matris from Elizabeth de Lecq. From Elizabeth Jeanne it passed to her son Frederick James de Lisle and then to his brother Richard, a doctor, who served in India before returning to Jersey. He sold it in 1885 to J. A. Seale, a former Constable, for £1,600; it was sold yet again in 1894, 1914 and 1952.

See *Victorian Voices*, J. Stevens.
A Jerseyman at Oxford, R. R. Marett.
B.S.J. 1968, p. 327.
Drawings 47, 61.
Plate XXb.

LE COIN COTTAGES
La Haule (B). (J. Vibert on Godfray.)

According to the Appairiement du Roi en St. Brelade, this group of cottages owes Prévôté as Chef No. 7, the owner in 1670 being J. Le Petevin dit Le Roux; in 1774–1786 it was Jean Vibert; and in 1872 J. B. Le Feuvre. The name Le Roux here cannot be unconnected with the hill, Le Mont au Roux.

It is rare in Jersey (outside the town) to have a pair of semi-detached houses of any age, and it may be that the smaller of the two cottages was built before the other. If either or both are as old as 1670, the actual sashes of the windows can hardly be original, but the window openings with their six-piece surrounds do not appear to have been altered. The left-hand cottage has but three windows, one on the ground floor and two above. The right-hand cottage has normal fenestration, though the actual sashes are rather unusual, with four panes across and two in depth, and are probably 18th century.

There are three granite chimneys, and in the façade there are two unexplained shallow recesses, perhaps small windows which have been blocked. The junction between the two units is a straight joint, though two large stones cross it to bond the wall. Additional rooms to the north are far more recent. The stonework is of a very pleasing colour.

See Plate Xa.

LE COLOMBIER
Near the church (L). (F. Payn on Godfray.)

In spite of a marriage stone of 1776 and the initials of Philippe Payn and Ann Marett, the interior fitments here seem later and are probably contemporary with the addition of the third storey. The stairs are elegantly curved, rising up to the third level; they are probably of the 1820 period, at about which time the older three-panelled doors were relegated to the upper rooms and replaced by something more modern.

Some extremely interesting documents of the Payn family have been preserved here, including the 1838–1839 diary of Augusta Maria Harvey of Guernsey, whose brother Thomas married Jane Elizabeth Payn. When Augusta came over for her brother's wedding, the passage from Guernsey took three hours. She stayed on for a while, having a very gay time with her cousins the Journeaux, and then became engaged to François Payn.

The artificial mound in the front garden was excavated in 1973 and found to have no prehistoric significance. It is probable that it was erected in the 18th century, and the name "The Proclamation Mound", by which it was known in the family, suggests that it was used as a venue for the Fief Jourdain Payn, of which the owners of Le Colombier are still the seigneurs.

See *Old Jersey Houses*, Vol. I, J. Stevens, p. 335.
B.S.J. 1927, p. 335.
Drawing 46.

LA CORNETTERIE
La Cache ès Demoiselles (Mt). (J. Mollet on Godfray.)

This farm takes its name from the Cornet family, despite the carved cornets on the roadside.

The main interest here lies in the lavoir (or douet à laver) which belongs to the farm and takes its name from association with the Fleury family. It is approached down a lane with a neat stone gutter on the left, at the entrance to which are granite gate posts; one of these is of such massive proportions as to suggest the activities of Constable Messervy; indeed T. W. Messervy bought the property from J. Mollet in 1898, Miss F. Messervy selling it in 1934.

At the end of this lane is the lavoir, perhaps second only to that at St. Cyr. It measures 13ft. 10in. by 9ft. 1in., and is fed to two springs, one on the north, the other in the south-east corner. The entrance is on the south and is 3ft. 1in. wide; it is flanked by pillars measuring 1ft. 1in. by 6in. by 2ft. 6in., that on the right bearing six names in initials, that on the left having seven sets of initials. Ten of these thirteen names can be identified with reasonable certainty as those of people living in the vicinity in 1849, the date of Godfray's map. The right-hand pillar bears the date 1832. The names are:

Right:

E E L S	Edouard Elie Le Sauteur (Devon Villa).
T A H	Thomas Ahier (near modern garage).
E D Q V	E. de Quetteville.
P V D	? Philip Vardon.
C M S V	C. Messervy (opposite Les Alpes).
1839	

Left:

P L G	?
P G D	P. Gaudin (Le Fleurion).
G P C	G. Picot (Les Chasses).
T M S V	T. Messervy (Les Alpes).
J M L	J. Mollet (La Cornetterie).
P H P C	?
T S H	T. Sohier (opposite Les Chasses).

See Plate Colour 3b.

LES CORVÉES
Mont Pinel (O). (J. Le Feuvre on Godfray).

Above a date stone with 17 I P E G B 38 is an armorial stone with an eagle for Priaulx, the name of the present owner; this was inserted fairly recently.

Behind the house is a most unusual sundial, mounted horizontally on a miniature tower about 8ft. 0in. high. The actual dial is 23in. in diameter, 3½in. thick and has Roman numerals round the perimeter. It is somewhat similar to a dial at Gorey Castle and another at Hamptonne (L), is probably sandstone, and of 16th-century date.

COUTANCHE FARM
Rue Coutanche (T). (C. Blampied on Godfray.)

Recent alterations have brought some new features to light, including a first-floor window with a cross as a chamfer stop. The stone with the initials of Renaud Coutanche and Jeanne Pinel is now visible in the back façade; he is said to have been the fifteenth of his line living there. A little room on the north has "Clara 1866" scratched on a window pane; she is thought to have been a dress-maker named Blampied who lived and worked there.

It now seems clear that, moving from west to east, there are three buildings, the first being 16th century, the middle section also 16th century, but reconstructed in 1725, and a dower wing added in 1812. The room east of the round arch has some good panelling, and a fireplace with a cross on one chamfer stop and decorated but unchamfered corbels.

On the first floor there is clapboard partitioning, and flooring with wide elm boards which show signs of considerable age. Almost all windows have been replaced by a late type of sash with large panes, with the exception of one on the north which has small square panes and the type of sash which was not made to open. Perhaps this, the panelling and many of the three-panelled doors were inserted at the 1725 period, though they would have been rather advanced for a country house at that date.

LA CROIX ÈS MOTTES
Maufant (S). (P. Baudains on Godfray.)

On the farm buildings is a stone with I N C J H P 1863, for Jean Nicolle who married Jeanne Hooper. It is interesting to note that the J of Jean is written traditionally as an I and the J of Jeanne in the modern manner. The dwelling house was built about then. Within the outbuildings, now converted, a great lintel 10ft. 0in. long, carved with "No. 10, 1821", has been inserted; it came from No. 10 Commercial Buildings in town.

A gate post to field No. S. 249, Le Paleron, has I M R M G D 1755.

DALE COTTAGE
St. Saviour's Road, St. Helier.

When this small cottage was being renovated, the Archaeological Section of La Société Jersiaise heard of it and dug some trial trenches, finding amongst other items a coin, a Louis XIV double, dated between 1643 and 1715, at a depth of some 10in. This was surprising in what appeared to be a late-19th-century cottage, but there were clues to show it was older than that, including the granite chimney, and the fact that the cellar had windows and a door (immediately below the present front door) which are now completely underground. It was clear from a 17th-century granite fireplace found in one gable wall that the floor level had at some time been a foot higher. As the cellar was, in part, too shallow for a normal person to stand upright, and as the archaeologists hit the water table at about 1ft. 6in., one may conclude that a two-storey 17th-century house was altered, probably more than once, the ground floor, which may have flooded in wet weather, becoming a cellar and a small front garden being built up in front of it. A drawing with suggested dates for the alterations may make this rather complicated story clearer.

See B.S.J. 1975, p. 320.
Drawing 62.

THE DEANERY
David Place, St. Helier.

The present Deanery was built in 1842 for the Dean who, since 1838, has always been the Rector of St. Helier also. It was François Jeune who made the move when he became Dean (1838–1844). The previous Rectory, not necessarily a Deanery, stood to the north of the parish church; the mediaeval one would have been very small and simple, perhaps replaced by another in the 17th century, but of these forerunners we know little.

It is a handsome house of simple design with a large garden at the rear. The Reverend E. Durell writing in 1847 says it is "a good substantial modern dwelling . . . the changes which have resulted . . . are highly advantageous to the benefice".

See *The Town of St. Helier*, E. T. Nicolle, p. 38.
Biographical Dictionary, G. R. Balleine, p. 335.
Victorian Voices, J. Stevens, p. 235.
B.S.J. 1888, p. 364; 1972, p. 362.

DIÉLAMENT MANOR
(T). (F. Pirouet on Godfray.)

The main house has been much altered over the years, and all but the north façade has been covered in stucco; it looks as if it was intended to cover it all, as there are handsome moulded pilasters at the corners, and the north face has brick shaping also intended to carry stucco, pilasters and a moulded cornice. Conversions here have taken an unusual course, as there are three storeys at the back (north) and two on the south, resulting in many steps and changes in level. In 1809 Stead remarked on the "majestic avenue of lofty beeches", which ran due south to the south gate of the manor, just north of Beaulieu, but deplored the dilapidation of the manor, adding: "and still it is said that the Lord of Diélament is opulent and not deficient of spirit or taste". Whether he meant the owner, then living at Rozel Manor, or Mr. Pirouet who was presumably the tenant, we do not know. But the beech avenue has quite vanished. The south gate to which it led is still there, and bears the inscription E L C N 1836, for Elizabeth Le Cornu who married Charles Renouf in 1827; it was they who put up on the farmhouse the stone which reads 18 C R N E L C N 42.

Earlier occupants of this site were Michel Lemprière and Jeanne Corbet, who married in 1713 and both died in 1762. They put up a stone over a stable door north of the house with 17 M L P ♡ I C 49.

A part of the farm buildings is reputed to contain the seigneurial chapel, but there is nothing to substantiate this except its size and the fact that it lies east-west. At the east end a window has been inserted with a 17th-century accolade lintel. A manorial chapel did exist here in 1537 and was dedicated to La Vierge.

See *A Picture of Jersey*, J. Stead, p. 165.
Old Jersey Houses, Vol. I, J. Stevens, p. 141.

LE DOUET
Near Hautes Croix (J). (J. Nicolle on Godfray.)

Years ago, in the time of the Doreys, this farm was a real centre of cider making. It also has the finest piggery seen anywhere in the Island, and a finely-made lavoir in which blue granite slabs like tables were mounted for scrubbing clothes. This "fontaine, douet et lavoir" was the subject of much litigation between 1739 and 1742, when

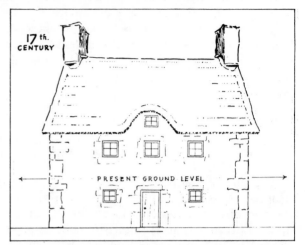
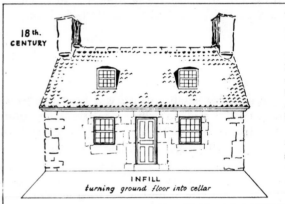
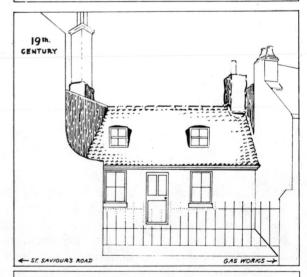

DALE COTTAGE, *St Saviour's Road.*
SUGGESTED EVOLUTION

62

neighbours disputed the right to use it, and the precedence of those who were approved. It was at that time a Romeril property.

The main house has a door lintel with 18 G D R ♡♡ E N C 75, for Dorey and Nicolle, and an older building behind it has 18 I P N ♡♡ A R R 14, for Pinel and Romeril. This latter may be the older house, though it is also suggested that the main house was built on the site of an earlier one.

See Plate XX d.

DOUET DE RUE
(My). (J. Hacquoil on Godfray.)

A fireplace lintel, broken at the left side, but otherwise a perfect fit, has been found for the hearth in the south room. It bears the date 1676 and an incised shield with I A, and T in the base. This suggests an Arthur ownership at that period, but one is inclined to think it was an addition, as the house appears to be before rather than after 1600. There is another instance, Le Nord (J) where the date, 1697, on a fireplace lintel, is clearly later than the house. On the left of the arch some faint initials can be seen, one apparently I L Q.

A door in the south wall of the oldest building on the property, the house in question, has been blocked at an unknown period and in the infill two small pottery jars were found, 5in. maximum circumference, and slightly under 3in. high. They are of Normandy ware, impossible to date accurately, put there to propitiate or repel witches incensed at finding a familiar door no longer open.

ELLISTON HOUSE
The Bulwarks, St. Aubin.

There is reason to think that this house was built before 1677, as in that year Jacques Pipon (d. ante 1706) bought some waste land from Sir Edouard de Carteret, between land he already held from Helier Mauger, "ou ledit Pipon a fait edifier", and going towards the high tide mark.

Although the front façade has been heavily stuccoed, there are chamfered windows on the back elevation which point to a 17th-century date. The stairs have enclosed stringers, bun moulding, slim urn balusters and a handrail curved into the newel. Panelling on the ground floor, with "Adam" style fireplaces, and plain round top niches in the back wall all indicate alterations at various dates. A small room which appears to be a powder closet is hard to reconcile with a date of 1677, but may have been contrived later.

A beautiful mahogany desk of about 1740 survived, to be bequeathed in 1863 by Nancy Pipon to Sir John Le Couteur. She was the daughter of Jacques Pipon, who inherited the house when his brother Thomas went to live in England, where he died in 1735, having been Constable of St. Brelade 1708–1713. There is a heraldic memorial to him in Bath Abbey. Jacques was among the signatories requesting States' permission to build a quay in St. Aubins in 1790.

See Actes des Etats, No. 15, p. 74.
    B.S.J. 1972, p. 36.
    An inventory for this house appears in Appendix 4.

THE ELMS
Rue Jean Lael (My). (J. Perrée on Godfray.)

This splendid property has now passed to the National Trust for Jersey, through the generous bequest of Mr. N. J. Perrée, who died in 1975.

It is likely that the existing house was built in or about 1774, for a stone now in the farm buildings, bearing the initials of Amice Balleine and Marie Le Hardy and the date 1774, was over the front door when La Société Jersiaise visited the property in 1904. Amice Balleine and his wife were grandparents of Sir R. P. Marett, Bailiff. Jacques Balleine fs. Amice sold it to Jean Arthur in 1810, and his son Charles Jean Arthur sold it in 1815 to Jean Perrée, whose second son inherited it; his fourth son built La Forêt, the adjacent property. In 1816 C. J. Arthur moved to Mont Mathieu, where Perrée was able to provide him with a property. In 1904 the proprietor of The Elms was Madame Hamon née Perrée.

The Fief of Câtelet in St. John, and Le Moulin de Gigoulande just south of The Elms, went with the property, through the descent from Philippe Balleine of St. Peter, who married Elizabeth Journeaux in 1735, and their son Pierre Balleine settled in St. Mary. The Journeaux family had been established in St. Mary since at least 1599, probably at The Elms. A chaplet of roses was due to them on their seigneurie, and one wonders if that is the explanation of the rose carved on the keystone of the big arch at The Elms.

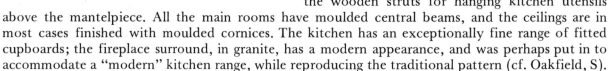

The Elms. (My).

rafter and wall heightened for the transition from thatch to slate.

63

The roof has been raised by about a foot, and the corner of the eaves has been manipulated to hide this; from inside the alteration in pitch can be seen in the timbers. The chimneys, and the dormer windows, must date from this alteration. The existing slate roof is very fine, the slates gradually decreasing in size as they approach the apex. A fine roof, inside and out, by any standards.

Many of the rooms, particularly on the first floor, have panelling and fielded panel doors consistent with the 1774 date, and several window sashes on the north have the wide glazing bars and fixed top sashes of the period. One room on the north, perhaps in origin the kitchen, has the wooden struts for hanging kitchen utensils above the mantelpiece. All the main rooms have moulded central beams, and the ceilings are in most cases finished with moulded cornices. The kitchen has an exceptionally fine range of fitted cupboards; the fireplace surround, in granite, has a modern appearance, and was perhaps put in to accommodate a "modern" kitchen range, while reproducing the traditional pattern (cf. Oakfield, S).

The stairs are somewhat anomalous. The turned balusters and panelling at the base could be contemporary with the décor in most rooms, but the open stringers with carved ends are later; the handrail could be Georgian survival or early Victorian. This staircase seems to be the work of a country carpenter of excellent craftsmanship who adapted several differing styles to a design of his own making. The mahogany appliqué is uneven in quality, that on the landings appearing to be coarser and later. The upper flight of stairs is interrupted by the insertion of steps leading to the roof space above the attics. The hall is paved with grey and white tiles, and it and the landings are of generous proportions. There is no "cabinet" bedroom over the front hall, which is unusual, nor does there appear ever to have been one, a peculiarity noted elsewhere only at La Haule Manor (1796).

When built, not later than 1774, this house had a thatched roof, an ashlar and granite façade, and no front porch, but a front door with a handsome door knocker, later demoted to the side wing, it is suggested. In about 1816 a major modernisation seems to have taken place both in and out; and at some later date the cement rendering was added, as is clear from the fact that it stands proud of the quoins. The dower wing to the west is hard to comprehend. In origin it may be older than any part of the main house, its main bedroom being virtually above the ancient round arch; but too many alterations have taken place for any definite explanation to be possible. A gate post on the other side of the road is dated 1746, while fragments of moulded granite on the property testify to the great age of this as an inhabited site.

See *Old Jersey Houses*, Vol. I, p. 144.
B.S.J. 1901, p. 395; 1905, p. 345.
Drawings 47, 63. Plates XId, XXIa.

ELMS FARM
Rue des Touettes (My); formerly The Elms. (T. de Gruchy on Godfray.)

The date stone I D G E E T 1796, for Jean de Gruchy and Elizabeth Estur, daughter of a French refugee family, puts the building of this house in the year after the Richmond map, and it consequently is not shown by the surveyors who so meticulously collected information for that map.

In about 1910 Jurat Guy de Gruchy visited the property in the hope of finding the keystone of an arch bearing de Gruchy arms which he had reason to think was there. He failed to discover it, but an hour after he left it was found, covered with ivy, in a derelict bakehouse; it had come from La Chasse, a de Gruchy property in Trinity; it has once again disappeared and its whereabouts are not known. It is possible that the round arch in the north façade of Elms Farm also came from La Chasse, where it is believed there was once an arch of this type. It is 6ft. 2in. high, 4ft. 2in. wide, and has a 4½in. concave chamfer. The keystone has 1799 roughly, and presumably retrospectively, incised. There are no chamfer stops. The arch is unusually broad, and one side stone of the uprights is so long that it also forms the side of a window; but the window seems later than the arch, which is of 17th-century type, and was quite out of fashion at the time the house was built. This arch, in fact, is a mystery, and one can only infer that it was brought here from elsewhere.

There was an interesting staircase with bun moulding enclosing the treads, turned balusters and the X crossing of the two flights. The windows and panes are slightly more square than one would expect at this date. There are some pleasing fireplace surrounds and panelling, all consistent with the date, though the grates are rather later. In a cupboard three decanters and two glasses were found, apparently of the same age as the house, and also four documents which establish the ancestors of the J. de Gruchy on the date stone. In a parish rate list of 1867 the property was called La Mare, the name of field No. My 289, to the east, though there does not appear to be marshy ground there. The name Close de la Mare has consequently been chosen as the trade name for the wine which the present owner is making there, the vines being already well established.

L'ESPINE
Rue de Haut (L). (P. Le Feuvre on Godfray.)

There are not many attached or semi-detached cottages in Jersey, but this is an example. On the Richmond map there is no building here at all, and all the surrounding fields are apple orchards. The property was previously called Euterpe Lodge, after the muse of music, a name chosen doubtless by an admirer of Greek mythology. Who was he? He may have been Philippe Le Feuvre fs. Richard, who in 1825 bought from Edouard Hamon a field named Le Jardin des Petites Fosses. He evidently built the house on the eastern part, retaining the western part as a garden, on which he had to erect a western stone wall, enclosing a plot of about one half vergée which is exceptionally sheltered and productive. It may be noted that this Jardin des Petites Fosses is very close to Le Jardin des Grandes Fosses (No. L. 867), where a hoard of bronze implements was found in 1871, and not far from the site where another hoard was found in 1976. The name of the house was changed to L'Espine in 1924 when Jurat (Senator) Collas bought it, and called it after his family's home in Brittany before they emigrated to Jersey in 1495.

It used to be said that the block was built as workmen's cottages, but this seems unlikely, and it is suggested that the owner intended it for his two daughters, or perhaps sisters.

It was originally a pair of cottages, with two staircases, each cottage having four very small rooms on each floor. It was converted by throwing the two cottages together and making each pair of south rooms into one, thus creating four good-sized rooms with fireplaces at each end. In some rooms slight changes of floor and ceiling level betray the change. What had been a shed and washhouse to the east became the kitchen, and its copper was brought back into valuable use during the German Occupation. A granite coach-house used to hold a loose box and two stalls, as well as room for a carriage, with a hay loft above. The interior woodwork is quite good, of a style in use from about 1830 onwards, but the stairs (one of the flights has now been removed), are steep and narrow owing to the small scale of the building. The façade, with small windows over the two staircases, is adorned with two niches above them, containing urns in which birds build their nests. Is must have been Jurat Gallichan, one-time owner, who planted the lovely row of camellias to the south of the house, and the magnolia, probably a Magnolia Soulangeana, on the roadside, a tree second only to the examples at Rozel in its spectacular display of ivory blooms in March.

See Plate XXId.

LA FERME
Vinchelez, Rue des Pallières (O). (J. Vibert on Godfray.)

This is a house where a square bottle, probably a Dutch gin bottle, was found embedded in a wall, with some stones, two at least of which were artefacts; there were also fragments of pots, and some seaweed. These objects must indicate "insurance" against witchcraft and lightning. There is a recess in the east bedroom wall which if invesigated could prove to be a "paûte"; it extends the full length of one's arm into the thickness of the wall, quite straight.

LA FERME GRANDET
(Previously Lowlands), Rue Golarde (L). (F. Helleur on Godfray.)

At the entrance is a gatepost with F H L M R D 1836, for François Helleur who married Marie Rondel in 1827. Their grandson Frederick Daniel Helleur, Centenier, still held the property, which later became part of the Hougue Boëte estate, but has since changed hands and gained its present name. Above a window on the north is the incised inscription H PN E A B 1837, not yet identified and perhaps coming from elsewhere; the N, as so often happens, has been reversed by the mason. Over the back door is a stone with N L C M M 1724 in raised letters, for Noé Le Cras and Marie Marett. The south front, which has no distinguishing features, must be 19th century. The inside partitions are wooden, most of the doors are two-panelled, and the stairs have had the appliqué added to the sides of the risers, perhaps at the 1827 period. The end gable shows no sign of the extension to the north, which undoubtedly took place, as may be seen from the very thick (now exterior) walls.

FERNSIDE
(Previously La Gallichanerie), Mont Sohier (S). (Jurat J. Pelgué on Godfray.)

A round arch dated 1824 is most unusual, as it is more than a century after the true vernacular arch had gone out of fashion, and rather before the later Victorian revival. The house has a stone with 18 G P G ♡ ♡ E L T 18, and an outbuilding bears the same initials with the date 1811. All these features are presumably the work of George Pelgué, father of the Jurat, and the Gallichan connection must be earlier.

FERN VALLEY
Les Mouriers (My). (J. Marett on Godfray.)

The original dwelling house, dated 1725, is now used for farm purposes. The well has the inscription P V B ♡ E R N 1765, and it is not common to find a dated well.

LA FÈVERIE
Maufant (S). (J. Godfray on Godfray.)

This house, taking its name from association with the Le Feuvre or Le Fèvre family, has two of the late, flattened type of arch, one bearing the date 1878, and the other bearing hearts but no initials—an expression of hope, perhaps, on the part of a bachelor. There are several similar arches in the near neighbourhood, perhaps the work of one mason.

On the north of the house is a stone with 17 J G F F V P 35, and over a window another with 18 P D G C M A G F 72. The former can surely be explained by a contract of 1732, by which Michel Lemprière of Diélament sold land on the Fief du Roi in St. Saviour to Jean Godfray fs. Edmond fs. Jean. The land includes "Le Clos de Noé Le Fevre ou était la maison anciennement appellée le Clos de Maufant . . .; le Clos Hardy au sud dudit clos, et le Clos des Fosses". Le Clos Hardy is field No. S.7, and is south of La Fèverie.

LE MANOIR DU FIEF ÈS NEVEUX
Mont Félard (L). (J. Denize on Godfray.)

In the façade of this house there is a series of initialled, dated stones, but all except the last appear to have been carved restrospectively. They are:

I D N F L C M N 1581,	for Jacques Denize (− −1609) who married Françoise Le Cheminant.
I D N M D S C 1670,	for Jean Denize (1647-1726) who married Marie de Ste. Croix (1650-1684).
I D N A F 1771,	for Jourdain Denize (1743-1827) who married Ann Fiott (1739-1805).
I D N M G B 1825,	for Jourdain Denize (1765-1825) who married Marie Gibaut (1789-1860).

An inscribed slate tombstone in the garden is likely to have come from the churchyard, being replaced there by a much more elaborate one. This, and the parish registers, confirm the identity of the people who lived in this house, but one suspects that it was the Jourdain of 1825 who commissioned these memorials. At the same time he may have altered and heightened the roof, and inserted the rather unexpected small windows high in the bedroom walls. There is a chamfered outer door at first-floor level, the house being built on a slope. This must originally have served an outer staircase, and could be the only remnant of the 1581 house.

LE FLEURION
(Mt.) (P. Gaudin on Godfray.)

The name Fleurion for the home of the Fleury family is a variation on the usual local manner of associating a family with a house, such as La Guilleamerie for the Guilleaumes, doubtless because Fleurerie would have made a clumsy word.

In 1646 Abraham Machon sold La Maison de Fleury to Marie Machon, wife of Philippe Payn. Le Grand et Le Petit Close de Fleury appear in the 1701 Appairiement de Sa Majesté for Jean Baal. The Richmond map of 1795 shows two buildings on this site. The date stone on the façade of Le Fleurion, reading 18 G L S L F M S V 20, seems to show that at that date the Le Seeleurs built a new house in place of an older one. By 1832 the property had passed to the Gaudins, as the initials P G D are carved with twelve others on Le Douet Fleury (q.v.) nearby, and it was still in that family in the parish records of 1889.

The central pediment is intended to add a classical finish to a standard local façade. The dower wings are presumably of the same date as the main house, 1820.

LA FONTAINE
Rue des Côtils (G). (T. Labey on Godfray.)

A gatepost at the entrance to the farmyard has T L B E B T 1769, and this is repeated on a flight of external stone steps in the outbuildings, representing Thomas Labey (1710–1785), Constable of Grouville, who married Elizabeth Bertram. Thomas inherited La Fontaine in 1744 from his father, Philippe, who married Jeanne Anthoine of Longueville.

The front door is of the type which opens to two-thirds of its width, leaving one-third for opening in emergency. The windows were very pleasing and must date from no later than 1830, a date consistent with the simple banisters and newels of the stairs. The proportions of the sashes and of each pane, the thinness of the glass and the type of catch all suggest this, though one would hesitate to put them as early as Thomas Labey's alterations of 1769, when he seems to have erected the farm buildings. On the top corner of the roadside gable the date 1697 appears, and doubtless records some event important to the family, perhaps the acquisition of the property by the Labeys.

A Baheur belonging to this family is now with a descendant in Canada, and details of it appear in another chapter.

LA FONTAINE
Grande Route de Ste. Marie (My). (J. Binet on Godfray.)

Facing east, with well dressed ashlar in the façade, in light coloured granite, this house has a stone with I B N ♡♡ E A T 1757, for Jean Binet and Elizabeth Arthur, a fairly early date for the double heart motif. The south-facing wing may be older than the main house, and it has one chamfered lintel over a door. The stable buildings, very good examples, are dated 1897, and have an attractive weathercock.

LES FONTAINES
Off Rue des Buttes (Mt). (E. Starck on Godfray.)

E. Starck has scratched 1812 E S T on a stone in an outhouse. Over the front door is 17 I L M M B T 32. Another stone on the property is dated 1753. A large standing stone in the front garden suggests a megalith, but this has not been substantiated; it is of Mont Orgueil granite.

This is a standard house, of the Guernsey pattern, having a single window on one side of the front door and two on the other side.

A spring near the entrance serves what was probably once a lavoir and is now a water-cress bed.

FONTIS
Near Carrefour à Cendre (P). (M. Binet on Godfray.)

On a lintel over the front door is M L F 1714 A L C, and the façade is in good agreement with such a date. A garden wall running north–south must have been part of an earlier house as it contains a pair of fireplace corbels, on either side of which a square gin bottle was found buried, one being broken and the other whole. These were no doubt placed there as protection against the ubiquitous witch.

Field No. P.383 is le Clos de L'Hermitte, and No. 384 is le Clos de la Montagne. In 1746 Thomas Binet sold, for the benefit of the poor, half of two fields so named on the Fief de Vingt Livres, St. Peter, for 13 cabots of wheat annually and £10 tournois cash, and the right to use the abreuvoir in the latter field. There can be little doubt that he was living in this house.

See St. Peter's Parish church documents.
Drawing 27.

LA FORGE
Rue ès Picots (T). (P. de Gruchy on Godfray.)

The Cabots, who claim to have had a Thomas in the family in direct line since the 16th century, bought this property from a de Gruchy early in this century. The stone over the front door has 18 P D G C A M T G 33, for Philippe de Gruchy and Anne Mattingley.

It is a satisfying façade, in that everything about it appears to be contemporaneous and to support the marriage stone. The front door has a heavy lock and the characteristic hinges stretching across its width. The architraves of the interior doors are good, though without corner bosses. The main bedroom has a hob-type cast-iron grate, and this must be a late example of that pattern. The floor boards are wide, and the stairs have stick balusters, plain sides to the treads, and a mahogany handrail returning in a chameleon twist at the base. In the kitchen is an apparently new granite fireplace of traditional type, and this continuity of design, after the introduction of iron ranges (which could be accommodated within the recess), has been noticed elsewhere.

LA FOSSE
Near Les Croix (T). (P. de Gruchy on Godfray.)

Although there are no definite features by which to date this house, it appears to be early 16th century. The windows are small and uneven, and there is a tourelle of very simple construction, similar to that of its near neighbour, Cambrai (q.v.). It has steep and narrow steps, worn smooth by generations of owners. The well water is exceptionally good, and it is noticeable how often the owners of country wells say this, for no chemicals interfere with their pure springs.

In the kitchen is a Grandin range, once so common in Jersey and now almost unknown; but this one is in constant use and is claimed to make more tasty food than any modern cooker.

See Plate XXIa.

LES FOUGÈRES
Rue des Chenolles (J). (D. Bisson on Godfray.)

Over the back door is the date 1838, and on a farm building 1886. In the 1890s Daniel Bisson, auctioneer and valuer, lived here. Within living memory there was a school in this house, the school-room being in an upper room.

When cement rendering was removed from the front façade the walls were shown to be granite, but with brick round the windows, while the back elevation is all stone. The farm buildings are very good, with a surprising hipped roof, and the roof timbers are fine, the cross-beams being morticed into the main timbers and secured with exceptionally large dowels.

In the grounds are the remains of a lime kiln. It is unexpected to find another example so close to that over the road, at St. Cyr.

LE FRANC FIEF FARM
Rue du Cônet (B). (F. Alexandre on Godfray.)

Far more interesting than one might suppose from the road, this is a most intriguing house. There are four very small windows at the corners of the south façade, three of which are now inside cupboards which may well have been powder closets. A fireplace on the ground floor has, in rather large letters, M R 1717 A F, for M. Renouf and Amelia Falle. Over the front door is M A L A R N 1760, showing that Renouf was written with one initial at the earlier date and syllabically later on.

Beside one of the ground floor fireplaces is a most curious recess with a shaft leading straight up to the attic, and this was probably used to supply bundles of fern stored in the attic to the lower room as fuel. But there is a door at first-floor level leading into a bedroom, with a latch which can only be fastened from within the shaft, which itself is only wide enough to accommodate someone on a ladder. The shaft is in the north-east corner of the ground floor room, but in the south-east corner of the bedroom above, the latter being rather wider than the former. The northern rooms appear to be a late addition, as so often happens. The explanation of this strange construction seems to be that the shaft was intended not only for the delivery of fuel, but also for the purposes of "La Fraude" (smuggling), and that even then it would have needed one person on the ladder and another to hold the door, which swings right across the shaft. This item has some affinities with Woodlands (My) and Les Ruettes (J), q.vv. The first floor has good doors with fielded panels, and panelled cupboards, and one room has a double door, as at La Vallette (J) and Les Potirons de Bas (My), q.vv. These features all appear to be contemporary with the 1760 stone, and thus offer a firm date for such décor. The building also shows that only the front façade was considered important, the north elevation being rather rough, with various older stones used in a somewhat haphazard manner.

There is another building, perhaps earlier, but also bearing the initials M R with the date 1707. It is said to have been a chapel, and had an altar stone incised with a cross, but this cannot now be found. An owner earlier in this century, a Mr. Alexandre, was a Swedenborgian and held services here.

LES GEONNAIS
Vinchelez (O). (A. Luce on Godfray.)

A small cottage, cement rendered, but appearing to be 17th century, has on its north wall the batter, or backward slope, typical of that period. The ground floor windows have been enlarged and have mid-19th-century sashes, but a small window on the first floor appears considerably older. The front door surround is chamfered but its lintel is cement covered. On the ground floor, east, is a granite fireplace with chamfered uprights and decorated chamfer stops, but a wooden lintel. The simple and rather steep stairs have the familiar X formation. The east bedroom shows the hood of the fireplace beneath it, and to the left of this hood are signs that there was a bedroom fireplace. Such a positioning is rare but not unknown (cf. La Porte (J) and Ville ès Philippes (G)). The roof was heightened and slated in about 1936, the pitch being made less steep, as was customary.

LE GEYT FARM
Five Oaks (S). (A Le Geyt on Godfray.)

This house has completely disappeared and its site has been re-used.

The main house had fine stonework with varied, bright coloured granite, and a date stone 18 A L G ♡♡ I E N 32. It is a sad reflection on current economic affairs that it paid better to demolish the whole structure rather than to make use of it. An older house at the back, facing east, had a stone-paved yard and a date stone with A L G ♡ A A L 1773, for Abraham Le Geyt, who married Ann Alexandre in 1741.

The A L G on the 1832 stone was the great-great-uncle of our member, the late Mr. Clement Leggett (derived from Le Geyt) of Ontario, son of William Clement (b. 1869), son of Clement William (b. 1833), who was the son or nephew of the Abraham on the stone.

See Drawings 30, 38, 47.

GLENROSE
(Now called Haut du Mont Farm.) Coin Varin (P). (P. Blampied on Godfray.)

A lintel in an outhouse is dated 1666, but it does not appear to be in its original position. There are three other initialled stones: P P C S B P 1763 over the main door; 18 P B P ♡♡ A R N 09 on the cottage (for Philippe Blampied and Anne Renouf married in 1778); and PBP ♡♡ NJ 1832 on an outhouse; all testifying to a lengthy Blampied ownership.

GOURAY COTTAGE (G).

On p. 150 of Volume I the limestone plaque on the road frontage of this house was illustrated. It has since been noticed that in 1809 Stead said: "Gouray was formerly the seat of justice; the House is yet standing where the sittings of the Royal Court were formerly held; against the Front of it the Arms are yet affixed". A pencil note in a copy of the book at the Museum, in the handwriting of the late Major Rybot, alters "formerly" to "occasionally". In special circumstances, such as an outbreak of plague, court sittings were held in the country, but in no other instance have the Royal Arms, crudely carved as these are, been erected, though it must be admitted that no such Court Sitting can be proved.

See *A Picture of Jersey*, J. Stead, p. 120.

GOVERNMENT HOUSE (S).

This is at least the fifth residence we have offered to our Governors and Lieutenant-Governors. The first was Mont Orgueil, followed by Elizabeth Castle in 1600. It is not clear when the Lieutenant-Governors ceased to live at Elizabeth Castle, but its remoteness and dependence on the tides must have made it a highly inconvenient headquarters, and no doubt individual Lieutenant-Governors bought or rented accommodation in the town. It may be remembered that until 1854 we still had a Governor, who was non-resident, and the post of Lieutenant-Governor was often held by a comparatively junior officer. It is known that Colonel Magnus Kempenfelt (1723–1727) lived in King Street in 1727 in the house of one Le Geyt. Peter Meade's map of 1737 shows "Residence of Lt. Governor" in that area. At the time of the Battle of Jersey (1781) Major Moise Corbet was living at Le Manoir de la Motte, subsequently called Old Government House. In about 1800, during the time of General Andrew Gordon, the site where Woolworths now stands, was bought for the Lieutenant-Governor, and in 1809 Stead described it as a "large, substantial and commodious stone mansion with appropriate offices, pleasure and kitchen gardens"; a decade later, in 1819, Plees wrote: "the town residence of General Don has a partial view of the Royal Square, and has been rendered more commodious than it was by the addition of offices appropriate to public business, and the gardens have likewise been enlarged".

Sir Colin Halkett, however, was far from satisfied with these quarters, and from November 1821 onwards he was writing to the English authorities urging an exchange between the King Street property and a house called Belmont on St. Saviour's Hill. His letters state that the King Street house had cost £1,575 14s. 10d. in repairs during the previous decade, that he anticipated further heavy expenditure, and that during the winter the garden and offices were frequently under water. One may recall that Le Grand Douet, then an open stream, would have run at the bottom of the back garden. He adds that "the rooms are ill calculated for public entertainment". In his opinion the Lieutenant-Governor "would, at Belmont, possess the desirable opportunity of seeing together, without apparent partiality, such of the inhabitants and strangers as naturally expect to be invited to the Government House".

Belmont had been built in or about 1814 by François Janvrin, a shipping merchant. He had bought the land from two owners, William Robertson and Philippe Aubin, and the Richmond map of 1795 shows that there was a house there already; the round arch in the garden wall may be a relic of it. In 1822 Janvrin sold the property to Mathieu Amiraux for 340 quarters of wheat, a large sum. The very same day Amiraux exchanged Belmont and some additional land for the King Street house and Le Pré du Roi in St. Clement. The building of the guard house, at a cost of £215, and some other improvements seem to have been undertaken at this time. It is interesting to speculate whether Amiraux was a public benefactor or whether he saw the advantage of a site in the busiest part of the town.

Not everybody was pleased with Belmont. After the exchange had been completed Sir John Le Couteur, then a young lieutenant, became A.D.C. to Sir Colin Halkett, and complained that the chimney in the small boudoir upstairs always smoked, and that "the masonry . . . is shamefully done, altho my f. in law spent so many thousands on the house". James Robin, Seigneur de

Grainville, on which fief Belmont stands, complained that he was deprived of his "année de jouissance" when George IV died without heirs, and he won his case. Writing of Belmont in 1838 Inglis said: "the view of it would not reward a walk up the avenue".

The idea of adding a third storey was considered long before it was accomplished, Sir James Reynett (1847-1852) saying he would "play it safe" (*sic*) on the subject. Photographs of garden parties held in the grounds, and other illustrations, show that the addition was made before 1894, and the interior woodwork supports this dating. The third storey no doubt added much needed accommodation to what is in fact a small house, to fit its new rôle, but architecturally this storey and other brick additions detract sadly from the building, which was in essence a French "pavilion", having nothing in common with the local vernacular architecture, as may be seen in Ouless's painting and the engraving made from it. It is somewhat similar in design to Beauvoir in St. Saviour, built in about 1840.

The wealth of mahogany in doors and stairs is evidence of the Janvrins' success as shipowners. The stairs are elegant, curved, shallow and wide, lit by a Venetian window. There may be a connection with La Haule Manor (1796), and alterations at Belle Vue (B), (*c.* 1810), for there were strong ties between the Marett, Janvrin and Le Couteur families. One suspects that the sturdy upright mahogany supports to the flying stairs were inserted later in the century.

Curtain pelmets in the drawing room have been made to match the pediments over the doors, as a photograph of the room in 1894 shows that the pelmets were not there at that time.

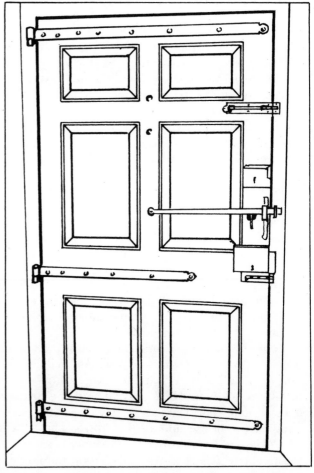

Architrave bosses with lion masks follow early 19th-century fashion, and are reminiscent of those at the Museum (1817) and Avranches Manor (1819).

I am much indebted to his present Excellency, General Sir Desmond Fitzpatrick for permission to quote from Sir Colin Halkett's letters.

See *A Picture of Jersey*, J. Stead, p. 93.
An Account of the Island of Jersey, W. Plees, p. 111.
Victorian Voices, J. Stevens, pp. 63, 112.
B.S.J. 1895, p. 309; 1900, p. 392; 1902, p. 34.
Plate XXIc.

GRAINVILLE MANOR

St. Saviour's Hill (S). (J. Poingdestre on Godfray).

It is sad that the needs of the present century have deprived us of this fine house, which took its name from the fief on which it stood. For long associated with the Poingdestre family, it passed to others in Victorian days. It had deteriorated badly in recent years, after being divided into flats, with little regard for its architectural features.

Most of the internal woodwork appeared to be of about 1830 or later, but the cellars, which were on ground level on the north, had far earlier woodwork of good quality. It seems as if the Poingdestres, who in the 17th century lived at Swan Farm in the valley to the north, moved up the hill in the first half of the 18th century and built themselves a new and larger house, facing north, as the slope of the land dictated. Stead described it in 1809 as "a good modern

inside of typical late 18th century outer door, from Grainville.

64

PLATE XXI

a. The Elms (My), perhaps 1774

b. Fliquet Bay and Tower (Mt)

c. Government House, as built *c* 1820; engraved
by P. J. Ouless

d. L'Espine (L), with its magnolia tree, *c* 1825

PLATE XXII

a. Highcliff cottage (La Maison du Becquet) (J) before restoration

b. La Hougue Boete (J) as now. Probably late 18th century

c. La Hougue Boete (J) in 1815, by Tobias Young

d. A pedigree on a chimney, apparently 1781. At Houguemont (G)

building". A little later, perhaps 1820-1830, a two-storeyed south-facing house was super-imposed, making the ground floor of the older house into the kitchens.

An undated water colour painted by Sir J. E. Millais (1829-1896) shows the house with a tiled pitched roof, and an early Georgian hood over the front door. The next piece of evidence we have is a photograph of about 1860, when it had a very shallow pitched roof behind a parapet, and a rather heavy front door porch added then by the Scotts, who bought the property in 1873. The house was subsequently acquired by Sir James Godfray, Q.A.D.C., whose grandson eventually sold it. The grounds are impressive, as are the trees, though one may have reserva-tions about the admittedly venerable oak which is said to have been there in 1066. A stone with a carved deer, crest of the Scott family, was saved and is now at Clos des Tours, Coin Varin (P).

See B.S.J. 1961, p. 111; 1969, p. 54.
Drawings 64, 65.

Grainville Manor in the mid 19th. century, after a water-colour by Sir J.E. Millais.

65

LA GRANDE MAISON
Sion (J). (P. Luce on Godfray.)

An imposing façade, dated 1852, fulfils the name of a house built at that date on the same, or nearly the same site as its predecessor, shown by Godfray in his map of 1849. There is a tradition that Mr. Luce built La Grande Maison in competition with Mr. Carcaud of Melbourne House, both being actually built by Philippe de la Mare, who was born in St. Martin in 1818, married Elizabeth Ferey in 1839 and died in Trinity in 1889. He was responsible for much quality workmanship in Jersey, and also in Guernsey.

The façade of the house has a granite string course, with pilasters, a porch with Ionic pillars, and a semi-basement ground floor. The attic windows are in the gable ends, which is rather unusual. The dower wing to the west may be a later addition.

THE GRANITE HOUSE
Rue du Hucquet (Mt). (P. Payn on Godfray.)

Apart from a good date stone with 18 P P ♡ ♡ A L S 34, there is nothing from the outside to suggest antiquity except the chamfered doorway, which has elaborate and matching chamfer stops looking rather like stunted palm trees. An accolade lintel has H M 1620. This is impossible to identify, but the most likely names with M in St. Martin are Malet or Messervy.

GREEN FARM
Mont Mado (J). (R. Barette on Godfray.)

This would seem to show the end of the fashion for chamfering, found here on all the ground floor windows and round the main doorway. This door has apparently been heightened, and the lintel, also chamfered, has T L S and the date 1709, with an indeterminate design cut at the apex of a low relief accolade. In the east ground floor room there is a fireplace with slight decoration on the corbels. An archway existed at the entrance until early in this century. A stable and bakehouse are attached to the farm.

GREEN FARM
Now called La Clochette. Queruée (Mt). (P. Gaudin on Godfray.)

"Nous sommes venus demeurer à ma maison de la Queruée le 30 juin 1679." So wrote the Reverend François Le Couteur, Rector of St. Martin (1672-1706), who died 1714. It is interesting to find a Rector living in his own house, and at some distance from the church. He and his wife, Sara Dumaresq (m. 1657), had thirteen children, only the last, Elizabeth, being born in this house, two months after the move. Sara, poor woman, died at the age of 52, but he survived to become an octogenarian.

Le Couteur must have been building or altering his house at least two years before he moved there, as there is an accolade lintel with F L C S D M 1677 over the old house. There are evidently three periods here: first the main 17th-century section; then buildings to the east which could be 18th century; and finally the 19th-century work. The first section has five windows with accolade lintels, but all sills have been dropped by the insertion of an extra stone. Inside there is a fine granite doorway with elaborate chamfer stops, though both it and the front door appear to have been heightened. The main room and the bedroom above it have traditional fireplaces. It has been suggested that the double arch now at the States Farm came from here, but this is doubtful.

The lintel of the later house has 18 P G D ♡♡ E A B 17, for Philippe Gaudin who married Elizabeth Aubin in 1781. There were Gaudins "de la Queruée" from 1659, when Philippe Gaudin married Catherine Jutize; a later Philippe Gaudin "of Green Farm" was Deputy of St. Martin 1875-1878.

See *Old Jersey Houses*, Vol. I, p. 218.
   B.S.J. 1913, p. 284.
   Notebooks of F. G. Collas in the author's possession.

GREENFIELDS
Pont ès Oies (T). (J. de Gruchy on Godfray.)

There is a gable stone in an outhouse with MH IC 1695, the MH being ligatured. It seems likely that the name was Hocquard, as a later stone is inscribed IHQ ♡♡ BHQ 1830, for Jean and Elizabeth Hocquard, married in 1794. Another stone reads J J D G C E P L 1890, for Jean Josué de Gruchy and Emily Pallot. It is fairly unusual to find two Christian names recorded on a stone. It is said that some early occupants of this property buried their money in wooden pots in the hedges, but that when dug up, within living memory, it was no longer legal tender.

GREENLAND
Rue de la Presse (P). (Agnes on Godfray.)

Here one notices granite of a very pleasing colour in a 17th-century façade, with four chamfered six-piece windows on the first floor, unaltered. Over the front door is a rather roughly incised P B 1660; the door surround looks rather later than that, and may have replaced a round arch. The ground floor windows have been much enlarged in recent times. The main living room has a modern granite fireplace which incorporates two far older stones.

The dower wing has a stone with P B 1704, but the wall in which it is set appears later in date. In the terrace floor is a stone, removed from the stable, inscribed with Ph B followed by a lozenge and I V N or I V M, and below this, E J ◇ 1705. This stone is a puzzle, as it may have been intended to be. It probably represents two Philip Balleines, of whom the former married I V N, so far unidentified, and the latter married Eliza-beth Journeaux. The contracted form of Ph for Philippe has not been recorded elsewhere in stone.

There is a tradition of this house being a manor. This may spring from the fact that in 1704 Philippe Balleine endeavoured to claim Le Fief Saval by right of kinship (retrait lignager) from Raulin Robin, who had bought it from Philippe Journeaux, Balleine's brother-in-law; Balleine succeeded in his claim, but swiftly passed the fief back to Robin.

See B.S.J. 1901, p. 397.
Drawing 66.

66

the Philip Balleine stone at Greenland, (P). incorporating his initials and those of his wife Elizabeth Journeaux, (m. 1673).

LES GRÈS

Ouaisné (B). (A. Le Brun on Godfray.)

A complex stone dated 1732 over the front door seems to represent Thomas Prideaux or Priaulx fs. Thomas, who had married Elizabeth Bechervaise in 1693, and may also have married M N (not yet identified) in about 1695; and their son, Jean Pridauld (*sic*), who was born in 1696 and married Katherine Alexandre in 1723.

In this typical early façade, with good chimneys, the window sills have all been dropped, presumably when sash windows were introduced. One room has a bread oven and hearth. The back elevation appears to be the oldest part, and may have been designed to be the front; if so, the owner in 1732 probably decided to reverse front and back, owing to the inconvenience of having his front door opening right on to the Ouaisné Hill road. The fenestration of the back or roadside elevation is utterly unsymmetrical. On the other side of the road are land, pig sties and the ruins of a building, all belonging to Les Grès, which thus occupied both sides of a public highway; but at the time of its building, less traffic passed Les Grès than it does nowadays.

See Drawing 28.

GREYSTONES

Upper King's Cliff (H).

Under the thick stucco of a three-storeyed façade a 17th-century house is buried, and it affords an interesting study in evolution. On the ground floor, to the right, is a fireplace of 1660 pattern, though the corbels bear a stylised decoration which is not traditional in design. The panelling in this room is modern, but the room on the opposite side of the hall is completely panelled in the 1750 style, even if the fireplace surround may be later. The door leading to the kitchen continues the panelling so that, when shut, it is unseen. There are interesting hinges to some of the cupboards. The room above has remnants of similar panelling, but incomplete, and the section left of the fireplace seems newer.

In the 19th century a vast alteration must have taken place, including the construction of a front door with a flattened rounded arch; this arch is chamfered, and its chamfer stops are copied from those on the granite fireplace.

GUINGEVAL

Or Gingueval. Coin Tourgis Sud (L). (C. Mauger on Godfray.)

Now demolished, this sad roofless house stood in field No. L.973. It had a window lintel with T M R 1782, the space presumably being left for the initials of Thomas Morel's future wife,

The staircase and very wide floor boards were probably contemporary with the lintel. There is reason to think that this was the home of the Morels before they bought Morel Farm. The name signifies a winding valley.

LA HAGUE MANOR
(P). (T. Pipon on Godfray.)

We know that a manor was built here in 1634 by François de Carteret, and that Thomas Le Breton (1707-1760) rebuilt it in the 1730s, a few years after he had bought the property from the de Carteret descendants. We know also that Colonel C. P. Le Cornu, who purchased it from Thomas Henry Pipon in or before 1871, undertook extensive alterations, during which time he rented and lived in Trinity Manor. But it is hard to see how much of the earlier houses remains, and whether all three manors have been built on the same site. A study of the Richmond (1795) map and Godfray's (1849), both dated between the Le Breton and the Le Cornu rebuildings, suggest that they have, as does the position of the colombier. The date 1872 can be seen on the central tower, which is rather reminiscent of the tower added in 1860 to the Seigneurie in Sark. The round-topped attic dormers, presumably of this date, help to date similar ones in other houses.

When Jean Pipon was Seigneur ca. ux., he arranged with the parish to close Le Mont du Chêne in exchange for sufficient land to straighten Le Mont de Veulle or Ruelle du Presbytère and widen it to 14 feet. This was agreed in 1811, but in 1822 complaints were still being received from inhabitants of Le Coin Varin, who said that the new route was far longer for them when going to church, or to St. Ouen's Bay for vraic. Le Mont du Chêne is the now disused drive to La Hague which enters St. Peter's Valley opposite Le Mont de l'Ecole. A newspaper advertisement of 1856 announced an auction sale of the contents of La Hague, including furniture ". . . in rosewood and acajou, pianos, silverware and oriental porcelain, carriages etc., . . . belonging to Thomas Henry Pipon".

In 1875 Colonel Le Cornu recorded in his diary: ". . . we removed the large stone cross socket from near La Hague gate and placed it on our lawn, and placed on it our large iron flower vase". The cross base is still there on the lawn, but it is disappointing to read in the diary that the de Carteret-Dumaresq arms on the colombier do not belong to La Hague, but came from La Caroline. The Colonel bought them there for 10s. in 1879. There was justification for their transfer, as Helier de Carteret and Sara Dumaresq were the parents of François who bought La Hague in 1602, and his family had also owned La Caroline (not the present house of that name).

See *Old Jersey Houses*, Vol. I, p. 158.
   Le Manoir de la Hague, R. Mollet.
   Chroniques de Jersey, 23 July 1856.
   La Hague documents in Library of La Société Jersiaise.

HAMLET FARM
Rue de la Hambye (S). (P. Quenault on Godfray.)

A door lintel of the accolade type, with the initials L A B and the date 1664, probably represents Lucas Aubin. The Quenault family owned this property for many generations, and until the sale to the present owner. The crushing stone of the tou à cidre is inscribed with C Q N 1835, probably the father of the P. Quenault on Godfray's map. This is the only recorded instance of initials appearing in such a place, where hard wear might be expected to obliterate them. Another remarkable thing about the apple crusher is that each section has tally notation scratched on the rim, to make sure that the right sections were joined to each other, a most efficient arrangement.

The frontage is of the Guernsey pattern, that is to say two windows on one side of the door and one on the other side, a variation not often seen here after the 17th century. There are corbels in one fireplace, wooden clapboarding partitions between rooms, good granite chimneys and various other features which suggest a date of about 1720 for the house. The stairs have nice pine balusters and rail, probably contemporary. On a beam in the main room the initials F M R are scratched, perhaps by the carpenter, and in this parish likely to be a Mourant.

HAMPTONNE
Le Hocq Lane (C). (P. Messervy on Godfray.)

The lintel over the door is inscribed P M S V 1833, for Philippe Messervy, born about 1801; he married Elizabeth Le Neveu, but apparently after he had put up his stone.

The north façade has retained the traditional 12-light sashes, but the windows on the south have been altered. Behind the house is a small building, apparently the original dwelling house, with a lintel reading P M S V ♡ E T Z 1786, for Philippe Messervy (b. 1751) and Elizabeth Touzel, grandparents of the Philippe mentioned above. It must have had thatch, and the window of the central bedroom shows evidence of the upward curve which the thatch took over it.

See Payne's *Armorial*, p. 284.

HAMPTONNE
Rue de la Patente (L).

Further investigation leads us to believe that La Chapelle de St. Eutrope was probably situated at Manor House (L), q.v., rather than at Hamptonne.

LA HAULE MANOR
(B). (P. Marett on Godfray.)

Here we have an example of a local landowner breaking away from tradition and building a more classical façade, with a Venetian window, pediment and oeuil de boeuf. It is believed to be on the exact site of the older house, and was built in 1796 by Philippe Marett who had married Ann, daughter of Brelade Janvrin of Le Coin (q.v.), a shipping magnate; their initials and the date are on a stone above the Venetian window. The dower wing to the west was added in about 1820, and has a contemporary front door and cornices.

In the main house the dining room has a fitted mahogany sideboard, the only other example so far recorded being in the merchant's house in Castle Street (q.v.). The overmantel and a gilded mirror over the sideboard are probably contemporary, and the shutters have retained fielded panelling. The windows of the second floor have contemporary slender glazing bars, quite an innovation in 1796, but others have been replaced by modern sashes with large panes of glass. The front door, now temporarily converted into a window, has a handsome pedimented doorcase. The custom of a first-floor drawing room, noted in many other houses, is seen here, the room occupying the whole depth of the house and thus having four windows, two on the south and two on the north.

There is a book preserved in the family entitled *Original designs, elevations and sections,* by John Crunder, 1791, showing Georgian designs in fashion at the time. Illustration No. 13 may well have been the basis for La Haule, with the addition of the Venetian window and oeuil de boeuf, the exclusion of ornamental urns on the roof, and the traditional gabled roof in place of the more English hipped roof. The ground plan of No. 13 is very similar indeed to that which Marett adopted at La Haule.

A secondary staircase behind the library has iron balusters, similar to the lowest flight at No. 9 Pier Road, and they may have been put in later when the dower wing was added. The main stairs have stick balusters, for which Sir John Summerson gives a date of 1770-1778 in England, and feels that they were part of a general revolt led by the Adam brothers against heavy detailing.

The manuscript material preserved in the Marett family is quite exceptional both in quantity and quality. From 1395 to the present time, documents testify to the activities and interests of the Dumaresqs, the Maretts and their collaterals. The diaries and letters of Edouard Marett, his son Philippe, and his grandson Philippe, give us invaluable information about the life of Jerseymen of their period, as Jurats, Seigneurs, farmers and militiamen, leading busy lives of the greatest variety. All this material has been generously lent to La Société Jersiaise for cataloguing and study.

See *Old Jersey Houses*, J. Stevens, Vol. I, p. 162.
   Plate, Colour 2a.

LE HAUT DE TOMBETTE
La Grande Rue (My). (J. La Gerche on Godfray.)

When the cement facing was stripped off, a façade was disclosed which had suffered severely over the years. Many windows had been enlarged with brick. One lintel, placed upside-down, is inscribed 1670 S M R, with an E below the M. These initials have not yet been identified.

There is a simple square tourelle staircase which does not reach the first floor level, and this is understandable as the roof has clearly been raised. An interior stone wall took a chimney when the roof was thatched. The present front door is not contemporary, but a round arch now in the carnation packing room to the west must have been removed when the plastering was done; at the same time the arch was heightened by the addition of one stone on either side. The current alterations are being carefully done.

An incised gable stone with the date 1670 picked out in paint, the same date as the S M R lintel above, was impossible to read with certainty. The date was clear, but the initials, which might be I R S A, were not.

See Drawing 26.

LA HAUTEUR
Faldouet (Mt.) (D. de Quetteville on Godfray.)

On the arch over the stable is E M L 1859, suggesting Mallet, but built into an outhouse is a window lintel with I L G 1662. In the fireplace of the main room another lintel is incorporated, and 1847 has been cut in the stone surround. This could be the date of the present house.

HEMERY ROW
La Motte Street (H).

This was a row of seven houses, all of which were in granite of a particularly pleasing warm brown colour. Only five now remain, Nos. 37, 39, 41, 43 and 45; No. 47 became part of a garage, and some of the walls of No. 49 survive. No. 45 was stripped of its plaster in the 1920s, an immense improvement. They were built by Jacques Hemery (d. 1831), and six of them were ceded to six of his seven nieces, the daughters of Clement Hemery, who each paid him £40 a year rent during his lifetime. His seventh niece, Anne, had married Jean Robin and gone to live in Ireland, and so was perhaps thought to be in no need of a house in Jersey. The last of the houses went to a nephew. Stead, in 1809, referred to them as "excellent houses". The handsome fanlights, some now destroyed, were notable examples of early 19th-century detailing.

See Drawing 34.
   Plate Ib.

L'HERMITAGE
Rue du Pont (J). (J. Robinson on Godfray.)

Here, as so often happens, the earlier house has become a stable building. It was single-storeyed, with one upper window which fitted under the curve of the thatch. The front door has become a window, and two windows are now doors. The building faces west and its south gable retains the uprights of a fireplace, chamfered on both sides.

The present dwelling house has a stone over the front door with P L C N♡ ♡M D M R 1813. In the attic many pottery vessels were found, as well as some documents belonging to a sea captain named de Gruchy. There is one most interesting item here, seen nowhere else; the pig sties are continuous with the bakehouse, so that the end sty was warmed by the bread oven, and there is a peephole through the wall enabling the farmer to watch his farrowing sow and to be ready to help her.

HÉRUPE
Near St. Cyr (J). (P. de Gruchy on Godfray.)

A second farm so named, west of the main Hérupe Farm, has two stones with 17 P G C R H 99, and P G C ♡ ♡ R H M 1807.

HIGHCLIFF
Bonne Nuit Hill (J). (J. Le Brun on Godfray.)

The main house here is a fine example of Jersey Georgian, with a good classical porch, and built of warm rosy granite.

In the farmyard is the older house, facing west. The main door and some windows are chamfered, and the central first-floor window has been enlarged into a loading bay. The left-hand ground floor room, with a beaten clay floor, has a nice fireplace with simply-carved corbels, and a shallow oven in the fireback. The front façade has sash windows, but of an early type, while the back façade has casements, one with elaborate leaded glazing. Several windows have bar holes in the side jambs, showing that the casements were in themselves an innovation when inserted.

There is no evidence of a tourelle; indeed there is scarcely room for one as the house is built close into a high bank. There is a stone dated 1661 in the back elevation with initials hard to decipher, but which might be I E G or I E C. The upper floor is level with the road on the south, and a now blocked door has a lintel with 17 H C I E 09, well carved in raised letters. No marriage can be found in the St. John registers to fit this inscription, but a Helier Chevalier and Jeanne Esnouf had three children baptised between 1716-1722. The only son, Charles Samuel (an early instance of two Christian names being given) was born in 1718. The registers give

67

leaded casement in old house at Highcliff, (J).

three Jean Esnoufs dying in 1667 and two in 1669, any one of whom could have been the father of Jeanne. This identification is strengthened by the discovery that the inscription on a fireplace lintel on the next property to the west, Hautmont, represents Thomas Chevalier and his wife Esther Vallepy (*sic*) married in 1656. On the farm buildings is a stone with J L B 1883, for Le Brun.

There are signs that there was a round arch at the roadside entrance, and fragments of one can be seen built into the later structures. The pig sties, now demolished, were of the type with a cement-hipped roof, and domed ceiling in each sty. An amusing scrap of information is the signature, on the plaster in the ground floor room, of John Luce, Carpenter 1877.

Is is satisfying to know that the old house is being saved and restored, as over the years it has become somewhat ruinous and one feared for its survival. It is to be called La Maison du Becquet.

See Drawings 27, 67.
Plates XIVb, XXIIa.

HIGHFIELD

Trinity Main Road. (D. Le Boutillier on Godfray.)

Were it not for the gable stone dated 1677 on the roadside, one would not expect to find traces of an old house here, as the buildings were cement rendered, probably in 1901, as a copy of the *Evening Post* of that year was found. Within, spanning the west ground floor room, there is a beam which forks into the north wall. There are several niches, some blocked windows, and one unexplained aperture, splayed as for a window but terminating in a blocking stone no larger than a fist. This may be one of the few examples of an opening in the kitchen wall through which waste water and scraps could be thrown out to the farmyard.

HIGHLAND

Grande Route de St. Laurent. (J. Dallain on Godfray.)

There is a complex of interesting houses here, four bearing the name Highland in some form, and three being marked with the name Dallain on Godfray. The main house in this group is most imposing and must have been built by a master mason, perhaps that maître charpentier Amice Norman who built the prison in 1811. Few other houses in the Island show such precision of stonework, and sturdy rusticated quoins. There is a string course in granite, as at La Hougue in St. Peter (1822) which is not common in local houses. The dower wing to the east is probably an addition, and the third storey may be also. If this is indeed an addition, a second string course was inserted, but the quoins were set flush with the façade, whereas the main section has them standing proud.

The porch is sumptuous, with an elaborate fanlight, repeated over the back door, and fluted columns with Corinthian capitals; but an unexpected economy was effected by omitting the decoration at the back of the capitals, where the unexpected economy was effected by omitting the unobservant visitor. The windows on the north elevation and one on the south are Gothic, with interlaced tracery in the sashes, as in one north window at Les Nièmes, St. Peter (1829). The gutter is also granite, rare, but not unknown.

The stairs are most elegant, rising the full three storeys to a circular ceiling, which makes it less likely that the upper level was added later. The balusters are lightly turned, and the sides of the treads have the familiar decorated mahogany appliqué. All the doors in the first two storeys are mahogany with six panels, but it is surprising that in a house of such opulence all the architrave bosses on the ground floor are plain, and but lightly decorated on the first floor. All the ceilings have decorated cornices, in some cases interrupted by subsequent alterations to rooms. A cellar extends under the whole site.

The main reception room used to be divided in two by large mahogany doors; but the extraordinary thing about them, not seen anywhere else, is that instead of swinging open as doors normally do they were lifted by a system of weights and chains, like a sash window, into

porch at Highlands, (L).

with detail of Corinthian capital.

68

an enclosed section between two bedrooms above. This rather lethal arrangement has been removed. In referring to this house, Stead said: "Mr. Dallain, a gentleman distinguished for mechanical ingenuity", and he may well have had in mind the unquestionably ingenious dividing doors.

There have been three Dallain Constables of St. Lawrence: from 1773 to 1786, Gidéon, who married Catherine Le Montais; from 1813 to 1816, Gidéon (1767-1847), who married Esther Simonet; and from 1841 to 1847, Jean (1807-1853), who died unmarried. The first of these Gidéons, who died in 1820, seems the most likely to have been the builder of this house, but one cannot guess what was the source of his prosperity.

See Drawing 68.

HIGHLAND COTTAGE
(J. Dallain on Godfray.)

The lintel has PDL MBQ1714, with the 4 reversed, which probably stands for Pierre Dallain (d. 1717), a Huguenot refugee, and his wife's name is likely to have been Marie Bosquet. They may have been married before coming to the Island, as the marriage cannot be found in the register.

The façade is contemporary with the lintel, though the windows have been enlarged. The stairs, which have no balusters, are very simple. The main room has fine dado panelling which can scarcely be as early as 1714, particularly in the country, and one may surmise that it was part of improvements undertaken in 1750 or later, after the family had become established and made some money. A subsequent generation, even more prosperous, foresook the charming old house and built the far larger one alongside it. Richmond shows a group of small buildings around the cottage, and one to the north is known to have been a blacksmith's forge.

HIGHLAND FARM
(A. Dallain on Godfray.)

On the front façade the main door is chamfered, as are some window surrounds, but those on the right of the entrance are original and those on the left more recent copies. Perhaps those on the left were considered too small, in an unsymmetrical façade, and invited alteration when some modernisation was taking place.

The position of the gable stones on the north shows that the roof has been raised. The fireplaces are simple, with wooden lintels, and in a recess in one of them were found a glass bottle, part of a cowhorn, and a stocking which must have been knitted locally; though rather tattered, it showed very fine stitching and well-made clocks in cinnamon brown wool. These objects were almost certainly concerned with witchcraft, cf. La Rigondaine.

HIGHLAND FARM
(L). (J. Langlois on Godfray.)

Situated off Mont Misère, and previously called Les Fontaines, this is another house with the name of Highland Farm. It is very secluded, with a lovely outlook to the south. The building itself is not spectacular and is probably early 18th century. The windows are mostly six-piece, nearly square, and have not been enlarged; the sashes are very old, and quite possibly original.

No. 16 HILL STREET (H).

On the façade is a small stone, seldom noticed, with I P 1748. This represents Jean Perrochon, who bought the land from Moyse Corbet in 1746, and evidently built his house immediately. In 1820 Elizabeth Perrochon, daughter of Jean, offered for sale a house and garden near La Pompe des Trois Pigeons, then occupied by a Mrs. Le Sueur, who kept a hotel or tavern. It is therefore very likely that No. 16 was the Hôtel des Trois Pigeons which gave its name to what later became Hill Street. No. 14 was owned by Jean Le Masurier; No. 18 was occupied by Nicholas Bott, whose descendants now live in New Zealand.

The interior of No. 16 has distinction. The stairs are elegant, with the flat curving balusters seen in a very few other instances. Ceiling cornices are decorated, and fine overmantels and panelling are in the traditional mid-18th-century style. Some of the contemporary doors have been encased under flush panels, but are safe within.

This is a good example of a town house of the period, as perhaps was the shop in Queen Street, lately Frederick Baker's and now totally demolished, which had a very similar stone with I H 1751.

See Aveux du Fief de la Fosse 1838–1849, in Library of la Société Jersiaise.
　　Drawings 28, 45.

THE HOLLIES

High Street, St. Aubin (B).

There is a gable stone dated 1683, but one dare not assign so early a date to the windows, old and venerable as they are, as that would be before the time of William III, who introduced sash windows to Hampton Court. Windows of this type, with the upper sash fixed and the top row of lights swinging forward to open, can be seen at Sausmarez Manor (1704) in Guernsey, and a few other instances. These examples could certainly date to well before 1750, and all the doors in the house could be of the same period, as well as the delightful circular staircase with its urn balusters, continuing up to the second storey.

The façade of the upper storey has been re-faced at some time, doubtless when the thatched roof was replaced and a less acute roof angle was needful. There is a cellar, as indeed there is in most houses in St. Aubin, to serve the needs of its busy and enterprising merchants.

See Drawing 43.
Plate XIc.

HOLLY BANK

La Ville Brée, Rozel (Mt). (J. Bellot on Godfray.)

Instead of adding rooms to the north, as is most usual, the owners of this property built on to the east, probably in 1715, the date of a very interesting and indeed unique stone representing Philippe Fauvel and Elizabeth Bandinel, and containing an early example of the heart motif.

The older, western, portion of the house has one straight topped door with chamfers and four chamfered windows, to which a fifth might be added, but it is not clearly visible as fillets of cement surround the sashes. In the west gable wall, high up, is a very small and extremely old window with minuscule panes of glass, six across and five vertically. The join between the 17th- and 18th-century houses is masked by creepers, but must be beneath the central chimney. One should not be misled by the very fine 17th-century fireplace in the eastern ground floor room, as this was incorporated recently from an unknown provenance.

There is a separate bakehouse. The bread oven, which has no flue of its own, is within the fireback instead of to one side, as is the common practice. The hearth is made of brick and is probably not very old, but the central oven door recalls one at La Hougue Boëte, which appears to be about 1680. The long-handled implements for shovelling ash, and inserting and extracting the loaves, have survived on the traditional rack in the roof. This hearth is similar to that at The Oaks, St. Peter, q.v.

The surrounding grounds are undulating, beautifully laid out, and fall to a small valley which leads down to Rozel.

See Drawing 27.

HOMESTEAD

Main Road (G). (C. Bertram on Godfray.)

There are three dated stones here: E B T $\heartsuit$ S E T 1758, for Elie Bertram (1698–1760) and Susanne Estur, who married in 1722; he was Constable of Grouville 1741–1760: 18 E B $\heartsuit$ A M 12, for Elie Bertram (1759–1817) and Ann Mourant; he was Constable of Grouville 1795–1798, 1805–1808 and 1817: C B $\heartsuit$ $\heartsuit$ F D, for Charles Bertram, son of the above, who married Frances Dalton; he was Constable 1823 and Jurat 1839–1862. Notes in the possession of the present owner suggest that a Philippe Bertram fs. Elie inherited the property in 1761. It is probable that the house was built in or about 1758, as suggested by the earliest of the stones, although it has been much altered over the years, and the gable must be quite recent. An arch on the roadside has 1852 in raised letters, but the arch itself appears to be a genuine 17th-century example.

HOMESTILL
Mont au Jubilee (P). (J. de Carteret on Godfray.)

Over the front door is 17 P A M S M 21. There is a small cross between the A and the M, and the last figure is doubtful. In the corner of the garden is a small, simple and private douet à laver.

LA HOUGUE
St. Ouen's Road (P). (P. Le Feuvre on Godfray.)

A stone on the east side of the house bears P L F 1822, for Philippe Le Feuvre, who built it. In 1840 he and his wife Ann Le Bas made a partage, dividing their property between their two sons, Philippe, the elder, inheriting La Hougue, and George William, the younger, Les Nièmes (q.v.). Les Nièmes came through Ann Le Bas, and was rebuilt by her and her husband. In the partage La Hougue is described as "la chefve maison de sondit père, communement appellée La Hougue, située en la paroisse de St. Pierre, avec les offices, tour d'échelle, les cours, le hogard, étangs, lavoir, chasses, issue et avenues . . .". The elder son also chose as part of his share the following land: Les Neufs Vergées; part of le Clos de Travers (P.129); le Clos ès Boeufs (P. 132a); le Pré de Jacques (P. 112a); le Clos de Hecq (P. 133); le jardin de devant ladite maison; le Clos du Télégraphe (P.132); le Clos du Sud; le Jardin de la Chasse; les prés de devant ou de Guillaume Robin (P. 110); le Clos de Jacques (P.128); le Clos de Devant; le Clos de Surelle nord et sud (P. 137); le Côtil du Mont Huelin; les Vingt Livres du sud (O.1929); land at Val de la Mare, and some land which Ann's father Nicolas Le Bas had bought from Pierre Alexandre. The lavoir mentioned almost certainly disappeared when the Germans made a cutting where the stream runs down to Val de la Mare.

The field called le Clos du Télégraphe does not of course refer to modern telegraphy, not yet invented, but to some kind of signalling. We know that in 1808 a Major Charles Le Hardy was awarded a silver medal by the Royal Society of Arts for his invention of a telegraph and read the Society a paper on the subject in that year, and an article on signals in the *Mariner's Mirror* mentions that in August 1809 "the stations in the Channel islands were equipped with semaphore apparatus imagined and supplied by Mr. Mulgrave, a commercial gentleman of ingenious ability". Mr. Mulgrave unfortunately found himself in the debtors' prison in 1808, and wrote a report on the conditions there which was partly instrumental in bringing about the replacement of the old prison in Charing Cross by the fine building, now in its turn vacated, in Newgate Street.

An older house stood on the site of La Hougue, and was inherited by Philippe de Carteret, first Governor of New Jersey, who by his will of 1682 left all his property in the Island to his mother, Rachel La Cloche, wife of Helier de Carteret, or, if she predeceased him, to his brothers and sisters, of whom there were eight. An inventory of the effects of Rachel, then a widow, dated 1686, shows a well-appointed house, and the list includes jewels, silver, pewter, linen, crops, livestock and a quantity of combed wool.

In the 18th century La Hougue belonged to the Fiot family. Daniel Messervy tells us that in 1769 Colonel Bentinck held a review of the North West Militia at Crabé (*sic*), after which he and some other officers dined with "Captain Nics. Fiot à la Haughe". An Appairiement of the Fief de Vingt Livres of about 1775 gives the Chef de Charette No. 18 as "Nicholas Fiot . . . sa maison communément appellée La Hougue". Some but not all of the field names are the same as in the 1840 partage. Nicolas had in 1758 married Elizabeth, daughter of Jean de Carteret, a distant relative of the Philippe of New Jersey. In 1793 Jean Fiot fs. Nicolas sold the house and some land to Mdlle. Margaret Le Couteur, with the Fief de la Hougue d'Hirvault. The house was then called La Maison de la Hougue, and the lavoir was mentioned.

It is interesting to compare the two houses which Philippe Le Feuvre built, La Hougue in 1822 and Les Nièmes in 1829. The earlier is the typical five-bay vernacular house with exposed quoins, a stucco façade flush with the granite, and a granite string course. The porch is quite elaborate, with fluted columns, decorated with circular paterae (as in the cornice in the Temple at Victoria College), Swanage stone steps and grey and white marble paving. There are small single-storey wings, with side louvres for ventilation of their roof space, and traditional gable stones at the corners. Were these two dower wings provided for two grandmothers?

Much as the ground plans and the exteriors of the two houses differ, the interior details are very similar. At La Hougue stairs have a slightly flattened mahogany handrail, appliqué decoration, and a pretty semi-circular "scoop" at the foot of the stairs, fully panelled. Most of the architrave bosses are formalised roses. Some of the panelling on doors and shutters is fielded, and some astragal. In the kitchen and in one bedroom are curious hybrid doors with four panels which are both fielded and reeded, a rare combination. The principal bedroom was designed as a drawing room, which is not uncommon, and it has a handsome ceiling rose and decorated cornice. The back door has an elaborate fanlight, and above a door on the landing of the stairs is a carving, presumably in granite, but now whitewashed, of a bull's head or bucranium. There are the traditional round-topped niches on the stairs. The back stairs, leading to the attic rooms are simple with stick balusters and square newels. The kitchen has a curious, and unexplained, small cupboard at a very high level, similar to one seen at Mainland (L).

The fine range of outbuildings has an unusual feature, in apertures closed with vertical slats spaced apart, to give ventilation to a hay loft.

slatted aperture for ventilating hay-loft, at La Hougue, (P).

69

See Payne's *Armorial*, p. 92.
    Balleine, *Biographical Dictionary*, p. 177.
    Old Jersey Houses, Vol. I, p. 166.
    B.S.J. 1893, p. 236; 1972, p. 363.
    Fief de Vingt Livres; La Hague MSS., in Library of La Société Jersiaise.
    Collas family MSS., No. 140, of 1793.
    Drawing 69.
    Plate, Colour I a.

LA HOUGUE
Near La Hougue Bie (S). (J. Amy on Godfray.)

The ownership shown on Godfray's map is supported by a stone in an outhouse to the east with I A M ♡ ♡ M P 1798 in raised lettering, and a doorstep has the same initials with the date 1803. On the house is a stone, not clear to read, with what appears to be E I I V 1742. A cottage at the side, with small upper windows now blocked, has a gable stone with the date 1757, which reappears on a gatepost.

LA HOUGUE BOËTE
Le Neuf Chemin (J). (E. G. Le Couteur on Godfray.)

Architecturally one of the most impressive houses in the Island, La Hougue Boëte remains a puzzle. Which of its many owners transformed a traditional 17th-century vernacular building into the grand 18th-century façade we now see and, more important, when?

There are affinities with Roger Morris's Lydiard Tregoze (1743), and Sanderson Millar's Hagley Hall (1753), though it is not suggested that either of these architects designed Le Hougue Boëte. The engraving in Payne's *Armorial* (1860) shows the flanking and projecting wings which can still be remembered; and another engraving shows a pillared porch at the front door level. But what is one to make of Tobias Young's painting (1815) showing three storeys under a pediment supported by four classical pillars? Were the painting not entitled "St. John's Manor", there would have been no temptation to regard it as a picture of La Hougue Boëte, nor of La Grande Maison de St. Jean, with which the former is sometimes confused. This is doubly disappointing, as one has accepted Young's work as faithful contemporary evidence. One notable expert has expressed the opinion that the house showed more French than English influence. Payne describes it as "built in the Italian style". Stead (1809) remarks on "the size of the mansion and offices, and the excellence and beauty of the ground and gardens".

The possible date of rebuilding may perhaps be narrowed down. It must have been before Stead's appraisal of 1809, and Tobias Young's fantasy of 1815, and may have been during the lifetime of Edouard Le Maistre, who married firstly Florence Patriarche and secondly Elizabeth Jacobson, and became Seigneur in 1768 on the death of his grandmother Ann, née de Carteret. On his death in 1826 the property was inherited by his great-grandson Edward George Le Couteur who, with his daughter Pauline Townsend née Le Couteur sold it in 1874 to Robert Venables. The auctioneer conducting the sale described the property in a press advertisement as "The Blenheim of the Channel Islands", and went on to state that the grounds contained a croquet lawn, a large cricket field, an archery ground, a rifle target with 350 yard range, a gravel pit on the estate and three pews in St. John's Church. The property was sold in 1911 by G. L. Venables to A. S. Raworth.

See *A Picture of Jersey*, J. Stead, p. 195.
Old Jersey Houses, Vol. I, p. 166.
Plate XXIIb and c.

HOUGUEMONT
Faldouet (Mt). (P. Mallet on Godfray.)

The fine 17th-century façade has a contemporary chimney at the east end and a far later one at the west gable. This latter is unique, for it appears to have a family tree inscribed upon it with only one date, 1781. The most diligent research has failed to read its message, except that it is a pedigree of a branch of the Mallet family, but they are too numerous in the eastern parishes for it to be possible to equate any of them with the initials on the chimney. In his *Armorial* Payne gives a Jean Mallet fs. James fs. Henry, of whom he says: "This branch is represented by Philippe Mallet of Faldouet". The house was still thatched in 1900.

See Plate XXIId.

HUE STREET
St. Helier

In the course of the last few years most of Hue Street and Old Street (La Rue de Hue et Le Vieux Chemin) have been demolished. There are two sides to this coin. The area had become very run-down; some properties were sub-standard, and in the interests of slum clearance had to go. On the other hand, some were very fine mid-18th-century houses, with dated stones, pantile roofs, granite chimneys and good interior woodwork; and the district could have been saved, upgraded and its historical atmosphere preserved, to the benefit of the whole town and Island.

"A quelqu'un, malheur est bon." Some of the demolition sites recently excavated have yielded evidence of domestic occupation centuries earlier than was ever suspected. At Nos. 13 and 13a Old Street foundations of a 13th-century house, probably a simple long-house, were found, built of water-worn Fort Regent granite. This date was later confirmed by the discovery of two much damaged coins, one of *c.* 1180 and one of *c.* 1250. A gulley caused by dripping from a thatched roof ran along the perimeter. The pottery fragments, the earliest dateable mediaeval material found in Jersey, originated from Beauvais and Rouen.

HUE STREET, St.Helier, west side, prior to demolition, 1974:
sketched from photographs by the Author and the Jersey Evening Post.

70

Philip / Shoosmith
n   Le Sueur Le 23° 76 "
                1748

Douard Le Sueur
Philippe Deslandes
                1749

Builders' signatures on a beam at 19. Hue Street, St.Helier, (now demolished).

71

It is not possible, nor necessary, to describe all the houses which have now vanished from Hue Street and Old Street, the two streets converging at the northern end, but some of them deserve an epitaph. The first Post Office was established in the house of Charles William Le Geyt in 1794; Hue Street came to be called La Rue de la Poste, though the Le Geyt house has yet to be identified with certainty. At No. 15 there was a most interesting stone with the initials of Pierre Luce and Sara Giffard, preceded by N D S X, presumably a Nicolas de Ste. Croix, and though no reason has been found for the juxtaposition, he could have been the grandfather or godfather of either of the married pair, and have given their house to them. The initials are followed by the cryptic message Ms 30, followed by a lozenge and the date 1739, which might mean the 30th of March 1739.

house and shop-front, now demolished, 21. Hue St. St. Helier.

72

Nos. 17 and 19 were rather similar, and both had tiled roofs and granite chimneys, with small dormers. The interior woodwork in doors, stairs and cupboards was all of good quality. The stairs in No. 19 were most interesting, but unfortunately all efforts to save them during demolition failed. They were in the form of a circular wooden staircase, a transition perhaps between the old stone tourelle and later wooden styles, and constructed to use as little space as possible. On a beam in the house three men, David Le Sueur, Shoosmith and Philippe Deslandes, the builders perhaps, wrote their names and the date 23rd September 1748, which must surely be the date of the house. It was purchased in 1919 by the late Mr. F. H. Foot, from Miss Victoria Deslandes Le Maistre. The Le Sueur family was connected with Hue Street until recent times. No. 6, on the opposite side of the road had a date stone with D L S 1767. Was he the David who worked in the construction of No. 19, and prospered and built himself a fine granite house? No. 19 had fine roof timbers throughout, and curious small windows to light the stairs from the attic bedrooms, an arrangement seen only here and at La Hougue in St. Peter. There is a tradition that this house once belonged to a doctor, and although this may be quite a modern memory of a doctor in recent times, it is not impossible that he was Dr. Philippé Chouêt de Vaumorel (1726–1789), the Jersey-born son of a French refugee. He is known to have lived in a large house in Hue Street, with enclosed courtyards and stables and a walled garden. The Richmond map shows houses on both sides of Hue Street, but none on the east of Old Street, as the Hue Street gardens extended backwards to it.

Some of the 19th-century shop fronts were delightful. No. 21 had an exceptionally fine front door, and No. 15 an elegant Ionic pillar beside the shop window.

See B.S.J. 1971, p. 226; 1974, p. 281.
   Newspaper advertisements.
   De Vaumorel family records.
   Drawings 28, 29, 42, 45, 46, 70, 71, 72.
   Plate XIb, XXIIIb, c, d,

LE HUREL
Queen's Road, St. Helier.

This small house, lately demolished, had two points of interest; a stone dated 1663, with a carved shield but no initials; and in the stable there was a bone set in the wall, about six feet above ground level, presumably used as a peg for hanging ropes or harness.

PLATE XXIII

a. Façade in Mulcaster St (H) shortly before demolition

b. Hue Street (H), detail in an attic

c. Detail in a drawing room

d. Street frontage during demolition

PLATE XXIV

Mainland (L)

a. Façade

b. Lantern over stairs

c. Pilaster at top of stairs

d. A ceiling rose, *c* 1830

LA HURETTE
Rue de la Bergerie (T). (P. Deslandes on Godfray.)

A fireplace 6ft. 8in. wide with decorated corbels has been uncovered, and is clearly older than the stone over the front door, which has 17 I G F E G F 30, for Jean Godfray fs. Thomas who married Elizabeth Godfray fille Jean in 1717. Another stone on an outhouse has 17 I L M 19.

LES IFS
Trinity Main Road (T). (J. Cabot on Godfray.)

Not long ago this house was completely demolished and rebuilt with the same stone, and some details of its previous appearance may be of interest.

Long before the ownership shown on its date stone, 1746, it was a Le Breton property, passing to Nicolas du Feu fs. Richard on his marriage with Marie Le Breton in 1709. There was a lovely round arch with a cross on the left chamfer stop, and on the right what appeared to be the initials P C B faintly scratched, from some Cabot owner. All windows in the façade had been enlarged, those on the ground floor by dropping the sills, and those on the first floor by raising the lintels. There was only one accolade lintel. Over the front door arch was a curious protuberance, not seen elsewhere, about 4in. in diameter and projecting 5in., possibly a peg for hanging a lamp. The window above the arch had a projecting sill. The beam in the main room forked where it entered the back wall, and some Cabot owner had tested out his branding iron by putting his initials upon it.

On the north elevation was the inscription 17 R D F 35, and on the south a stone with complex carvings, as illustrated, represting Richard du Feu who married Elizabeth Gruchy in 1737. On the wing to the east was another with I C B E D F 1789, suggesting that the property passed by marriage from du Feu to Cabot. On the roadside was a gatepost with I F C B ♡♡ M A J N 1852, for Jean François Cabot and Marie Ann Journeau.

See *Old Jersey Houses,* Vol. I, p. 169.
B.S.J. 1906, p. 36.
Drawing 28.

IVYSTONE FARM
Samarès Lane (C). (J. Le Jeune on Godfray.)

This farm stands in an interesting area. The "ivy stone" is the menhir named La Dame Blanche, and field No. C.118 is Le Clos de la Chapelle, referring to a mediaeval chapel dedicated to St. John the Evangelist. This chapel has disappeared, but in the grounds of the farm there are fragments of deeply moulded stone, and three stones in a doorway on the north have heavier mouldings than usual, and the owner thinks, probably quite correctly, that they are ecclesiastical. They could have come from this chapel.

The house is in three units, the central block being the oldest. On the north the five-sash windows are of a pattern older than the date stone inscribed I L I 1820, for Le Jeune. There is a fine door measuring 6ft. 1in. by 3ft. 4½in., with nine panels, long drop hinges and a large lock.

See Drawing 73.

LES JARDINS
La Verte Rue (My). (J. Trachy on Godfray.)

Three sets of initials here testify to Trachy ownership for over a century. On a barn is P T C I C B 1748; on the house is P T C M H Q 1777, for Philippe Trachy and Marie Le Hucquet; and on another barn is 18 I T C ♡♡ I R R 34, for Jean Trachy who married Jean Romeril in 1807.

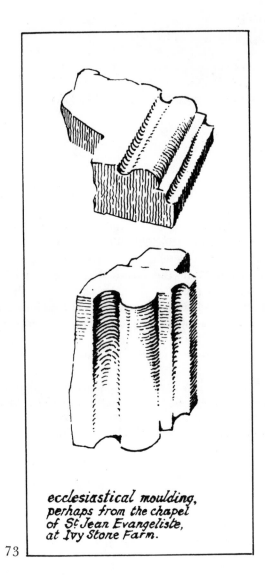

ecclesiastical moulding,
perhaps from the chapel
of St Jean Evangeliste,
at Ivy Stone Farm.

73

There is a small square sundial, in sandstone, on the western chimney, the date of which cannot be read with certainty, but it might be 1808.

See B.S.J. 1974, p. 272.

KING'S FARM
Rue du Bocage (B). (J. Le Cras on Godfray.)

There is a gable stone dated 1666 with initials which are hard to decipher, but might be I L S. In 1799 the occupant was a Mrs. Leigh, and years later, on a plan of the Belle Vue land, field No. B.807 is called "Mrs. Leigh's field". The house has the standard façade of the period, with no particular distinguishing details, but a very good example of the local style. Its name must refer to the fact that it is on the Royal Fief, and it may well have been the home of one of the feudal officers of that fief.

KINGSTEAD
Mont les Vaux (B).

This charming little 17th-century cottage has has recently been renovated and the granite exposed, which is a great improvement. A new stone bearing the date 1577 has been inserted.

LES LANDES FARM
Rue des Landes (O). (P. Le Gresley on Godfray.)

From the outside none could guess what an interesting property this would prove to be. On a door at the east end, clearly an addition, is a stone with 17 P L C M ♡ E G B I L C M 16, presumably parents and their son, in large raised but not very clear letters. The M may be intended to be N, because of long-standing Le Cornu ownership in the district. On the ground floor west is a 17th-century fireplace with moulded unchamfered corbels, and chamfer stops top and bottom of the uprights; the bottom stops are good stylised motifs, though that on the right appears to have been broken. Above this on the first floor is a plainer fireplace, the hood of which appears in the attic. A three-foot interior wall suggests that all the building east of it is a later addition, perhaps made in 1716, to a very small house with interior measurement of only 25 feet. In the attic the slope of the gable for thatch can be clearly seen and the earlier roof timbers are still there. In what would have been the exterior east wall there are some projecting stones, in a curve. Are they a witches' staircase? The northern additions to the house and the stairs are about 1850 in date.

LANDSDOWN
Millbrook (L). (F. de Carteret on Godfray.)

It is believed that a previous house on this site was built in 1704 by a privateer named William Snow, who put up a stone with W.S. and M.M., the initials of himself and his wife Marie Mauger.

(His father's initials appear at Albany House, q.v.) This house was demolished, and another built on or near the site by Mr. Jean Laurens, somewhere around 1880. He died in 1913 and his widow, Laura Elizabeth Clement, sold it to G. A. Romeril, and his widow in turn sold it to Sir Jesse Boot in 1924. It is now called Springland, and has been considerably altered. It was the model for La Pompe, St. Mary, as we have seen in chapter ten. In 1861 Colonel Peter Hemery, Q.A.D.C., and President of the R.J.A. and H.S. lived there; he was the ancestor of David Hemery, the Olympic runner.

See *Jersey in the 18th and 19th centuries*, A. C. Saunders, p. 150.

L'AUGÉE
Mont à l'Abbé (H). (T. Laugée on Godfray.)

There are gateposts at the end of a short drive, that on the right being a plain granite block; that on the left is broken, but is chamfered, and incised with the date 1686 in figures 2¼in. high and 1in. wide, the 86 being below the 16. It is likely that this is one of a pair of porch pillars (cf. Hamptonne (L), and Augrès Farm (T)), and that the twin would have carried initials. The house has two chamfered windows, though with cement lintels, and all windows on the first floor have been enlarged. Inside a modern porch is a round arch, cement covered. The shape is not quite of the regular pattern, yet the evidence quoted above makes a rounded entrance way highly probable. On an addition to the west is an undated stone inscribed T P N ♡ M L G.

In 1755 Josué Blampied fs. Nicolas sold to Rachel, procuratrice of Edouard Laugé, a house on the Fief of Mélèches in St. Helier, and it seems more than likely that this is it.

LAUREL LANDS FARM
Maufant (S). (Ahier or Falle on Godfray.)

At the entrance stands a gatepost with the roughly incised inscription I B M 1790 (or possibly 1750).

The main house has been much altered. All windows, which originally had eight-piece surrounds, have been enlarged above, below and laterally. The roof pitch was changed when thatch was replaced by slate, and small brick chimneys were erected. There have also been alterations inside, though the main beams survive. The most remarkable feature is the staircase, which is a circular wooden flight within a stone tourelle, which has its customary small windows. The treads are not boxed in, as sometimes occurs, as the space beneath them, often used as a larder, shows that the treads are wood on the underside also. This must be a transition in construction, devised by someone who wanted the warmer and more convenient steps, but clung to the old tourelle design.

At right-angles is a single-storeyed building, originally thatched, but now tiled, which contained the boulangerie; the bread oven has been retained and its iron door, much encrusted by years of use, has embossed upon it, "G. Le Feuvre, Ironfounder, 1861, Jersey"; the date is not clear and could be read as 1801. Doors from West's Cinema in town, built in the 1920s and now demolished, have been incorporated in the façade of the wing.

The title Laurel Lands must testify to political adherence to the then Liberal party by the owner who chose the name.

LEDA HOUSE
Rue de la Fontaine St. Martin (L). (T. Morel on Godfray.)

The Richmond map shows no building here at all, and this must be one of the rare errors in this otherwise excellent survey.

The modern house has a good marriage stone with 18 T M R ♡ ♡ A M R 41, for Thomas Morel and Ann Mourant. A portrait of this Thomas Morel, painted in Italy, hangs in the house, and shows him holding an envelope addressed to Dlle. Mourant, St. Laurens, Jersey, that is his fiancée. The owners also have a picture of his ship the *Leda,* after which he named his house; it is unsigned, but is a fine painting showing the vessel in full sail in a choppy green sea with the Cliffs of Dover behind. They also have a silver watch, thought to be about 1770 in date, which belonged to him and perhaps to his father before him. Some details of the building of Leda House have been preserved and are mentioned in the chapter on building.

Behind this 1841 house there is a far older structure. Its windows have been enlarged, though happily with granite, and there are simple fireplaces on the ground floor, one of which has a bread oven beside it, with a slightly concave fireback, as noticed at Les Ifs (T). There are several niches in the house, one of them curved, and it may have been a paûte (hiding place). It seems possible that there was a tourelle here before the addition of the northern rooms. At the top of the wooden stairs there is a double door which led to the three bedrooms, now just one attic; this, though simple and rather rough, seems to be the lineal descendant of the double stone doorways found in stone tourelles.

A gable stone at the east end has T M R well carved, with a date above it, but only the figures 170 can now be read. There have been too many Thomas Morels for one to be dogmatic about the date, which could be between 1700 and 1709, the former on the whole being more likely.

THE OLD LIBRARY
Library Place, St. Helier.

We have here a building with claims to our attention on both historical and architectural grounds. It must be one of the very first buildings in Jersey to be made of brick. The cistern heads are embossed with P F 1736, for the Reverend Philippe Falle (1656–1742), who devoted much time and money to establishing a public library in the Island. He first made his offer of a library and books in 1729, but the project met with much difficulty, and building was not begun until 1737, being completed in 1742 shortly after the death of the benefactor. Another gift he made, outside Jersey, was of a valuable collection of music to Durham Cathedral Library in 1722.

The staircase is particularly fine with globe stops, urn balusters and elaborate newels, with the end baluster applied like an architrave. The main first floor room, which was the original library, is very fine, with typical Georgian woodwork, a high pediment and entablature over the fireplace. The window sashes with their thin glazing bars are not original, dating probably from 1830 when the attics became a third storey, to accommodate more books. Above this there are attics with dormers, invisible from the road. The ground floor was intended as living quarters for the librarian, who from 1791 to 1821 was the noted silversmith Jacques Quesnel.

The public library was moved to its present venerable and dignified quarters in 1886, constructed by Messrs. Ansell and Orange, architects, on the site of the Union Hotel. A fine marble tablet dated 1736, designed by Falle himself, used to grace the façade of the old library, and one can still see a difference in the colour of the bricks where it was. This was moved to the new building and can now be seen on the stairs leading to the present library.

A few years ago Falle's Library was in imminent danger of demolition, but the various pressure societies in the Island persuaded the States to retain it, as being something which had been given for the use of the public in perpetuity, as well as being a very early example of awareness of the need to make literature accessible to the community.

See *States of Jersey Libraries,* R. Falle.
      Biographical Dictionary, G. R. Balleine, p. 273.
      Old Channel Islands Silver, R. Mayne, p. 50.
      Actes des Etats, numerous references.
      B.S.J. 1885, p. 138; 1937, p. 259; 1969, p. 60.

LITTLE GROVE
Rue de Haut (L). (M. Wood on Godfray.)

Known originally as Myrtle Cottage, then as Petit Grove and now as Little Grove, to distinguish it from The Grove, a much larger house on Mont Cambrai above, this house was formerly owned by the de Gruchy family, who erected the series of traditional type arches along the Rue de Haut, bearing de Gruchy arms on the keystones. At least two stones, on the right of the easternmost pedestrian arch, are far older and must have come from an early building. The stone with 18 E H M A L R 06 represents Edouard Hamon (d. 1808) who married Ann Le Rossignol (d. 1813) in 1771, and it was no doubt he who built Myrtle Cottage at about the date of the stone. In 1890 the property was sold to Edward Voisin by William Lawrence de Gruchy, who at the same time sold The Grove to Francis Néel Gaudin, a doctor who ran it as an asylum.

LONDON HOUSE
Le Mourier (J). (F. Ahier on Godfray.)

This is a small house, having but two rooms, but it shows a well carved lintel stone with Ed A H 1842 E D V G, for Edouard Ahier of St. John who married Esther Dauvergne of St. Ouen in 1806. The valley stream which separates the parishes of St. John and St. Mary runs at the bottom of the garden, and behind the house rise steep and very early côtils. The steep track to the south of the house is named Petticoat Lane, perhaps to strengthen the illusion that this is the metropolis.

See Drawing 30.

LONGUEVILLE
Rue St. Thomas (S). (T. Anthoine on Godfray.)

One thought that there were no more round arches to be found but here, at "La Maison qui fut à Aaron Stocall", is one, and the keystone of another. The former, with a 4½in. concave chamfer, is but 35in. wide; it has been blocked and any chamfer stops which it may have had are invisible; it is probably not in its original position.

The present house is dated 1840, but the Anthoine family have been there since c. 1600. It had passed to them through the marriage of Estienne Anthoine to Elizabeth Stocall fille Aaron in 1617. The Stocalls were a wealthy family and Elizabeth's brothers may have inherited other property. Estienne is doubtless the E A T whose initials, with the date 1648, the year before he became Constable of St. Saviour, appear on a solitary keystone which was found at Rouen House, another Anthoine property. As the Anthoines were Royalists and the Stocalls Parliamentarians, Elizabeth, who married long before the Civil War, may have found herself in a difficult position.

The house contains a portrait of Falle the historian, as is mentioned in Payne's *Armorial*. An Anthoine ancestress was a Le Caumais, and field No. S.696 is le Clos de Caumais. A sword which belonged to Jean Anthoine in about 1780 was made by Jacques Quesnel, and it is rare to find a locally-made sword. What is now a garden pond used to be a fountain with an abreuvoir.

See *Old Channel Islands Silver*, R. Mayne, Pl. 57.
B.S.J. 1899, p. 258; 1905, p. 330.

LONGUEVILLE FARM
(S). Rue à Don. (P. Labey on Godfray.)

A stone in the façade of this handsome house has PLB EAT1776, representing Philippe Labey and Elizabeth Anthoine (1750-1825). This date is consistent with many internal features such as doors with fielded panels on both facets, panelling on the end wall of the north bedroom, early hinges, some internal partitions, and a beam measuring approximately 25ft., which appears to be all in one piece and is probably chestnut. The window recesses have the same panelling on their ceilings as on their shutters. The actual window sashes have been replaced about a century later, perhaps when the roof was changed from thatch to slate. The staircase is most interesting; the newels are flat-topped and square with corner beading and the handrail is flat-topped, but the balusters are straight and 2in. wide, a cross between the rare serpentine version and the usual stick type. At the intersection of each flight these wide balusters form a criss-cross pattern not seen elsewhere. One bedroom has an early hob grate with blue and white tiled surround, and one would have been tempted to think this was contemporary but for a large expanse of the same tiles in the south bedroom, combined with a much later mantlepiece.

The corbels of a stone fireplace in the drawing room were taken from one in the south dower wing. This extension was rebuilt in recent years, the best of the granite from the back and side being used to heighten its façade. It must have been but a two-roomed dower appartement with the main hearth on the first floor.

This is a satisfactory house having succeeded in becoming comfortable by modern standards with a minimum of alterations in its two centuries of life.

LOWLANDS
La Retraite (P). (J. Vincent on Godfray.)

Although this house has been heightened and much altered, the façade retains four finely cut accolade lintels, two of them initialled. Over the window left of the entrance is A L F 1675, possibly for Abraham Le Feuvre dit Filiastre who married Katherine Hullin (*sic*) in 1642. Over the front door the lintel bears the inscription A L F I I 1747 for Abraham Le Feuvre dit Filiastre who married Judith Jean in that year, and on the opposite side of the lane is a building, previously another house, with a lintel with A L F E L C 1782, for Abraham Le Feuvre dit Filiastre who married Elizabeth Le Cour in 1773. The property passed to the Vincent family through the marriage of Françoise Le Feuvre to Jean Vincent in 1756, who have their initials at Parklands q.v.

See Colour Plate Ib.

MAINLAND
Bel Royal (L). (M. Gibaut on Godfray.)

This house was representative of a number of grand houses built by the "Cod Barons" in the middle of the last century, and although totally divorced from any relation to vernacular architecture, such houses did constitute a part of the local scene. Mainland, however, no longer does so, having been demolished during the first half of 1975, and attracted a good deal of publicity in the process. A full range of photographs and notes were taken before the demolition hammers got to work, and a ground floor and first floor plans were drawn.

We had here a design in which everything was sacrificed to the grand entrance, the hall and the entertainment rooms. There were but two bedrooms apart from those on a third floor, invisible from ground level and approached by a side staircase. The front porch was stately, with Corinthian capitals to the pillars, and grey and white marble flooring. A central glass dome, some of the glass being red, lit the stairway, which swept up in an elegant curve, with six small arched niches and ten scagliola pilasters, with capitals of Tower of the Winds style: they were 13½ins. wide, each with five concave ribs. The balusters were heavy, but when in good order and painted in pastel shades the whole entrance must have been very impressive. A cloakroom on the ground floor and one halfway up the stairs probably provided such convenience as could be contrived in the country at that period. Most of the first floor on the south was given to a ballroom with parquet flooring, in elaborate patterns in shades of brown; there were double doors at its entrance, and a marble fireplace. The room to the north had a cupboard with shelves made of granite. Was this a

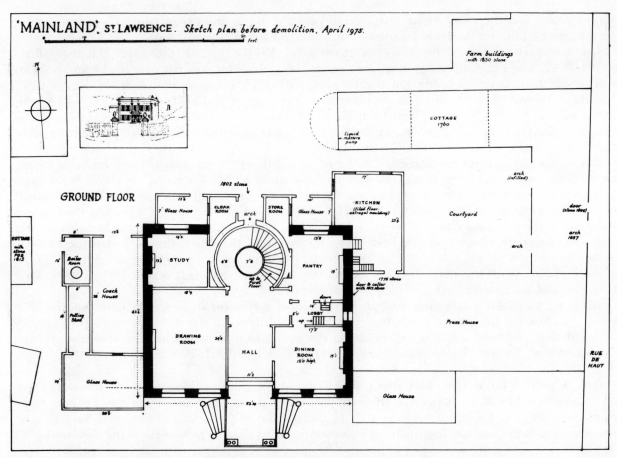

'MAINLAND'. ST LAWRENCE. *Sketch plan before demolition. April 1975.*

GROUND FLOOR

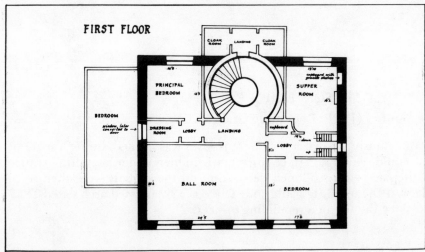

FIRST FLOOR

74

supper room, and the stone shelves installed to keep the drinks and sweets cool? The drawing room on the ground floor was scarcely less imposing, and again with parquet flooring.

On the back elevation there was a stone with P G B ♡ ♡ E D 1802, for Philippe Gibaut (1764-1842) and Elizabeth Dean, but one cannot think that this was the date of the house. There was a wealth of initialled stones on the property: P G B 1812 on one cottage; M G B A P 1762, for Moise Gibaut (1732-1796) and Ann Payn, on the cottage just behind. The latter had a gable stone with 1749, and the unexplained initials M L G. An arch on the Rue de Haut was dated 1857, with the Gibaut arms, a castle. In the press house leading to the cellar there was another stone dated 1812, and yet another with 1775 in the kitchen.

The wings to the main block seemed to be of very different dates, that to the west being clearly an addition, and indeed the bricks used in its construction were Copps, while those in the main house (most of which was in fact granite under its stucco rendering) were unnamed and obviously older. This western wing comprised a coach house with a service room, and a potting shed serving the conservatory to its south; above was a large room, perhaps a nursery, approached down some steps, as the coach house had not been given the full height of the main block. On the east was what must have been the kitchen, with two servants' bedrooms above it, and this seemed a rather older building than the main house, one of the bedrooms having a small 18th-century style fireplace, and the kitchen having 1815 style woodwork.

In origin Mainland was a large and prosperous farm, noted for its apple orchards, and in 1856 when the Société Centrale d'Agriculture de la Seine Inférieure de Rouen visited Jersey, they reported that the best managed orchards and the heaviest crops were found at Mainland, farmed by Mr. Moise Gibaut. Later Moise was almost ruined by the failure of the Mercantile Bank in 1873.

One is glad to know that some items were saved at the time of the great demolition. The two staircases, two entrance gateposts with their decorative pineapples, and some dated stones, have found new homes. The woodwork, superb in quality and in perfect condition, was hard to save, for who wants a door ten feet high? All the same, many Islanders witnessed the destruction of this landmark with sorrow.

See *Victorian Voices,* J. Stevens, p. 167.
    B.S.J. 1970, p. 164.
    Drawings 29, 74. Plate XXIV.

LA MAISON BRÛLÉE
Le Mourier (J). (P. Renouf on Godfray.)

It was only when this house (previously known as Prospect House) was burned during a spate of fires in empty buildings, that one could detect a 17th-century fabric hidden under late-19th-century stucco. The remains of a good fireplace with scalloped decoration on the corbels were then seen, and traces of a first-floor fireplace at the opposite gable end. There is a suppressed arch dated 1887 in the outbuildings, incorporated since the fire in a rebuilding project.

LA MAISON CARTERET
The Bulwarks, St. Aubin.

A yard in front of this house is shared by it, by another house on the roadside, and by a very small cottage alongside. High above the ground level is a surprisingly large and sheltered garden.

The main bedroom has good early 18th-century panelling and doors. The ground floor beams are very large, and the back door is of enormous thickness. Some of the woodwork on the ground floor appears to be about 1830 in date. There are some interesting little lights on the stairs and in one of the cupboards, with sliding panels which could close them off; they are rather similar to lights noticed in now demolished houses in Hue Street (q.v.).

This appears to be the house which belonged to Philippe de Carteret in 1785, and was sold by Amice de Carteret fs. Jean to Jean Le Bas fs. Philippe in 1813.

See B.S.J. 1949, p. 136.
St. Ouen's Manor document, 1813.
Plate XXV c.

LA MAISON CHARLES
Bel Royal. (A. de Ste. Croix on Godfray.)

It is much regretted that in Volume I the names of this house and of Le Bel Royal, which stands at right-angles to it, were mistakenly reversed.

A notebook compiled by Jean Maugier in about 1719, which embodies information of 1650 or earlier, mentions "la maison Charles le Roux", apparently near Bel Royal. This could be the origin of the name La Maison Charles.

Although this house does not exhibit definite 17th-century features, the thickness of the walls, the size of the windows, the height of the rooms, and the local design of staircase all point to a date late in that century. According to the Richmond map of 1795 it was virtually the only house in the vicinity, and before the sea wall was built it must have been almost on the beach at high tide.

See Drawing 45.

LA MAISON DU BUISSON
Rue de la Pièce Mauger, Maufant (S). (T. Binet on Godfray.)

·Traditionally this was the home of Mathieu de Gruchy (1761-1797), a Jersey boy who became a Roman Catholic priest and was shot at Nantes at the age of 36 as a rebel against the Revolution.

At the back of the house is a stone with P D G   M H C 1733, for Pierre de Gruchy fs. Mathieu and Marie Hocquart, married in 1719. He was clearly the brother or son of Philippe de Gruchy who in 1732 bought two fields on the Fief du Roi in St. Saviour, le Clos de Bisson and le Clos de Messervy, now in one field as No. S.9, for 4 quarters of wheat rente, 2 quarters of oats, 12 hens, 216 hens' eggs and £40 tournois; de Gruchy was obliged to build a house on this land, which he seems to have done. The proprietor still holds a Livre de Quittance for this rente, showing Philippe de Gruchy fs. Philippe paying it in 1764; in 1796 it was received from Ann du Feu, mother and procuratrice of Mathieu de Gruchy fs. Philippe. This Mathieu was the priest, who had by then inherited the property on the death of his elder brother. An entry for 1812 shows that it had passed to Philippe de la Haye, who sold it to Thomas Binet. There is a stone here with 17 B B N I L B 19, for Beniamin Binet of Trinity who married Jeanne Le Brock of St. Ouen in 1711. Perhaps the Binets brought this stone from elsewhere when they bought La Maison du Buisson.

The Binet family have bred many carpenters, whose signatures may be found on woodwork in the neighbourhood. Several signatures of 1877 appear under the stairs in this house. It is an interesting staircase for its date, as it continues a traditional design, curving elegantly up to the top floor, but with a later type of newel post.

In the farmyard is an auget (trough), used for pouring water from the well to fill the abreuvoir where the animals drank; it bears the date 1737, and is the only recorded instance of such an object being dated.

a trough or conduit (aûget) at La Maison du Buisson. (T).

See Balleine, *Biographical Dictionary*, p. 201.
B.S.J. 1917, p. 268.
Drawings 27, 28, 75.
Notice sur la famille de Gruchy, p. 5 (1920).

75

LA MAISON DU COIN
Le Couvent (L). (E. Mauger on Godfray.)

There is a long traditional association here with the Mauger family, and a reference in Payne's *Armorial* to "Mauger of Handois" may be relevant, as no other identification seems likely and this house is on the Handois Fief. Perhaps it was this which moved George Mauger to put up a stone on a lintel over the kitchen door, inscribed retrospectively with G M G 1565.

To the right, and slightly set back, are the ruins of an older house with P M G 1751 roughly carved on a lintel, for Pierre Mauger who married Elizabeth Marett. Within the ruins, now restored, is a fireplace with a wooden lintel and several niches. There is a suggestion that this was a dower wing, an early example if 1751 is the date of the whole range of buildings.

LA MAISON LE MAISTRE
Mont les Vaux, St. Aubin.

Here is a further example of a fine staircase in St. Aubin. The stairs have one central newel post rising the full height of the house, and oak urn balusters, much worn but well worthy of preservation.

The name of this house implies a connection with the Le Maistre family, but this has not yet been established. The theory that Le Maistre refers to a schoolmaster is most improbable.

The marriage stone reading I L P △ A D 1706 stands for Jean Lemprière (b. 1654) and his wife Ann Durell. He it was who received a gold medal from Queen Anne in 1703 for "zeal in Her Majesty's service". The medal, which passed into the Anley family through the marriage of Lemprière's daughter Elizabeth with Philippe Nicolle, was still at Maitland Manor (Le Manoir d'Elie) when Payne's *Armorial* was written, but its present whereabouts are unknown. In 1704 Lemprière was made Intelligence Officer for the French coast near Jersey. He appears to have built his house in 1706, and the younger of his children were born there. There are granite fireplaces in the two first floor rooms, and sturdy beams extending the full depth of the house.

See Payne's *Armorial*, p. 235, 248.
  Biographical Dictionary, Balleine, p. 418.
  Drawing 27.
  Plate XIII a, XXV a.

MANOR HOUSE
Rue de Bas (L). (H. Coutanche on Godfray.)

There is reason to think that the Chapelle de St. Eutrope was in fact situated here, and not at Hamptonne (or La Patente). De la Croix states that "Cette chapelle a fait partie d'une maison jadis habitée par l'ancienne famille des Hamptonne, des Bissons etc. On y trouve encore un champ qui porte le nom de la chapelle". These facts fit Manor House, where field (L. 757a) is Le Jardin de la Chapelle; there is also, in what is now an outhouse, in its north wall a structure which can only be a bénitier (piscina). It is approximately 26in. high and 15in. wide, but a window has been inserted in such a way that it is hard to reach it and take measurements. This same building also contains two chamfered windows, clearly from an earlier structure. There is a Clos de la Croix (L. 650), and the combination of manor, fief, croix, chapelle, fontaine and bénitier cannot be mere coincidence. There is a most attractive fountain in the Jardin de la Chapelle, containing a little recess at the back, said to be a shelf on which to rest a drinking cup.

As to the fief, the owners held the Fief Luce de Carteret in whole or in part since the 15th century, but the title probably refers mainly to the small Fief ès Hastains, held in 1490 by Guille de Hamptonne. The fields at that time included Le Clos de Horman (L. 649) as at present, and Le Val Hubaut which was mentioned in the Rapport des Commissaires in 1515 in connection with Nicolas Hamptonne fs. Guille. The family association is further confirmed by an early carved

The Hamptonne window-lintel at Manor House, (L).   76

window lintel, now built into the north wall of the new house, which bears the Hamptonne arms; the shield is flanked by what appear to be initials, which are far from clear, but could be an E and an H, or B, either of which could be appropriate.

From the Hamptonnes the property passed to the Bissons by sale in 1601, Edouard Hamptonne (Constable of St. Lawrence 1587-1592) selling to Edouard Bisson, his cousin (Constable of St. Brelade 1581-1591, 1593-1601, and of St. Lawrence 1604-1616); Edouard established his family in St. Lawrence from then on; his great-great-grand-daughter, Susanne Bisson, died without heirs, and it passed to her sister Sara's son, Richard Le Feuvre. He died in 1803 and in 1810 his son sold it to François Carrel, who in turn sold it to Pierre de Caen, who again sold it, in 1845, to Henry Coutanche (d. 1895).

The rolls of the Fief ès Hastains show that the court took place on this property in 1846, the Seigneur of the fief then being Charles Laurens, and by then ès Hastains had become a sub fief of Mélèches.

The present house was built in 1875 by Henry Coutanche. Some of the internal detailing in the semi-basement level is of mid-18th-century date, which suggests that the present large Victorian house was built up on an existing base, perhaps in itself on the original 15th-century site. Members of the family still living have heard mention of a "tower" which used to exist. One wonders if this was a colombier.

There is a very fine cedar tree in front of the house, planted when it was built, and thus just a century old. Who could guess that a large late Victorian house could hide so much fascinating history in its past?

See B.S.J. 1928, p. 102.
    Payne's *Armorial*, p. 177.
    de la Croix, Vol. I, p. 187.
    O. J. H., Volume I, p. 158.
    Rapport des Commissaires 1515, p. 12.
    Drawing 76.

LE MARAIS
(My). (Jurat J. Le Couteur on Godfray.)

This is a house which has been much altered at different dates. The dormers and perforated ridge slates must be late Victorian. The windows have been enlarged in brick, and in recent years the traditional twelve-pane sashes have been removed. The interior, however, speaks of greater age, with Swanage paving in the hall, thick gable walls, and what can only be racks for storing wine or cider, in brick, in a service room attached on the west.

In 1787 John Wesley was in Jersey, on a visit which was to have a profound effect on the life of the community. On 23 August he preached in this house, which then belonged to the Le

Couteurs, the whole service being translated by Mrs. Marie Arthur née Vibert of Le Puits (later named La Pompe) opposite. In 1809 Le Marais was described as "the elegant and commodious house finished in the cottage style" of Mr. Le Couteur. Jean Le Couteur, Constable of St. Mary 1836–1840 and Jurat 1840–1867, lived here, and is credited with inserting projecting stones in his field walls to make it easier to climb them.

    See Drawing 15.

LE MARINEL
Rue des Chenolles (L). (P. Vaudin on Godfray.)

Deeper study of this most interesting property prompts a further entry. We have already seen that it had passed to de la Cour ownership by 1759, and from that family it passed to the Vaudins, who still hold it. What has not yet been revealed is who owned it before the de la Cours. The answer is the Lemprières of Diélament.

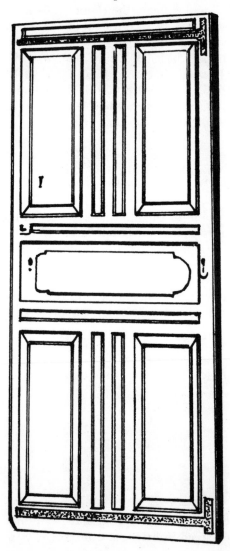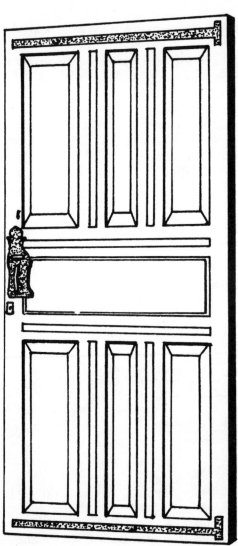

mid-18th. century panelled doors at Le Marinel, (J).

It appears as "La Maison du Marinel" in the Extente of 1749, when Françoise de Carteret of La Hougue (d. 1764) owed 4 cabots of wheat upon it. At her death her grandson Philippe Lemprière (1718–1787) inherited from her Le Fief Chesnel in St. John and, having no surviving heirs, sold the fief to his nephew Thomas (1756–1823) in 1786; he had already in 1784 sold La Maison du Marinel to this same Thomas. On Philippe's death in 1787 the Court annulled these sales, passing the inheritance to his brother Charles, father of Thomas. But it seems that this decision was not maintained, as Thomas's son George Ourry Lemprière inherited the fief in due course. Thomas lived for a while in St. John before moving into town, where he was at the time of the Battle of Jersey in 1781, being wounded in the engagement.

Both Philippe and his nephew Thomas had French wives, and perhaps their influence may be seen in the décor which still survives in some of the rooms they occupied. One bedroom retains some of its hand-painted wall coverings, with a design of flowers and birds; the woodwork still shows that it was painted light blue, and the four-post bed which was there until recent years had its hangings in faded blue cotton material, the panel behind the pillows being pleated into a central point, giving the effect of sun's rays. Tiles which have been saved from the fireplace surround, within its bolection moulding, have biblical scenes in clear blue on white, and perhaps this gives us the shade of blue the bed hangings would have been. Was this room first chosen by Philippe's wife, Julie Catherine de Varignon, married in 1739, or by Thomas's wife, Elizabeth Charité Beuzeville, married in 1783? The former seems the more likely date for this room, and accords with the elaborate panelled doors and fragments of panelling in other rooms in this range of buildings, one of which contained a second bed with slender, elegant posts. It is indeed remarkable that one can enter a room which has remained virtually undisturbed for over two centuries, and share the enjoyment of its simple but highly civilised furnishings with those who put them there.

After Thomas Lemprière moved to town the property was sold to Jean de la Cour, who put up his date stone in 1795. He had no sons, and his eldest daughter married a Vaudin. The new house, built in 1870, is a fine example of its period, and still has some of its original furnishings and wallpapers. As it faces north, the pleasantest rooms are at the back. The entrance gateposts, which so excellently match the style of the house, come from the house now called Burfield on the main St. John's Road, the birthplace of the mother of the present owner; that house is shown for C. Hocquard on Godfray's map.

See Extente 1749, p. 61.
   Old Jersey Houses, Vol. I, p. 180.
   B.S.J. 1904, p. 269; 1917, p. 258.
   Drawings 38, 77. Plate XXVd.

MECHANIC LODGE
Rue des Landes (P). (T. Bodnaham on Godfray.)

On the Richmond map there is no building at all where St. Peter's Ironworks, founded in 1859, now stands. A house immediately to the south dated 1794 was just in time to be included in that map, which was produced in 1795, and the man who built it put his initials, I L B (? Le Brun) on his lintel stone, leaving a space for those of his wife, which were never added.

The house named Mechanic Lodge has been in the Le Cappelain family for four generations, and its name proclaims a justifiable pride in the family's achievements. It was a single-storey building when the present owner's grandfather George Philippe acquired and altered it, probably in the 1880s, as he became the owner of the business on the death of his father Théophile John in 1882. A testimonial given to George Philippe Le Cappellain (*sic*) by his employees in 1892 has amongst the signatures that of S. M. Stuart Turner, a member of the famous firm of pump makers; this man had served his apprenticeship with the Le Cappelain firm, and the bell shown on the testimonial was made by them, and is still there. The alterations to the house gave it an elaborate Victorian Gothic finish, great attention being paid to detail.

The firm was founded by Théophile John (b. 1828), who was followed by his son George Philippe (b. 1859), his son Théodore George (d. 1959), his son Cyril George, and his son Cyril, who also works in the business. The founder Théophile came from St. Brelade's, and served his apprenticeship in a shipbuilding yard at Gorey. In 1873 he was awarded a silver medal, and given a testimonial from several farmers who presented him with a screw-cutting lathe, valued then at £90, as a reward for having introduced steam threshing and straw elevators. He must have made hundreds of wooden ploughs with steel breasts and shares. Théodore George who took over the business in 1936 was admitted in 1939 an Associate of the Institute of British Agricultural Engineers. Through this firm, St. Peter's was the first parish to experiment with electric lighting.

George Philippe was educated at Le Brocq's school at La Chasse, St. Mary, and then at Boyer's at Beaumont. In 1874 he went to work at C. Vautier's, at La Place, St. Peter, and then at Grandins of Commercial Buildings. In 1882 he took over the family business and manufacture of all iron ploughs, followed by the twin-breezing plough, which remained a standard implement for many years, and the first iron- and steel-planting plough. At that time such a plough could be made in a day and a half for the price of £4 10s. The firm used to keep five steam threshing machines at work during harvest, as well as one at Portbail and one in Guernsey. One of them was still in use at the beginning of the second war. The firm maintained a steam pulsometer (vacuum pump) for P. N. Gallichan when he was building the sea wall in St. Ouen's Bay, and also for Charles Le Quesne when the wall in St. Aubin's Bay was being built. In 1914 the Jersey Lily potato digger was introduced and the firm supplied many of them, with slight modifications to suit local conditions. This machine was a break-through and an immense help to farmers, remaining the standard mechanical digger until fairly recent times.

See *The Islander*, October 1940.
Plate XXVIa.

MELBOURNE HOUSE
Rue de la Mare Ballam (J). (A. Vautier on Godfray.)

Like La Grande Maison (q.v.), Melbourne house was built by Philippe de la Mare, a most able craftsman, and there is a story of competition between the two owners, Mr. Luce and Mr. Carcaud, in the manner of Hugh Walpole's novel *The Fortress*. Mr. Carcaud won with Melbourne House, if sheer grandeur was his object. It is a large square house with a verandah on the south supported on pillars. Pilasters at all angles of the building have composite capitals in which the designer has taken liberties with the orders. Some of the leaf decoration is similar to that employed on internal pilasters at Mainland (q.v.).

The choice of the name Melbourne does not establish a firm date for the house, but the great statesman retired from public life in 1841, and the town of Melbourne was named after him in 1835. The Le Rossignol family chronicle published in 1917 refers to the house as Caesarea Court. The cottage to the west is still called Caesarea Cottage.

Within living memory Miss Maria Carcaud kept a school in the very fine granite stables, which were converted for the purpose. Her sister Louisa, the housekeeper of the family, is remembered in her bonnet and cloak with an ebony walking stick, driving to town in Murphy's bus.

See Plate XIVd. Colour 2b.

LE MÉNAGE
Ville Emphrie (L). (E. Laffoley on Godfray.)

78

The plastered façade of Le Ménage gave little clue of what was underneath. When the stucco was removed a very fine granite frontage was disclosed with a gable stone dated 1695 (the last digit is unsure). There are also two window lintels, one with M H, and the other with M Bt on one side of a central stylised motif of a cross,

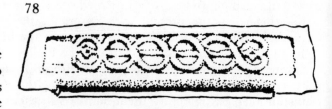

window lintel at Le Ménage, (L).

and an H on the other side. Over the front door is another lintel, elaborately carved. Although the door and all the windows have been heightened, these features are consonant with a date of 1695.

The geological formation of the terrain is remarkable, for the steep hillside immediately behind the house has about one foot of soil and two feet of clay, and below that is sharp-fissured shale with horizontal stratification. The house is built on this bed of shale.

Mathieu Berteau had children born between 1690 and 1700 in the parish, and his wife, whose name is not given, died in 1715. It is quite possible that he was the M Bt and that her name was perhaps Helière, but this is only supposition. No other entries in the St. Lawrence register approximate to this inscription.

See Drawing 78.

MERRIVALE
Rue Végueur (O). (J. Le Rossignol on Godfray.)

The pig sties, of the type with a vaulted or corbelled ceiling within a pitched roof, are very fine, and are built in two sections so as to separate the farrowing sow and piglets from the remainder. All the farm buildings are of quality workmanship, and the stables are paved with granite "bricks", that is to say granite trimmed to the shape and size of a brick, which is very rare. Ships' masts may be seen as beams. Under the kitchen there is a low cellar containing a pig salting trough, and in one window embrasure of the kitchen there is a lead sink, no doubt the last word in labour-saving when the house was built.

The outer doors of the main house are unusual in design and are very fine; there is an attractive door knocker on the back door, and an elaborate fanlight over the front door, somewhat masked

pig-sty with vaulted ceiling at Merrivale, (O).   79

by a more modern porch. In the front garden is a very grand conservatory. This whole group of buildings constitutes the superior residence of a prosperous farming family, believed to be the Le Rossignols, and associated with the man after whom Mont Rossignol in St. Ouen's was named.

The far older single-storey house, now demoted to farm sheds, is undatable, but one early accolade window lintel has survived as a pointer to its age.

See Drawing 79.

MON PLAISIR
La Haule (B). (P. Marett on Godfray.)

This delightful little "romantic" house, an early version of the modern split-level construction, was built by Philippe Marett of La Haule in about 1820. He may have intended to let it, but he frequently lived there and it was La Haule Manor which was rented.

The house is constructed into the slope of the hill, so that one enters on the level of the principal bedrooms and descends to the living rooms. A central window in the façade is in fact a dummy, with its shutters permanently closed. The stable block behind, with a ship's bell atop the roof, is in true Georgian tradition. The dining room lies to the east of the main block and must have been an addition to the original design, though probably added at an early stage. The architect who designed the very symmetrical façade would not have disturbed the balance by the inclusion of this extra room, which also obstructs the view from the bedroom behind it. Everything here is contemporary; one notes acanthus leaf moulding on ceiling cornices, the elegant curved stairs and the decoration on the sides of the risers adjusted to the curve.

It is disappointing that the diaries of Philippe Marett for 1818 to 1820 do not mention Mon Plaisir, although they include minute detail of expenditure in other directions. One item dated 27 December 1818 may be relevant: it reads, "Paid Ed. Carrel's bill £37.17, and for the mahogany rails £5". During this period he was buying many shrubs, trees and fruit trees, and this may be reflected in the camellias, mimosa and fruit in this garden, which enjoys really panoramic views of St. Aubin's Bay.

See Plate XXVIb.

MON PLAISIR
Coin Motier (L). (N. Arthur on Godfray.)

There is a stone built into a stable with R B and S B H within a shield, flanked by the date 1676, and it stands for Raulin Benest who married Sara Bailhache in 1663. It is curious that he gave his wife syllabic initialling but was content with one letter for his own surname; R B N would have been more correct. This stone probably came from the west wing of the house, which has three accolade lintels over windows which have been enlarged.

The main house is impressive, with a good entrance gate, approach avenue and nicely-kept gardens. The house itself appears to be about 1870 in date, and displays round-topped dormers, a granite gutter supported on brackets, a pediment with generous curves, and a charming little iron balcony to the central first-floor window.

See Drawing 26.
Plates VIc, XXVIc.

LES MONTAGNES
Les Charrières de Malorey (L). (J. Le Sueur on Godfray.)

Here the dower wing to the west may be contemporary with the rest of the building, as there is no sign of a join in the masonry; if so, it is a rare example of a 17th-century "maison douaire". There is a salting trough in a back room, a plain fireplace on the ground floor west, and a rather

PLATE XXV

a. La Maison Le Maistre (B), 1706

b. Maupertuis (My) shortly before demolition

c. La Maison Carteret (B), early 18th century.

d. 18th century biblical tiles from the old house at
Le Marinel (J)

PLATE XXVI

a. Mechanic Lodge (P), *c* 1890

b. Mon Plaisir (L), *c* 1870

c. Mon Plaisir (B), *c* 1820

better one in the first-floor room east, a further instance of the best room in the house being off the ground floor.

A right-hand gatepost bears the initials E D S X and 80; its twin, now in use as a lintel over a door near the road, bears I L G and 17; though invisible, the I may be taken for certain, as representing Jean Le Gallais who married Elizabeth de Ste Croix in St. Lawrence. In 1839 their granddaughter Jeanne Le Gallais, wife of Charles Mauger, sold to Jean Le Sueur a house and land on the Fief de la Reine, which no doubt were Les Montagnes. Her mother Jeanne Le Grand, widow of Jean Le Gallais fs. Jean, had the enjoyment of her living quarters at the west of the house for her lifetime, with 4 perches of land, as well as the right to draw water from the fountain. It was also stipulated that as the bake-oven was situated in her part of the house, she had to permit the purchaser to use it, provided he gave six hours' notice.

See Drawing 29.

MONT DES VAUX COTTAGES (B)

This secluded row of cottages lines what is now a cul-de-sac, but was previously the main hill, Le Mont des Vaux. At the north end is Hibernia Vale, the home of the schoolmaster and mistress before the present primary school was built. Further along is West View, which has a lintel inscribed F I ♡ ♡ M C 1775, for François Jeune and Marie Carcaud, great grandparents of François Jeune, later Bishop of Peterborough. The Jeunes were Huguenots, and became early supporters of the Methodists; indeed in 1787 a shed near this house was used for meetings during the period when Methodism was most unpopular among the majority. Later this couple went to Grenada in the West Indies as missionaries.

Further to the south are a pair of still older houses in a bad state of disrepair. The lower one, called Lugano, has an outside staircase, and the left-hand section has a lintel inscribed 1648. There are three good granite chimneys on this pair.

See Balleine, *Biographical Dictionary*, p. 334.
    B.S.J. 1949, p. 131.

MONT MILLAIS HOTEL
Formerly Claremont House (H).

It is hard now to visualise the original house, buried as it is behind massive enlargements, but when Lieutenant John Collas, R.N. (1779–1834) built it in about 1820, he wanted it to look like a ship. So, no doubt, it did, with an unusual façade and stairs in imitation of companion ways. The stairs are still there, to remind one of this sailor's fancy. The only room retaining its original décor is the drawing room, now the television lounge, where the 1820 woodwork shows the combination of various types of moulding, fielded, astragal and reeded, sometimes found during a transition from one style to another. Here and there original doors and door frames can be seen, with moulded architraves and bosses decorated with formalised roses.

John Collas was captured by the French when serving in H.M.S. *Calcutta,* and remained a prisoner-of-war until 1814. It is told in the family that some of his colleagues broke parole and escaped, but that he refused to do so, and worked out the design for his house during his years of captivity. He probably did not build it until after his marriage in 1821 to Charlotte de Vaumorel, heiress to both her father and her uncle. Between them they acquired a considerable amount of property in the College Hill area, including all Claremont Terrace, Claremont Place, five other small houses and eight vergées of land. In 1862 a valuation of the contents of the garden alone amounted to £54. The house was sold in 1879, and has changed hands many times since then.

See B.S.J. 1974, p. 272.

MOSS NOOK
Rue de Podêtre (H). (P. Anley on Godfray.)

The façade of this house is an excellent specimen of ashlar facing. Its date stone reads P A L ♡ ♡ I P N 1823, that on the dower wing reading P A L ♡ ♡ M B N 1832. The latter stands for Philippe Anley, who married Marguerite Binet in 1797. They were probably the parents of the Philippe Anley on the 1823 stone, and must have put up the 1832 stone when they moved to dower quarters in their retirement.

The ground floor room east is in uncovered granite, not originally meant to be exposed, containing two small fireplaces and various recesses.

On the north elevation is an early lintel with the initials M L, and above it a stone with three shields, one with M L, one with M M, and the central one with the date 1666 and some decorative motifs. The M L on the lintel is surely Moise Luce "of Mont à l'Abbé", one of the twelve men chosen in St. Helier to report and advise on the property and lands of "delinquents", the title chosen by Cromwell for any who did not support his cause. The upper stone no doubt represents Moise Luce junior and his wife Marguérite Messervy, who had three children, Moise (1664), Mathieu (1667) and Jeanne (1670).

See Jean Chevalier's Journal, 1645, p. 218.

No. 15, LA MOTTE STREET, St. Helier

Now demolished, this house bore a stone exempted from the surrounding stucco with the initials I L T and F L T and the date 1699. It was one of the earliest surviving dated stones in town. No marriage has been found to accord with these initials, but Le Tubelin or Lestel are likely names.

LE MOURIN
Maufant (S). (F. Journeaux on Godfray.)

Perhaps the most interesting thing here is the square bottle found buried in the north wall, when a beam had to be replaced, and it is fortunate that it was recovered unbroken. In that position it was certainly intended as a specific against witches. Although popularly supposed to be gin bottles, such a design could be used for any sort of beverage. It is of 17th-century date.

80

At the entrance gate a well-carved inscription reading P D M   A L M 1766 represents Philippe Dumaresq (b. 1701) and Ann Le Maistre (b. 1706), who were married in 1724, his family originating from Vinchelez de Bas. The couple had five sons who all died young, and three daughters of whom the youngest, Françoise, inherited the property. She married Jean Collas of Les Carrières, a descendant of the Collas' of St. Martin's House, and their initials I C L   F D M 1766 are carved rather roughly on the house.

It seems likely that the wing on the east is the older part, as it has a stone inscribed P D M E M and a date which is partly covered with plaster, and might be 1634; but 1684 is more likely, in which case the stone would represent Philippe Dumaresq (b. 1659) who married Elizabeth Messervy. His parents were Philippe Dumaresq (1632-1669), Solicitor General, and Susanne de Frotté of Normandy. Payne in his *Armorial* gives an account of her arrival in Jersey, and one wonders what she thought of the very small house to which she had come. In the 1671 list of payments for fortifications in this vingtaine of St. Saviour we find "les hers Philippe Dumaresq, £10", the guardians of his children no doubt paying on their behalf. The name Mourin, variously spelled, appears in the Extentes of 1331, 1528 and 1607.

17th. cent. bottle found buried in a wall at Le Mourin.

The main house is small and attractive. Its windows have all been enlarged. It suggests a late-17th-century date, altered perhaps in 1776.

See Payne's *Armorial*, p. 146.
   Journal of Glass Studies, Corning Museum of Glass, N.Y., p. 106.
   St. Ouen's Manor MS. 1671.
   Drawing 80.

LA MOYE VILLA
Route du Sud (B). (J. d'Aubert on Godfray.)

The proportions here suggest antiquity, concealed under the plaster rendering. The round-topped doorway may well hide a traditional round arch. The two first floor rooms have evidence of granite fireplaces.

The Appairiement de Ste Brelade 1774, and surrounding field names, suggest that this was the property of "les hoirs de Jean Orange".

NEW STREET
St. Helier

In October 1838 Augusta Maria Harvey of Guernsey received an invitation to a ball at "Mr. Journeaux of New Street" in St. Helier. A few months later Augusta came again for the wedding of her brother Thomas to Jane Elizabeth Payn of Le Colombier (L), and she then fell in love with François Payn, Jane's brother, and married him soon afterwards. The house where the ball was given was No. 18 New Street.

It belonged to François Journeaux and his wife Jeanne Thérèse Pradié Desarnauds, a French girl from Bordeaux, François having exchanged it for one in Mulcaster Street belonging to Pierre Patriarche in 1797, but it is a far older house than that. It can be located on the Richmond map, and is indeed almost the only house then shown in New Street, which at that time was called La Rue Durell. The interior shows that it was built no later than 1750. The stairs have a flat-topped handrail, bun moulded stringer, square newels and well-turned balusters, with fielded side panelling all up the wall. All doors have fielded panels, and all the main rooms are panelled, with good overmantels. On the first floor is what must have been the ballroom, with five windows stretching the full width of the façade. The overmantel is topped with a pediment, similar to that in the actual library room in Falles's Old Library.

The house was built right on Le Grand Douet, which now flows underground, and some of the manuscripts studied are concerned with the use of an access to the stream, and the obligation of adjoining landowners to keep it "nettoyé" as far as Durell's bakery.

See B.S.J. 1901, p. 403.
   MSS. from La Haule Manor and Le Colombier Manor.
   Plate XIIIc.

LES NIÈMES
Grande Route de St. Pierre (P). (G. Le Feuvre on Godfray.)

There is evidence that Philippe Le Feuvre (1764-1855), who married Ann Le Bas, thereby inheriting the property, built this house in 1829 and La Hougue (q.v.) in 1822 for his two sons. Internal details are in good accord with such dates. At the partage in 1840 of the estate of Philippe and Ann between the two sons, the younger, George William, was allocated "la neuve maison des Nièmes", which Ann's father Nicolas had bought from Jean Le Brun fs. Jean. He was also allocated "la maison que ledit Philippe Le Feuvre" had bought from Nicolas Le Marquand in 1828, perhaps Arcadia, now demolished, and a house he had bought from Amice Carrel in 1813, this being La Carrellerie, just north of Les Nièmes. "L'assiette de la vieille maison", measuring one vergée, is also mentioned, and the field names in this partage seem to suggest a site on the west of the road where Les Nièmes Farm now is. The very fine barn there has a suppressed arch with the inscription P L F

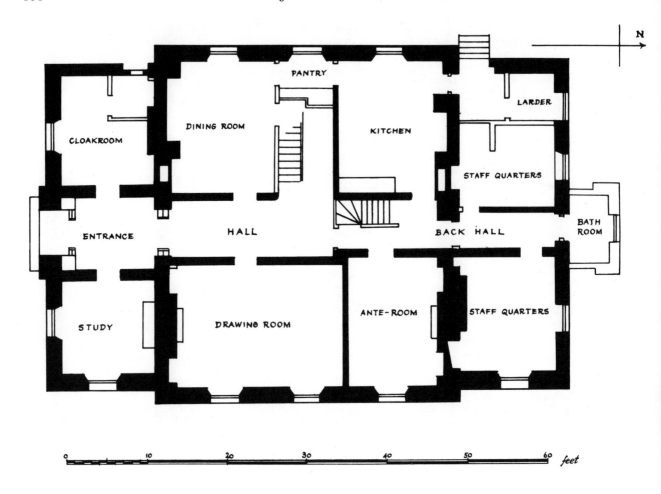

N

CLOAKROOM

DINING ROOM

PANTRY

KITCHEN

LARDER

STAFF QUARTERS

ENTRANCE

HALL

BACK HALL

BATH ROOM

STUDY

DRAWING ROOM

ANTE-ROOM

STAFF QUARTERS

0   10   20   30   40   50   60   *feet*

81

A departure from the
traditional ground-plan.
LES NIÈMES,
St. Peter.
BUILT 1829.

1837 ALB, in italics, both sets of initials written in monogram. Another barn is dated 1867 and has an unusual chequered pattern in the colour of the granite blocks. The farmhouse is probably late 19th century, and has a round arch, heightened with two additional stones, which clearly comes from a much earlier structure. There was a house on the land bought from Le Brun, by Ann's father in 1817 and this may have been in the sunken garden immediately west of the present Les Nièmes; names of neighbours given in the contract of sale accord with the names on Godfray's map.

Les Nièmes house is unusual for Jersey in several ways. The front door, which faces south, is at the side of the house, and the stairs are not opposite to it. There are single-storey rooms projecting on the north and south and it has been suggested that these are later additions. If so, the internal details have been remarkably well copied in the case of the southern section, including doors, architraves, corner bosses and fanlights. It seems more likely that they are contemporary, that on the south giving an entrance porch flanked by small rooms, and that on the north providing extra service rooms.

A cellar extends under the main structure but not under these wings. On the west it is on ground level and has the date 1829 over its entrance door. There is a tradition that this was big enough for a horse and cart to enter, so that the contents could be unloaded secretly, but this seems unlikely as the entrance is only six feet high and five feet wide.

The window lighting the stairs is Gothic revival in feeling and is surrounded by granite on the inside. Recent alterations have been few, and to judge by photographs, have definitely enhanced the property. A large drawing room has been created by throwing the two east rooms into one, and an ugly and apparently pointless gable above the front door has been removed.

The family retains an elaborate silver kettle presented by the parish of St. Peter to Jean Le Brocq of Les Fontaines in 1870. His daughter Jeanne married George William Le Feuvre. The kettle is English silver bearing the overstamp of Le Gallais.

Le Fief des Nièmes, now a dependency of La Hague, includes an area surrounding the house, going east just beyond La Croix au Lion, north round La Carrellerie and along La Neuve Rue west to St. Ouen's parish boundary and south to St. Peter's village. In a Court Roll of the fief, dated 1851, there were only eight tenants to testify, the court being held in the house of George William Le Feuvre "appellée Les Nièmes". The aveu of Nicholas Le Bas in 1792 totalled 66¾ vergées of land, the names being substantially the same as in the 1840 partage, and by 1851 "les enfants de George William Le Feuvre" owned 69 vergées, the difference probably being the addition of the small property bought in 1817. The death of the last of a very long line of male Le Bas cannot be traced, but must have been between 1817 and 1840. It is surprising that Godfray's map of 1849 omits the drive leading east from the house to La Croix au Lion cross roads. Presumably it was made at a later date.

See Drawings 30, 47, 81.
Plate XXVIIc.
Registre Publique L.121 F.201.
Documents in La Hague collection.
Le Feuvre family documents.

NONPAREIL

Grande Route de St. Pierre. (Dr. Cuquemelle on Godfray.)

With a Gothic revival façade of perhaps 1840 this house belonged to a Dr. Cuquemelle who lived in St. Peter until 1856. By 1858 he was in Grove Place, and was in contact with Eugène Duprey, an outstanding pharmacist, to whose influence can perhaps be attributed the curious symbol in relief in the apex of the central gable. Dr. Cuquemelle must have been the son of Benjamin Cuquemelle, adjutant d'Etat Majeure à la Légion Departementale du Calvados, who married Françoise Gaudin in 1818, at St. Martin. There are statues in oblong niches flanking the symbol, and dormer windows, the roof having a shallow pitch. Detailing inside the house is disappointing, but the room within the central gable has a remarkable vaulted ceiling, and the present owner has heard that it was used for Masonic meetings. The kitchen has a copper and bread oven, both with interesting iron doors.

In 1872 the house passed to the Dickson family, Mr. Dickson being the first manager of the Jersey Western railway. His daughter, Miss Dickson, showed much spirit in refusing to be hustled

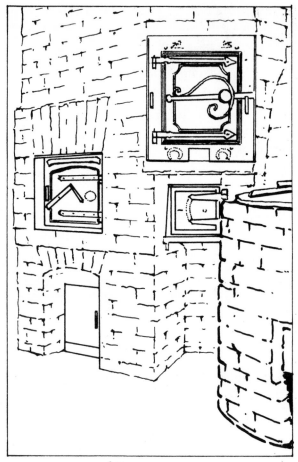

high-quality fittings in furnace-room at Nonpareil, (P), including bake-oven and copper: the oven-door on the left is inscribed: 'C. Le Feuvre, Iron Founder, Jersey'.

82

out of her home when it was threatened by airport extensions which in the event were not proceeded with. There is a striking and very large camellia bush to the left of the front door which, like its owner, refuses to be dismayed by the low-flying aircraft and blooms serenely.

See Drawing 82.
Plate XXVIIb.

OAKDALE
Rue des Buttes (J). (P. Nicolle on Godfray.)

Over the back door is a finely carved stone inscribed   E G L B T ♡♡ E P N 1866,   for Le Boutillier and Pinel. The stone step leading to this door incorporates two early chamfered window lintels, and on one of them, in raised figures, is the date 1590. This is a great surprise but appears to be entirely genuine, and places this lintel among the small number of pre-1600 stones in the Island.

See Drawings 30, 83.

OAK FARM
Ville ès Gazeaux (L). (P. Bigrel on Godfray.)

The bénitier has now been fully uncovered and is thus much improved. Recent alterations have shown yet another round arch directly above that on the ground floor. This suggests that the east wing is contemporary with the main house; otherwise, to what did the upper arch lead? As they are directly above one another they cannot have served either a tourelle or a straight flight of steps.

There was great modernisation here, perhaps in about 1750. The stairs are extremely good examples of their style, continuing up to the attic floor. The cabinet at the top of the stairs has contemporary panelling, and also a row of five hooks on each side of the ceiling, which have not yet been explained. Some door frames have Georgian-style architraves, consistent with the stairs,

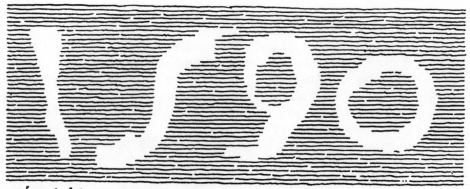

83

embossed date 1590 on window-lintel in use as a step, at Oakdale, (J).

and the hall and main ground floor room have Swanage paving stones. This house has the most complete stair and panelling seen outside the town, and the most similar in style is the house described in New Street.

See Drawing 44.

OAK FARM
Rue de Sorel (J). (J. Renouf on Godfray.)

This house, which has long been in possession of the Renouf family, has a stone dated 1588 in its north wall, but the initials following the date are indecipherable. An outhouse has a gable stone dated 1610 with the initials I L Q, surely Le Quesne in this parish. A John Renouf copied this stone, inscribing his initials I R N and the date 1813, which is likely to be the date of the house as it now is. At some time the roof was slightly raised, and thatch replaced by slate, perhaps in 1869, a date found on the staircase (now replaced). There is a bread oven in an outhouse at the side, and another outhouse has fragments of an early window, but one which was designed to take glass and therefore not as early as the 1610 stone.

There are few 16th-century dated stones on domestic property, and amongst them five are dated 1588. Can this be associated with jubilation at the defeat of the Spanish Armada?

OAKFIELD
St. Saviour's Hill (S). (J. Perchard on Godfray.)

The south façade here has a fine arched doorway and fanlight, and above it a stone with 18 I P C ♡♡ I V P 17, probably for Perchard and Valpy, though so far no marriage has been found to confirm this. The stairs, with stick balusters and decorated sides to the risers, are consistent with this date.

A three-storey dower wing to the east, built perhaps in about 1850, contains six very small rooms, but the wing to the west may be the oldest part. Its west facing wall has a round arch, of eleven stones instead of the regulation nine, and rather narrow voussoirs, but there is no sign that it has been altered. This wing contains a fireplace which was evidently copied, with great care and precision, in the fireplace in the west ground-floor room of the main house. The copyist has gone so far as to reproduce a single corbel projecting through the main gable into the living room of the wing, in perfectly dressed stone, and in imitation of the projecting "witches' stones" seen on the outside of gable walls. It is extremely interesting to find the traditional arch and fireplace being so conscientiously copied as late as 1817, by when they were quite outmoded. The Richmond map shows just one small building on this site in 1795, and it looks as if a humble early house with a round arch was welded into a more ambitious building in which, however, all the traditional features were faithfully copied.

OAKLANDS
Route de l'Eglise (L). (C. Godfray on Godfray.)

A bénitier has survived here, built into the original north wall of the house; it is on the first floor, as at Cap Verd (L) and Greystones (O). It is a simple and rather large example, and it is not possible to say from whence it came, but the proximity to the parish church is significant.

In the farmyard there is an impressive rugged exterior stone staircase, and what may be a cross base. Among the field names are le Côtil de la Croix, le Vivier and le Jardin des Buttes. This is clearly a site occupied and frequented for many purposes from the earliest times. There are many stone items here to illustrate this, including a circular pebble bearing the date 1790, and that rare type of trough, half in and half outside the house, for feeding animals from within the kitchen. A bakehouse and oven have survived, and the owners hope to restore them to use. The ceiling

bake-house, with oven, hearth and copper, at Oaklands, (L).

84

of the cow stable is plastered, which is most uncommon. The roof timbers of the main house are also noteworthy.

The main bedroom has a late-18th-century fireplace, set to the south of the gable apex to avoid collision with the hood of the hearth on the ground floor, a rare arrangement which has been recorded in few other cases. Many of the doors in the house have two fielded panels. It seems likely that the east facing range of buildings is the earliest part, perhaps the Fiott house, for there is a stone dated 1679 with the initials P$_o$F within a shield, probably for Philippe or Pierre Fiott.

There was once a "paûte" here but it is now covered over. Another stone in these buildings reads I L G 1806 for Jean Langlois. A much later wing on the east of the main house was a ballroom, which still has its elaborate ceiling rose, and its supper room behind.

Oaklands was a Langlois property in the 18th century, and was named La Maison de Bas, or lower house of that family, their Maison de Haut being at Ville au Veslet. It passed from Jean Langlois (1712–1755) to Philippe (b. 1747); to Jean (1770–1848) who was Constable of St. Lawrence; to Jean (1794–1833); to his daughter, Marie (1827–1822), who in 1848 married Charles Godfray (1826–1898). Their son Henry Nicolle Godfray (1851–1920) had a granddaughter who sold it to Mr. E. J. Pipon.

Philippe Langlois (1817–1884), the younger son of Jean Langlois (b. 1794), was the second President of La Société Jersiaise, being in office from 1877 to 1881. His great-nephew, Henry Nicolle Godfray, mentioned above, had a distinguished local career as Advocate, Constable of St. Saviour, Jurat and Lieutenant Bailiff, and was also joint Honorary Secretary of La Société Jersiaise from 1878 to 1883.

See Drawings 5, 84, 85.

85

a king-post roof-truss at Oaklands, (L), showing timber inserted between rafters and purlins to raise pitch of roof.

THE OAKS

St. Peter's Main Road (P). (M. Alexandre on Godfray.)

This property is outstanding for its remarkably fine outbuildings, dated 1837, perfect inside and out in every detail. Great prosperity and house-pride are indicated here. Even the bakehouse and fuel store have fine doors with fanlights.

The hearth of the boulangerie is of the style where the bread oven with its iron door is set in the centre of the fireback. The routine was first to put furze, then thorn faggots, in the oven, light them up, and close the door, sealing it with clay. When it was judged that the oven was hot enough, having been tested with a sprinkling of flour to see how quickly it browned, the loaves were introduced. They were placed on cabbage leaves and were lifted on a long-handled wooden shovel, the hot ash having been raked with an implement resembling a sickle on a long handle. Mr. F. Perrée recalls that his mother used to have a big baking once a fortnight, cooking bread, buns and apple pies in this capacious oven.

Over the front door of the main house is I D L I A L 1773, representing Jean Dallain and Judith Alexandre, who are mentioned in the Appairiement du Fief de Vingt Livres in 1775. In the base of the front façade is an inverted undated stone with the inscription I D L ♡ ♡ I B, thought to be a Dallain-Bauche marriage. The late Mrs. Perrée, née Alexandre, was descended from the Alexandres of Les Ormes, St. Brelade, home of Mathieu Alexandre, the printer.

See Balleine, *Biographical Dictionary*, p. 11; Plates Va and b.

THE OLD FARM
St. Clement's Road (C). (P. Le Maistre on Godfray.)

This house was formerly known as La Maison du Moignan. On the east chimney is a sundial with the initials H D M in ligature and the date 1720, and a shield showing Dumaresq arms quartered with de Carteret. At the base E C M de C 1884 has been added, for Edouard Charles Malet de Carteret. The property descended to the de Carterets of St. Ouen through Jeanne Le Maistre, née Dumaresq.

By the gate is a heraldic stone with Payn trefoils, dated 1714, and an incision on a corner stone has H D M. These can be explained. Jeanne Le Maistre (1733–1806) was the daughter of Debora Dumaresq (m. 1731) and Jean Dumaresq of Augrès (1705–1747). Debora was the daughter of Helier Dumaresq, Constable of St. Clement (d. 1725) and Jeanne Collas. Helier was the son of Clement Dumaresq, Constable 1702–1705, who married Marie de Carteret, daughter of Philippe de Carteret "of Grouville" and Marie de la Place. In 1723 the Royal court ordered Helier to appear before the court of the small Fief au Sauteur, which belonged to the widow of François Payn. This is not a very convincing explanation of the Payn arms on the gatepost, and a more likely one is that here, as elsewhere, the Dumaresqs followed the curious custom of using the Payn trefoils instead of their own three cockle shells.

In the western ground floor room there is a simple granite fireplace. A granite bowl in front of the house is reputed to be a font, but its side lugs and outlet hole place it among the collection of such bowls or stoups which are discussed in Volume I, and whose purpose has not yet been determined. At the back of the hall there is an unusual slightly pointed arch, chamfered, and now blocked with a window inserted.

Opposite the Old Farm, to the south, in field No. C.246, le Jardin à Ozier, there is a very large stone, suggestive of a menhir.

See B.S.J. 1906, p. 14; 1967, p. 221.

OLD FARM
Verclut. Fauvic (G). (No name given on Godfray.)

There was here a single-storeyed house exhibiting 17th-century features, rare indeed. It is now demolished. There were a chamfered door and windows on the north or roadside façade. The south had been altered, and brick inserted round the windows.

LA PALLOTTERIE
Now called Vale View. Les Varines (S).

In the garden wall of a modern house is a round arch with a keystone inscribed 1617, and the initials I H below the date. The arch has been heightened by the addition of two stones at the base. In the farm buildings are three windows with carved lintels, but their size and the eight surrounding stones suggest that they are more recent than their lintels. It seems certain that the initials I H represent Jean Herault, Bailiff 1616–1626, a tumultuous figure who liked to refer to himself as Monsieur de St. Sauveur, and was the first Bailiff to wear red robes.

See Balleine, *Biographical Dictionary*, p. 317.

PARKLANDS
Panigot (P). (P. Rive on Godfray.)

To the left of the front door are inscribed the letters L D D D, and below then I V C ♡ F L F 1764. The I V C and F L F are for Jean Vincent (b. 1727) and Françoise Le Feuvre whom he married in

1756. The L D D D reminds one of the I A P D D at Les Pigneaux, in which the D D probably stands for the Latin formula "dono dedit" (gave as a gift); if the same applies to the Parklands inscription, one may guess that a benefactor named L D gave the Vincents this stone, or possibly the house itself. The 1828 inscription on Bouley Bay pier also seems to have been composed by a Latin scholar, who chose to leave a riddle for posterity to solve.

On the right of the drive are a pair of gateposts; one is of water-worn St. Mary's granite and is strongly suggestive of a menhir, and in this context one may note that fields to the north of the house, Nos. P. 592–594, are named La Hougue. The grey-coloured stone of the window surrounds comes from Sorel or Ronez, and the yellower stone from Mont Mado or Gigoulande. This is an early example of dressed ashlar from Sorel.

The descendants of Jean Vincent distinguished themselves academically. The grandson Frederic (b. 1788) taught at St. Anastase's school close to Parklands. His son John Charles Frederick (1814–1910) was Regent at that school from 1842 to 1850, and his brother, Frederick Augustus, also taught there. The three sons of J. C. F. Vincent were all scholars of Winchester College. All eventually left the Island, Charles becoming a master at Radley, Reginald emigrating to New Zealand and George to Melbourne.

See *Old Jersey Houses*, Vol. I, p. 193.
   Victorian Voices, p. 77.
   Winchester College Register, 1836–1906.

PATIER
Patier Lane (S). (M. Amy on Godfray.)

The sword of Damocles hung over this property for some years. Preservationists have visited it and put in suggestions, developers have prepared their schemes, and the Island Development Committee have struggled to find a compromise between the opposing camps, while the parish have hoped to widen and straighten the road where the farm buildings of the oldest part of this complex jutted out. Meanwhile the old house, already neglected, fell into further disrepair, and since the newer farmhouse, situated behind it was vacated, every pane of glass was smashed. There was a door lintel dated 1755 here.

In the end the 1823 house saw its last days. It presented an awkward social and administrative problem, argument being balanced evenly between those who sought its destruction and those who did not. It was said that the house and garden were far too large for modern living, but was this true? It had only four bedrooms and four small attics. It was said that no one wants a large garden, but is this necessarily true? It was said that it would cost a fortune to make it habitable, but it was being lived in until months before the axe fell, and was in excellent condition. It is however true that a purchaser seeking a house of this standard might prefer a more private and secluded position. It was also claimed that in place of the one large house, small farmhouse and older buildings now derelict, over twenty modern residences could be built. So they could, but they would be expensive, and beyond the resources of many local families who are now in search of homes. The developer tends to cater for purchasers in a higher income bracket, and in their mutual interest has no qualms about the removal of a fine 19th-century houses, an 18th-century farm cottage, all the outbuildings necessary to a farm, a perfect example of a 17th-century courtyard house, and a wealth of mature timber and shrubs.

So speaks the preservationist. Different people will answer such questions in different ways, but one sighs to think of more fine doors, shutters, windows and floors feeding more bonfires, and hundreds of granite quoins and lintels being scattered and scarred by the bulldozer, slates and tiles broken as they fall. This is indeed a consumer age, which will be remembered by posterity for its destructive zeal.

The 1823 house, presumably built by Philippe Amy in that year, had a stately flight of granite steps leading to a porch supported on four Roman Doric pillars, its roof having elegant railings, and behind this was a window with narrow side sashes, a style seen more in Guernsey than in

Jersey. The chimneys were in pale coloured brick, as at the Museum and at Beechfield in Trinity (1822), and the roof was double gabled. The main rooms had astragal moulded doors and shutters, again as at the Museum, the first floor rooms having simpler mouldings, but all with the well-made shutters of the period. Every room, even the attic bedrooms, had a fireplace and each surround was different, that in the drawing room being white marble. The hall had parquet flooring, and the flying staircase followed the fashion of the time.

Patier was a good example of a local proprietor retaining the basic vernacular style and adding classical details, while eschewing the more flamboyant type which was soon to appear on the Jersey scene.

See Payne's *Armorial*, p. 27.
Old Jersey Houses, Vol. I, p. 191.
Plate XXVIIIb.

PEACOCK FARM
Rue de la Pièce Mauger (T). (F. Amy on Godfray.)

This house was formerly known as La Crepinerie, and is shown as such on the 1849 map.

On the sill of the window above the front door is the inscription 18 E A M E B P 21, the same initials appearing with the date 1832 on a barn to the east. An early photograph shows elaborate topiary in the form of peacocks, hence the name, a monkey puzzle tree, a porch and twelve-paned window sashes.

See *Jersey through the Lens*, p. 67.

LA PELOTTE
Rue à Don (G). (W. Payn on Godfray.)

In French "pelote" means a ball of wool, which seems an unlikely name for a house, but "faire sa pelote" can mean "to make one's pile". So perhaps the building of La Pelotte in 1710 (the last digit is not clear) was the result of a successful business career. The man who built it put his initials P P with E A (for Elizabeth Alexandre whom he married in 1692), and the date on the right-hand gable stone. There is little doubt that his name was Payn, for Philippe Payn, Constable of Grouville 1814–1817, is mentioned as "fs. Philippe Payn de la Pelotte près de l'Eglise de Grouville, et Marie sa femme, fille puisnée d'Elie Falle", and it must have been his son or grandson who owned the house in 1849.

There are here two small houses alongside one another and one suspects that the house to the west is slightly older, though the evidence is not very clear. The roof is now part slate, part tile, but was at first all in thatch, and the chimneys are good, with clear thatch stones. With one exception all the windows have been enlarged. The stairs are cramped and undistinguished. The stone corbels of three hearths are visible, two of them having wood lintels which probably replace

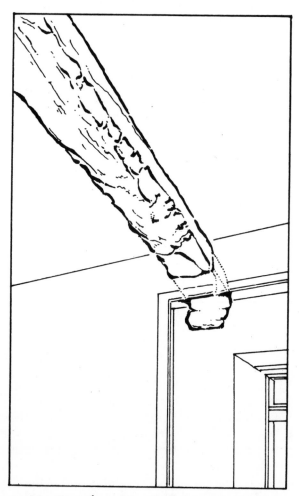

a curving tree-trunk, trimmed, and installed as a beam; at La Pelotte, (G): (the beam is intersected by a modern partition).

86

the original stone. The living room to the extreme east has a moulded mantel shelf sitting self-consciously over the earlier corbels, and this room has fine cupboards flanking the hearth and along the opposite wall. These are of mid-18th-century date, as are many of the doors in the house with their contemporary hinges and, in one case, an early brass lock. A small fireplace on the first floor east has traditional corbels in wood, clearly not meant to be seen, as fragments of early 18th-century panelling and fireplace surround enclose it. There is not a right-angle in any room, and the beams are as twisted as any yet seen. Some of the first floor boards, probably of elm and in perfect condition, are as much as 13in. wide, and wooden partitioning between rooms is also of exceptionally wide panels.

A cannon ball about the size of an apple has been found in the garden. It has not yet been dated, but the geographical position of the house makes it possible that the ball was connected with de Rullecourt's landing. The owners have also found a metal spike with the remnant of a wooden handle, which might be the end part of a halberd, and it is quite likely that La Pelotte was a holding which owed halberd service. Though the original duty of a halberdier was to escort prisoners from Mont Orgueil to the Royal Court for trial, this ceased in 1693 when a town prison was built, but other duties still fell to the halberdiers.

See Le Quesne, *Constitutional History*, p. 44.
de Gruchy, *Medieval Land Tenure*, p. 140.
B.S.J. 1906, p. 24.
Drawing 86.

PETERBOROUGH HOUSE

High Street, St. Aubin.

This house is so called because it was the birthplace of Dean François Jeune (1806–1868) who became Bishop of Peterborough. Over the years it has been much altered. The main staircase is quite plain, but that leading to the upper floor is certainly 18th century and similar to others in St. Aubin. There are some fine 18th-century doors and fireplace surrounds in the house.

The property on sea level is now in separate ownership, but no doubt this house in origin was one of the High Street houses which went down to the beach on the south.

See Balleine, *Biographical Dictionary*, p. 334.

LE PETIT CÂTELET

Rue du Muet (J). (P. Romeril on Godfray.)

The earliest stone here, over the front door, reading I B N S P T 1753, records the marriage of Jean Benest and Sarah Pithon in 1723, who is known to have built a house in 1768 on an 8 vergée field, probably No. J. 327–329, which he bought in 1728 from Jean Journeaux.

The owner in 1806, Philippe Romeril, and his wife Marie Mauger (m. 1778) put up their stone high in the façade with P R R M M G. Not long afterwards another Philippe Romeril put up his initials and the date 1829, with double hearts in anticipation of his marriage. In 1931 Philippe Josué Romeril, sometime Senator in the States of Jersey, put up his marriage stone at the east end of the house.

There is another house nearby named Le Petit Câtelet, which has a stone reading P R D 1831, probably the date when the house was built, and the initials represent P. Rondel who is shown as the proprietor on Godfray. There are four stone hearths here, and one embodies a window lintel inscribed I C S A R B 1716, but this could well have been brought from elsewhere.

LE PETIT PONTERRIN
Rue du Ponterrin (S). (J. Starck on Godfray.)

The most interesting thing here is the sundial on the roadside chimney with R D M 1726, for Richard Dumaresq (1684-1758), father of Richard Dumaresq who was Dénonciateur 1720-1733 and Constable of St. Saviour 1740-1744, and in 1728 married Judith, daughter of Charles Le Hardy, Constable of Grouville. A shield-shaped stone built into the wall of the meadow south of the house bears the inscription TLHDY 1782, for Thomas Le Hardy, Constable of St. Saviour 1773-1776 and 1779-1782, who died in 1798. Stead mentions Le Petit Ponterrin as the seat of Thomas's son Charles Le Hardy, Advocate (d. 1815), "whose library is such an one as becomes the man of learning and of science". (See p. 140.)

The house has been much altered in this century, and little of its former quality remains. In a bakehouse there is a fireplace with an unusually decorated corbel, far older than the building itself, and it must have been brought from elsewhere to serve this humbler use.

See Drawing 29.

LA COMMUNE FARM and LA PETITE COMMUNE
Rue des Pigneaux (S). (Noel and J. Pelgué on Godfray.)

In the roadside wall is I P G ♡ M M R 1805 in raised lettering with one heart, and 17 I P G M M R 54 in incised lettering. The Jean Pelgué of those days seems to have celebrated his marriage and his golden wedding in these two stones.

The second house of this name has a stone over a door on the north with I N E H 1842, and in front there is a much weathered gable stone in use as a garden step, with the initials I P C and the probable date of 1604. These initials confirm the knowledge that this was once a Perchard property, and add the information that it passed from Perchard to Hue, and then by marriage to Noel.

LA PETITE FERME DES JARDINS
Rue du Douet (O). (P. Jean on Godfray.)

This property is now called La Cigale. An estate of three houses here was sold by Mr. Jean to Mr. Le Feuvre, and this house, becoming empty, was used as a potato shed for the first half of this century. On the north-east corner of the house 1889 has been incised, and this could be the date of a thorough rebuilding of a much older structure, of which traces remain in the very thick walls. The western part appears to be the oldest section, and the Richmond map shows no north wing.

In a shed to the south is a stone dated 1607, which might have been brought from elsewhere. Near it is a bakehouse, not very old, but extremely well built, with brick floor and corbelled brick roof, probably of the 1889 period. A quadrant-shaped shed with raised floor and no window, now demolished, may have been an "aîre à vraic" or shed for storing vraic ash, for use as fertilisers.

No. 7 PIER ROAD, ST. HELIER

Recently demolished for Museum extensions, and before that very run down, this must in its heyday have been a house of quality. Most of the rooms were panelled, with elaborate and beautifully wrought overmantels, though all the actual grates were of far later date. A few of the windows had retained their sashes with the heavy Georgian glazing bars, but most of them had been replaced. The most oustanding feature was the great central staircase (dismantled with great care and now in store for some future use) with its flat-topped handrail, square newels, classical urn balusters, and generous landings. But its very spaciousness was at the same time a great

at Nº 7, Pier Road, St Helier.

87

handicap, the area sacrificed to it being so great that the rooms it served were inconviently small.

The date of the building is established by a stone dated 1750, found over the back door of the basement. The mason had evidently been told to leave plenty of room for the initials of the owner, but these were never added. He did, however, put them on a cistern head (now in the Museum) in 1751, with those of his wife. He was Nicolas Fiott, who in 1748 had bought "un emplacement de maison" from William Dumaresq fs. Jean, situated between the house of Philipe Mauger and that of Charles Hilgrove fs. Charles. The site had been acquired in a partage of 1714 by Jean Dumaresq. The cistern head inscription, N F M A D M 1751, stands for Nicolas Fiott and Anne Dumaresq, married in 1740. She died in 1763; the M at the beginning of her initials has not been explained.

In 1792 No. 7 was sold by Edouard Fiott fs. Nicolas to Elie Durell for 105 quarters of of wheat rente, and an undertaking to transfer to Durell a pew in St. Helier's Church. According to the records of Le Fief de la Fosse, Durell was still its owner in 1797. By 1828 it belonged to Clement Hemery who had married Anne Susanne Durell. In 1835 the owner was William Cuming, who had bought it from her; in 1849 Cuming again appears as owner, owing 95 quarters of rente on the property, 53 quarters of this sum being due to Clement Hemery. He was the father of Jacques Hemery (1814-1849), Dean of Jersey, who died in office. In 1858 the Cuming brothers appear in Almanacs as wine merchants at No. 7 Pier Road. However there was a bankruptcy later on and the property reverted to Clement Hemery fs.

Clement, who in 1875 sold it to Josué George Falle.

See Drawings Nos. 43, 87.
    B.S.J. 1916, p. 186; 1899, p. 407.
    Biographical Dictionary, p. 285.
    Payne's *Armorial*, p. 160.

No. 9 PIER ROAD, ST. HELIER

Headquarters and Museum of La Société Jersiaise

Here we have the finest possible example of a prosperous merchant's town house, superbly well built. The builder was Philippe Nicolle, born 1769, at the family home, Hérupe, St. John. His business expanding, he moved to town and established a ship-building yard on land which is now a tidy herbaceous garden at the rear of the house which he built soon after 1817. The sea came right up to the garden.

It is ingriguing to speculate how the rooms were used when it was a family house. One can assume that the kitchen was on the level which is basement on the Pier Road side, and this was flanked by various domestic offices, opening to a paved court, with deep vaults under the present lawn for storing wines, cider and fuel. The front room on that level was probably the shipping office, and the outer buildings would have been stable, coach-house and hay loft.

On the Pier Road level the largest room would perhaps have been the dining room, served by the back stairs leading from the kitchen quarters. The double room facing the harbour would have been a drawing room, while the extra room on the left of the front door is thought to have been a billiards room, a later addition, on the site of what was No. 11, which no longer exists. On the first floor one imagines the large room with its view over the harbour to have been the master's bedroom, opening through an arch (now blocked) to a dressing room with a small cabinet behind perhaps used to accommodate a hip bath, for which water was carried up the narrow back stairs. A similar arrangement is suspected at Mainland (q.v.). Alternatively the large room may have been the drawing room for formal occasions, with a boudoir opening off it as at Belle Vue (B). The double room opposite must have supplied one or two bedrooms. On the second floor

kitchen overmantel, fitted with pegs for hanging crockery and utensils, in vogue from c. 1815.

88

would have been nurseries and above them attics for household servants.

Testimony to the shipbuilder's craft is shown in the fine mahogany doors throughout the building, as well as in some outstanding pieces of furniture believed also to have been made in the shipyards. The woodwork is uniformly excellent, with deeply moulded architraves, decorated corner bosses of great variety, and astragal moulding on the well-made window shutters and cupboard doors. It is interesting to note that the stairs, which from the Pier Road level upwards are all timber, continue down to the Caledonia Place level with stone treads, and cast-iron balusters, but still with the mahogany handrail. At the foot of these stairs monumental marble pillars support the upper floor, no doubt impressing clients who came to do business with the shipowner.

La Société Jersiaise was founded in 1873 as a local antiquarian society, but lacked satisfactory headquarters. On 22 April 1893 Jurat Josué George Falle (1820-1903), a founder member, passed a life interest in the property to La Société (together with No. 11) so long as it should exist and function. He was promptly and rightly elected a membre d'honneur. No. 9 has remained the Société's headquarters ever since and is in itself one of the most noteworthy of its possessions, and it has most excellently adapted itself to Museum needs.

As it has passed through many hands since the first mention in 1714, with a rather tortuous history, it may be best to give this in strict chronological sequence.

1714   The site was allotted to Charles Hilgrove, and later passed to George Hilgrove. It is not known what buildings were erected, nor when.

PLATE XXVII

a. The Jersey Museum (H), 1815

b. Nonpareil (P), *c* 1840

c. Door at Les Nièmes (P), 1829

d. Gate at Les Potirons (My)

PLATE XXVIII

a. Le Quai des Marchands (H), 1810–20

b. Patier (S), 1823

1791 The tenants après décret of George Hilgrove, Matthieu Gosset and Jean Benest, sold "la maison, magazins, terrain et appartenances . . ." to Laurens Ahier. After his death his son, also Laurens, sold, re-purchased and re-sold it.

1803 Philippe de Heaume, who had acquired it, sold it back to Laurens Ahier.

1817 Laurens Ahier died, and the property reverted to Philippe du Heaume, perhaps through a renunciation. December. Philippe du Heaume sold to Philippe Nicolle. The contract refers to a gable as "vieux" which was to be rebuilt within four months, but it is clear that Nicolle demolished and built anew. Following his death his property passed to his daughter Jeanne, wife of Dr. Charles Adolphe Ginestet, who went "en décret" and left the place. A nephew, Sidney Nicolle, mentioned in 1868 that it was forlorn and awaiting a sale of all the contents. In the census of 1861 Dr. Ginestet was the householder, with his sister-in-law Anne, and nephew Sidney, living there. In 1871 the house was uninhabited. Philippe Nicolle had himself died in 1835, his widow Esther Winter remaining there until her death in 1849, and their son retaining it until 1863.

1873 Pierre Philippe Guiton, tenant après décret of Madame Ginestet, sold to Josué George Falle.

1893 Josué George Falle transferred life usage to the Société, together with No. 11.

As regards No. 11, which was really two properties,

1811 Philippe Nicolle bought the front part from William Gosset. (This comprises the room which was later built as a billiards room, and the lawn in front.) At this time the house at the back, the access to which would have been down steep steps to Caledonia Place, belonged to Nicolas Hocquard, while the site of the museum proper, as we have seen, belonged to Laurens Ahier. After Nicolle's death this passed to his daughter Esther Elizabeth, and in the fief aveu of 1838 she owns land on which "il existe encore quelques débris de maisons". Both the Nicolle and the Hocquard properties were acquired by a Gosset, though the house at the back, it seems, never belonged to the Nicolles.

1870 Charles Hilgrove Robin Gosset sold the whole block to Josué George Falle.

1893 Josué George Falle transferred this part also to the Société. At this time No. 13 seems to have belonged to the Le Feuvre family, and is now the Museum warden's house.

Philippe Nicolle had been a very prosperous merchant, and in the aveux of the fief we can trace his other holdings. He held numbers 3, 4, 13, 16, 28, 29, 30 and 31 on Le Quai des Marchands as well as the house in Pier Road, which in 1828 is described thus "La maison et offices que ledit Nicolle occupe dans la rue ou chemmin de haut qui conduit de la ville de St. Helier audit Havre, joignant d'un côté à la maison, offices, etc, de Clement Hemery écr, causa uxoris, de l'autre côté à la maison de Monsieur Nicolas Hocquard et à une propriété appartenant audit Nicolle et aboutissant sur les avants dits quais. Item un emplacement de maison, cour et offices, aussi dans ladite rue joignant d'un côté à ladite dernière maison, cour et offices et aux maisons dudit Monsieur Nicolas Hocquard et de Monsieur George Le Feuvre . . .". It is through a combination of these details, and the efficient and patient searches of Mr. Peter Bisson that it has been possible to build up this complex history.

See A portrait of J. G. Falle, B.S.J. Centenary number, p. 16.
B.S.J. 1894, p. xiv; 1906, p. 77; 1966, p. 131.
Drawing No. 88.
Plate XXVIIa.

LA PLACE. ROUTE DE LISLE
(B). Now Del Sol Hotel. (W. Weary on Godfray.)

A stone with I P P F D L P 1726 represents Jean Pipon and Françoise, daughter of Thomas de la Place, and the name of the house suggests that it passed by marriage to Jean Pipon. In the Appariement de St. Brelade 1796 the 16th Chef de Charette was Richard Pipon, probably their son, and at that time the property comprised 24 vergées. The house now has but vestiges of an 18th-century structure, and a few of the window lintels could be of the 1726 date.

See Extente 1749, p. 75.

LA POINTE
Vinchelez (O). (P. Perrée on Godfray.)

This is an example of a small farm complete with all its appurtenances, including accommodation for horses, cows, heifers, pigs, hay and potato lofts and bakehouse. The cement cladding of the house masks its age, but careful examination suggests that it is early 18th-, if not 17th-century, and that it almost certainly had a tourelle stairway. Late 19th-century alterations inserted an unworthy staircase, but fitted the main bedroom with a most attractive range of built-in cupboards, slightly Gothic in design and painted in light coloured graining.

An adjustment of rents in about 1780 shows that the house then belonged to Amice Perrée, having previously belonged to Jean Le Cornu fs. Lean of Les Landes. A stone let into the stable wall is hard to decipher but is clearly dated 1734.

See La Hague MSS., Les Landes section. Société Jersiaise Library.

LA POINTE
Near Croix ès Bruns (P). (V. Villain on Godfray.)

The remarkable thing here was a section of an octagonal cross shaft, converted into a stone weight, which has been generously given to the Museum by Mr. Pipon. The situation of the house is so close to La Croix ès Bruns, where there is a cross base now belonging to La Société Jersiaise, that it cannot but be part of that wayside cross. This is perhaps the only instance of a cross base remaining in its original position, and certainly the only recorded case of part of a cross becoming a farm weight.

See Drawing 89.

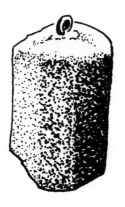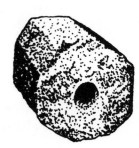

part of a cross-shaft, probably from La Croix ès Bruns, formerly used as a stone weight at La Pointe, (P); shown upright, and lying flat.

89

LE PONT
Rue des Cabarettes (Mt). (P. Le Gros on Godfray.)

The stone with I L G E L F 1775 represents Jean Le Gros who married Elizabeth Le Feuvre in 1771. There is a stone fireplace with lightly decorated corbels, and a "cranne" for hanging cooking pots remains in position.

LA PORTE
La Rue du Pont, Maufant (S). (E. Billot on Godfray.)

The outside appearance here would lead no one to suspect a round arch, but there is one in the north wall of the central section; this has now become an inner wall on account of later additions to the north. The arch is of the flattened "Tudor" style, as at Le Pissot in St. Peter, is certainly no later than 1600 and could be considerably earlier. A small upper door in the east of this section of the house probably served an outside staircase. People still living can recollect their mothers or grandmothers telling them how they had to go outside the house to go upstairs to bed. There is another arch of the late-19th-century type in the farm buildings, which are all of dressed granite and good workmanship. Large well-made gateposts are carved with E B L A R N 1891, for Elie Billot and Ann Renouf.

LES POTIRONS DE BAS
La Rue des Potirons (My). (E. Renouf on Godfray.)

The date 1755 appears over the front door, with no initials. Some of the interior woodwork could be of that date, or perhaps a generation later. The entrance to the main room has a door in two sections, the smaller part being opened only when need arose, in order to introduce, for example, a large piece of furniture or a portly relative, a feature noted only very seldom.

There used to be a well-head in front of the house, and efforts were made to preserve it when it was demolished, but once taken apart such an item loses its identity and becomes but a heap of stones.

LES PRAIRIES
Rue des Issues (J). (P. Gibaut on Godfray.)

Over the doorway is MGB ♡♡ APD 1800, for Moise Gibaut and Ann Poingdestre. This is a fine house of its style, and a comparatively early instance of a "double pile" house. The porch has Roman Doric columns, and in the front garden is a notable tulip tree. The north window lighting the stairs is round topped, with interesting tracery, seen elsewhere in houses of this date.

Behind, and now converted into farm buildings, is the earlier house. In its north wall is a round arch, rather lower than usual, on the keystone of which 1819 has been scratched, but of course the arch is older than that. On the south façade there are at least three accolade window lintels, and the base stones of a wide chamfered doorway with well-carved chamfer stops, one being a fleur-de-lys and the other a cross. No early internal features have survived. At the east end of this range of buildings are some interesting steps, serving an upper doorway, which can be ascended from either side.

The property passed into the Le Gallais family, and remained in their possession until 1942.

LES PRÉS
Green Farm Lane (Mt). (P. Nicolle on Godfray.)

On the lintel of a door in an outbuilding are the initials E AT MAB within a shield, flanked by the date 1675. The E AT for Estienne Anthoine is raised, and the M A B for Marthe Aubin and the date are incised, though they were married in 1664, so this is not a case where the husband waited until marriage to add the wife's initials.

In the north wall is a 17th-century oak window frame, and a ground floor fireplace shows its corbels, lightly decorated, and part of the uprights; but the present floor level cuts right across them, and must have been at least two feet lower originally. Two moulded stones project at the present floor level, and would thus have been about three feet above the ground, and one can only guess what their purpose would have been. A gable stone at the east end repeats E AT 1675.

A stream flows through the property, coming under the road from Le Mourin, and a side stream feeds cress beds and what may have been a lavoir or abreuvoir.

LE PRÉ DU PORTIER
Fauvic (G). (J. Godfray on Godfray.)

Is is most unusual to find an old house facing north as this one does. The façade has a decorated gable stone on the left, that is the east, and a dated one on the right. The date is probably 1706, though the last digit looks like a hook above a triangle. The door and three of the windows are chamfered, and all window apertures are small, square and deeply embrasured. The back façade is not noteworthy. It is a pity that large sheets of glass have replaced the previous small-paned windows, though doubtless they allow more light into the rooms.

(the seagull is poised over No.12).

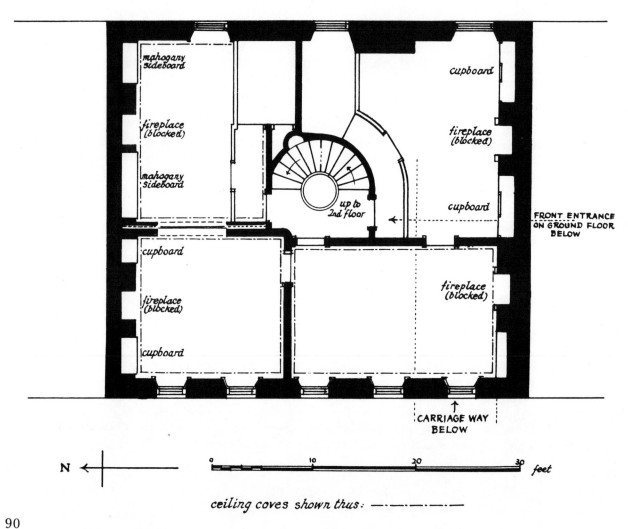

mahogany sideboard

cupboard

fireplace (blocked)

fireplace (blocked)

mahogany sideboard

cupboard

up to 2nd floor

FRONT ENTRANCE ON GROUND FLOOR BELOW

cupboard

fireplace (blocked)

fireplace (blocked)

cupboard

CARRIAGE WAY BELOW

N ←

0   10   20   30   feet

ceiling coves shown thus: — · — · — · —

90

A MERCHANT'S QUAYSIDE APARTMENTS IN ST. HELIER.

No. 12. QUAI DES MARCHANDS, built c. 1820: First Floor.

(from plan drawn by J. N. Stevens.)

The name Pré du, or au, Portier stems from the Master Porter at the Castle, and is first noted for this area in 1614. It appears again in 1749 when the Extente for that year was being prepared. In spite of being the property of the Crown, it was recorded that the banks on the west of the 18-vergée field were in a bad condition, and the meadow flooded as the canal draining it was full of sand, and also that there were no gates or barriers nor had been for some time.

See *Jersey Place Names Dictionary*, p. 614.

LE QUAI DES MARCHANDS
Or Commercial Buildings, St. Helier.

This dignified row of merchants' buildings was erected, in granite, between 1818 and 1831. There are thirty-one premises, numbered from south to north, and extending from near La Folie Inn almost to the modern tunnel under Fort Regent. Their ownership was largely in the hands of the Nicolles, de Quettevilles and a few other families. To begin with each unit, either 40 or 50 feet wide, had a granite lintel with its number and often its date, in beautifully carved raised lettering, but only five of these lintels have survived, three of them dated. That from No. 10 has been removed and is at La Croix ès Mottes in St. Saviour; it is ten feet long and bears the inscription "No. 10. 1821".

The records of Le Fief de la Fosse have given much information about these properties and made possible the identification of many of them and their owners. Designed as they were for the business affairs of merchants, who were often also shipbuilders, these units followed a fairly uniform pattern in which the ground floor of the building was used for offices and the first floor for residence, while the area between the building and the rock face of Fort Regent was occupied with the equipment and installations which each owner required for his business.

Examination of No. 12, which has been but little altered internally, shows that the first and second floors formed a luxurious maisonette for the owner, with large rooms, and windows looking across the harbour to St. Aubin's Bay, and with lavish use of mahogany in doors and cupboards. This was indeed a case of "living over the shop" in comfort. The first floor was probably devoted to reception rooms, a dining room at the back with fitted sideboards, and sliding doors leading to a front room, which in turn led to a larger salon. The upper floor presumably contained the bedrooms.

The ground floor entrance to No. 12 is paved in square tiles of grey and white marble, and the circular staircase is very handsome, if steep; the balusters are lightly turned and the ends of the risers decorated, all, as well as the rounded handrail, in mahogany.

The census of 1851 shows that only a few of these units were occupied by the same owners as had answered for them in the aveux of the Fief in 1849: that is to say No. 2, David de Quetteville; No. 7, George Jean Valpy; No. 12, F. Charles Clarke; No. 14, Jean Anthoine; No. 22, Philippe Nicolle; and No. 23, George Deslandes. That census shows Nos. 1, 5, 6, 9, 10, 15, 18 and 24 as uninhabited but in use as stores; all but one of these had been shown as de Quetteville properties in the aveux, No. 24 having belonged to Nathaniel Westaway. Since those days there have been many changes in the ownership of this fine range of premises, and the uses to which they have been put, the trend being away from residential occupation, and towards a greater variety in their function.

See Balleine, *Biographical Dictionary*, p. 55.
     B.S.J. 1975, p. 313.
     Drawing 90.
     Plates XIIId, XXVIIIa.

RADIER
(G). (P. Simonet on Godfray.)

This is a case where the old house has been almost, but not quite, swamped by subsequent alterations. The Richmond map of 1795 shows a group of four buildings, and Godfray's map of 1849 shows the pond and stream, which now forms a focal point to a most beautiful garden, containing every imaginable tree, creeper and flower, and a spectacular camellia walk.

The original house faced south, and appears to be 18th century. The west wing must have been added a century later, and considerable improvements have been made in recent years.

See *Victorian Voices*, pp. 126, 130.
　　B.S.J. 1968, p. 331.

LE RÂT

Mont l'Evesque (L). (G. Le Ruez on Godfray.)

This is an example of a really small house of the 17th century if not earlier which is double storeyed. It is surprising that it has a name, for until postal services were introduced house names were unnecessary and therefore uncommon. There is some carving on a gable stone, but it is hard to decipher. The house has stone fireplaces. A well is said to exist below a ground level recess inside the south wall of the house. There are indications that there used to be a tourelle. The main bedroom has an interesting and very old door.

In 1548 Martin Langlois sold to Edouard Estur and Jeanne his wife "la petite maison et ménage, Fief du Roi en St. Laurent, par l'aest du doyet au dessous de la fontaine de St. Martin". This is no doubt le Rât, and may well be the same building that we see there today. In 1559 a further document refers to the houses of Clement Langlois and Edouard Estur, and there is reason to think that this refers to La Perrine, later named Old Fallings, and Le Rât.

See Gibaut MSS.

REDWOOD

Five Oaks (S). (C. Le Sueur on Godfray.)

The stone was C L S　M J P 1845 almost certainly stands for Clement Le Sueur junr., who married Marie Payn in 1826.

An older stone has been found, the keystone of an arch inscribed with P L C and the date 1685. With little doubt this is Philippe Le Caumais, who appears in a 1671 list of subscribers to the cost of fortifications, where no other name with the initials L C figures in the Pigneaux vingtaine. The name Le Caumais appears in Extentes, and in parish registers in the 17th century, but not later.

LA RETRAITE

Millais (O). (E. Vautier on Godfray.)

Here we are in the vicinity of the lost Hougues de Millais, and one is bound to notice the many large stones used in building this house. No mounds can be seen in the locality on the Richmond map of 1795, but they had probably been pillaged and flattened by them.

The façade is simple and the windows have not been altered. In the north wall there are a chamfered window and door, now blocked and extraordinarily large and wide for their period; the door is 6ft. 3in. high and 4ft. 5in. wide. A recess to the left of the east fireplace poses problems, and may have been intended to take a jonquière seat. The floors are clay, and there is a bread oven in the west wall. Blocked doors in the east gable suggest that there may have been a straight exterior flight of stairs. A possible sequence of events is a rebuilding in about 1720 of a 17th-century house, with the dower wing added a century later. The more modern house is immediately to the south and this juxtaposition, so often found, discourages the owners from keeping the older house in repair. There is an interesting well, and a stone-lined stream in a lane immediately to the north-east.

See *Archaeology of the Channel Islands*, J. Hawkes, p. 228.

LA RIGONDAINE
(G). (J. Graut on Godfray.)

Stones of many dates give evidence that the Graut family held this property for a minimum of three centuries. Its position is most commanding, but the two attached houses have suffered considerably over the years and have now been demolished. The house to the west had an incised inscription IG EAM1786 for Josué Graut and Elizabeth Amy, who married in about 1774. The eastern portion had in raised letters JG ♡♡ MJ1841, for Josué Graut and Marguérite Jennes, who married in about 1822. In the north wall of the western portion there was a round arch with IG, surely another Josué Graut, on the keystone; its position suggested the entrance to a tourelle staircase, perhaps removed when modernisation was done in 1786, as the stairs could well have been of that date. Sections of another arch exist, with J G 1870 in raised letters.

When uncovered, a niche beside a fireplace in the earlier house contained a curious assortment of objects, suggestive of folklore. Amongst them was a clay pipe with a macabre and emaciated face and prominent cheek bones, probably about 1850 in date, but a type not otherwise recorded in the Island. This motley collection of objects was probably intentional as a charm to avert evil spirits, or as a specific for curing an illness, such as rheumatism. The inclusion of an egg in the collection is a reminder that eggs were regarded as a charm against whooping cough.

The two houses have now disappeared, but the round arch and dated stones have been incorporated in the new structure.

See B.S.J. 1975, p. 356.
Drawing 30.

ROCHEBOIS
Mont du Boulevard, St. Aubin. (F. Hocquard on Godfray.)

Before the 19th century addition was built this property was called La Maison du Val Essart, a house of about 1630. The old part has a round arch measuring 7ft. 3in. by 4ft. 0in., higher than was normal but apparently unaltered. The right-hand side stones are partly masked by the newer house, as well as some windows on that side of the façade; a similar masking occurs at Gouray Cottage (G). Two ground floor windows have their original accolade lintels, but all those on the first floor have been heightened. To the left is a wash-house, with one of the accolade lintels ejected at the time of the alterations. The rooms at the back of the building are almost certainly later additions. The interior woodwork is good, with clapboard partitions and three-panel doors with drop latches. The main bedroom has its end wall panelled in the typical early 18th-century manner. Blue and white Dutch tiles of this date were round the fireplace, as seen at Les Câteaux (T), and Le Marinel (J). The designs are usually biblical. The newer house, built by Hocquard, has mahogany doors and an imposing curved staircase which intrudes into two rooms, forming a curved buttress within them. In the garden wall is a stone dated 1648, and another with 1634. A large lintel, in use in the dining room of the new house, is also dated 1634. The Richmond map suggests that the approach to the house in 1795 was up Ghost Hill, not Bulwarks Hill.

Jurat Guy de Gruchy lived in this house as a child, from 1875, when his father, W. L. de Gruchy, bought it from Jean Carrel, and scratched his initials in monogram on the window of an attic, a room with round-topped dormers which accord with a date of about 1880.

ROCKSTONE
Rue des Vaux (Mt); previously called Les Vaux. (J. Buesnel on Godfray.)

This is an extremely secluded and sheltered house of great charm, situated just above the tiny Commune du Fief de l'Abbesse de Caen. The front façade is built of well-dressed granite, but the sides and back have a mixture of conglomerate, which also composes all the steep banks surrounding the house. The windows have been enlarged, some with brick, though some chamfered

surrounds have survived. At some period the
thatch was removed, the roof heightened and
brick chimneys built. Evidence of this is clear in
the two gable stones a foot below the gutter,
and dated 1606; that on the left has the initials
GM, that on the right IM, or possibly IMT,
and what is probably PHB. Another stone, above
a window, very hard to decipher, appears to read
1588 ELE. It has not been possible to identify

these. There is a fireplace with a niche and a *twin gable-stones at Rockstone, (Mt).*   91
hinge for a cranne; the lintel is wooden, its
granite predecessor having broken. There is evidence of another fireplace, now blocked, in one
of the bedrooms. The west gable has two very small windows. The position of doors on the north
and a curved section of wall indicates that there was a tourelle. There are no outbuildings, nor
evidence that this was ever a farm, which is rather surprising in such a rural context.

See Drawing 91.
    Plate XXIXa.

RONCEVILLE
St. Clement's Road (C).

This very superior house was bought in or about 1860 from the Amy family, by François Le
Maistre. It has a fine fanlight and entrance on the west, and a pillared verandah to the south. It
is suggested that it was built in about 1850 partly because the gas pipes are built into the construction in a manner that looks as if they are original, gas being first mentioned in Jersey in 1849.
One would have thought it was earlier. It is also suggested that Ronceville may have been built
by the same architect as Melbourne House and the present Metropole Hotel in Roseville Street,
once a Hemery house. Road widening here has reduced the size of the garden. The house
presumably took its name from the Rue des Ronces, St. Clement's Road.

See Plate XXIXb.

ROSEDALE FARM
Rue des Issues (J). (A. Le Couteur on Godfray.)

This farm provides another example of vaulted pigsties. They are in three sections in a row,
which is the most common pattern, but have a pitched roof covered in rough cement; attached to
the end of the row is a privy, with matching roof and the same interior ceiling, cunningly
constructed in beehive manner.

The main room of the house has a beam which forks when it enters the north wall, a comparatively rare feature. On the south wall is the broken remnant of a fire insurance badge. In front
of the main door, and very rare, is a simple porch supported on slender chamfered pillars of
granite, clearly copied from some 17th-century example.

The present outhouse to the west has a first-floor granite fireplace of simple design.

ROSELANDS
Croix Besnard (S). (A. Aubin on Godfray.)

This typical 18th-century house almost certainly stands on the site of a far older building, La
Ville ès Tubelins, which would seem to be the property bought by the Seigneur de Lerrier in
Brittany, ancestor of the Lerrier family in Jersey, after his defeat in the Battle of St. Aubin du

Cormier in 1495. His great-great-granddaughter Rachel (b. 1610) married Jean Le Tubelin. In 1743 Abraham Aubin fs. Abraham bought a property in St. Saviour from his mother, Marie Le Tubelin, on the Fiefs of La Motte and Longueville, and it is probable that it was the predecessor of Roselands, though one would not have expected those fiefs to extend so far north. An advertise-met in *Le Soleil de Jersey* on 3 March 1798 states that Mrs. Le Tubelin is offering for sale "le Clos de Rouvet et le petit Clos de Gallais . . . ils sont aussi bien commodes à faire de la brique, l'argile est sur les lieux"; and half a century later Godfray showed three brickfields in the immediate vicinity.

High in the west gable is a stone with I L P 1731, which does not seem to accord with what we know about this house, and it may have been brought from elsewhere. The façade has been modernised by the introduction of french windows and round-topped dormers. The stairs, curving round a continuous central newel, and much of the internal wood partitioning, could be early 18th century. Some panelling and doors are very skilful copies of the style which would have fitted such a staircase. A delightful house with a prolific garden.

See Payne's *Armorial*, p. 252.

LES ROUTEURS
Off St. Martin's Road (S). (J. Perchard on Godfray.)

A stone with 18 T P C E G L 89, for Thomas Perchard and Elise Gallichan, is in the side of the house, and above it is a far older stone, apparently a gable stone from an earlier building, with 1692 IPC MG; these point to a continuous Perchard ownership for two centuries. A fireplace with unusually deeply moulded corbels must have come from the first house, this perhaps being the small building to the south-east. A gatepost in the front garden is inscribed I P C 1772, and another, dated 1773, leads into field No. S. 301, whence it is said there used to be a lane leading to La Fosse à l'Ecrivain.

ROYDE HOUSE
Midvale Road, St. Helier

This house has been chosen as an example of the many town houses and terraces of good quality which were being built in the Regency and early Victorian periods. The Richmond map shows fields with scarcely a house in the northern part of the town; fifty years later Godfray shows us dense building over the whole area. These town houses were in great demand by the many retired army and navy officers who flocked to the Channel Islands in search of what was then inexpensive living, combined with good education for their sons, a mild climate and a fairly gay social atmosphere.

Royde House has a classical façade, a sizeable back garden, with coach house and other offices opening on to Clairvale Road. Internally the lofty rooms are well finished with decorative cornices. It was built in 1836 by one William Much who had bought the land on which it stands from Edouard Nicolle. Much's son William Thomas sold it to Philippe Sorel, whose daughter Agnes Mary, wife of Charles Vatcher, sold it in 1921 to Dr. H. J. Shone.

ROZEL MANOR
(Mt). (P. R. Lemprière on Godfray.)

A little more may be added to what was said in Volume I. Daniel Messervy's mention on Friday, 25 May 1770 of the new manor being built by Charles Lemprière is well known. In 1820 his grandson Philippe Raoul made extensive alterations, covering the granite walls with Roman cement and adding towers and castellations. His grandson Reginald Raoul Lemprière (1851–1931) in his turn undertook internal improvements, inserting in about 1896 the reproduction linen-fold panelling and a plaster ceiling which embodies his and his wife's initials, R R L and CvG, in the design. It is hard to be sure about the stairs, but in their present form they also seem to be of that period, though if so they are very good reproduction work.

In the chapel the pews, of wood from the estate, also appear to be late Victorian, but the stalls and altar are composed of panels of about 1600. The designs include St. John, St. Bartholomew, St. Thomas and several representations of St. Peter, as well as a prophet with a book.

Information from Mr. E. C. Rouse, F.S.A., the ecclesiastical expert, who visited the chapel in 1972.

LA RUETTE
Near Carrefour Jenkins (L). (E. Bisson and C. Romeril on Godfray.)

There are two adjacent houses of this name, situated above Quetivel Mill in St. Lawrence.

The western house has the inscription P R M R   E C T 1716, for Philippe Rummeril (sic) and Elizabeth Coutanche, married in 1714. A threshold stone in a brick stable is inscribed – N ♡ S V T I B N 175-, with decorative symbols between the T and the I, and between the N and 175-; the stable door jambs cover the beginning and end of the inscription, which is for Philippe Benest who married Sara Vautier in 1735, and their second son, Jean, born in 1737. There is reason to think that this stone has been brought from elsewhere, possibly Mon Plaisir, though within the parish.

This property presents some other problems which are harder to solve. One is a block of stone inscribed with E B S 1884, both the S and the 4 being reversed, on the top. It is a cube of dressed granite with a rough base, and must have been intended to be sunk into the ground up to the level of the dressing. It clearly represents Edouard Bisson, who bought the property from Jean Edouard Martel in 1843, Martel having inherited it through his mother, Madeleine Romeril (b. 1777), great-granddaughter of the Philippe Romeril on the 1716 stone. But the purpose of the 1884 stone is obscure.

Another problem is that above the first floor windows there are hints of another row of openings, the lintels of which are visible within the attic at floor level; but this attic also has beams apparently designed to support another ceiling at floor level. This enigma remains unexplained by several architects consulted, and one can only surmise that a number of changes have been made over the years which altered floor and roof levels.

The more easterly house has been much altered, but there are signs that there was a tourelle, and sundry clues point to an original 17th-century date. The dower wing is a later addition, perhaps of about 1870, when it is likely that the round-topped dormers were added.

LES RUETTES
Rue de la Sceletterie (J). (H. Le Ruez on Godfray.)

Noted principally as the birthplace of Richard Valpy (1754–1836) and Edouard Valpy (1764–1832), this is a very good example of a superior vernacular house of the mid-18th-century, following the accepted pattern of the period, but with interesting features which give it individuality.

In the façade are the initials R V P   C C V 1756, for Richard Valpy and Catherine Chevalier, parents of the two famous schoolmasters mentioned above. The front door is most unusual, in that what seems to be a fanlight is in fact part of the door. The hall is paved with Swanage stone, and the banisters are of the unusual flat two-dimensional type, seen only in four other instances. They are probably the personal whim of a particular carpenter. Some of the doors have six fielded panels with reeded moulding, a transitional design of about 1800. The main bedroom has the end wall panelled, and the north-east corner has a cupboard with a small window; it used to have oak shelves, and in it a mirror and a wig stand were found, showing that it had been a powder closet. All this is likely to be contemporary with the date stone. In the north of this bedroom there is a "paûte" within a cupboard. In the west bedroom, also panelled, there is a cupboard opening to a shaft which could be reached through a window in what was the outer gable wall, now blocked by the later addition of a farm cottage; the object of this arrangement was to enable farm produce to be stored in the attic without going through the main house. The roof timbers are very fine, and extremely old floor-boards have survived in the attic and in the east bedroom. In the north bedroom there are the corbels of a simple fireplace. In about 1853 Moise Orange, the then owner, had an office built to the north, and also inserted a small window in the back ground floor room, from whence he could watch his workers, he being a consumptive and unable to work himself.

Les Ruettes was bought in 1811 from Josué Le Sueur by Philippe Le Ruez (b. 1783), Le Sueur having bought it from Jean de Ste Croix, who bought it from the Reverend Richard Valpy.

His ownership is marked by a lintel, now in use as the step into the stable, with incised initials, E D S C with a reversed N over the E. Philippe Le Ruez married Sophie Rachel du Pont (b. 1800), who came of a French refugee family which had settled in Hue Street, then at Vieux Ménage (S), as is testified by dated stones there. She is reputed to have established a herb garden in the walled garden at Les Ruettes, and it is said that people came from all over the Island to obtain her herbal cures. It was her daughter, Sophie Elise Le Ruez, who married Moise Orange (1827–1867), who sold it to her future husband in 1857. In 1879 it was again sold to one Emanuel Galodé fs. Casimir, and later it returned to the ownership of Philippe Le Ruez's grandson-in-law. Sophie Elise Orange (b. 1864) married John Stephen Orange Arthur of La Pompe (My), and Les Ruettes remains in the Arthur family.

When Moise Orange died in 1867 the contents of the house were sold, as well as wood (oaks from le Clos de la Cache), farm animals and equipment; the sale list shows it to have been a well furnished house with much silver. Curtains were still not mentioned, but there were carpets in some of the rooms, and the furniture was mainly mahogany, though walnut, oak and rosewood also appear. The item "wash stand", in English, appears for each bedroom, but is not found in earlier inventories.

ancient roof-timbers at Les Ruettes, (J).

92

This house has greatly benefited from the fact that its owners have always been able to keep it in good repair, but have not had the wherewithal to make drastic alterations. It has thus retained many interesting features, and with them the serenity which must have existed in Sophie Rachel's healing herb garden.

See Drawing 92.
Plate, colour 3a.

ST. BRELADE'S HOSPITAL
Mont des Vaux (B).

A prosperous and benevolent shipowner and merchant named Thomas Denton, or d'Enton (1701–1770), with his wife Jeanne (1697–1770), daughter of Pierre Le Bailly, founded this charitable establishment. They were very St. Aubinais people, and Pierre Le Bailly has his initials on La Vieille Maison (q.v.). When the Chapel of Ease was built in St. Aubin in 1750, Thomas and Jeanne were among the founders and presented a baptismal dish 13in. in diameter, with the maker's mark I G (probably Jean Gruchy) under a crown. Being childless the couple decided in 1757 to found a "hospital" or almshouse for the poor of their parish. Thomas predeceased his wife, and in her will she left a further £1,500 to the hospital, which was so well endowed that a larger house was bought for it on the opposite side of the road, from Thomas Pipon. There is a portrait here of Thomas Denton, but it is in a sorely damaged condition.

The façade bears a stone inscribed G P B Connétable 1853, for George Philippe Benest, who was Constable 1844–1860. The left-hand part of the building was used as a parish hall for a while,

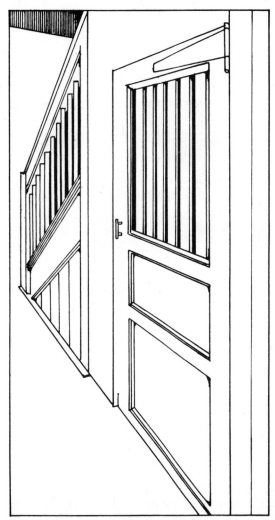
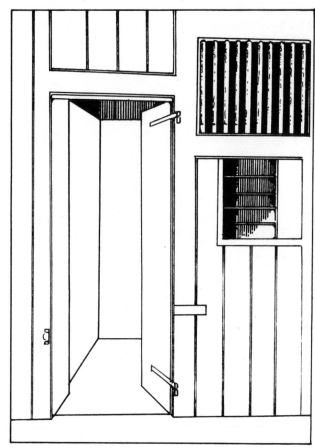

93

ST. BRELADE'S HOSPITAL, St. Aubin.
left: a ventilated store-room under the stairs:
right: a detention cell, in the portion formerly
used as the Parish Hall.

and interior features, such as stairs and doors, accord with such a date. This fact accounts for the three cells which used to be in a back room, one of which survives. They have wooden partitions, with grilles admitting but little light, and primitive sanitation in the form of a drainage hole in one corner. They were not of course intended for the hospital inmates, but for short-term detention of any persons arrested by the Constable and awaiting trial, or simply as a "cooler" for the un-cooperative.

The right-hand portions of the building had good panelling, three panelled doors, and fine stairs, borne on one great newel post 6in square and perhaps 30ft. high; all of this accords with a date of 1750–1770. It was recently considered necessary as a fire precaution to cover over the panelling with plaster board, and one hopes that when the building is no longer an Old People's Home, it may all be uncovered again.

In the attics are small windows to light the stairs, such as we have seen in Hue Street and a few other places. The windows of the front façade have slightly curved granite lintels, and the gutter is also in stone. The back garden has a door leading to what was the railway line, and in earlier times the mill leat, and the percage path, making it a richly historic door.

See Balleine, *Biographical Dictionary*, p. 213.
    Balleine, *Bailiwick of Jersey*, p. 104.
    Old Channel Islands Silver, p. 14.
    B.S.J. 1917, p. 326.
    Drawing 93.
    Plate XXIX c.

ST. MAGLOIRE
High Street, St. Aubin

The outside appearance of this house belies its true age. It is known as having been the home of the famous Charles Robin, who was born in 1743 and died there ummarried in 1824. It seems likely that its first occupant was his father Philippe (1703–1754), from 1736 when he married Ann, heiress of Jean Dauvergne; he was amongst the original donors who had St. Aubin's Chapel erected. It was probably here that the two younger Dauvergne sisters and their brother-in-law (Ann having died) carried on their "mestier de marchandise", for at that time the little house stood on land which fell to sea level on the coast road, an area now densely built over. We are not told in the family's mutual agreement of 1751 what type of merchandise they stocked, but in that position it was probably an all-purpose shop with a bias towards ships' chandlery.

The house is reputed to date from 1640, as well it may, though considerable alterations in the form of panelling were made, perhaps at the time of the Dauvergne-Robin marriage, and even more extensive work was undertaken in the 1800–1820 period. As Charles Robin, when he returned to Jersey in 1802, was a very rich man, it may have been he who built on to the south, installing a spacious flying staircase with rounded handrail and unusually thick balusters. At the same time a large and imposing drawing room was added, with a huge bow window commanding a view over the whole of St. Aubin's Bay, such as a retired seaman would have loved. The woodwork and windows of this room are in agreement with such a date. A window sash in what has now become a passage bears names of the Robin family scratched on the glass.

See Balleine, *Biographical Dictionary*, p. 562.
    B.S.J. 1907, p. 156.
    Form of Family Agreement, in La Haule MSS.

ST. MARTIN'S HOUSE
Near the Church (Mt). (P. Collas on Godfray.)

Recent alterations, which included stripping the façade of its plaster, have revealed a round arch, a good deal mutilated, of the 1620 period. One can also see that the window apertures were of the six-piece chamfered type, later enlarged vertically with brick.

The room in the south wing, dated with apparent accuracy at 1763, has had all its granite exposed, showing that it originally had a north window, and a granite fireplace of simple type, where the stone was probably never meant to be exposed. The main beam, which had later been boxed in and painted white, was stripped and found to be padded with a newspaper of 1864, a period of known alterations. A decade earlier an imposing staircase had been inserted, and a silver medallion in the newel post records the name of the owner, the date and the name of the architect, J. Jacobs, perhaps a son of a builder J. Jacobs of Old James Street listed in an 1834 almanac.

In 1867 an inventory was made, the house then being let. The sole item in the pantry was a barrel of gooseberry wine, and in the back porch we find "stone cross", which is surely the top of a pre-Reformation cross originating from La Chapelle de Sire Augustin Baudains; this relic is still to be seen in the garden of the house.

At the date of the inventory carpets appear in most of the rooms, as do curtains and blinds. The "nineteen likenesses" in the drawing room must be the collection of Le Hardy portraits in oil, no longer at St. Martin's, but preserved by the descendants and their heirs. A later inventory of 1877 shows, in the hall, a "long family spear". This was the ancient halberd which disappeared some fifteen years ago, a relic of the days when certain houses in the eastern parishes had the duty of halberd service, that is to say conducting prisoners from Mont Orgueil Castle to St. Helier for trial, before there was a town prison.

See B.S.J. 1960, p. 325; 1972, p. 361.
       p. 83, specification for alterations.
       Collas family MSS.

ST. MARY'S RECTORY

Curiously little is known about our Rectories and none, with the exception of St. Saviour, is of any age. Indeed several are quite modern, and even the site has been changed. There are occasional references to individual rectories in old documents. For example, there is a mention of the cost of repairs, in 1585, to St. Martin's Rectory, which was on or near the site of the present one. In 1606 David Bandinel, Rector of St. Brelade, cut some trees for repairs to his rectory without permission; he was fined, and the wood returned, to be used for the church. In 1705 Jean Clement, a mason, was paid £3 4s. 9d. tournois for five days' work on the rectory at St. Clement. In 1715 the heirs of Clement Le Couteur were charged a third of the cost of repairs to St. John's Rectory.

Details regarding St. Mary's Rectory can be followed in the parish records, and are probably representative of the situation in all the parishes. Repairs at St. Mary's in 1766 mainly concerned the cider-making room, which the parish was renovating, including treating a smoking hearth and renewing most of the roof. There was a "maison appellée le colombier" where it was necessary to lay a stone floor as the lower part was used as a stable. The cider press was said to be useless. The total repairs were estimated to cost £666 d'ordre, to be raised by parish rate. If wood was needed, ash and elm were to be felled in the rectory grounds. Further repairs were carried out in 1771, and in 1777 the Rector asked for gates instead of doors in the grounds. In 1776 the Rector, François Le Breton, received £600 d'ordre to put a ceiling in the main room, to build another room at right angles with a tiled roof, and a kitchen measuring 18ft. by 10ft. with another room over it. In 1783 the Rector, François Valpy, appealed to the Privy Council against a Royal Court verdict in a case in which the parish accused him of irregular proceedings and infringement of the rights of the parochial officers; but the following year Rector and Constable made up their quarrel and the parish paid £36 costs. In 1798 repairs were done in "coeur de chêne du clou de Jersey", and two coats of paint. The Rectory was re-thatched, the necessary wood for repairs again being cut in the rectory and cemetery grounds. In 1801 shutters (the English word is used) were fitted to the four ground floor windows, and in 1805, in order to render the front façade uniform, sash windows were inserted, all to be of equal size. This is an important point. In 1836 the church-wardens were ordered to plant oaks in the rectory grounds.

It is said that the present Rectory was built by the Reverend Philippe Guille, Rector 1838–1856, with his wife's money, and the lay-out on Godfray's map shows it to have been done before 1849. Mrs. Guille is said to have held meetings in the big upper room, making bandages for the troops during the Crimean War.

See B.S.J. 1893, p. 193; 1908, p. 317.

ST. PETER'S HOUSE
Mont des Routeurs (P). (P. J. Simon on Godfray.)

There is a heraldic stone on the façade here quartering Payn and Dumaresq arms, with a date, hard to see, but probably 1754. The property had come to Sir John Dumaresq (1749–1819) in

1784 through his mother Marie (1716-1784), daughter of Raulin Robin; her grandfather, Raulin Robin, had bought it in 1708 from Jean Arthur fs. Jean, fs. Charles, in which connection it may be noted that field No. P. 460 is le Jardin d'Arthur. Arthur had inherited it from his grandmother, Catherine Robin.

Sir John's daughter, Marie Dumaresq, married General John Le Couteur. Among the Le Couteur papers is a vellum bound book used for gardening notes, and a torn and faded entry reads: "La néscence de mon fils Jean et Ph. estai garite dans un livre qui fut consumé dans l'embrasement de notre maison". (The birth of my sons Jean and Philippe were put for safety in a book which was destroyed in the burning of our house.) This indicates that St. Peter's House was burnt down some time after 1751, when Philippe was born, and rebuilt a few years later. In 1809 Stead says: "The gardens and grounds are laid out with great taste, and the mansion is well adapted for the use of a large and opulent family". In 1831 George Dumaresq, grandson of Sir John, sold the house to François Wheeler Armstrong, who had married Esther Françoise de Quetteville. Armstrong sold it in 1841 to Pierre Jean Simon, who in 1850 sold it to the Hon. Eliza Grace Vernon née Coke, niece of the Earl of Leicester. She was the grandmother of Sir William Venables Vernon, Bailiff (1852-1934), who made drastic alterations and enlargements.

See *A Picture of Jersey*, J. Stead, p. 202.
    Victorian Voices, p. 5.
    B.S.J. 1905, p. 156.

ST. PETER'S RECTORY

St. Peter's is a peripatetic Rectory; originally it was on Le Mont du Presbytère, the little hill rising from St. Peter's Valley to La Hague Manor. It then moved to a site near La Croix au Lion, and in recent years what is now known as The Old Rectory was sold, and the Rector moved to the present modern house near the church.

Already in 1790 it was found that the old Rectory just south of La Hague was inconvenient and in bad condition; in 1813 payments were made for thatch and tiles to repair the roof, but in 1815 it was sold to Jean Pipon of La Hague for 38 quarters 7 cabots of wheat rente, and it was decided that a house must be bought, nearer the church, for the Rector. After some searching a choice was made and the house of Elie Le Grand was bought. This was what is now known as La Croix au Lion, immediately west of the "Old Rectory", Le Grand having bought it from Jacques Payn. The committee formed to transact this business found the house entirely satisfactory, but there is then a gap in the records, and the contractor then announced that it would be most unwise to rebuild on old walls, and so it was decided to build anew, and Le Grand's house became the stables, presshouse and coach-house. The Rector, Reverend George Balleine (Rector 1815-29) was allocated £24,000 tournois "pour la bâtisse de la maison presbyteriale". The plans are given in great detail, with brick being imported from England for the window surrounds, red deal to be used as well as Portland stone, all imported. In 1817 the Assembly met at the new Rectory, and they found that the Reverend Balleine had exceeded the estimate by putting lead instead of "papier tarré" on the roof, marble instead of ordinary stone for the fireplace surrounds in several rooms, and making the handrail of the stairs in mahogany, as well as adding a wash-house and bake-house; however as all this was done at his own expense, the parish was delighted and felt that the new Rectory would be a great asset.

In 1818 a parish rate of 800 francs annually was raised to reimburse the mortgages on the Rectory, and in 1821 it was already being re-painted. It is interesting to note that in 1815 Jacques Payn's widow was receiving an annual sum of £80 tournois from the Trésor for her dower rights on the older house.

This latter house, now in separate ownership, and re-established as a dwelling house, has six chamfered lintels, four of them accoladed, and within the house there are two dated stones, one 1633 and one 1645. A window sill has I P   I L B 1773, for Jacques Payn who married Jeanne Le Brocq in 1763, and it may be noted that field P. 642 is called Le Clos de Jacques Payn. On the apex of an outhouse abutting onto the road is a granite cross, shaped to fit such a position; this is an important point as it shows that it was not the top part of a wayside cross at La Croix au Lion cross-roads, as one might otherwise have supposed, but was designed for the roof of an ecclesiastical building, and one wonders what this was? The answer is offered by another field name. The fields opposite (P. 553-556) are named La Flocquetterie, a proof that this area was the headquarters of Robert de Flocques, stationed there during part of the French Occupation of 1461-1468. It is on record that the monks of St. Peter's Priory complained that the invaders had turned them out of their house, and there can be little doubt that La Flocquetterie was at or near the site of this Priory, and this strongly suggests that the cross on the outhouse came from the priory chapel.

In spite of the great pains taken with the 1815 house it seems to have needed constant attention, like its precedessor, and perhaps it was not as well built as the records would have one think. For instance considerable repairs were undertaken in 1848, it was painted inside and out in 1855, and in 1857 the then Rector, Clement Le Hardy offered to pay £30 sterling for a new coach-house, the existing one being in a ruinous condition. In 1864 3 "grilles bivalves" (gratings) were fitted in the two parlours and the library, and galvanised iron was put to replace zinc along the apex of the roof, and in 1872 it was decided to plaster the whole frontage with Portland cement. However in 1877 its condition was found to be very bad, due to damp caused by the lack of ventilators (soupirails), drain pipes and drains (égouts et saignées). The estimate for what was needed included a second staircase, and amounted to £133 10s. sterling. The Rector, the Reverend William Brine Le Maistre, Rector 1877-1897, offered to pay for other improvements, amounting to £200; these included gate pillars for £40, bay windows (fenêtres cintrées) for £20 and a portico for £20. Later the same year the parish decided to enlarge the north-west room, to match that on the north-east which the Rector had already enlarged, so that the house would be symmetrical, but finally the Rector offered to pay for that too. At the same time he inserted a doorstep with A D 1877 inscribed in bold figures.

> See Cartulaire No. 272.
>   Extente 1528 (Floktre), 1607 (Flocktree).
>   St. Peter's parish and church records.
>   La Hague manuscripts, No. 47 of 1815, *et alia.*
>   MSS. belonging to descendant of Le Feuvre family.
>   B.S.J. 1912, p. 137.
>   Drawing 29. Plate XX c.

ST. SAVIOUR'S RECTORY

The birthplace of Lillie Langtry née Le Breton (1853-1929), the famous Jersey Lily, must hold a place in any review of Jersey houses. On a window pane in the study she scratched her name on the evening before her marriage in St. Saviour's Church to Mr. Edward Langtry on 9 March 1874.

The evolution of the house seems to stem from a traditional four-roomed south-facing nucleus, which contains one granite fireplace with lightly decorated corbels. The fireplace in the east room has been infilled and little that is original remains. The woodwork of these ground floor rooms is of the 1830 style, with varied mouldings. On the first floor there are remnants of older styles in door mouldings and hinges, and some doors have a most unusual arrangement of panels, with two small ones above, two high narrow ones below them, and only one at the base, a transition between the 18th- and 19th-century fashions. Some wall cupboards have early wooden hanging pegs. One suspects that a wing was added to the west, perhaps in the early 18th century. One window is what is now the kitchen testifies to this age. During the time of Dean Le Breton, Rector of St. Saviour 1850-1875, a study and a drawing room above it were added to the north. They are fine rooms with big windows, marble fireplaces and ceiling roses. At some period the east-facing wing running southwards was converted, its upper floor becoming additional bedrooms, and the windows being surrounded in modern brick. Canon Luce, Rector 1895-1912, is known to have made some improvements at his own expense. The tiled roof, replacing thatch, dates from 1802.

The stable block was added to the north and retains the stalls, manger and hay rack, and in the adjoining tack room is a very small fireplace, more to prevent damp damaging the leather than to

PLATE XXIX

a. Rockstone (Mt), 17th century house, altered later

b. Ronceville (H), early 19th century

c. Near St Clement's church

d. St Aubin's Hospital (B), *c* 1750

PLATE XXX

a. Seafield (L)

b. Slate Farm (C)

c. The Temple at Victoria College and detail of ceiling moulding (taken before the fire. It has since been restored). All early 19th century.

warm the coachman. Alongside there is a bakehouse. These probably date from 1876. In the sheltered well favoured garden were noticed one piece of moulded stone, probably of the 15th century, and a roughly octagonal stone trough with an outlet hole, of a type often found in an ecclesiastical context.

See *The Parish Church of St. Saviour*, F. de L. Bois.

SEAFIELD
Millbrook (L). (J. Le Gros on Godfray.)

Not surprisingly, no house was shown here on the Richmond map, and the area was sand dunes down to the seashore.

The house was built by Jean, father of Gervase Le Gros, M.A., F.S.A., Seigneur of Mélèches, who lived there and had a long career of legal service, being an Advocate in 1853, Greffier 1861–1875, Vicomte 1876–1894 and Jurat 1895–1913. From 3 September to 6 October 1887 the Princess Stephanie of Austria stayed at Seafield with a retinue of sixteen persons, some of whom had to be found accommodation in the village. On her arrival the Vicomte's carriage was put at her disposal to take her to the house.

She was the daughter of Leopold of the Belgians. Born in 1864 she married the Archduke Rudolph, Crown Prince of Austria Hungary, only son of Franz Joseph, in 1881. Her husband, as the world knows, was found dead at Mayerling, near Vienna, in 1889, and in 1900 she married Count Lonyay of Hungary, and she lived until 1945. When in Jersey she used the title of Countess of Lacroma, the name of an island off the coast of Yugoslavia which belonged to the royal family, and which she had much loved.

This is a very splendid house, and unlike any other in the Island, and with a lingering feeling for Georgian proportions and symmetry. The interior, though the two main reception rooms are very fine, is less opulent than the exterior would lead one to believe. But the ceiling roses and cornices are elaborate, particularly in the hall, where some of the motifs are like those used at 9 Pier Road. The dining room is fitted with mahogany sideboards, and the hall repeats the Ionic pilasters on the outside by producing them in its four corners, divided to fit into a right angle, a novel treatment.

The two surviving fireplace surrounds are in veined marble, a pattern one sees in relatively humble farmhouses, and the door architraves are simple, with no corner bosses. The stairs are not very impressive, though the mahogany decoration on the sides of the risers is intricate. The rooms on the upper floors are very simple in décor, though some detailing may have been removed over the years. The central room in the dome is a perfect circle and the bedroom below is a semi-circle. Most of the windows are round headed and some are in three sections with Ionic pilasters between the sections, and the north verandah is supported on four Ionic pillars backed by pilasters. The south façade is even more imposing, with rusticated arches to the basement entrances, round-headed windows behind six Ionic pillars on the first floor, and deep, complex moulding with dentils between it and the second floor, the whole flanked by wings, and all embellished with cast-iron balconies. In all, a house of great distinction.

See Drawing 47 Plate XXX a.

LA SERGENTÉ
La Pulente (B). (J. Le Boutillier on Godfray.)

There are houses called La Sergenté in several parishes, and no doubt they existed in every parish which had a Royal Fief upon it.

In the Appairiement de St. Brelade for 1774, Chef de Charette No. 1 is Jean Le Boutillier ca. ux. Jeanne Martel; in 1670 it had been Thomas Martel fs. François. Herein lies a fascinating story of the Martels of Cognac fame.

The name Martel has been recorded in Jersey since 1299, but the family first appeared in St. Brelade when Brélade Martel fs. Lorans (1564-1631) bought "les terres de la Sergenté" from Pierre Laell. It is believed that he demolished Laell's old house in the meadow, remnants of which could still be seen in this century, and built a house on the present site. The west gable wall, which is 8ft. thick, speaks of great antiquity, but the date 1681 and the initials of François Martel indicate a considerable restoration, and there have been other more recent changes. François was great-grandson of Brélade, who had two grandsons, Philippe, father of François, and Thomas (1652-1698), who had two daughters, Marthe and Catherine, and one son, Jean (1694-1753). Marthe married William Kastell and Catherine married Henry Marett. François's brother Edouard had a daughter Ann who in 1769 married Jean Le Boutillier (1740-1823). Jean Martel emigrated to Cognac with Kastell and Marett, then spelt Kastel and Maret, and all three decided to double the last letter in their names to prove their British nationality, and the famous brandy firm became Martell from then onwards.

The word Sergenté means the feudal function of a Sergent and the land, on which there might be a house, which went with it. The duties of the Sergent included the carrying out of any orders made by his feudal Court, and appearance at the Assise d'Héritage on behalf of his Fief.

See *La Famille Martell*, Roger Firino.
    Balleine, *Biographical Dictionary*, p. 486.

LA SERGENTÉ
La Grande Route de Rozel (Mt). (P. Pallot on Godfray.)

There are two houses here, the more northerly having a stone with 18 I P L   E P C 21 over the door in raised letters, no doubt for a Pallot-Perchard marriage. The corbels of a stone fireplace have survived in a west ground floor room, and there are signs in the north wall of one of those apertures through which food scraps were thrown from the kitchen to the yard. The westward extension, demoted into a stable, may have had habitable rooms on the first floor. Unexpectedly there is a round arch in the north façade. In view of the name of the property, this is probably the remnant of a far older house.

Only slightly newer is the house to the south, with the inscription 18 P P L   E D S 34, showing the property to have remained with the Pallots in the next generation. The kitchen had a fireplace with corbels and a wooden lintel, and the customary side niches. A bakehouse, retaining its copper and bread oven, has a fine granite chimney, but the main house has brick chimneys.

This property has recently undergone much restoration.

See Drawings 30, 38.

LA SERGENTÉ
Les Grupieaux (P). (P. Bigrel on Godfray.)

The front façade is slightly chequered in the colouring of the granite, but the shades are so harmonious that the result is delightful. Over the door is the date 1794, with ligatured initials which represents Philippe Le Boutillier who married Douce Balleine in 1779.

LA SERGINE
Rue des Issues (J). (J. Pinel on Godfray.)

There is a conglomeration of initials here, probably representing Le Quesnes, on two attached cottages, with a western addition which could have been a bakehouse or presshouse. From west to east the inscriptions read: 17 C L Q   M G F 28;   17 E L Q   A L C 08;   and 17 C L Q 08.

See Drawing 27.

SLATE FARM
St. Clement's Road (C). (J. de Veulle on Godfray.)

It is generally believed that this house derived its name from being the first in the district to be roofed in slate. From the curious position of the granite gutter, it would appear that the roof was raised at the same time, leaving the gutter to masquerade as a string course. The bedroom windows are unusually low, indicating that the floor level was raised. It is a double-pile house, and its appearance suggests a date of about 1800. At the outer corners there are pilasters, a foretaste of the breakaway from the truly vernacular house towards the grander classical façades of the middle of the century. The porch over the front door is a wooden platform resting on four-sided granite pillars, one of only two examples seen of blending 17th-century porch pillars with the classical porch which was soon to become universal. The west gable of the house is exceptionally thick.

Over a door in the farm buildings is a stone with A D V (the A D being ligatured) I M G F 1786, for Aaron de Veulle, born 1741 and grandfather of Sir John de Veulle, Bailiff, and Jeanne Marguerite Godfray (b. 1745). It is not impossible that 1786 is the date of erection of the house, the alterations being a generation later. In 1809 Stead considered it a "commodious mansion". The farm building on the west, formerly a stable, is very fine, with brick string courses deftly inserted in granite walls. It is said that it was rebuilt after a fire about a century ago.

At the roadside is a well-built abreuvoir fed by a never-failing stream, claimed to be exceptionally pure.

The Richmond map shows only one small building, right on the roadside. It will be recalled from Volume I that there was a cottage just behind the present house with a stone dated 1634.

See *A Picture of Jersey*, J. Stead, p. 117.
    Old Jersey Houses, Vol. I, p. 217.
    B.S.J. 1917, p. 214.
    Plates V d, XXX b.

SPRINGVALE
Rue Mathurin (G). (T. Hooper on Godfray.)

Chef No. 39 in the Appairiement de Grouville of about 1770 was Jean Payn fs. Jean, holding over 33 vergées of land, and another 13 vergées away from the farm. He certainly believed in putting up date stones, and we find: I P ♡ M A M, for Jean Payn and Marie Amy from Le Câtillon, on the front of the house; adjacent to it is another inscription, I P ♡ M V V 1778; and on either side of the further entrance, now blocked, a third, I P ♡ M V V 1784, for Jean Payn and Marie Vivian.

Extensive repairs were undertaken in 1973, in the course of which some stone fireplaces were found, of the simple undecorated style which were perhaps never meant to be uncovered. Some nice mid-18th-century panelling in the west ground floor room was removed in order to expose the stonework. There was a dado rail all round the room, and the window surrounds, shutters and sashes were all contemporary, as indeed were two other windows on the first floor. The partitions in the hall were of clapboarding, and it is surprising that they are not of stone in

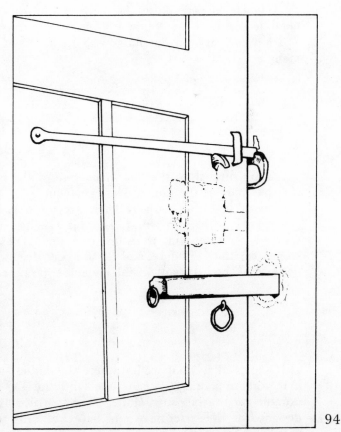

94

draw-bar for securing front door at Springvale, (G).

such a superior house. The front door, with some bottle glass in the lights above it, has six panels and is exceptionally wide, measuring 49in. This door is secured by an extremely simple and effective device, a block of wood measuring 2½in. by 2½in by 9in., which slips over the door frame into a recess in the wall. This has not been seen anywhere else. There are many contemporary doors and hinges.

The addition to the east, perhaps a dower wing, has casement windows, and bears the inscription I P and M V V with the date 1790, an identical inscription appearing on one of the farm buildings. The stairs, later removed, had stick balusters and a heavy newel post, but a flat-topped handrail; this could be a transitional design, or an older handrail may have been re-used.

See Drawing 94.

SURVILLE
Ruettes Pinel (H). (M. Le Gallais on Godfray.)

A further examination has disclosed some massive stonework in the tourelle. The first floor landing is in stone, as occasionally occurs. Immediately west of the tourelle, on the ground floor, are two very small rooms, literally roofed in stone. The ceiling of the room nearer the stairs measures 6ft. 6in. by 5ft. 0in., all in one piece, and looking up at it one is automatically reminded of La Hougue Bie.

Five steps up the stairway is a recess, now blocked, which would have opened out beside the stone-roofed store-room, and must have been designed for loading produce destined for the upper storey or the attic, without going through the main living rooms.

On a gatepost is J L G 1841, and on an outhouse 17 M L G L   M P D 56. Two successive Mathieus Le Gallais married Maries Poingdestre. In the garden wall of the modern house is a coloured heraldic plaque with "Surville 1841", and arms which appear to be those of the Poulet family, and have nothing in common with those of the Le Gallais, a family which had held Surville for many generations.

See Payne's *Armorial*, p. 210.

SYCAMORE COTTAGE
Market Hill, St. Aubin.

A slate sundial on the right-hand side of the house is inscribed 1794, which seems a likely date for that part of the house. The east-facing wing is the older part, and the upper room retains the corbels of an early fireplace. There are some nice early doors, one, in this same room, with bottle glass panes in the upper part. There is a well in the secluded, sheltered garden. To the right of the door of the older wing is a stone inscribed P D 1597, which is something of a mystery as the initials seem later than the date, and the P is cut deeper than the D. This stone is difficult to photograph because of the luxuriant wistaria which covers the house.

LE TAILLIS
Rue de la Croix (Mt). (E. Payn on Godfray.)

It seems likely that we have here the earliest dated dower wing to a house, 1751. There is also here a 16th-century dated stone with initials, which is sufficiently rare to make the property notable on that account alone. Found in use as a fireplace lintel, for which it cannot have been designed as the lettering would have been the wrong way up, it is inscribed C B 1588. It is more than likely that this stands for Colas (Nicolas) Baudains, whose first wife died in that year. The succession of Laurens Baudains, the famous benefactor, fell to the descendants of his brothers and sisters, represented by the Payns of Le Taillis through Colas's niece Laurence.

A fireplace in the internal wall has two paûtes (hiding places), one within the recess of the hearth and the other in the wall to the right. In each case you put your hand into a hole, and at a depth less than the length of your forearm is a rounded pot. The first pot contained a clay pipe of the period 1700-1770 with the initials R B, and the maker may have been Richard Bryant, active in England in 1733. The pot in the second paûte was found broken but was expertly mended by our archaeologists, who recognise it as Normandy ware of any date from the late 16th to the 18th century.

An early oak window with four upright members, found in the north wall of the west room, has been saved and is preserved behind glass. There is a tourelle, the steps turning to the left. A low doorway exists which would have served as a loading bay, as at La Tourelle. The landing is in stone, with granite chamfered doorways to the main bedrooms. In the dower wing there are signs that there were two hearths superimposed.

One wonders what is the date of the façade. It appears to be older than the 1751 on the dower wing, yet certainly not as old as the 1588 stone. One may suggest a date early in the 17th century, when a rebuilding was done for some purpose we cannot know, perhaps a fire, a collapse from lack of lime in the mortar, or the whim of a fashionable wife. The initials on the dower wing must represent Edouard Payn (b. 1706) who married Elizabeth Nicolle in 1744.

The property is No. 6 in the lists of Chefs in the Appairiement de sa Majesté 1701. It was then held by Michel Payn (b. 1635), grandfather of the Edouard mentioned above, who also appears in the Extente for 1668.

See Payne's *Armorial*, p. 313.
B.S.J. 1903, p. 143.
Appairiement de Sa Majesté 1701 (St. Martin only).
Drawings 26, 28.

TERREBONNE
Rue du Puits (G). (C. Aubin on Godfray.)

The date stone here, reading 17 C A B   I F 78, is for Clement Aubin and Jeanne Falle. Higher up on the façade is another stone with S N, well carved in raised letters, which has not yet been explained, but may be presumed to record ownership previous to that of the Aubins.

The mahogany stairs must have been inserted about a century ago, though they are morticed into a far older central post. The hall is tiled in buff, terra cotta and black squares. The main bedroom has the end wall completely panelled in a style which could be as late as 1778. The hinges and locks on the cupboards are contemporary and there is a paûte in one of them. The west bedroom clearly used to have similar panelling. Over the stable door is a stone with S N 1751, unidentified, and a stone dated 1825 without initials. As is so often the case, extra ground floor rooms were added to the house in about 1820, and the dower wing is dated 1825.

The private lane, La Ruelle de Ravenel, may refer to wallflowers growing there, but Ravenel does appear as the surname Raveney in 1668, a more likely if less romantic explanation.

See B.S.J. 1906, p. 84.
Drawing 38.

LA TOMBETTE
Rue d'Enfer (My). (P. Rondel on Godfray.)

Under dull grey stucco Tombette only invited a passing glance, but the façade has now been stripped and reveals nicely coloured dressed stone blocks. The fenestration is irregular, some window surrounds being early, and all having been heightened. Those which have retained their complete chamfered surrounds are unusually large and the chamfer is lightly moulded, as on some round arches. There is evidence of a tourelle in two adjacent chamfered doorways in the north wall, with remnants of a doorway above them on the first floor, and a portion of a newel step found on the property. On the ground floor, east, is a fireplace with deeply moulded corbels and concave-convex chamfering on the uprights. On the first floor, west, is a fireplace with its corbels and lintel missing, but the uprights have two chamfers; both chamfer stops on the left are Calvary crosses; those on the right have a fleur-de-lys and a cross on an orb. Three doorways in the north wall measure 2ft. 8in. by 5ft. 0in; 2ft. 4in. by 5ft. 6in.; and 3ft. 2in. by 5ft. 6in.; they all have 4in. chamfers. This house is probably unique in having six chamfer stops in the form of a cross, a feature which must give it a pre-Reformation date in origin.

There is a stream in front of the house now, a feature in an elaborate ornamental garden. On both the Richmond and Godfray maps the road seems to twist at this point, but has since been straightened, giving the house a short approach drive.

TRÉOVILLE
Rue de la Hague (P). (P. Le Couteur on Godfray.)

The stone over the front door reads PT♡SCT 1743, which could well be the date of the staircase, now replaced, and the panelling in the upper east room. All window sills have been dropped, perhaps when the present sash windows were installed late in the 19th century. A Philippe Toque fs, Jean was born in 1707 and a Jeanne Tourgy fille Pierre in 1734, and either name is a possibility.

It is almost certain that this is the house sold by Philippe Le Couteur fs. Josué to Marie Le Rossignol in 1836, in which case it seems to have returned to Le Couteur ownership by the time of Godfray's map.

See La Hague MSS. No. 69 of 1836.

TY ANNA
St. Aubin.

A grey-coloured stone over the front door inscribed R R B   M D C 1715 represents Raulin Robin (1668-1731) and his second wife Marie de Carteret (d. 1734), the grandparents of Charles Robin the Newfoundland pioneer.

The house has an attractive but simple staircase, and many pieces of 17th-century stonework are incorporated in the building. These may have been taken from an older house, and there is evidence that there was another house to the right, showing projecting bonding stones as well as fireplace corbels.

See B.S.J. 1907, p. 165; 1949, p. 131.
    Plate XVIII b.

VALE FARM COTTAGE
Mont Fallu (P). (G. de Carteret on Godfray.)

This tenement owed the duty of "faicturier" of Gargate Mill, that is responsibility for keeping the roof in good order; a little surprising, as Quetivel is the mill at the foot of Mont Fallu and Gargate is some distance away.

The property belonged to a de Carteret, descended through Bailiff Helier de Carteret (c. 1490-1580), since 1730. On 20 December in that year Jean de Carteret of St. John and his wife Susanne Nicolle bought a house and land on the Fief du Roi in St. Peter from Jean Simon fs. Philippe. Simon had purchased it from Nicolas Bisson and Elie Falle, and de Carteret had to promise dower apartments for the mother, Elizabeth Romeril. Simon retained the life use, for himself and his wife, of the east end of the house "haut et bas", without responsibility for the upkeep of the roof, as well as ground to the south of the house and its crops and fruit.

Comparison with the 1795 map shows that the road used to go behind the small Simon house, whereas the airport traffic now rushes past its front windows. It seems likely that the present Vale Farm, which was built in 1855, stands where Bisson's house was, and indeed there is in an outbuilding a reversed window lintel inscribed P B S I L C 1729. Over the front door is the inscription I S M ♡ F L F 1714, an early date for the heart motif. Though no marriage has been found to fit these initials, the I S M must surely be Jean Simon, who died in 1739, and had four children baptised in the parish, Philippe (b. 1688), Marie (b. 1694), Elizabeth (b. 1696) and Edouard (b. 1703). The parish register is tantalising in witholding the name of their mother, but these are the only Simon entries appropriate.

In 1832 George de Carteret fs. Jean bought a house with farm buildings and land from Nicolas Bisson fs. Nicolas. Jeanne Tourgis, widow of Nicolas Bisson senior, had the usufruct of the rooms she occupied at the time, and Jeanne Fleury, wife of Nicolas Bisson junior, renounced her dower rights. It seems as if the de Carterets continued to live in the smaller house for some time.

This cottage is now undergoing repairs. The plaster has been stripped and one can now see that the western end is the older part. The main room at this end has a ceiling supported on a great beam, forked at the north end, not unknown in early houses but sufficiently rare to be of great interest. A unique feature is that in the south-east corner of this same room an area of about 3 feet square in the ceiling is in stone, and this is repeated immediately above in the bedroom ceiling. Could this have been a landing at the top of a flight of stairs?

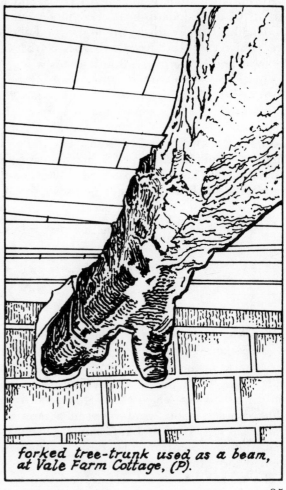

forked tree-trunk used as a beam, at Vale Farm Cottage, (P).

95

See Drawings 27, 95.
Plates VIb, XXXIb.

LA VALLETTE (or VALETTE)
Bellozanne (H). (D. Hamon on Godfray.)

In the 1607 Extente we find Edouard Le Porque paying Thomas Stockert (Stocall) 19 cabots of wheat annually for ground and an old house, which by 1678 had been sold to Philippe de Ste Croix fs. Philippe; he was instructed to "faire bastir et edifier une maison sur icelle et de planter un jardin à pommiers dans la vallette dans deaux aux prochains . . .". The successions of known owners, and the testimony of dated stones make it certain that this is the property concerned.

An unusual feature here is that the latest house has been built behind the earlier, for it is usually the other way round. The earlier house, now called La Pepinière, has on the north a lintel with 1706 E D S X for Edouard de Ste Croix. There are small windows and inside the beams are huge and the joists are curved, features which are often thought to suggest ships' timbers. There are three simple fireplaces with undecorated corbels and wooden lintels. It is recalled that there were no internal stairs, and to go to bed it was necessary to go outside to the external steps, and this in the lifetime of the present owner's great-great-grandmother.

An initialled stone is inscribed P D S X and R A for Philippe de Ste Croix and Rachel Ahier, the parents of the Edouard mentioned above, who had married Anne Langlois in 1704. In plaster along the length of the south of the house, and above the upper windows and with a continuous decorative design are the initials E D S X K L B L 1759, for Edouard de Ste Croix fs. Edouard fs. Philippe, and Katherine Le Boutillier his wife.

This is de Ste Croix territory, and although probably not the actual house concerned in an inventory of 1757, of the effects of the late Philippe de Ste Croix, this is a suitable place in which to refer to it. This Philippe married firstly, Elizabeth Gibaut and secondly Susanne Le Blancq. The house where the inventory was taken consisted of a salle, kitchen, despence (pantry), a small bedroom and two main bedrooms. The linen cupboard was well stocked, having 18 pairs of sheets, 15 pairs of pillow cases and 5 bolster cases; there were 19 fine ladies' caps, 12 coarser ones and 6 small ones. There was silver and pewter, and, most unusual at that date, 9 pictures "tableau des prospects de l'isle de Jersey et Guernsey".

The new house referred to has attractive dormers with barge boards, probably early Victorian.

See B.S.J. 1972, p. 361.
Extentes 1607, 1668.

LA VALLEUSE
St. Brelade's Bay. (J. Piton on Godfray.)

Over the front door is a stone with E L B and the date 1766, and a raised plaque apparently awaiting the initials of a wife. This was Edouard Le Brocq, who was Aide to the Quinzième Chef de Charette in the Appairiement of 1774, and his house was then referred to as "sa maison au pie de la Valeure", implying that Valeure was the name of the hill above the house. There is some confusion between Valleuse, a Norman word for a small dry valley, and Valeure, probably meaning value or price; or the word might be a form of Vallaire, a rampart or palisade. Valeure is the form found in 1774, 1786 and 1858, and is likely to be the correct form. The property was bought by Jean Allez in 1858 from Jean Piton fs. Thomas, a relative, the latter family having inherited it from the Le Brocqs through the female line.

The stairs are most interesting, and somewhat reminiscent of those at No. 7 Pier Road, though no stair well has been allowed here, and so the banisters of the lower flight intersect the string course of the upper. The present owner has heard a tradition that the stairs were made from ships' timbers; it seems more likely that they were constructed in a local shipyard, as one knows was the case with locally-made furniture. Other woodwork in the house is contemporary.

See Drawing 44.

LES VARVOTS
Rue des Varvots (L). (D. Le Riche on Godfray.)

The only item of real age is a gable stone now inserted beside the front door with 1676 N Q R, though the central letter is not very clear. This stone, and the irregular angles of the house plan, may be evidence that in origin the building is older than it looks. There is a bakehouse with hearth, copper and chimney, all in brick. Beside this hearth is a shallow scooped-out area in the wall, such as has been noted in very old houses, intended to make a bench more comfortable for someone leaning back against the wall.

LES VAUX
Rozel (Mt). (? P. Renouf on Godfray.)

Varied conglomerate is used in the walls of this house, with quoins in dressed granite. A small building behind the present house may well have been its precursor. The Richmond map shows buildings which do not accord with what is there now. One suspects that a Renouf owner became prosperous and built his new house in about 1840, still making a traditional type of kitchen fireplace with a wooden lintel.

The beautiful garden, enriched by a stream, was recently featured in an article in *Country Life* by Mr. A. Hellyer.

LE VERT CHAMP
Rue du Hucquet (Mt). (G. Vardon on Godfray.)

A threshold stone leading to the pigsties is inscribed 17 I R D ♡ I A M 27.

During repairs a bottle was found buried behind a main beam, as at Le Mourin (q.v.) and elsewhere, but this is of a different type: it is flat, with three angels' heads embossed in the glass, and a rather large outlet, and is probably a baby's feeding bottle.

THE TEMPLE. VICTORIA COLLEGE (H).

The story of the building of the College is well known, but less so, until its restoration, was the building known as the Temple. It was a gazebo or folly, built for the owner of Mount Pleasant (later Victoria College Preparatory School), long before the College was contemplated. It is composed of a main room with a domed ceiling, with an entrance lobby and stairs down to a further room. A verandah has classical columns, and the whole has some affinity with Flitcroft's temple at Stourhead in Wiltshire, built in 1745. But the interior decoration of our Temple, excellent though it is, suggests a date no earlier than 1810.

The site of Mount Pleasant was almost certainly farmland when Mathieu Amiraux bought it in 1815. In 1824 he sold it to William Le Breton fs. François (1774–1853), grandfather of Lillie Langtry. In 1847 Le Breton sold the whole property to the States for £5,000, plus a sum for 16 vergées of additional land, and the contract refers to "les edifices que ledit Sieur Le Breton a fair ériger sur ladite propriété". The diary of Clement Hemery, who was closely related to William Le Breton, speaks of going to the Temple to smoke after dinner parties at his parents' house in Colomberie, in about 1840.

There is good reason to think that the Temple was used for musical recitals, notably by Hartung and Hegemann, two German musicians living in the Island; and it was here that the Bailiff and Jurats robed for the formal opening of the College on 29 September 1852, an incident vividly recounted by Sir John Le Couteur in his diary for that day.

A garden retreat was no new idea in the early 19th century, nor was the adoption of the Greek style of architecture, though unexpected in Jersey. The dramatic siting of our Temple speaks of classical influence, such as one might have found in the Le Breton family, which produced men of culture and learning.

The interior was sadly damaged by a fire some years ago, but enough remained for careful restoration to be effected. This has been done, and the serene little building, standing so close alongside the main college and the modern science block, retains its Georgian elegance, even if it was built in the Regency period, in an island where new fashions came but slowly. Small as it is, its commanding position and its classical excellence rank it among our most prestigious buildings.

See *Victorian Voices*, p. 238.
Registre reference 195, 22; 16 Oct. 1847.
Plates XXX c and d.

LA VIEILLE MAISON
The Bulwarks, St. Aubin

This is one of the finest, though not the oldest, of the houses along the Bulwarks. It must have been built by Pierre Le Bailly in 1687, and he has left his initials and the date above the front door. He sold the house to Jean Villeneuve in 1705.

The fourth storey has been re-made recently, with the granite so well matched that it is not possible to notice the addition; it had already been heightened in rough, unmatching stonework, and would originally have contained low rooms under a steep roof, perhaps thatched. The windows of the front façade have heavy glazing bars, but can hardly be contemporary with the 1687 date stone, though they could be very early Georgian. On the stairs there is one small casement window, which may be the sole survivor of a complete set of casements; the apertures are fairly large, and may always have been so as there is no sign that they have been enlarged.

The pride of this house is the staircase, surely contemporary; it is in dark wood, probably oak, the walls being panelled in a simple manner. It rises to the full height of the house, twisting round and round, with every flight resting on the great newel which soars up from the base. The balusters are heavy and turned, with turned finials, and the whole is very reminiscent of the staircase at Sausmarez Manor in Guernsey. It seems to be the direct descendant of the circular stone staircase.

One of the bedrooms has a wood-lined recess, which may have been a powder closet, contrived at a later date. There are five very simple stone fireplaces. The front door, now replaced, was very fine, but not 17th century. There was a considerable amount of 18th-century panelling in the ground floor rooms, but unfortunately it was found to be in bad condition and had to be removed.

In a tiny back yard there is a pump, a stone trough and a well 15ft. deep, and therefore below sea level. There is a story that the owner's horse used to be led through the house into this back yard, but this may be apocryphal.

See *English Interiors in Smaller Houses*, M. Jourdain, p. 118.
Drawings 26, 43.
Plate XXXIa.

LA VIEILLE MAISON
Rue du Temple (J). (A. Barette on Godfray.)

The fireplace in the south-east ground floor room is so similar to examples at Les Buttes (1669) and Don Farm (1673) now at the Museum, that one may suppose all three to be the work of one mason. A bedroom retains remnants of another fireplace of similar date, and a small upstairs window may be contemporary. The western bedroom has cupboards with fielded panel doors. This house provides further proof of the excellence of the granite, and of the masons' skill, in the Mont Mado area, a skill still manifested three centuries later.

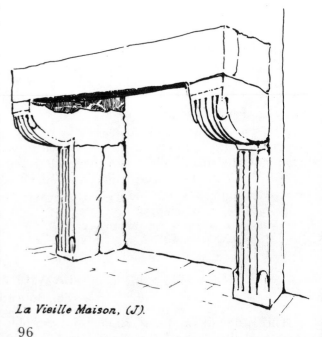

Floor levels suggest that the southern part of the house is earlier than the northern, though both the front and back façades have been altered over the years. The ashlar of the south façade, with the extreme ends of the house still in rougher stone, is reminiscent of La Vallette nearby, which was re-faced in 1796. It looks as if a four-roomed house was built in about 1670, the façade re-faced about a century later, and additions built to the north with a different floor level perhaps a century after that. Considerable changes have been made in this century, making four drastic changes in four hundred years. There is a large flat stone near the well which is said to have been a platform for gutting fish, though it would also have been an aid in lifting heavy weights.

La Vieille Maison, (J).

96

It is thought that at the time of Godfray's map this was the home of Abraham Poingdestre, a wealthy merchant, father of Elizabeth who married Colonel E. C. Malet de Carteret, though the map gives the name of Barette for it.

See Drawing 96.

LA VIGNETTE
Maufant (S). (F. Gaudin on Godfray.)

We had here examples of buildings of three centuries. What had been demoted into a stable was clearly the earliest house, certainly 17th- and perhaps 16th-century. A lone corbel of a fireplace survived in a cow stall. Many early fragments survived also, including a window under the arched entrance, made up from four carved lintels.

A later house has a corbel with a fleur-de-lys design, and above it is a room with very fine panelling, the farmer's safe being built into it. One stone has D G D ♡ E M R and a date hard to decipher; another has D G D S G D and the date 1785. Alongside these older buildings is an imposing Victorian house. Outside the farmyard is a stream and what may have been a lavoir, or an abreuvoir.

See Drawings 38, 97.
Plates XIIc, XXXIIa.

fireplace corbel in the 18th century building at La Vignette, (S).

97

LA VILLE AU VESLET
Near Mont Isaac (L). (J. Gallichan on Godfray.)

Though the façade is plastered over, a series of interesting lintels have survived, three with a scalloped design and an incised cross at the apex of the accolade; two more, reversed, are in use as sills. The main door has a hollow chamfer with an incised cross, which is most unusual, the cross almost always being carved in relief. The stable door also has a wide hollow chamfer. The gable walls are 6ft. thick.

The house was badly burned in 1910, after which the roof was raised. There was formerly an approach road on the east, but the house can now only be approached from the west.

LA VILLE ÈS GROS
Le Couvent (L). (A. Le Gros on Godfray.)

On a lintel over a side door is 17 IGD ♡ IHM38, for Jean Godel and Judith Hamon. On the south-east corner of the roof apex, on the gable side (which is unusual) is 17AGD ♡ IGL48, for Abraham Godel and Jeanne (Le) Gallais, who married in 1729. In the side of a pigsty is a reversed stone with the date 1664 and initials which are almost illegible, the second set perhaps MHM. Two gateposts, pentagonal in section, could have been the uprights of a fireplace.

The field behind the building is called Le Vieux Château and there is much stone débris there. The next field, No. L.349, is le Clos de la Vieille Maison, and it is not impossible that we have here the site of John Walsh's 14th-century stronghold.

See Volume I, p. 208.

LA VILLE ÈS NORMANS
Rue de Bechet (T). (J. Norman on Godfray.)

Considerable alterations have taken place here in the last century. Over the front door, but reversed and plastered over, is the inscription 17 I N M ♡ E M R 44, for Jean Norman and Esther Marett. The gatepost at the entrance reads P N M ♡♡ R N Bk 1834, for Philippe Norman fs. Philippe who married Rachel Naurcombe Baker in Sark in 1833. Her three sons inherited her property, Le Petit Dixcart, which had been bought by her father Jean Baker in 1794 from Thomas Le Feuvre, and it is one of the original 40 tenements in Sark, first granted to Pierre Le Brocq. A stone over a window in a barn is dated 1824, and the sill of another window, perhaps brought from elsewhere, is inscribed 17 I R 42.

The indications are that the 1744 house was altered in about 1834, the ground floor becoming a semi-basement, the first floor becoming the main level, and a third storey being added. At the same time a tall flight of steps was built leading to the new front door. The front façade is plastered, so no join can be seen, nor can it be found on the north, but it is likely that the north rooms were added at the time of the second alteration and built to the full height. In fact a small and very simple four-roomed cottage became an impressive Victorian or near-Victorian house. Ours is not the only generation to go in for the aggrandisement of modest homes.

See *The Fief of Sark*, de Carteret and Ewen, p. 130.

LA VILLE ÈS PHILIPPES
Rue du Puits (G). (P. Mourant on Godfray.)

The date stone over the front door, reading 17 T A B I T Z 78, represents Thomas Aubin and Jeanne Touzel née Le Couteur. It is most unusual to find a widow's initials on a stone, the custom being for the wife to put her maiden name. Jeanne was the mother, by her first marriage of Lieut.-General Helier Touzel (1779–1865), who was Receiver General over the period 1814–1863, and also acted as Deputy Governor to three Lieutenant Governors, Generals H. M. Gordon, Colin Halkett and Thornton, on many occasions.

The doors on the ground floor have six fielded panels and this shows, at that date, a transition stage from the two- and three-panelled door to the ubiquitous six-panelled version of the 19th century, with varied mouldings. The stairs appear to be contemporary.

The name of this delightful group of farms probably derives from a Mariot Philippe who held land on the Fief du Roi and the Fief Astelle in Grouville in 1558, and indeed the boundary between those fiefs passes through the farmyard. Land calle La Clôture is mentioned as being west of Philippe's house, whilst field No. G. 56a, where there used to be some ruins, is La Couture. The site may well be far older even than this, as the Assize Roll of 1309 shows a Carucate ès Phelipes in Grouville.

See B.S.J. 1902, p. 27; 1903, p. 101; 1913, p. 275.
Book of Messervy contracts belonging to Mr. P. E. Le Couteur.

LA VILLE MACHON
Côtes du Nord (T). (P. de Gruchy, Maison de Haut; P. Renaut, Maison de Bas; G. Guille, house now demolished; on Godfray.)

The presumed association with the Machon family must be earlier than any of the dated stones.

This property has the distinction of being situated on at least five fiefs, "Diélament, Triguel, Petit Rosel, Saval, Vanesse ou autres fieux", from which quotation it will be noticed that the men who compiled our ancient documents often played safe, when in doubt, by adding the words "or other fiefs".

In the meadow to the south there is a rough lavoir. There are in fact three houses here, and one contract refers to "La Maison de Bas de la Ville Machon appellée Le Colombier". This colombier is mentioned again for one of the patches of land, and was presumably the dovecot of one of the five fiefs. The Maison de Bas was towards the east, where a third small house was recently demolished.

The Maison de Haut has three inscribed stones, reading P R N ♡♡ M A M, for Renaut and Amy; 18 PDG ♡ MMRN 14, for Philippe de Gruchy and Marie Renaut; and 17 IDG   EDG 83, for Jean and Elizabeth de Gruchy, married in 1757. The appearance of the façade belies its age, which can be deduced from the granite fireplaces and from the thickness of the walls, which measure 5 feet at the west gable.

The Maison de Bas is rather an enigma, and its dated stones suggest sundry alterations; they read 17 P R N M D G 89; 18 P R N ♡ M A M 24; and 1813. There is also a stone here reading 18 P R N M A M 05. The first floor woodwork is very pleasing, with good fireplace surrounds and cupboards, perhaps dating from the 1789 era. One very deep small cupboard was probably the family safe.

LA VILLE MARS
Mont au Prêtre (H). (P. Richardson on Godfray.)

There is no end to the interesting discoveries to be made about Jersey houses, which we are sometimes told are so dull because they are all alike. How under-informed our critics can be.

We find here an earlier single-storeyed house facing south, with granite chimneys, built or bought by Philippe Richardson fs. Hugh in about 1698, when his father was living at or near Ponterrin Mill in Trinity, a little to the north.

In 1768 Philippe's son Jean built the present west-facing house and put his initials with the date over the front door, leaving room for those of his wife. It is probably Jean with whom the diarist Daniel Messervy spent an afternoon on 29 March 1770. It is a small house, only one room deep, with a slate roof, and brick chimneys put there about a century ago. The casement windows have the early type of L hinge, and it is so unusual to find casements in a Jersey house that, combined with their appearance and texture, one is tempted to think that they are original. The doors, of the fielded six-panel type, certainly are, and only lately did they have their wooden drop-hinges removed. The stairs are most interesting and have the serpentine balusters so far recorded only at Les Ruettes (J); 16 Hill Street (H); Bellozanne Abbey (H); and Les Chasses (J). They suggest the work of one carpenter, and in fact much of the interior décor here is reminiscent of Les Ruettes, built but twelve years earlier. The front door, with bottle glass lights over it, is of the type where two-thirds open normally, the remaining third opening only in special circumstances, as at La Vallette (1796) and Potirons de Bas (1755). A very attractive sampler worked by Rachel Richardson in 1834 at the age of 13, is preserved in the family.

The name of the farm is somewhat mysterious, but is probably derived from a family recorded as Mars in 1617, in which case Ville Mars would indicate their home, as with Ville Bagot, Ville Brée and many others.

Plate XXXIc.

VINCHELEZ DE BAS
(O). (J. de Carteret on Godfray.)

The original manor house was sited north of the vivier, approximately where the stables now are, and the new manor was built on higher ground in about 1820, with severe simple lines, a pillared porch and a pediment enlivened by the de Carteret arms.

The builder was John Daniel de Carteret (b. 1782), and after passing through the female line to the Le Sueurs of Hamptonne in St. Peter, the house was bought back by Colonel Malet de Carteret in 1885, and it was he who put in the front door, flanked with heraldic glass. The

the manor bell, Vinchelez de Bas.
98

interior woodwork before recent renovation was pleasing but not outstanding. There are fine sea views to the north, and tales are told of smuggling contraband goods up from le Douet de la Mer. An old resident of the district thought that pepper was one of the forbidden items. In this context, there is a curious hole in the floor of a pantry on the north-east, which may

well have been a secret hiding place; and in the north-west attic is an unexplained and rather mysterious corner cupboard. The fields leading down to le Douet de la Mer are criss-crossed with walls which, with the name La Brébis which some of them have, tells of many sheep once penned and grazing there.

A farm bell hanging high between the west chimneys was recently brought down for examination, and found to bear the inscription: "Abraham de Carteret Fescvyer (*sic*) Seignevr de St. Ian, 1692. Recast 1888". As all the lettering is identical, one must assume that the original legend was copied in 1888. This Abraham was Seigneur de la Hougue Boete, dying childless in 1701, and it seems that Colonel Malet de Carteret acquired the bell, had it re-cast and brought it to Vinchelez. It has been re-erected in a position where it is accessible and more visible than it was before.

See Drawing 98.
Plate XXXII b.

at Wayside, (My).
99

WAYSIDE

Near La Forêt (My). (J. Malzard on Godfray.)

Much demolition has been suffered here. There was a shed behind the main house with the remains of a 17th-century fireplace, one unchamfered corbel with a two-piece upright bearing a shortened cross as chamfer stop. Several other chamfered lintels proved an early house, dating before the building bearing the stone inscribed I L B M R M 1722.

See Drawing 99.

WINDSOR CRESCENT
Val Plaisant (H).

This is a group of eight houses with nicely projecting eaves, built in a gentle curve in 1835. The builders must have taken a Regency design and given it their own interior woodwork. The appearance of such a design at this late date gives a neat example of the provincial time-lag.

Each house is on four levels; a semi-basement of four rooms with Swanage stone floors; a ground floor with a double drawing room, a dining room, servery, entrance hall and cloakroom; a first floor with four bedrooms; and an attic level with three rooms, the attic stairs being shut off at first-floor level. The rooms are light with large windows, though the verandah rather shades the drawing room, which has beautifully-made shutters in narrow sections hinged together. The verandahs are continuous along the crescent and are supported on slender fluted columns with no bases. The stairs, steep but elegant, have the usual round-headed niches in the walls. It is helpful to find a range of houses so firmly proclaiming the date of their erection.

Plate XXXII c.

WOODLANDS
La Verte Rue (My). (J. Esnouf on Godfray.)

The rather rough tourelle staircase appears to be the oldest part of this house, and a date of 1723 with the initials I R M on a lintel between the main room and what was later the kitchen annexe supports this theory. A larder under the slope of the stairs is like those seen at Les Arbres (L), La Tourelle (Mt), and elsewhere, and it has several deep niches in it, the storeroom cupboards of the time. A mysterious feature is a narrow passage leading from the hall to the west gable; at a high level is a small window with diamond-leaded lights, now invisible from the outside; in the north of the passage, of which one could easily be unaware, is a rather wide door, now blocked. Everything about this tall narrow passage suggests some secret activity.

In the garden is a triangular stone slab, said to have been used for beating leather, some former owners having been cobblers. There is also a quern, possibly neolithic, and perhaps associated with the field La Houguette on the other side of the road.

The property has passed through the families of Le Cronier, Jolin, Esnouf, Le Rossignol, Le Marquand and Bisson. The Le Croniers came to Jersey from "des parties de Normandie", and Pierre Le Cronier married Susanne Barbey in Jersey in 1688. A bible, of which the title page is unfortunately missing, still survives, and on its metal clasp are the initials S B B, for Susanne Barbey. It contains a note that their daughter Abigail could read the bible in 1715 at the age of 16. Several documents are preserved with it; one gives the recipe for a "sirop de pas d'ane", said to be good for pneumonia; another gives the words of a song "Sur la chute de Malakoff Ecclesiastique partant pour la Syrie", which refers to the efforts of the Rector of St. Mary, the Reverend Le Couteur Balleine, to stop the traditional bell ringing at Christmas, and the parishioners' violent efforts to continue it. It is said that they threatened to tip the poor Rector into the pond at Le Marais, and that during this troubled period he brought the church silver to La Pompe for safety. He was Rector from 1856 to 1879. The title of the song shows an awareness of events in the Crimean War of 1854-1855.

WRENTHAM HALL
La Grande Route de Rosel (Mt). (Dr. Nicolle on Godfray.)

It was Dr. Nicolle (b. 1824) who lived in this house at the time of Godfray's map, a man who could trace his direct ancestry back to 1500 according to the *Armorial*. But his family did not build Wrentham Hall.

By a fortunate chance a newspaper cutting has been found at the Museum giving details of its origins, telling us that when a kitchen range was being fitted in 1916, a letter was found under the mantelpiece. The newspaper translated it as follows: "The 14th day of August 1822. Mr. Ph Hubert has asked me to write a little note to be enclosed in this mantel board so that those who find it later will know that there were people in my day who could perform work with taste and facility. It was Mrs. Marie Barbenson, wife of the Rev. Charles Le Touzel who caused this house to be built. Will you, dear relatives or friends who find this letter, think of me and remember that much has taken place since I wrote it. I am young now, but when you discover the letter I shall, perhaps, have been long dead. Man, as you know, is born to die, and those who pass away in their youth avoid much trouble. Four years ago my father died, leaving a widow and twelve children to mourn his loss. If you seek to know more, go to the church and read the inscription on the stone which stands in front of the pulpit; it will give you all the information you desire. I close by embracing you heartily. I am and will be until my death, Henriette Le Touzel".

The Reverend C. Le Touzel (1774-1818) was Rector of St. Martin 1799-1818, and was a son of Jean Le Touzel and Elizabeth du Parcq.

This is a house on a grand scale, three storeys high, five bays wide with side wings and a paved portico supported on eight Ionic pillars. There is a good mahogany staircase rising the full height of the house, and as Miss Le Touzel said, it is constructed with taste, although now converted into flats. It is surprising to find that it was built quite so early, and even more surprising to find a parson's widow with twelve children constructing such a large and imposing house. The memorial stone referred to cannot now be found in St. Martin's church. There have been other houses on this site and this is discussed in Volume I of this work (pp. 106, 230).

PLATE XXXI

a. La Vieille Maison (B), 1687

b. Windsor Crescent (H), 1835

c. La Ville Mars (H), 1768

PLATE XXXII

a. La Vignette (S) before demolition, probably 16th century

b. Vinchelez de Bas (O), *c* 1820

c. Ville ès Phillipes (G). The unchanging face of Jersey. The house is dated 1778, the scene is 1976

APPENDIX I

SOME INITIALLED AND DATED STONES, and Other Domestic Inscriptions

Readers may welcome a check list of some of these interesting "marriage stones" and related inscriptions, which are such a distinctive feature in Jersey buildings. The list is not, of course, complete. There will always be more inscriptions to find, record and interpret, and the author of this book will be grateful to hear of others. Most of the initials have been identified, but this has not always been possible where a marriage took place in a distant parish or where, as may be seen, the carving of the stone was commissioned 30 or more years after the marriage; or indeed where the inscription is illegible through age, damage, or inaccessibility.

Most of these stones are mounted in conspicuous positions on the façade of a house, as lintels to doors or windows or as gable stones, but initials and dates are also to be found on the keystones of entrance arches, on sundials, on field gateposts, on troughs and, indoors, on the lintels of fireplaces. They are ubiquitous. Those who had them erected were proud of their identity and ancestry, and of the dates which seemed to them important in their lives.

Section 1 is an alphabetical list of surnames recorded, with reference to serial numbers in Section 2. Section 2 numbers the inscriptions alphabetically by the first initial of each. Where a surname is presumed but not proven, the reference number in Section 1 is given in brackets. Names given in Section 1 do not reappear in the general index to this book.

The letter I almost always stands for J. The 12 parishes are shown by their initial, e.g., (B) St. Brelade; (Mt) St. Martin; (My) St. Mary; (O) St. Ouen. A few simple abbreviations are used: b. (born); c. (about); d. (died); Fm. (farm); m. (married); v. (see).

Section 1

Ahier: 127, 219, 327, 331, 680, 849, 877.

Alexandre: 24, 45, 306, 551-3, 775, 886.

Amy: 110, 112, 191, 262, 264-5, 336, 457, 585, 620-1, 631-3, 790, 900.

Anley: 263, 351, 625-6, 628-630, 812.

Anquetil: 38, 277.

Anthoine: 113-4, 726.

Arthur: 47, (267), 268-9, 274, 319, 376, 586, (594), 806, (820).

Aubert: 523.

Aubin: 43-4, 114, 173, 261-2, 543, 697, 848, 879.

Badier: 212, 799.

Bailhache: 813.

Baker: 772.

Balleine: 2, 233, 635-6, 703, 730.

Bandinel: 213, 686.

Barette: 90.

Bauche: 308.

Baudains: 48, 117-8, 271, 278, 505, 588.

Baudet: 693.

Beaugié: 506, 851.

Becquet: 277.

Benest: 275, 286, 639, 640, 813, 869.

Berteau: (556), 708.

Bertram: 1, 49, 50, 116, 124, 270, 390, 645, 867.

Bichard: 504.

Billot: 119, (120), 272, 638, 648.

Binet: 40, 274, 630, 768.

Bisson: 91-2, (115), (121), 122, 153, 382, 510-1, 603, 643-4.

Blampied: 3, 112, 265, 276, 395, 508-9, 530, 641-2, 719, 777.

Bois: 192.

Bosquet: 669.

Brée: 231.

Cabot: 5, 279, 280, 332, 406, 519, 568, 590, 647-8, 854-5.

Carcaud: 199.

Carey; 53.

Carrel: 632.

Chapelle: 163.

Chepmell: 757.

Chevalier: 241, 589, 835, 852.

Clement: 796.

Collas: 1, 50, 71, 169, 195, 214, 248, 278, 282, 366, 434, 558, 646, 649, (650)

Corbel: 193.

Cotillard: 718.

Coutanche: 15, 51-2, 77, 239, 287, 493, 512, 788, 815-6.

Dallain: (101), 306, 308, 514, 669, 670.

Dalton: 49.

Dauvergne: 127.

Dean: 691.

de Caen: 379, 656.

de Carteret: 4, 6-8, 53, 65, 70, 133, 215, 225, 242, 312, 468, 591-3, 653-4, 797, 834.

de Faye: 295.

de Gruchy: 35, 94, 128, 130, 177, 191, 297-9, 300, 302-5, 527, 659, 661-4, 666-7, 728,

(820), 838, 857-60.

de la Cour: 92, 310, 550, 684.

de la Garde: 558.

de la Haye: 243, 809.

de la Lande: 130, 309, (311).

de la Mare: 36, 515, 672, 872.

de la Perrelle: (607).

de la Place: 476.

de Lecq: 41.

Denize: 314-7.

de Quetteville: 134.

de Ste Croix: 10, 54, 137-9, 195, 316, 321, 387, 517, 595, 677-80, 694, 710.

Deslandes: 131, 193, 709.

de Veulle: 11, 12, 322.

Dolbel: (287), 288, 291-2, 294, 513, (817), (874), 884.

Dorey: 135, 217, 472, 516, 557, 675-6.

Dowton: 288.

Du Bois: 289, 293.

du Feu: 279, (340), 818-9, 859.

du Fresne: 638, 657.

du Heaume: 129, 200, 668.

Dumaresq: 133, 202, 244-5, 282, 312, 380, 597, 673-4, 821, 870-1.

du Parcq: 616.

du Pont: 232, 645.

du Pré: 58, 216, 318-20, (594).

Durell: 409.

Durell, Le V. dit: (710).

Effard: 776.

Emily: 518.

Esnouf: 241, 327, 424, 502, 681.

Estur: 124, 299, 822.

Prideaux: 886.

Quenault: 86.
Querrée: 181–3, 272, (615).

Remon: 210, 291, 294, 486–7, 539, 701, 720, 771, 786–7.
Renaut, Renault: 168, 184, 320, 664, 790–1.
Renouf: 17, 64, 87, 119, 158, 480, 488–9, 540, 551–2, 578, 582–3, 617–8, 641, 891.
Richardson: 107, 343, 481, 616, 782.
Rive: (795).
Robin: (9), 834.
Rogier: (549).
Roissier: 557.
Romeril: 39, 473, 490, 494, 538, 718, 788, 792–4, 802.

Rondel: 69, 198, 394, 511, 702, 783–5.
Rouet: (549).

Sarre: 493.
Seale: 796–7.
Servant: 344.
Shoosmith: 708.
Simon: 492.
Skelton: 239.
Snow: 897–8.
Sohier: 238, 799, 892.
Sorsoleil: 490.
Starck: 185.
Stocall: 559.
Syvret: 304.

Tapin: 495.
Thoreau: 804.

Touzel: 76, 466, 519, 761, 848.

Trachy: 494, 801–3.

Valleur: 416.
Valpy: 214, 338, (346), 463, 835, 852, 883.
Vardon: 186, 807–8.
Vautier: 640, 804, 809.
Venement: 98, 110.
Vibert: 205, (353), 441, 496, 806, 860.
Villeneuve: 255.
Vincent: 499.
Vivian: 459, 810.
Voisin: 502, 550.

Wadham: 503.
Whitley: 188–9.

Section 2

1. AB.CCL.1733. Abraham Bertram and Collette Collas; Grasfort (Mt).
2. ABL. MLH.1774. Amice Balleine and Marie Le Hardy; The Elms (My).
3. ABP.MLR.1757. Abraham Blampied and Marie Laurens; Stanford (L).
4. Abraham de Carteret Fescvyer Seignevr de St. Ian. 1692; farm bell, Vinchelez de Bas (O).
5. AVB.MP.ICB.1679. Aaron Cabot, Jean Cabot; on arch; ACB.MP, on porch pillars; Augrès Fm. (T).
6. ADC. Abraham de Carteret; La Hougue Boëte (J).
7. ADC.1730. Amice de Carteret; Vinchelez de Bas (O).
8. ADC.IDG.1681. Abraham de Carteret jr.; Les Buttes (J).
9. ADP.SR.1726. ? and Robin; Robin Place (H).
10. ADSX.EPD.17..... Abraham de Ste Croix and Elizabeth Poingdestre; Penny Cottage, Douceville (H).
11. ADV.IMGF.1786. Aaron de Veulle and Jeanne Marguerite Godfray; Slate Fm. (C).
12. ADV.MLN. Aaron de Veulle and Marguerite Le Neveu; Beachside, Le Hocq Lane (C).
13. AF.1688. Sundial from Bel Royal, at Le Tilleul, Rue de Haut (L).
14. AF.MN.1715. Clairfield, Maufant (S).
15. AGB.ECT. 1900. Abraham Gibaut and Elizabeth Coutanche; Les Vaux (L).
16. AGD.IGL.1748. Abraham Godel m. Jeanne Le Gallais 1729; La Ville ès Gros (L).
17. AGLB.FLR.1920. Le Brun and Renouf; Beaulieu (T).
18. AGP. ? Goupil; Ivy House, St. Aubin (B).
19. AH.1707. Hue; Les Buttes (J).
20. ALC.ILC.1743. La Pierre des Trois Milles (S).
21. ALF.1675. ? Abraham Le Feuvre who m. Katherine Hullin 1642; Lowlands (P).
22. ALF.ELC.1782. Abraham Le Feuvre dit Filiastre m. Elizabeth Le Cour 1773; Lowlands (P).
23. ALF.II.1747. Abraham Le Feuvre dit Filiastre and Judith Jean; Lowlands (P).
24. ALG.AAL.1773. Abraham Le Geyt m. Anne Alexandre 1741; Le Geyt Fm. (S).
25. ALG.IEN.1832. Abraham Le Geyt; Le Geyt Fm. (S).
26. ALG.RLHQ.1798. Abraham Le Gros m. Rachel Le Hucquet 1786; Meadowside (My).
27. ALHQ.1846. Abraham Le Hucquet; Fontaine de Gallie lavoir (Mt).
28. ALM.1631. ?? La Ronce, Trodez (O).
29. ALR.1848. Le Riche; Pont ès Oies (T).
30. ALR.MGL.1733.PLR. Augustin Le Rossignol, Marguerite Guillet and their son Pierre; Brampton Fm. (O).
31. AM.1623. ? Mallet; La Chasse (Mt).
32. AMP.SDM. Greenhill (P).
33. AMR.1813. Abraham Marett; St. Cyr Lavoir (J).
34. AMSV.EPMSV.1897. Alfred Messervy and his son; Le Carrefour (T).
35. AMSV.MDG.1895. Alfred Messervy and Mary de Gruchy; Ville à l'Evêque (T).
36. APF.DLM.EDET.1828. ? Abraham and François de la Mare (or ? artifices pontis, familia de la Mare, eximia diligentia, exiguum tempus); Bouley Bay Pier (T).
37. APL.KN. Sir Anthony Poulet and Katherine Norreys; Gorey Castle (Mt.).
38. AQT. Anquetil; Le Marais (O).
39. AWPN.MJRR.1887. Augustus William Poignand and Mary Jane Romeril; Clos des Toùrs, Coin Varin (P).
40. BBN.ILB. Beniamin Binet m. Jeanne Le Broc 1711; Maison du Buisson (S).
41. BIV.EDL.1762. Brelade Janvrin and Elizabeth de Lecq; Le Coin (B).
42. BLeF.SF.1676. Palm Grove (H).
43. CAB.AG.1740. Charles Aubin and Anne Gourey or Godfray; La Tourelle (Mt).
44. CAB.IF.1778. Clement Aubin and Jeanne Falle; Terrebonne (G).
45. CALX.1820. C. Alexandre; Beaupré, Boucterie (T).
46. CAMSV.MMDF.1907. Messervy; Clos Durell (T).

47. CAT.1742. Charles Arthur; sundial, La Grange (My).
48. CB.1588. Colas Baudains; Le Taillis (Mt).
49. CB.FD. Charles Bertram and Frances Dalton; Homestead (G).
50. CCL. 1725. Collette Collas who m. Abraham Bertram; Grasfort (Mt).
51. CCT.1813. Charles Coutanche; St. Cyr lavoir (J).
52. CCT.ILB.1812. Charles Coutanche and Jeanne Le Bas; Coutanche Fm. (T).
53. CDC.MCR.1747. Charles de Carteret and Marthe Carey; Le Câtelet (J).
54. CDSX.MLP.1761. ? de Ste Croix and Le Porcq; Bellozanne Priory (H).
55. CELC.EN.1699. ? Le Clercq; Carrefour au Clercq (S).
56. CGC.MLBT.1814. Charles Gruchy m. Marie Larbalestier 1810; repeated 1826, and CGC.1817; Champs Clairs (T).
57. CGLC.1834. C. Gallichan; Bouley Bay Hill lavoir (T).
58. CH.EDP.1749. Charles Hue and Elizabeth Dupré; Perry Fm. (My).
59. CH.MCR.1884. ? Clement Hemery; Carteret Fm. (G).
60. CHM.JMZ.1828. ? Hamon and Malzard; La Vallette, Le Mourier (J).
61. CIG.1803. Clement Ingouville; Alphington House (now Priors) (S).
62. CIG.FEG.1825. Clement Ingouville and Frances Elizabeth Godfray; Alphington House (now Priors) (S).
63. CLB.ELG.1769. Le Blancq and Le Gresley; Le Coin (O).
64. CLBTL.MRN.1821, repeated 1835; Le Boutillier and Renouf; Les Lauriers (T).
65. CLC.IDC.1678. Clement Le Couteur m. Jeanne de Carteret 1664; oak plaque, Mont à l'Abbé Manor (H).
66. CLGL.AMG.1825. Route du Mont Mado (J).
67. CLM.1808. Charles Le Masurier; La Vallette (J).
68. CLM.EPN.1796. Charles Le Masurier and Elizabeth Pinel, repeated 1807 and 1824; La Vallette (J).
69. CLM.ESRD.1826. Charles Le Masurier and Elizabeth Sophie Rondel; La Vallette (J).
70. CLM.R. Clement Le Montais and Rachel, sister of Sir George Carteret, m. 1636; La Chaumière du Chêne (P).
71. CLP.SCL. Charles Lemprière and Susanne Collas. Stirling Castle Fm. (H).
72. CLQ.1708, and CLQ.MGF.1728. ? Le Quesne; La Sergine (J).
73. CLS.MJP.1845. Clement Le Sueur m. Marie Payn 1826; Redwood Hotel (S).
74. CM.RN. ? Mallet and Noel; Devon Villa (Mt).
75. CMC (or G).ECB.1767. Blanc Pignon (Mt).
76. CML.ETZ.1741. Charles Mallet m. Elizabeth Touzel 1719; Home Fm. (G).
77. CML.ICT.1817. Charles Malet m. Jeanne Coutanche 1786; Home Fm. (G).
78. CMR.1702. Charles Maret; La Maison Maret (T).
79. CMR.AM.1755. Charles Maret m. Anne Messervy 1742; La Maison Maret (T).
80. CMS.1832. Messervy; Douet Fleury lavoir (Mt).
81. CNC.IPN.1803. Nicolle and Pinel; The Limes (H).
82. CP.c.1687. Clement Pinel; La Vallette (J).
83. CP.1846. La Chapelle Méthodiste; Fontaine de Gallie lavoir (Mt).
84. CPC.1832. Picot; Douet Fleury lavoir (Mt).
85. CPN.1743. ? Clement Pinel; opposite La Girette (J).
86. CQN.1835. Quenault; cider crushing stone, Hamlet Fm. (S).
87. CRN.ELCN.1842. Charles Renouf m. Elizabeth Le Cornu 1827; Diélament Manor (T).
88. CSR.AD.1748. Highfield (T).
89. DA.1725, and DA.IA.1741; Ashley Court (J).
90. DBR.1813. David Barette; St. Cyr lavoir (J).
91. DBS.EM.1785. Daniel Bisson m. Esther Marche 1776; Le Mottais Fm. (J).
92. DBS.FDLC.1819. Daniel Bisson m. Florence de la Cour 1801; Le Mottais Fm. (J).
93. DC.1676. Gable stone, near Maison St. Louis (H).
94. DDG.MMR.1797. Daniel de Gruchy m. Marie Marett 1788; Whitton (J).
95. DFR.EL.1801. David Fleury m. Elizabeth Luce 1796; Elmdale (L).
96. DGD.1724. Denis Guerdain; La Guerdainerie (T).
97. DGD.EMR. Gaudin; La Vignette (S).
98. DGD.MVM.1810. David Gaudin m. Marie Venement 1800; Chambard (C).
99. DGD.SGD.1785. Gaudin; La Vignette (S).
100. DHM.MAHM.1862. Daniel Hamon m. Mary Ann Hamon; Beauvoir, Mont Cochon (H).
101. DL.B. preceded by X. ? 1598. ? Dallain; La Chasse, Sion (J).
102. DLC. Beechleigh (P).
103. DLS.1767. David Le Sueur; No. 6 Hue Street (H).
104. DLS.PHB.1775. ? Le Sueur; No. 4 Hue Street (H).
105. DMAM. MLCN.1792. Monamy; La Fontenelle, Samarès Lane (C).
106. Douard Le Sueur. 1749; on beam at No. 19 Hue Street (H).
107. DPL.1706, and DPL.MRS.1728 and 1742; Daniel Pellier m. Marguérite Richardson 1714; Mont Pellier (T).
108. DPL.EGF. Daniel Pellier; Mont Pellier (T).
109. DR.EFB.1726. Sundial, Shady Cottage, Augrès (T).
110. DVM.RAM.1754. Daniel Venement m. Rachel Amy 1752; Chambard (C).
111. E. at Val au Bec (P).
112. EAM.EBP.1821, and EAM.1832. Amy and Blampied; Peacock Fm. (T).
113. EAT.1648. Estienne Anthoine; keystone from Rouen House, now at Longueville (S).
114. EAT.1675, and EAT.MAB.1675; Estienne Anthoine m. Marthe Aubin 1664; Les Prés (Mt).
115. EB.ALF.1712. ? Bisson; Old Fm., Mont an Prêtre (H).
116. EB.AM.1812. Elie Bertram and Anne Mourant; Homestead (G).
117. EBD.1813. Elie Baudains; St. Cyr lavoir (J).
118. EBD.SBD.1717. Baudains; Beaupré (J).
119. EBL.ARN.1891. Elie Billot and Anne Renouf; La Porte (S).

120. EBL.EHM.1819. ? Billot; Sunny Corner (J).
121. EBS.1742. ? Bisson; Old Fm., Mont an Prêtre (H).
122. EBS.1884. Edouard Bisson; La Ruette (L).
123. EBS.EBD.1615, with 1811 added; St. Lawrence's Rectory (L).
124. EBT.SET.1758. Elie Bertram m. Susanne Estur 1722; Homestead (G).
125. EC.I.Maret.1646. La Maison Maret (T).
126. ECB. La Chasse (T).
127. EdAH.EDVG.1842. Edouard Ahier m. Esther Dauvergne 1806; London House, Le Mourier (J);
128. EDG.EDQ.1807. de Gruchy; La Chasse (Mt).
129. EDH.RGL.1857. Edouard du Heaume and Rachel Gallichan; Millais Villa (O).
130. EDL.EDG.1700. Edouard de la Lande and Esther de Gruchy; La Chasse (T).
131. EDL.MHM.1741. Elie Deslandes and Marie Hamon; La Courtinerie (L).
132. EDM.1739. At the Museum.
133. EDM.EDC.1741. Elie Dumaresq and Elizabeth de Carteret; Les Augrès (T).
134. EDQV.1832. de Quetteville; Douet Fleury lavoir (Mt).
135. EDR.MLC.1835. Dorey; Valley Fm., Le Mourier (My).
136. EDRM.1747. At Le Câtillon (Mt).
137. EDSC.N. de Ste Croix; Les Ruettes (J).
138. EDSX.1704. Edouard de Ste Croix; La Vallette (H).
139. EDSX.KLBL.1759. Edouard de Ste Croix and Katherine Le Boutillier; La Vallette (H).
140. EDVM?LFLV?1718. Les Chasses (P).
141. EELS.1832. Edouard Elie Le Sauteur: Douet Fleury lavoir (Mt).
142. EF.SLC. At Beaupré (J).
143. EGD.EGD.1807. Gaudin; La Chasse (Mt).
144. EGD.FNC.1753. At Beauchamp (Mt).
145. EDG.MPC.1771. Gaudin and Perchard; Le Câtillon (Mt).
146. EGLBTL.EPN.1866. Edouard Le Boutillier and Elizabeth Pinel; Oakdale (J).
147. EGLC.IPC.1793. Les Grès (T).
148. EH.Hamptonne; Manor House (L).
149. EHL.ALMT. At Beaumont.
150. EHM.ALR.1806. Edouard Hamon m. Anne Le Rossignol 1771; Little Grove (L).
151. EHM.ELR.1719. Edouard Hamon and Elizabeth Le Rossignol (d. 1772); near La Valleuse (B).
152. EI.IV.1742. At La Hougue (S).
153. EIN.KBS.1766. Edouard Journeaux m. Caterine Bisson 1740; Les Câteaux (T).
154. EJLB.ACLC.1890. Le Blancq and Le Cerf; sundial, Le Coin House (O).
155. ELB. ? Le Brun; Beechleigh (P).
156. ELB. 1766. Edouard Le Brocq; La Valleuse (B).
157. ELB.EBL.1890. Le Pré Cottage, Rue des Raisies (Mt).
158. ELCN. 1836, and CRN. Elizabeth Le Cornu m. Charles Renouf; south gate, Diélament Manor (T).
159. ELCN.EF.1805 and 1814. Le Cornu; La Guillaumerie Cottage (S).
160. ELE.1588 (perhaps LB); at Rockstone (Mt).
161. ELeG.1819. Sundial, St. Cyr (J).

162. ELG.BLG.1823. Le Gresley; near St. Ouen's church.
163. ELG.MCP.1745. Edmond Le Gallais m. Marie Chapelle 1736; Les Ormes, Ville Emphrie (L).
164. ELM.1650. Elie Le Montais; Chaumière du Chêne (P).
165. ELM.MB.1719. At Oakdale (S).
166. ELQ.ALC.1708. ? Elie Le Quesne (b. 1665); La Sergine (J).
167. ELR.1714. At Ville Bagot (O).
168. ELR.ERN.1805 and 1816. Edouard Le Rossignol and Elizabeth Renaut; Les Arbres (L).
169. ELRT.NCL.1819. Edouard Le Rougetel and Nancy Collas; Rock View, La Rocque (G).
170. EM.1636. At Les Mars (G).
171. EML.1859. ? Mallet; La Hauteur (Mt).
172. EM.RF.AF.WLM. ? Faultrat, Le Marchant; fireplace, Handois (L).
173. EMR.MAB.1678. Etienne Mourant m. Marie Aubin 1647; preceded by HAPDD (? hoc amoris pignus dono dedit); Les Pigneaux (S).
174. EMZ.1793. Elizabeth Malzard (b. 1716, m. Richard Dolbel); Le Vivier (J).
175. EN.1694. ? Edmond Noël; Summerville (Mt).
176. EN.EMP.1760. At La Retraite (S).
177. EN.MDG.1723. Edouard Nicolle m. Marguérite de Gruchy 1701; Ville à l'Evêque (T).
178. ENC.LNC.1868. Nicolle and Nicolle; La Fontaine, Ville à l'Evêque (T).
179. ENC.1803 and ENC.MLB.1811. Nicolle; Boulivot de Bas (G).
180. EP.ENC.1751. Edouard Payn and Elizabeth Nicolle; Le Taillis (Mt).
181. EQR. Querrée; La Vallette, Mourier (J).
182. EQR.SB.1818. At Highfield (T).
183. EQR.SB.1829 and EQR.1858. Querrée; Boulivot (G).
184. ERN.ARN. Edouard Renault; La Sergenté (My).
185. EST.1812. E. Starck; Les Fontaines (Mt).
186. EVD.1846. Elie Vardon; Fontaine de Gallie lavoir (Mt).
187. EVD.MLB.1733. At L'Aiguillon (G).
188. EW.1790. E. Whitley (b. 1748); salting trough, La Haie Fleurie (Mt).
189. EW.ELH.1805. Elie Whitley m. Elizabeth Le Hucquet 1776; La Haie Fleurie (Mt).
190. FA.NDP.1659. At L'Ancienneté (My); v.NDP.FA.
191. FAM.SDG.1825. François Amy m. Susanne de Gruchy 1804; Belle Vue, near le Câtel Fm. (T).
192. FB.NFV.1819. François Bois and Nancy Fauvel; La Maison du Moulin de Pol (now Alphington House) (S).
193. FCB.JDL.1813. François Corbel and Jeanne Deslandes; Highview, Coin Hâtain (L).
194. FDPL.PG.1673. At 31 Broad Street (H).
195. FDSC.MCL and FDSC.EDSC.1777. François de Ste Croix m. Mary Collas, and François de Ste Croix m. Elizabeth de Ste Croix; Pied du Côtil House (now Santa Monica Hotel) (H).
196. FGC.ELB.1774 and 1776; François Gruchy and Elizabeth Le Bas; Champs Clairs (T).
197. FHB.ELGL.1743. ? Hubert and Le Gresley; La Voûte, L'Etacq (O).

198. FHL.MRD.1836. François Helleur m. Marie Rondel 1827; La Ferme Grandet (L).

199. FI.MC.1775. François Jeune and Marie Carcaud; Mont des Vaux Cottages (B).

200. FLB.IDH.1756. François Le Boutillier and Jeanne du Heaume; No. 3 Hue Street (H).

201. FLB.MMG.1847. François Le Brocq and Marie Mauger; Homestead (P).

202. FLC.SDM.1677. Rev. François Le Couteur m. Sara Dumaresq 1657; Green Fm. (Mt).

203. FLCT.1760? (date partly covered); at Montrose (P).

204. FLF.EN.1844. ? Le Four; Elsingham, near La Forge (Mt).

205. FLG.AVB.1818. François Langlois and Anne Vibert; Ville au Veslet (L).

206. FLS.1687. At Vaucluse (H).

207. FMR. ? Mourant; on beam, Hamlet Fm.(S).

208. FN. At Les Pigneaux (S).

209. FPD.JML.1884. Poingdestre; near Carrefour au Clercq (S).

210. FRM.1694. François Remon m. Jeanne Pinel 1690; Ville au Veslet (L).

211. GAM.MAB.1759. At Sion Villas, Longueville (S).

212. GBD.1669. George Badier; on colombier, Colombier Manor (L).

213. GB.1731. George Bandinel; Old Bagot Manor Fm. (S).

214. GCL.EVP.1799. George Collas and Elizabeth Valpy; Les Pigneaux (S).

215. GDC.1855. George de Carteret; Vale Fm.(P).

216. GDP.1744. George Dupré; on sundial, Inverness Lodge (L).

217. GDR.ENC.1875. Dorey and Nicolle; Le Douet (J).

218. GGD.JGD.1812. George Gaudin m. Jeanne Gaudin 1805; La Maitrerie (Mt).

219. GGD.SAH.1824. George Gaudin m. Suzanne Ahier 1820; Le Câtillon (Mt).

220. GIG.1788. ? George Ingouville (1760–1828; m. 1789); The Museum (H).

221. GJ.1623. In plaster between beams; Les Ormes (Mt).

222. GLB.1675. George Le Brun; Market Hill, St. Aubin (B).

223. GLB.MLCN.1837. Le Brun and Le Cornu; Beaulieu (T).

224. GLBT.1770. Le Boutillier; Elmwood, Trodez (O).

225. GLC.IDC.1684. George La Cloche and Jeanne de Carteret; Longueville Manor (S).

226. GLHQ.1846. George Le Huquet; Fontaine de Gallie lavoir (Mt).

227. GLSL.FMSV.1820. Le Seelleur and Messervy; Le Fleurion (Mt).

228. GM.1606, IM or IMT 1606, and PHB; gable stones, Rockstone (Mt).

229. GMG.1565 (retrospective). George Mauger; Maison de Coin (L).

230. GMR, preceded by Greek letter phi; La Fontaine, Ville à l'Eveque (T).

231. GMSV.EB.1832. George Messervy and Elizabeth Bree; Grande Maison (Mt).

232. GNC.SDP.1826. George Nicolle and Susanne du Pont; Vieux Ménage (S).

233. GPB. Connétable.1853. George Philip Balleine; St. Brelade's Hospital (B).

234. GPC.1832. G. Picot; Douet Fleury lavoir (Mt).

235. GPC.ELS.1884. La Fosse à l'Ecrivain (S).

236. GPG.ELT.1811 and 1818. George Pelgué; Fernside (S).

237. GPLP.ACL.1801. At Waterloo House (L).

238. GSH.1846. George Sohier; Fontaine de Gallie lavoir (Mt).

239. GST.ACT.1843.1873. George Skelton m. Anne Coutanche 1842; Elmwood (My).

240. HAPDD. v.EMR.MAB.

241. HC.IE.1709. Helier Chevalier and Jeanne Esnouf; Highcliff (J).

242. HD.Lan.1580. Tombstone of Helier (or Hugh) de Carteret; Handois (L).

243. HDLH.1891. Hugh de la Haye; Bushy Fm. (H).

244. HDM.1714. Helier Dumaresq; The Old Farm (C).

245. HDM.1720. Helier Dumaresq; ECMdeC.1884 added below for Edouard Charles Malet de Carteret; on sundial, The Old Farm (C).

246. HFV.AP.1831. Helier Fauvel and Ann Payn; Val Feuillu (S).

247. HG.RML.PG.1686. Helier Godfray m. Rachel Mylays 1663, with their son Philippe; The Hollies (C); now at Mont Pellier (T).

248. HHT.MCL.RHT.1731. Henry Hamptonne and Marguerite Collas, with their son Raulin; Eastfield (My).

249. HLP, or HLR; at L'Aiguillon (G).

250. HLR.ELB.1751. Helier Le Rossignol m. Elizabeth Le Bas; Le Bocage (B).

251. HM.1620. At The Granite House (Mt).

252. HM.1664. At La Boiserie (J).

253. HML.1859. On field pillar, Water Lane (O).

254. HML.SR.1812. At L'Aiguillon (Mt).

255. HMR.AVN.1764. Henry Marett m. Anne Villeneuve 1753; Brook Fm. (B).

256. HNC.1834. H. Nicolle; on trough, Bouley Bay Hill lavoir (T).

257. HP.1822. At Hillcrest, L'Etacq (O).

258. HP.EGF.1811. Helier Payn m. Elizabeth Godfray 1808; L'Abri (Mt).

259. HPN.EAB.1837. At La Ferme Grandet (L).

260. I. v. also J.

261. IAB.AF. Isaac Aubin and Anne Filleul; Maison de la Hougue Bie (G).

262. IAB.?SAM.17?5. Jean Aubin m. Marie Amy 1730; States Experimental Farm (T).

263. IAL.1626. Anley; Highfield (P).

264. IAM.MP.1798, and 1803; Amy; La Hougue (S).

265. IAM.RBP.1847. Jean Amy m. Rachel Blampied; Dronfield (L).

266. IAMT.1806. Jean Amice Martel; La Ferme Martel, Glencoe (L).

267. IAT.1676. ? Arthur; Douet de Rue (My).

268. IAT.MLVC.1841. Jean Arthur m. Marie Le Vesconte 1810; La Place (O).

269. IAT.RLC.1720. Jean Arthur and Rachel Le Couteur; La Pompe (My).

270. IB.IT.1730. Bertram; cottage at La Rocque (G).

271. IBD.1668. Baudains; Beaupré (J).

272. IBL.EQR.ILS.1797. Josué Billot m. Elizabet Querest 1764 and Jeanne Le Sueur 1784; La Billotterie (T). Father and son.

273. IBM.1790, or 1750. Gatepost, Laurel Lands Fm. (S).

274. IBN.EAT.1757. Jean Binet and Elizabeth Arthur; La Fontaine (My).

275. IBN.SPT.1753. Jean Benest m. Sara Pithon 1723; Le Petit Câtelet (J).

276. IBP.SL.Jean Blampied and Susanne Luce; Blampied Fm. (L).

277. IBQ.MAQ.1819. Jean Becquet m. Marie Anquetil 1811; gatepost, Les Quatre Carrefours (Mt).

278. IC.RB.1688. Jean Collas m. Rachel Baudayne 1678; La Préférence Cottage (Mt).

279. ICB.EDF.1789. Cabot and du Feu; Les Ifs (T).

280. ICB.MMTG.1838. Cabot; at La Commune (T).

281. ICH.ELP.1682. Gouray Lodge (Mt).

282. ICL.FDM.1776. Jean Collas and Françoise Dumaresq; Le Mourin (S).

283. ICM.FB. at La Porte (T).

284. ICR.1788. La Chênaie des Bois (Mt).

285. ICS.ARB.1716. Fireplace, Le Petit Câtelet 2 (J); ? from elsewhere.

286. ICT.EBN.1721. Jean Qoutances m. Elizabeth Beney 1698; opposite Le Vivier (J).

287. ID.1626. ? Dolbel; roadside arch, Les Carrières (Mt).

288. IDB.AD.1747. Jean Dolbel m. Anne Dowton; La Colomberie (H).

289. IDB.ALG.1700. Jaque de Bois m. Anne L'Anglois 1699; Lilac Cottage, Ville Emphrie (L).

290. IDB.ATV.1739. On Rue Militaire (O).

291. IDB.EMRM.1884. Jean Dolbel m. Elise Marthe Remon 1863; Fair View (L).

292. IDB.IGN.1805. Jean Dolbel m. Jeanne Gasnier 1798; Chestnut Grove (J).

293. IDB.MDB.1684. Jean Du Boys m. Marguerite Du Boys 1671; Les Perquages Fm. (P).

294. IDB.TRM.1703, or 1701, 1705; Jean Dolbel m. Thomassine Remon 1699; Chestnut Grove (J).

295. IDF.MLGL.1800. Jacques de Faye and Marie Le Gresley; Rose Fm., Grouville village (G).

296. IDG.1679. At Le Câtel (T).

297. IDG.1800. de Gruchy; La Chasse (T).

298. IDG.EDG.1783. Jean de Gruchy m. Elizabeth de Gruchy 1757, La Ville Machon (T).

299. IDG.EET.1796. Jean de Gruchy and Elizabeth Estur; and a stone weight with IDG; The Elms Fm. (My).

300. IDG.ELM.1827. de Gruchy; La Raulinerie (T).

301. IDG.ILP.1744. at Le Câtel (T).

302. IDG.ILQ.1744. Jean de Gruchy m. Jeanne Le Quesne 1730; Le Câtel (T).

303. IDG.MDF.1751. de Gruchy; La Pièce Mauger (T).

304. IDG.MSV.1820. Jean de Gruchy and Marguerite Syvret; Le Carrefour (My).

305. IDGC.JDGC.1855. Jean de Gruchy; La Chasse (T).

306. IDL.IAL.1773. Jean Dallain and Judith Alexandre; The Oaks (P).

307. IDL.EDL.ADL.1838. At La Fontaine, Ville à l'Evêque (T).

308. IDL.IB. Dallain and Bauche; The Oaks (P).

309. IDL.ILG.1778. Jean de la Lande m. Jeanne Le Gros 1772; La Chasse (T).

310. IDLC.1795. Jean de la Cour; Le Marinel (J).

311. IDLL.EGF.1812. ? de la Lande; Rose Fm., Ruettes Pinel (H).

312. IDM.EDC.1739. Jean Dumaresq and Elizabeth de Carteret; Les Colombiers (My).

313. IDM.IPR.1824. At Fauvic Fm. (C).

314. IDN.AF.1771 (retrospective). Jourdain Denize m. Ann Fiott; Manoir du Fief ès Neveux (L).

315. IDN.FLCMN.1581 (retrospective). Jacques Denize m. Françoise Le Cheminant; Manoir du Fief ès Neveux (L).

316. IDN.MDSC.1670 (retrospective). Jean Denize m. Marie de Ste. Croix; Manoir du Fief ès Neveux (L).

317. IDN.MGB.1825. Jourdain Denize m. Marie Gibaut; Manoir du Fief ès Neveux (L).

318. IDP.ELB.1825, and 1832. Jean du Pré m. Elizabeth Le Bas 1812; Les Augerez Fm. (P).

319. IDP.F.1645. Jean Dupré and Foy Arthur; Plaisance (My).

320. IDP.SR.1675. Jean Dupré m. Sara Renaut c. 1660; Plaisance (My).

321. IDSX.MB.1662. de Ste Croix; Le Trésor (L).

322. IDV.ENM.1815. de Veulle; Les Tours Fm. (C).

323. Iean Payn, Marie Payn.PP.FP.IP.1635. Jean and Marie Payn and their sons Jean, François and Philippe; La Maletière (G).

324. IEC. or IEG.1661. At Highcliff (J).

325. IEC.1699. On stone weight of 101lbs. at The Museum (H).

326. IEL.1680. At Beauverd (J).

327. IEN.IAH.1753. Esnouf and Ahier; Alphington House (S).

328. IF.1646. Jacques Filleul; Fauvic Nursing Home (G).

329. IF.1659. Jean Fautrat; Handois (L).

330. IF.EF. Jean Fautrat and Elizabeth Fondan; fireplace, Handois (L).

331. IF.RAH.1740, and 1750; Jean Falle m. Rachel Ahier 1735; Val Feuillu (S).

332. IFCB.MAJN.1852. Jean François Cabot m. Mary Ann Journeaux 1846; gatepost, Les Ifs (T).

333. IFR.1846. Jean Ferey; Fontaine de Gallie lavoir (Mt).

334. IG.1819. Jean Godfray; Les Grandes Rues (Mt).

335. IG.1678. Gruchy; Crossbow House (T).

336. IG.EAM.1786. Josué Graut m. Elizabeth Amy c. 1774; La Rigondaine (G).

337. IG.EF.1741. At Patier Lodge (S).

338. IG.IVP.1834. Jean Grault and Jeanne Valpy; Greenhill, Samarès (C).

339. IGCB.MST.1830. At Beaupré, near Brooklyn (Mt).

340. IGD.1640, or 1646. ? Jean Grandin who m. Marie du Feu; Mont Pellier (T).

341. IGD.EGD.1739. Jean Godel m. Esther Godel 1732; Les Chasses Cottage, Rue du Servais (J).

342. IGD.IHM.1738. Jean Godel and Judith Hamon; Ville ès Gros (L).

343. IGD.MRS.1764. Jacques Grandin m. Marie Richardson 1741; Shady Cottage, Augrès (T).

344. IGD.MSV.1761. Jean Grindin m. Marguerite Servant 1752; Maupertuis (My).

345. IGF.EGF.1730. Jean Godfray m. Elizabeth Godfray 1717; La Hurette (T).

346. IGF.FVP.1735. ? Godfray and Valpy; La Fèverie (S).
347. IGLC.1834. J. Gallichan; on trough, Bouley Bay Hill lavoir (T).
348. IGLC.SGLC.1742. At Mon Caprice (T).
349. IH.1617. Bailiff Jean Herault; La Palloterrie (S).
350. IH.1666. Jean Hue who m. Philippine Le Geyt; La Porte (J).
351. IHC.IAL.1786. Hocquard and Isobel Anley; L'Abri (J).
352. IHD.1619. Near La Vieille Maison, La Hougue Bie (G).
353. IHL.CLF.1728, with ? IVB. Jean Huelin m. Catherine Le Feuvre c. 1728, and ? Jean Vibert, godfather to their child; Les Charrières (P).
354. IHL.FLB.1623, or NHL. ? A Nicolas Huelin m. a Félice; Les Charrières (P).
355. IHL.MLB.1827. At Beaumont cross-roads (P); see 522.
356. IHM.BHM.1797. ? Jean Hamon who m. Betsy Hamon 1772; Le Câtel (T).
357. IHP.1774. ? Hooper; at Le Boulivot (G).
358. IHP.ISS.1803. ? Hooper; at Le Boulivot (G).
359. IHP.MGF.1785. ? Hooper; at Le Boulivot (G).
360. IHQ.BHQ.1830. Jean Hocquard m. Betsy Hocquard 1794; Greenfields (T).
361. IIN.1734. Jean Journeaulx; The Elms (My).
362. IIV. Jean Janvrin; L'Ancienneté, High Street, St. Aubin (B); recurring as IIV.1818 on the harbour jetty.
363. IL.EL.PL.1718. Jean Laurens m. Elizabeth Luce 1681, with their son Philippe; Fernhill, Mont à l'Abbé (H).
364. IL.MFL.1776. In lane behind Wesley House, St. Aubin's Bulwarks (B).
365. Il y a plus de plaisir à pardonner qu'il n'y a à se venger, 1823. Windsor House, Gorey Village (G).
366. ILB. Jeanne Labey, widow of George Collas (1746–76); St. Martin's House (Mt).
367. ILB.1794. Near Mechanic Lodge (P).
368. ILB.EHQ.1777. Le Boutillier and Hocquard; Mont Pellier (T), from Le Binaud (T), now demolished.
369. ILB.MLF.1775. Jean Le Brun m. Marie Le Feuvre 1769; La Fragoniele, Le Coin (O).
370. ILB.MMR.1737. Jean Le Boutillier and Marie Mourant; Alphington House (now Priors) (S).
371. ILB.MRM.1722. At Wayside, near La Forêt (My).
372. ILBLT (for ILBTL).1834. I. Le Boutillier; on trough, Bouley Bay Hill lavoir (T).
373. ILBT.AS.1838. Le Breton; Le Vallon (T).
374. ILBT.BALX.1807. Le Breton; Le Vallon (T).
375. ILBTL.EDCC.1814. Le Boutillier; Le Carrefour (T).
376. ILC.EA.1696. Jean Le Couteur m. Esther Arthur 1689; fireplace, Le Nord (J).
377. ILC.EFL.1757. Josué Le Cornu m. Elizabeth Filleul; Clairmont, Mont Cochon (H).
378. ILC.MGB.1767. Jean Le Cras and Marie Gibaut; La Ferme Martel (L).
379. ILC.RDC.1765. Jean Le Cornu and Rachel de Caen; Maison de Portinfer (O).
380. ILF.MDMR.1808. Jean Le Feuvre m. Marie Dumaresq 1801; La Croix (G).
381. ILF.SLB. Jean Le Feuvre m. Susanne Le Brocq 1753; La Caumine, Le Coin (O).
382. ILFL.CBS.1858. Jean Laffoley m. Caroline Bisson 1858; Le Trésor (L).

383. ILG.1649. At Chestnut Fm. (B).
384. ILG.1662. At La Hauteur (Mt).
385. ILG.1806. Jean Langlois (b. 1770; Constable 1810–13, 1816–28); Oaklands (L).
386. ILG.ADC.1833. At Belmont (P).
387. ILG.EDSX.1780. Jean Langlois m. Elizabeth de Ste Croix 1766; gateposts, Les Montagnes (L).
388. ILG.ELF.1775. Jean Le Gros m. Elizabeth Le Feuvre 1771; Le Pont (Mt).
389. ILG.ERN.1826. At Petit Coin, Rozel (Mt).
390. ILG.IBT.1720. Jean Le Geyt m. Jeanne Bertram 1718; La Guillaumerie Cottages (S).
391. ILG.MH.1678. Jacques Le Geyt m. Marie Hue 1654; Sunningdale (H).
392. ILG.RLC.1744, and 1746. Jean Langlois and Rachel Le Cras; Broadfields (L).
393. ILG.SLG.1727. Josué Le Gros m. Sara Langlois 1717; Handois (L).
394. ILG.SRD.1802. Jean Le Gros and Susanne Rondel. Le Hurel (L).
395. ILGL.SBP.1848. Jean Le Gresley and Susanne Blampied; Hampton Villa (L).
396. ILI.1820. Le Jeune; Ivy Stone Fm. (C).
397. ILM.1619. Jean Le Manquais, who m. Anne La Cloche 1612; Bandinel (Mt).
398. ILM.1672. Le Maistre; Milton Fm. (Mt).
399. ILM.1719. At La Hurette (T).
400. ILM.1818. Le Marinel; St. Blaise (J).
401. ILM.EDC.1769. At Les Ormes, near le Câtel (T).
402. ILM.ELM.1737. Josué Le Masurier m. Elizabeth Le Masurier 1722; La Porte (T).
403. ILM.ELM.1748. Jean Le Masurier m. Elizabeth Le Masurier 1742; La Porte (T).
404. ILM.MBT.1732. At Les Fontaines (Mt).
405. ILM.MLM.1690. Le Maistre; Milton Fm. (Mt).
406. ILMT.ACB.1755. Josué Le Mottais m. Anne Cabot 1753; La Chasse (J).
407. ILMT.SCL.1713. At Rectory View (J).
408. ILP.1731. At Roselands (S).
409. ILP.AD.1706. Jean Lemprière and Anne Durell; Maison Le Maistre, St. Aubin (B).
410. ILP.ELC.1696. Jean Lemprière m. Esther Le Couteur 1693; Maison de St. Jean (J).
411. ILQ.1610. Le Quesne; Oak Farm (J).
412. ILQ.APD.1745. Jean Le Quesne and Ann Poingdestre; Mont à l'Abbé House (H).
413. ILQ.ELR.1798. Jean Le Quesne and Elizabeth Laurens; Mont à l'Abbé House (H).
414. ILR.1776. At Milton Fm. (Mt).
415. ILR.ELR.1790. Jean Le Riche m. Elizabeth Le Riche 1767; Hillside, Rozel (T).
416. ILR.EVL.1777. Jean Le Rossignol and Elizabeth Valleur; Magnolia Hotel, Bel Royal (L).
417. ILR.MLB.1692. At L'Ecluse (My).
418. ILS.1660. Illustrated by Payne, p. 17.
419. ILS.1666. At King's Fm. (B).
420. ILS.1734. At Les Issues Fm. (J).
421. ILS.ILS.MLQ.1726. At Les Houguettes (J).
422. ILS.IN.1662. Jean Le Sueur m. Jeanne Norman 1652; Les Lauriers (T).
423. ILS.MLM.1767. At Lloyd's Bank (H).
424. ILS.REN.1819. Josué Le Sueur m. Rachel Esnouf 1795; La Porte (J).
425. ILT.FLT.1699. At 15 La Motte Street (H).

426. ILVC.1846. Jean Le Vesconte; Fontaine de Gallie lavoir (Mt).

427. IM.1663. ? Maret; La Porte (T).

428. IM.1665 on lintel, and IM on salting trough; Jean Marche, who m. Jeanne le mot Motey 1668; Le Mottais Fm. (J).

429. IM.1671. Jean Millais; Le Tapon (S).

430. IM.SLS.1656. Jean Messervy and Sara Le Sueur; Linden Hall (H) (now at The Museum).

431. IMC.1834. I. Machon; on trough, Bouley Bay Hill lavoir (T).

432. IMH. Jean Mahaut; Les Arbres (L).

433. IML.1832. Mollet; Douet Fleury lavoir (Mt).

434. IML.MCL.1728. Jean Mallet and Marie Collas; La Ville Brée (Mt).

435. IMR.1723. Woodlands (My).

436. IMR.EDR.1793. Mourant; Oakborne, behind Grouville Church.

437. IMR.MCB.1732. At Mont Pellier (T).

438. IMR.MF.1755. Jean Mourant and Marie Falle; La Ferrière (S).

439. IMR.MGD.1755. Gatepost, Croix ès Mottes (S).

440. IMR.SLG.1826. Jean Mourant and Susanne Le Gros; Middlehall (L).

441. IMR.SVB.1738. Mourant and Vibert; Rectory Fm. (now Ladies' Walk) (My).

442. IMR.TMR.1698. At Oaklands (My).

443. IN.EH.1842. Noel and Hue; La Petite Commune 2 (S).

444. IN.?M.1718. ? Nicolle; Bishopstown (T).

445. INC.1834. I. Nicolle; on trough, Bouley Bay Hill lavoir (T).

446. INC.1846. Jean Nicolle; Fontaine de Gallie lavoir (Mt).

447. INC.ELS.1819. Jean Nicolle and Elizabeth Le Sueur; China Quarry Fm. (L).

448. INC.JHP.1863. Jean Nicolle and Jeanne Hooper; Croix ès Mottes (S).

449. INC.MGB.1747. Jean Nicolle m. Marie Gibaut 1741; Oak Fm. (L).

450. INL.1785. At La Retraite (S).

451. INM.EMR.1744. Jean Norman and Esther Marett; Ville ès Normans (T).

452. INM.EMR.1831. Jean Norman m. Elizabeth Marett 1826; Fauvic (G).

453. IP.1632. Jean Pipon (Constable); L'Aleval (P).

454. IP.1748. Jean Perrochon; 16 Hill Street (H).

455. IP.EGB.1738. At Les Corvées (O).

456. IP.ILB.1773. Jacques Payn m. Jeanne Le Brocq 1763; Croix au Lion (P).

457. IP.MAM. Jean Payn and Marie Amy; Springvale (G).

458. IP.MP.1740. At Highfield (H).

459. IP.MVV.1778, and 1784, 1790. Jean Payn and Marie Vivian; Springvale (G).

460. IPC.1604. Perchard; La Petite Commune 2 (S).

461. IPC.1772. Perchard; gatepost, Les Routeurs (S).

462. IPC.1797. Jean Perchard, who m. Marie Gabourel; Augrès Manor (T).

463. IPC.IVP. ? Perchard and ? Valpy; at Oakfield (S).

464. IPC.MG.1692. Perchard; Les Routeurs (S).

465. IPC.MLF.1771. Jean Perchard m. Marthe Le Feuvre 1736; Augrès Manor (T).

466. IPD.ETZ.1817. Poingdestre and Touzel; Les Côtils, near Electricity Station (H).

467. IPD.MBT.1750. Poingdestre; gatepost, Vieux Ménage (S).

468. IPD.SDC.1738 or 1758. Jean Poingdestre and Sara de Carteret; Vieux Ménage (S).

469. IPG.MMR.1754, and IPG.MMR.1805. Jean Pelgué; La Petite Commune (S).

470. IPL.APC.1797. Jean Pallot m. Anne Picot 1798; La Chouquetterie (Mt).

471. IPL.EPC.1821. Pallot and Perchard; La Sergenté (Mt).

472. IPL.JDR.1860. Jean Pallot m. Jane Dorey 1841; Rozel Fm. (T).

473. IPN.ARR.1814. Pinel and Romeril; Le Douet (J).

474. IPP.1790. Opposite Grouville Church.

475. IPP.EMB.1794. On sundial, Le Bel Royal (L).

476. IPP.FDLP.1726. Jean Pipon and Françoise de la Place; La Place, Del Sol Hotel (B).

477. IPR.ITZ.1790. Near Central House (G).

478. IR.1742. At Ville ès Normans (T).

479. IR...17... At Dale Cottage (H).

480. IR.EPQ.1680. Jean Renouf and Elizabeth Picquet; La Pompe (My).

481. IRCS.SLHQ.1820. Jean Richardson m. Susanne Le Hucquet 1790; Le Villot (Mt).

482. IRD.IAM.1727. At Le Vert Champ (Mt).

483. IRM.1723. At Woodlands (My); note also IMR. 1724 on trough.

484. IRM.ID.1747, and IRM.BL. At Chestnut Fm. (My).

485. IRM.IGD.1732. Gateposts, Daisy Fm. (P).

486. IRM.RPD.1739. Jean Remon m. Rachel Poingdestre 1727; Ville au Veslet (L); (son of FRM. No. 210).

487. IRM.SGC.1684. Jean Remon m. Sara Gruchy 1676; Badier Fm. (L).

488. IRN.1813. Jean Renouf; Oak Fm. (J).

489. IRN.ELB.1761. Renouf; Highfield (now Clos des Tours), Coin Varin (P).

490. IRR.JBSSL.1865. Jean Romeril m. Jane Betsy Sorsoleil 1858; Midlands (L).

491. ? IRSA.1670. At Haut de Tombette (My).

492. ISM.FLF.1714. Jean Simon; Vale Fm. Cottage (P).

493. ISR.MCT.1821. Josué Sarre m. Marie Coutanche 1810; Maple Grove, Route du Mont Mado (J).

494. ITC.JRR.1834. Jean Trachy m. Jeanne Romeril 1807; Les Jardins, near Six Rues (My).

495. ITP.CLQ.1721. Tapin; Route du Mont Mado (J).

496. IVB.1826. Vibert; at Bas du Marais (O).

497. IVB.RDH.1717. At Montrose (P).

498. IVB.KI.1700. ? Vibert and ? Jeune; Les Escaliers, near Frémont (J).

499. IVC.FLF. Jean Vincent m. Françoise Le Feuvre 1756; with LDDD (? the gift of LD) above; Parklands (P).

500. IVD.MSR.1850. At La Saline (J).

501. IVP.SAB.1713. At Neuilly (Mt).

502. IVS.AEN. 1788. Isaac Voisin m. Anne Esnouf 1775; Les Mauves (T).

503. IW. John Wadham, who m. Andrie Messervy 1585; Governor's House, Elizabeth Castle (H).

504. JBC.SLB.1820. Jean Bichard and Suzanne Le Brocq; Seaview (L).

505. JBD.1813. Jean Baudains; St. Cyr lavoir (J),

506. JBG.EGD.1849. J. Beaugié and Esther Gaudin; gatepost, Le Pavilon (Mt).

507. JBN.MCL.1831. At Highlands, La Boucterie (T).

508. JBP.MAGLC. Jean Blampied m. Mary Ann Gallichan 1854; Three Oaks Fm. (L).

509. JBP.RBP.JBP.ECB.1820. Blampied; Maison des Croix (T).

510. JBS.1813. Jean Bisson; St. Cyr lavoir (J).

511. JBS.AMRD.1932. Bisson and Rondel; Don Fm. (J).

512. JCT.1813. Jean Coutanche; St. Cyr lavoir (J).

513. JDB.1805. Jean Dolbel; Chestnut Grove (J).

514. JDL.JHL.1891. Jean Dallain and Jeanne Huelin; La Chasse, Sion (J).

515. JDLM.JGF.1823. Jean de la Mare m. Jeanne Godfray 1823; Aston House, opposite St. Clement's Church (C).

516. JDR.JDF.1882. Dorey; opposite Diélament (T).

517. JDSC.1813. Jean de Ste Croix; St. Cyr lavoir (J).

518. JEML.MMTG.1832 and 1836. Jean Emily m. Marguerite Mattingley c. 1816; Beechfield (T).

519. JFTZ.LMRCB.1900. John Francis Touzel and Louise Marguerite Renouf Cabot; Homestead (L).

520. JG.1870. Josué Graut; La Rigdonaine (G).

521. JG.MJ.1841. Josué Graut m. Marguerite Jennes c. 1882; La Rigondaine (G).

522. JHL.MLB.1827. On corner house at Beaumont (P).

523. JHM.AAB.1805. Jean Hamon and Anne Aubert; Les Chasses, Coin Hâtain (L).

524. JHM.MPN.1840. Jean Hamon and Marie Pinel; Les Chasses, Coin Hâtain (L).

525. JHM.NGC.1848. At Beau Regard (J).

526. J. Jacobs, Archt. 1854. On newel medallion, St. Martin's House (Mt).

527. JJDGC.EPL.1890. Jean Josué de Gruchy and Emily Pallot; Greenfields (T).

528. JLB.1883. Le Brun; Highcliff (J).

529. JLG.1841. Le Gallais; gatepost, Surville (H).

530. JLM.ABP.1827. Jean Le Maistre m. Anne Blampied 1792; La Vielle Demeuthe, Bel Royal (L).

531. JLR.MAL.1839. At South View (L).

532. JML.1832. J. Mollet; Douet Fleury lavoir (Mt).

533. JMSV.SLR.1874. John Messervy; Ville Brée (Mt).

534. JNC.ALG.1869. Jean Nicolle and Jeanne Le Grand; China Quarry Fm. (L).

535. JNC.ELC.1806. Jean Nicolle m. Elizabeth Le Cras 1794; Le Passage (L).

536. JPF.FAP.1835. Falle; at Waverley Fm. (Mt).

537. JPF.MSW.1885. Jean Philippe Falle m. Marie Susanne Whitley; Waverley Fm.(Mt).

538. JPRR.AJMR.1891. John Philip Romeril and Alice Jane Marett; Oaklands, Coin Varin (P).

539. JR.AM.1827. James Remon and Anne Marett; St. Aubin's Institute (B).

540. JRN.BRN.1820. Renouf; gateposts, Old Fm., Mont au Prêtre (H).

541. KLS.ECSA.1699. At La Chasse (J).

542. KQR. At Midlands (L).

543. LAB.1664. Lucas Aubin; Hamlet Fm. (S).

544. LAN.1580. v.HD.

545. LB.1588. v.ELE.1588.

546. LDDD. v.IVC.FLF.

547. LH.EH.1637. Laurens and Edouard Hamptonne; at Hamptonne (L).

548. LP.BI, or BJ. Lemprière; on stoup at Rozel Manor (Mt).

549. LR.RR.1660. ? Louys Rouet who m. Rachel Rogier 1654; Mont à l'Abbé Fm. (H).

550. LV. RDLC.IPV.1745. Louis Voisin m. Rachel de la Cour 1725, with their son Jacob Philippe, b. 1726; at Albany House (L).

551. MAL.ARN.1707 and 1717. M. Alexandre and Anne Renouf; Franc Fief Fm. (B).

552. MAL.ARM.1760. Alexandre and Renouf; Franc Fief fm. (B).

553. MALX.1790, and MALX.SGL.1804. Moise Alexandre m. Susanne Gaillard 1796; Chestnut Lea, Mont à l'Abbé (H).

554. Maufant 1837. At Maufant Manor (S).

555. MB.MAH.1763. At St. Helier Boys' School (H).

556. MBt.H. ? Berteau; at Le Ménage (L).

557. MD.E.1647. Matthieu Dorey and Elizabeth Roissié; fireplace, Stirling Castle Fm. (H).

558. MDLG. Marie de la Garde, wife of Philippe Collas (1646–1717); on garden steps, St. Martin's House (Mt).

559. MG.1618. Michel Guerdain, who m. Marie Stocall 1600; on trough at La Guerdainerie (T).

560. MGB.AP.1762. Moise Gibaut and Ann Payn; Mainland (L).

561. MGB.APD.1756. Moise Gibaut and Ann Poingdestre; Les Prairies (J).

562. MH. At Le Ménage (L).

563. MH.IC.1695. Hocquard; Greenfields (T).

564. MIN.1786. ? Journeaux; Half-way House (now The Spinney) (G).

565. ML.1666. Moise Luce; Moss Nook (H).

566. ML.MM.1666. Moise Luce m. Marguerite Messervy c. 1664; Moss Nook (H).

567. MLB.1720. Labey; on trough, Home Fm. (G).

568. MLB.MCB.1686. Michel Larbalestier m. Marie Cabot 1671; La Fosse (T). At The Museum.

569. MLF.1696. Moyse Laffoley; at Auvergne (P).

570. MLF.ALC.1714. At Fontis (P).

571. MLG. ? Michel Langlois; Morel Fm. (L).

572. MLG.1669. Bushy Fm. (H).

573. MLG.1749. At Mainland (L).

574. MLGL.MPD.1756. Mathieu Le Gallais and Marie Poingdestre; Surville (H).

575. MLP.IC.1749. Michel Lemprière m. Jeanne Corbet 1713; Diélament Manor (T).

576. MLVC.ML.1708. Michel Le Vesconte and Marguerite Lael; Les Buis (My).

577. MMB, MMG or MMLB.1692. Le Feugerel (J).

578. MPD.1715, with RRN near by. Michel Poingdestre m. Rachel Renouf 1692; China Quarry Fm. (L).

579. MPD. 18th century. ? Poingdestre; at Animals' Shelter (H).

580. MPD.IRN.1730, or IPD. Poingdestre; The Olde House, Rue de Friquet, Mont à l'Abbé (H).

581. MPL.ICB.1683. At Les Sts. Germains Fm. (L).

582. MR.1707. Renouf; Franc Fief Fm. (B).

583. MR.AF.1717. M. Renouf m. Amelia Falle 1717; fireplace, Franc Fief Fm. (B).

584. MSV, or MSW. at Ivy House, St. Aubin (B).

585. NAM.1663. Amy; Maison de Bas (L).

586. NAT.1813. Noé Arthur; St. Cyr lavoir (J).
587. NB.Fecit.1765. On sundial, Le Marinel (J).
588. NBD.MVP.1784. ? Nicolas Baudains; Beaupré (J).
589. NC.KLM.1727. Nicolas Chevalier m. Katherine Le Montais 1717; La Retraite à l'ouest, Beaumont (P).
590. NC.L.1619. Nicolas Cabot; La Chasse, Maufant (S).
591. NDC. ? Nicolas de Carteret; near St. John's Church (J).
592. NDC.1664. Nicolas de Carteret; Les Buttes (J).
593. NDC.1669. Nicolas de Carteret; fireplace, Les Buttes (J).
594. NPD.FA.1659. ? du Pré and Arthur; L'Ancienneté (My).
595. NDSX.PL.SGF.Ms.30.1739. Nicolas de Ste Croix, Pierre Luce, and Sara Giffard, ? 30 March 1739; 15 Hue Street (H).
596. NER.EDL.1718.
597. NF.MADM.1751. Nicolas Fiott m. Anne Dumaresq 1740; cistern head, No. 7 Pier Road (H).
598. NG.SN.16?8. Noé Germain m. Susanne Noel 1677.
599. NGF.1688. At Fontaine de Bas, near St. Peter's Church (P).
600. NGF.1813. N. Giffard; St. Cyr lavoir (J).
601. NH.1651. ? Hue; lintel from St. Aubin's (B), now at The Museum.
602. NHL.FLB. v.IHL.
603. NJBS.ABR.1875. Bisson; Les Ruettes, near La Fontaine (T).
604. NLB.IDC.1731. ? Le Brun; Beechleigh (P).
605. NLC.MM.1724. Noé Le Cras and Marie Marett; La Ferme Grandet (L).
606. NLQ.ELF.1768. Nicolas Le Quesne and Elizabeth Le Feuvre; Beaufort House (H).
607. NLR.EDLP.1715. ? Le Ruez and de la Perrelle; Greystones (O).
608. NLR.EGD.1710. Le Rossignol; Château des Roches, near L'Horizon (B).
609. NM.LDCGN.1721. On Ancient House at Plémont, near Léoville (O).
610. NN.1670 and NN.1681. Noel or Nicolle; Le Rué (Mt).
611. NO.AM.ARP.1940. An Air Raid Precaution inscription, on boulder in lavoir near L'Amiral (O), just before the Occupation.
612. NPC.MMC.1740. At Georgetown (H).
613. NPL.ILS.1820. Nicolas Pallot; Les Landes Lodge (Mt).
614. NPM. Gable stone, at Greenhill (P).
615. NQR.1676. ? Querrée; at Les Varvots (L).
616. NR.SDP.1675. Nicolas Richardson m. Sara du Parcq c. 1664; fireplace, Don Fm. (J), now in The Museum.
617. NRN.1815. Renouf; La Gallierie (Mt).
618. NRN.1846. Nicolas Renouf; Fontaine de Gallie lavoir (Mt).
619. NVD.VMH. At Les Mauves (T).
620. PA.EC. or EG.1680. Philippe Amy; Patier (S).
621. PA.MMR.1823. Philippe Amy and Marguerite Moreau; Patier (S).
622. PA.MSM.1721. At Homestill (P).
623. PAB.ILN.1770. At Central House (G).

624. PAB.MAH.1733. At Appledore, Boulivot (G).
625. PAL.1677. Philippe Anley; fireplace, Les Aix (P).
626. PAL.1718. Philippe Anley; Les Aix (P).
627. PAL.ERN. ? 1769. At Le Hurel (T).
628. PAL.SLM.1689. Philippe Anley m. Susanne Le Maistre 1684.
629. PAL.IPN.1823. Philippe Anley; Moss Nook (H).
630. PAL.MBN.1832. Philippe Anley m. Marguerite Binet 1797; Moss Nook (H).
631. PAM.1732. Philippe Amy, who m. Marie Amy; Câtillon de Haut (G).
632. PAM.ECR.1802. Philippe Amy and Esther Carrel; Câtillon de Bas (G).
633. PAM.EMR. Philippe Amy m. Elizabeth Mourant 1699; Câtillon de Bas (G); repeated 1772.
634. PAT.SLC.1683. Pierre Anthoine and Sara Le Couteur; Maison de Haut (S).
635. PB.1660. Balleine; Greenland (P).
636. PB.1704. Balleine; Greenland (P).
637. PBL.1605, or PBD, PBN (stone broken). ? Badier or Benest; La Bruyère Fm. (L).
638. PBL.DDF.EGF.1822. Philippe Billot m. Douce du Fresne 1820; Holmdale (Mt).
639. PBN.MHQ.1811. Benest and Hocquard; Bel Respiro (H).
640. (PB)N.SVT.IBN.175.... Philippe Benest m. Sara Vautier 1735, with their son Jean, b. 1737; stone from ? Mon Plaisir (L), now at La Ruette (L).
641. PBP.ARN.1809. Philippe Blampied m. Anne Renouf 1778; Glenrose (P).
642. PBP.NJ.1832. Blampied and ? Juste; Glenrose (P).
643. PBS.ILC.1729. Bisson; Vale Farm Cottage (P).
644. PBS.MGC.1780 and 1781. Bisson; Les Ruettes, near La Fontaine (T).
645. PBT.RDP.1823. Bertram and du Pont; gatepost, Maufant (S).
646. PC. Philippe Collas (1668-1748); garden bench, St. Martin's House (Mt).
647. PCB. Cabot; Les Ifs (T).
648. PCB.JBL.1883. Cabot and Billot; Le Câtel Fm. (T).
649. PCL.1762, and 1763. Philippe Collas (1740-90); St. Martin's House (Mt).
650. PCL.RLR.1776. ? Collas; at Chandos, St. Aubin (B).
651. PCRD.1671. On apple crusher from Les Grandes Rues (Mt), at La Chaumière, Millbrook (L).
652. PD.1597. At Sycamore Cottage (B).
653. PDC.1661. de Carteret; St. Ouen's Manor (O).
654. PDC.1707. Philippe de Carteret; Le Câtelet (J).
655. PDC. or PDG.EG.1747. At Fliquet Mill, Bellozanne Valley (H).
656. PDC.ILB.1723. Pierre de Caen m. Judith Le Brun 1701; Ville au Bas (L).
657. PDF.IN.1797. Philippe du Fresne m. Jeanne Noel; Cintra, Rozel (Mt).
658. PdG.1686. Near Hotel de France. (H).
659. PDG.EDG.1800. Philippe and Elizabeth de Gruchy; Pièce Mauger (T).
660. PDG.EG.1761. At Mont à l'Abbé Manor (H).
661. PDG.ELG.1773. de Gruchy; Cowley Fm. (S).
662. PDG.MDG.1822. Philippe de Gruchy m. Marie de Gruchy 1791; Le Câtel, Rozel (Mt).
663. PDG.MHC.1733. Pierre de Gruchy m. Marie Hocquart 1719; Maison du Buisson (S).

664. PDG.MMRN.1814. Philippe de Gruchy m. Marie Renaut 1799; Ville Machon (T).

665. PDG.RMSV.1803. At Hautmont (J).

666. PDGC.AMTG.1833. Philippe de Gruchy and Anne Mattingley; La Forge (T).

667. PDGC.MAGF.1872. de Gruchy and ? Godfray; La Féverie (S).

668. PDH.ELB.1826. Philippe du Heaume and Elizabeth Le Breton; La Robeline (O).

669. PDL.MBQ.1714. Pierre Dallain and Marie Bosquet; Highland Cottage (L).

670. PDL.MNC.1765, and 1772, 1796. Pierre Dallain m. Marguerite Nicolle 1765; gatepost, La Chasse, Sion (J).

671. PDLCN.MALB.1899. Philippe David Le Cornu m. Mary Ann Le Brun; Le Trésor (L).

672. PDLM.1846. Philippe de la Mare; Fontaine de Gallie lavoir (Mt).

673. PDM.ALM.1766. Philippe Dumaresq m. Ann Le Maistre 1724; Le Mourin (S).

674. PDM.EM.1684. Philippe Dumaresq and Elizabeth Messervy; Le Mourin (S).

675. PDR.1772. Dorey; La Fontaine, Ville à l'Evêque (T).

676. PDR.EGD.1882. Dorey; Maison Maret (T).

677. PDSC.1743. Pierre de Ste Croix, who m. Elizabeth Mahaut 1743-4; Eden Grove (L).

678. PDSC.EF.1759. Philippe de Ste Croix m. Elizabeth Fiott 1760; La Roussetterie (now Hollydale) (L).

679. PDSX.1683. de Ste Croix; at Eden Grove (L).

680. PDSX.RA. Philippe de Ste Croix and Rachel Ahier; La Valette (H).

681. PEN.1694. Pierre Esnouf; La Porte (J).

682. PF.1711. Philippe Falle; Rev. P. Falle's House (S).

683. PF.1736. Rev. Philippe Falle; cistern heads, The Old Library (H).

684. PFDLC.ILL.1825. Philippe François de la Court m. Jeanne Le Lièvre c. 1821; Ville au Veslet (L).

685. PFO.1679. Pierre Fiott; Oaklands (L).

686. PFV.EBD.1715. Philippe Fauvel and Elizabeth Bandinel; Holly Bank (Mt).

687. PG.1638. At Haut du Rué (Mt).

688. PG.c.1675. ? Philippe Gourré; Bel Air (S).

689. PG.SM. At Anneville, Faldouet (Mt).

690. PGB.1812. Philippe Gibaut; Mainland (L).

691. PGB.ED.1802. Philippe Gibaut and Elizabeth Dean; Mainland (L).

692. PGC.1813. Philippe Gruchy; St. Cyr lavoir (J).

693. PGC.MBD.1746, and 1756. Philippe Gallichan and Madeleine Baudet; Bon Air (L).

694. PGC.MDSX.1760. Philippe Gallichan and Marguerite de Ste Croix; Sunnyside, Ville au Veslet (L).

695. PGC.RH.1799, and PGC.RHM.1807. Pierre Gruchy m. Rachel Hamon 1785; Hérupe (J).

696. PGD.1832. Gaudin; Douet Fleury lavoir (Mt).

697. PGD.EAB.1817. Philippe Gaudin m. Elizabeth Aubin 1781; Green Fm. (Mt).

698. PGF.SM.1754. ? Godfray; fireplace, Devon Villa, Faldouet (Mt).

699. PGLC.1807. Gallichan; field wall, La Chouquetterie (Mt).

700. PGLC.1813. Pierre Gallichan; Fontaine de Gallie lavoir (Mt).

701. PGLC.CRM.1788. Philippe Gallichan and Catherine Remon; Bel Air (L).

702. PGLC.MRD.1810. Philippe Gallichan m. Marie Rondel c. 1800; Bel Air (L).

703. PhBL.IVN.EL.1705. Philippe Balleine 1 and IVN; Philippe Balleine 2 and Elizabeth Journeaux; Greenland (P).

704. PhGC.EPN.1836. At Le Pont (J).

705. PhLG.1649. Philippe Le Geyt; on stairway, Fernhill (H).

706. PH.AC.1737. In Hill Street (H).

707. PH.IG.1669. At Junction of Kensington Place and Lewis Street (H).

708. Philip Shoosmith, Le 23e.7bre.1748 (who m. Catherine Bertaut 1780); on beam at 19 Hue Street (H).

709. Philippe Deslandes. 1749. On beam at 19 Hue Street (H).

710. PHLDX.ELVdD. de Ste Croix and ? Le V. dit Durell; Rosedale (H).

711. PHM.EIV.1776. Philippe Hamon and Elizabeth Janvrin; Sables d'Or, High Street, St. Aubin (B).

712. PHM.EN.1824. Pierre Hamon and Elizabeth Noel; St. Clair (L).

713. PHM.JNM.1875. Pierre Hamon and Jane Norman; gatepost, St. Clair (L).

714. PHM.MBP.1693. Hamon; Les Câteaux (T).

715. PHPC.1832. Douet Fleury lavoir (Mt).

716. PH.RN.E.M.PD.1909. At Le Rué (Mt).

717. PHT.1813. Pierre Hotton; St. Cyr lavoir (J).

718. PJR.LAC.1931. Philippe Josué Romeril and Lily Ada Cotillard; Petit Câtelet (J).

719. PL.ABP. Philippe Luce and Anne Blampied; Greenland (L).

720. PL.MR.1707. Philippe Lael m. Marguerite Remon (? Marie Renouf) 1697; Valley Fm. (My).

721. PLA.ILQ.1716.1816. Opposite Ivy Fm. (J).

722. PLB.1659. Larbalestier; Holmbury (T).

723. PLB.1671. At La Fontaine, Ville au Veslet (L).

724. PLB.1687. Pierre Le Bailly; La Vieille Maison, St. Aubin (B).

725. PLB.AG.1668. Philippe Larbalestier and Andrée Gallie; La Fosse (T).

726. PLB.EAT.1776. Philippe Labey and Elizabeth Anthoine; Longueville Fm. (S).

727. PLB.ERD.1870. Le Brun; Les Sts. Germains Fm. (L).

728. PLB.SDG. Pierre Le Breton m. Sara de Gruchy 1640; Beechfield (T).

729. PLBLG.MLVC.1824. Le Boulanger and Le Vesconte; Roseland (G).

730. PLBT.DBL.1794. Philippe Le Boutillier m. Douce Balleine 1778; La Sergenté (P).

731. PLC.1685. Philippe Le Caumais; Redwood Hotel, Five Oaks (S).

732. PLC.ELVC.1770. Pierre Le Cras m. Elizabeth Le Vesconte 1766; Prospering Fm. (My).

733. PLCD. and PLCD.1662. Philippe Le Couteur, Doyen; St. Martin's Rectory (Mt).

734. PLCN.EGB.ILCN.1716. Pierre Le Cornu and Elizabeth Gibaut, with their son Jean (d. 1743); Les Landes Fm. (O).

735. PLCN.MDMR.1813. At L'Hermitage (J).

736. PLCT.MLB.1721. ? Le Couteur; opposite La Caroline (P).

737. PL.EP.1699. ? Philippe Laurens and Elizabeth Poingdestre; Les Sts. Germains Fm. (L).
738. PLF. At La Citadelle (L).
739. PLF.1822. Philippe Le Feuvre; La Hougue (P).
740. PLF.ALB.1837. Philippe Le Feuvre and Anne Le Bas; Les Nièmes (P).
741. PLG.1716. Philippe Langlois; Morel Fm. (L).
742. PLG.1832. On Douet Fleury lavoir (Mt).
743. PLG.HB.1768. Le Gros; Les Câteaux (T).
744. PLG.IIB.1777. Philippe Le Gros m. Jeanne Joubaire 1751; Les Câteaux (T).
745. PLGC.EPN.1836. At Le Pont (J).
746. PLM.IL?.1659. Le Maistre; Fosse à l'Ecrivain (S).
747. PLR.MAG.1896. At Le Carrefour (J).
748. PLR.RLBTL.1811. At Beauverd, Rue au Poivre (J).
749. PLS.1674. or 1679.IN.CB. Jersey Farmer's Trading Union, Esplanade (H) v.833.
750. PLS.1767. ? Le Sueur; Hue Street, St. Helier (H).
751. PLS.AJD.1902. At La Ronde Porte, Maufant (S).
752. PLV.On Fireplace, Les Augerez Fm. (P).
753. PM.1734. ? Pierre Mauger; La Fontaine 2, Ville au Veslet (L).
754. PM.MP.1628. Philippe Messervy m. Marie Pipon 1616; Old Bagot Manor Fm. (S).
755. PMG.1751. Pierre Mauger who m. Elizabeth Marett; Maison du Coin (L).
756. PMG.SLF.1790. Pierre Mauger m. Susanne Le Feuvre 1789; Maison de la Ruette (O).
757. PML.MC.1762. Pierre Mallet m. Marie Chepmell 1759; at Hambros, Broad Street, St. Helier (H).
758. PMR.AIV.1796. Philippe Marett and Anne Janvrin; La Haule Manor (B).
759. PMR.RLR.1867. Philippe Mourant m. Rachel Le Riche; Haut du Mont au Prêtre (H).
760. PMSV.1833. Philippe Messervy, who m. Elizabeth Le Neveu; Hamptonne (C).
761. PMSV.ETZ.1786. Philippe Messervy and Elizabeth Touzel; Hamptonne (C).
762. PM?T.P&?8.1606. At Rockstone (Mt).
763. PN.1609. At Le Câtelet (J).
764. PN.1682. ? Nicolle; at La Biarderie (T).
765. PN.MV.1805. At L'Aiguillon (G).
766. PNC.1766. Nicolle; Hérupe (J).
767. PNC.LPT.1873. ? Nicolle; at La Biarderie (T).
768. PNC.MBN.1737. Pierre Nicolle m. Marie Binet 1736; La Hauteur, Rue de la Chênaie (T).
769. PNC.MFV.1816. Pierre Nicolle and Marie Fauvel; Bu de la Rue, Coin Hâtain (L).
770. PNC.MLG.1796. ? Nicolle; Ville à l'Evêque (T).
771. PNM.MRM.1756. Philippe Norman and Marie Remon; near Pierre des Bessières (L).
772. PNM.RNBk.1834. Philippe Norman m. Rachel Narcombe Baker 1833; Ville ès Normans (T).
773. PP.ALS.1834. Payn; The Granite House (Mt).
774. PP.AMR.1776. Philippe Payn and Anne Marett; Le Colombier (L).
775. PP.EA.1710? Philippe Payn m. Elizabeth Alexandre 1692; La Pelotte (G).
776. PP.I.1632. Pierre Pipon m. Judith Effard 1623; La Retraite (S).
777. PPC.SBP.1763. Perchard and Blampied; Glenrose (P).
778. PPD.1852. At Cherry Tree Cottage, Bel Royal (L).
779. PPD.ILS.1815. Philippe Poingdestre and Isobel Le Sueur; Champ Collin (S).
780. PPL.ELS.1834. Pallot; La Sergenté (Mt).
781. PR.GM.1?19. At La Rosière (J).
782. PRCS.ELS.1816. Richardson; Rue des Côtils (Mt).
783. PRd.1831. Philippe Rondel; Le Petit Câtelet 2 (J).
784. PRD.ae.8a's.1795; IRD.ae.19a's.1796. Philippe and Jean Rondel; La Guerdainerie (T).
785. PRD.ELR.1795, and 1817. Philippe Rondel; La Guerdainerie (T).
786. PRM.1660. Philippe Remon; Broadfields Cottage (L). .
787. PRM.1774. Philippe Remon; Broadfields Cottage (L);
788. PRMR.ECT.1716. Philippe Rummeril (sic) m. Elizabeth Coutanche 1714; La Ruette (L).
789. PRN.1742. At Prospering Fm. (My).
790. PRN.MAM; PRN.MAM.1805, 1813, 1824. Renaut and Amy; La Ville Machon (T).
791. PRN.MDG.1789. Renaut; La Ville Machon (T).
792. PRR.1829. Philippe Romeril; Le Petit Câtelet (J).
793. PRR.ALF.1791. Philippe Romeril and Anne Le Feuvre; Windsor House (L).
794. PRR.MMG.1806. Philippe Romeril m. Marie Mauger 1778; Le Petit Câtelet (J).
795. PRV.1740. ? Philippe Rive, who m. Marguerite Paris 1779; La Maison des Côtils, St. Peter's Valley (P).
796. PS.1611. Pierre Seale, who m. Sara Clement 1598; fireplace, Old Court House Hotel, St. Aubin (B).
797. PS.1668. Pierre Seale, who m. Marie de Carteret 1675; fireplace, Old Court House Hotel, St. Aubin (B).
798. PS.CI.1732. On cottage behind The Hollies, St. Aubin (B).
799. PSH.SBD.1712. Philippe Sohier m. Suzanne Badier 1684; Milton Fm. (Mt).
800. PT.SCT.1743. At Tréoville (P).
801. PTC.ICB.1748. Trachy; Les Jardins, near Six Rues (My).
802. PTC.JRR.1834. Trachy and Romeril; Les Jardins, near Six Rues (My).
803. PTC.MHQ.1777. Philippe Trachy and Marie Le Hucquet; Les Jardins, near Six Rues (My).
804. PTR.SVT.1830. Philippe Thoreau and Susanne Vautier; October House, Mont des Routeurs (P).
805. PVB.ERN.1765. On well, Fern Valley (My).
806. PVB.IAT.1746. Philippe Vibert and Jeanne Arthur; Beech Fm. (P).
807. PVD.1832. Philippe Vardon; Douet Fleury lavoir (Mt).
808. PVD.1846. Philippe Vardon; Fontaine de Gallie lavoir (Mt).
809. PVT.EMDLH.1889. Vautier and de la Haye; Sion Villas, and Sion Cottage, Longueville (S).
810. PVV.MMR.1729. Philippe Vivian m. Marie Mourant 1710; St. Mannelier (S).
811. PW.1767. On drinking trough, from Le Marais, now at La Pompe (My).
812. RAL.1761. Anley; Beau Séjour, opposite Maitland (H).
813. RB.SBH.1670 and 1676. Raulin Benest m. Sara Bailhache 1663; Mon Plaisir (L).

814. RBD.1711. At Rozel Manor Fm. (Mt).
815. RC.IP.1696. Renaud Coutanche and Jeanne Pinel; Coutanche Fm. (T).
816. RCT.MMG.1725. Renaud Coutanche m. Marie Mauger 1704; Coutanche Fm. (T).
817. RDB.EGN.1742. ? Dolbel and Gasnier; Le Vivier (J).
818. RDF.1735. Richard du Feu, who m. Elizabeth Gruchy 1737; Les Ifs (T).
819. RDF.EG.29 Mo.8br.1746. Richard du Feu m. Elizabeth Gruchy 1737; Les Ifs (T).
820. RDG.IAT. ? de Gruchy and Arthur; Le Carrefour (My).
821. RDM.1726. Richard Dumaresq; on sundial, Le Petit Ponterrin (S).
822. RET.MLB.1766. Richard Estur m. Marie Labey 1762; Rev. Philippe Falle's House (S).
823. RF.MLF.1791. In Gorey Village (G).
824. RHM.1663. Richard Hamon; Les Câteaux (T).
825. RI.R.1608. At Longueville Manor (S).
826. RJTL, also read as ROSE or NOTE; on sundial, Picket House, Royal Square (H).
827. RLB. At Les Colombiers (My).
828. RLB.1794. On sundial, Maison Charles (L).
829. RLF.MLF.1734. Rolin Laffoley and Marie Lafolley; Mon Séjour, Augerez (P).
830. RLG.1666. Richard Langlois; Morel Fm. (L).
831. RLG.1676. Raulin Langlois; Broadfields (L).
832. RLM.MLS.1687. St. Saviour/Trinity boundary stone.
833. RLS. Alternative reading of PLS in No. 749.
834. RRB.MDC.1713. Raulin Robin and Marie de Carteret; Ty Anna, St. Aubin (B).
835. RVP.CCV.1756. Richard Valpy and Catherine Chevalier; Les Ruettes (J).
836. S-.1664. Gable stone, South View (S).
837. SD.NLG.1624. At Trafalgar Hotel, St. Aubin (B).
838. SDG. PLB. TLB. MLB. SLB. ELB. ELB. Sara de Gruchy, who m. Philippe Le Breton 1640, with their five children, Thomas, Marie, Sara, Elizabeth, and Esther; Beechfield (T).
839. SI. ? Saint Jean; at le Câtelet (J).
840. SLF.SHB.1715. At Les Chasses (J), brought from elsewhere.
841. SLG.EFL. Gatepost of field (P.527) on Mont de l'Ecole (P).
842. SLM.NLF.1700. At La Croûte, near Le Marais (O).
843. SLP.MMG.1715. Simon Lemprière m. Marie Mauger 1707; near St. Mary's Garage (My).
844. SMR.1813. Samuel Marett; St. Cyr lavoir (J).
845. SMR.E.1670. At Haut de Tombette (My).
846. SN. and SN.1751. At Terrebonne (G).
847. TAB.ELG.1825. At Mon Plaisir (My).
848. TAB.ITZ.1778. Thomas Aubin and Jeanne Touzel; Ville ès Philippes (G).
849. TAH.1832. Thomas Ahier; Douet Fleury lavoir (Mt).
850. TB.1766. Guerin fecit. On sundial at The Museum (H).
851. TBG.MSV.1909. Beaugié and Messervy; Le Pavillon (Mt).
852. TC.EV.1670. Thomas Chevallier m. Esther Vallepy 1656; fireplace, Hautmont (J).
853. TCAH.IHC.1820. At Rosedale, Gorey (G).

854. TCB.MCELV.1903. Cabot; Le Carrefour (T).
855. TCB.RCB.1764. Thomas Cabot m. Rachel Cabot 1742; Champs Ravet, near La Planque (T).
856. TCLG.1879. Jersey Farmer's Trading Union, Esplanade (H).
857. TDG.1683. Thomas de Gruchy; Sous les Bois (T).
858. TDG.1743. Thomas de Gruchy; gatepost, Sous les Bois (T).
859. TDG.MDF.1765. Thomas de Gruchy and Marie du Feu; Pièce Mauger (T).
860. TDG.RVB.1728. Thomas de Gruchy and Rachel Vibert; Pièce Mauger (T).
861. TF. Thomas Falle, ancestor of the historian; on family home (now demolished) near St. Mannelier (S).
862. TFL.MNM.1810. At Vicq Fm. (G).
863. TFL.HGB.1834. Thomas Falla and Harriet Gibaut; Les Buttes (J).
864. TGF.1689. Godfray; Meadow Vale (G).
865. TGM.RLS.1640. Thomas Guillaume m. Rachel Le Sueur 1669; La Boucterie (S).
866. TLB.1669, 1671, 1673, and TLB.SPD. Thomas Le Breton m. Sara Poingdestre 1678; Beechfield (T).
867. TLB.EBT.1769. Thomas Labey and Elizabeth Bertram; La Fontaine (G).
868. TLC.MGB.1701. Thomas Le Cras and Marie Gibaut; La Ferme Martel, now Glencoe (L).
869. TLG.MB.1606. Thomas Le Goupil dit Guerdain m. Marie Benest 1606; Portelet Inn (B).
870. TLHDY.1782. Thomas Le Hardy, who m. Françoise Dumaresq 1768; in field wall, Le Petit Ponterrin (S).
871. TLHDY.FDMR.1793. Thomas Le Hardy m. Françoise Dumaresq 1768; site of Maison du Roux, Springfield Road (H).
872. TLHQ.EDLM.1827. Thomas Le Huquet m. Elizabeth de la Mare 1808; L'Ecurie, Rue des Côtils (Mt).
873. TLM.MR.1889. Le Marinel; St. Blaise (J).
874. TLP.ADB.1820. Lemprière and Dolbel; Eileenid Villas, Route du Mont Mado (J).
875. TLS.1709. At Green Fm. (J).
876. TM. At Faldouet Lodge (Mt).
877. TM.E.1661. Thomas Mourant m. Elizabeth Ahier 1637; La Ferrière (S).
878. TMfB.EL.1632. At Maison Pelgué (S).
879. TM.SAB.1683. Timothée Mourant m. Susanne Aubin 1681; Champ Collin (S).
880. TMR.170-. Thomas Morel; Leda House (L).
881. TMR.1782. Thomas Morel (b. 1745); Guingeval (L).
882. TMR.AMR.1841. Thomas Morel and Ann Mourant; Leda House (L).
883. TMS.EVP.1751. Thomas Messervy m. Elizabeth Valpy 1745; Les Alpes Cottages (Mt).
884. TMS.MDB.1741. Thomas Messervy m. Mary Dolbel 1705; Les Alpes Cottages (Mt).
885. TMSV.1832. T. Messervy; Douet Fleury lavoir (Mt).
886. TP.MN.IP.KAL.1732. Thomas Pridaux and MN; Jean Pridauld m. Katherine Alexandre 1723; Les Grés (B).
887. TP.SP. Thomas Pipon (Constable 1708-13) and Suzanne Pipon. near Wesley House, St. Aubin's Bulwarks (B).

888. TPC.EGL.1889. Thomas Perchard and Elise Gallichan; Les Routeurs (S).

889. TPE or PTE.1737. Cistern head, L'Ancienneté,
High Street, St. Aubin (B).

890. TPN.MLG. At L'Augée, Mont à l'Abbé (H).

891. TRN.SGD.1883. Thomas Renouf and Suzanne
Gaudin; Le Câtillon (Mt).

892. TSH.1832. T. Sohier; Douet Fleury lavoir (Mt).

893. WCR.AER.1899. At La Ville Brée (Mt).

894. WF. William Fortescue; Governor's House, Elizabeth Castle (H).

895. WGQ.1664. William Jenkins (whose son was
baptized at St. Lawrence in 1663); inside cottage
at Carrefour Jenkins (L).

896. WK.1700. ? William Kastell; L'Armistice, S.
Aubin (B).

897. WS.1644. William Snow; Albany House (L).

898. WS.MM. William Snow m. M. Mauger 1704; Springland, Millbrook (L).

899. X.1598. v.DL.B. No. 101.

Inscriptions in which the opening letters are illegible

900. -AM.MML.1818. Amy and Mallet; Câtillon de
bas (G).

901. -ILM.1716. At Chestnut Fm. (B).

902. -MHM.1664. At Ville ès Gros (L).

903. -R.MN.1740. On step in garden, Chestnut Fm.
(B).

APPENDIX II

For the funeral of Phle de Carteret Esqr
Performed by the Society of upholsterers att Exeter Change London.

	£	s.	d.
A fine Puikt shroud sheet Pillow & Gloves	1	10	0
a double lid elm coffin covered with fine cloth and sett off with silver work and inscriptions	4	0	0
for lining the coffin with seare cloth to preserve the body	1	10	0
6 men in mourning & a flambeau to move the body to the Change		10	0
for hanging a Roome for the body with Cloth & floor covered	2	0	0
The next Roome for Relations hung with Cloth & floor covered	1	0	0
6 sylver candlesticks & stands by the body		10	0
24 large silver sconies for the Roomes	1	4	0
18 black ditto for ye great Roome & staircasse		4	6
20 lb ½ wax lights & tapers att 2	2	1	0
a large velvet pall		10	0
a velvet lidd & white plumes of feathers on the body	1	0	0
10 silk escutchons for the Pall	2	10	0
a hearse & six horses	1	0	0
6 mourning Coaches & 2 horses each	1	10	0
Paid to lady's frethwell coachman		5	0
17 plumes best white feathers for the hearse and horses	2	10	0
Coverings for the herse & howsings for the Horse of velvet	1	10	0
12 buckrum escotchons 12 shields for ye horses	3	0	0
3 fine cloakes for Gentl^m mourners		6	0
2 crape scarves for Dr London & Dr. Place	1	6	0
a crape Girdle for Dr London		8	0
7 best hadbands for Minister & mourners 3/6	1	4	6
8 paire best shamy gloves for ditto 3/6	1	8	0
5 pre womens best reble (?) shamy 4	1	0	0
4 pre white kids for ye 3 mst Philips & nurse		8	0
6 white sarsenet scarves for palbearers 13	3	18	0
6 white favors & 6 pre white kid gloves for do.	1	4	0
10 p^{re} white topt kid gloves 2	1	0	0
2 porters in mourning with gowns staves and white sarsenet scarves to attend att ye doore & hearse.		10	0
24 branch lights of white wax — 3/	3	12	0
24 men in mourning to carry them 18d.	1	16	0
7 cloakes for coachmen 18d		10	6
7 hatbands for ditto		14	0
10 white favours for do postilion & porters		10	0
24 do for the men that caryed the branch lights		12	0
35 prs white sheep Gloves for ditto Coachmen Postilion & porters	1	15	0
Printed tickets & wax & 2 men to deliver them		5	0
a Gold ring enameld with white	1	0	0

continued on the next page

	£	s.	d.
a Silver dish & rosemary		1	6
Pd for 4 quarts of Canary 3 q^rts of claret		15	0
a Silver server		1	0
Pd for the Parish of St Clement	5	0	0
4 white favours & 4 paires sheeps gloves for the Ladys frethwell Coach^n & foat^m & Sir Edm^d Andros. footmen & Mr Seales footmen		8	0
6 paires sheeps gloves for parish bearers		6	0
2 payres ditto for attendants		2	0
Gave the Poore att ye Church doore per order.		5	0
	£58	10	0
Returned in wax ends 13lbs.		13	0
	£57	17	0

Att the funerall of Phle de Carteret Esqr

Pale bearers.

Captn Charles Hardy	Mr. Edwd Maret	Mr. Edwd touzel.
Mr London Jones.	Mr John Seale se^r	Mr Durel.

Ministers.

Dr London.   Dr Place.

Dr Spaven ye minist^r that officiated.

Mourners.

Phle Pipon	Mr John Seale ju^r	M^ste Scott
Sr Edmond Andros	M^ste Rayford	M^ste Vautiere

Company.

Mr La fosse	Mr. Abram le Cornu.	Mr. Mulins per Ld Carteret
Mr Janoret	Mr Philips	Pr Philips. M^ste Philips
Mr Daniel Lafosse a favor	Mr Peter Maret a favor	2 daughters of M^ste Philips.
Mr. Harrison	Mr. Tapin	

From the inventory of Anne Seale (1703), grandmother of Philippe de Carteret. (In Société Jersiaise Library.)

APPENDIX III

Chart of Christian names in use

Boys	St. Martin			St. Peter		
Name	1700–09	1750–59	1800–09	1700–09	1750–59	1800–09
Aaron	5	2	1	—	—	—
Abraham	6	1	4	5	1	5
Alexandre	—	—	1	—	1	—
Amice	2	—	—	3	7	3
Benjamin	1	2	—	1	—	1
Charles	1	4	12	2	4	3
Clément	21	9	8	—	5	—
Daniel	2	2	2	2	1	2
David	4	2	4	—	1	1
Denys	1	—	—	—	—	—
Edmond	1	—	—	—	—	—
Edouard	5	7	4	9	14	10
Elie	9	5	11	11	14	8
Estienne	1	—	—	1	—	—
Ferdinand	—	—	1	—	—	1

continued on next page

Appendix III—Chart of Christian names in use—*continued*

Boys Name	St. Martin			St. Peter		
	1700–09	1750–59	1800–09	1700–09	1750–59	1800–09
François	11	10	12	9	7	18
Fréderick	—	—	4	—	—	2
Germain	—	—	—	1	—	—
George	10	10	29	1	2	20
Gidéon	—	—	—	1	—	—
Guillaume	2	1	—	—	2	—
Helier	1	—	3	1	—	2
Henri	—	—	2	3	2	2
Hugh	4	—	—	1	—	—
Isaac	2	1	—	—	—	—
Jacques	1	—	—	7	5	7
James	1	2	2	—	—	2
Jean	41	33	56	39	53	50
John	—	—	3	—	—	4
Joseph	—	—	1	—	—	—
Josué	—	3	9	—	4	9
Laurens	1	1	—	—	—	—
Martin	1	1	—	—	—	—
Mathieu	1	—	—	1	—	1
Michel	4	—	—	2	1	—
Moise	4	2	—	1	—	1
Nicolas	6	4	2	13	6	9
Noé	5	1	—	—	—	—
Philippe	30	30	41	27	33	33
Pierre	3	—	—	11	12	14
Raoul/Raulin	—	—	—	2	1	—
Renaud	2	—	—	—	—	—
Richard	1	—	1	—	3	—
Robert	1	—	—	—	—	—
Samuel	2	2	1	1	1	—
Simon	—	—	—	1	2	1
Sylvanus	—	—	—	—	—	1
Timothée	1	—	—	—	—	—
Thomas	19	9	24	3	10	7
Tom	—	—	1	—	—	—
Victor	—	—	1	—	—	—
William	1	2	4	—	2	5

Girls Name	St. Martin			St. Peter		
	1700–09	1750–59	1800–09	1700–09	1750–59	1800–09
Alise	—	—	—	1	—	—
Andrée	2	—	—	1	—	—
Anne	21	13	19	6	28	24
Apoline	1	—	—	—	—	—
Barbara	—	—	1	—	—	—
Betsy	—	—	7	—	—	7
Caroline	—	—	2	—	—	—
Carterette	—	—	—	—	—	3
Catherine	3	2	—	2	5	2
Debora	—	—	—	—	—	1
Douce	—	4	2	1	4	1
Eliza	—	—	1	—	—	—
Elizabeth	37	55	33	26	44	40
Esther	1	4	2	—	6	17
Françoise	3	5	9	1	2	2

continued on next page

Appendix III—Chart of Christian names in use—_continued_

	Girls	St. Martin			St. Peter		
Name		1700–09	1750–59	1800–09	1700–09	1750–59	1800–09
Harriet		—	—	—	—	—	1
Helena		—	—	—	—	—	1
Henriette		—	—	—	—	—	2
Hester		1	—	—	—	—	—
Jane		—	—	2	—	—	3
Jenny		—	—	4	—	—	—
Jeanne		30	23	24	11	24	31
Jeanneton		—	—	8	—	—	2
Mabel		1	—	—	—	—	—
Magdelaine		—	2	—	2	2	—
Marguerite		9	—	1	8	9	7
Maria		—	—	1	—	—	—
Marienne		—	—	1	—	—	—
Marie		51	30	50	16	35	34
Marthe		8	1	—	1	2	—
Mary		—	—	5	—	—	7
Molly		—	—	2	—	—	—
Nancy		—	—	7	—	—	8
Rachel		21	15	6	7	7	8
Sara		10	4	2	5	4	1
Sophie		—	—	3	—	—	4
Susanne		19	11	16	8	4	14
Suky		—	—	1	—	—	—
Totals							
Boys		214	317	453	159	194	222
Girls		218	169	209	96	176	229
Baptisms		432	486	662	255	370	451

APPENDIX IV
An inventory dated 1763

The inventory of the effects of Thomas Pipon fs Thomas, a merchant and ship owner, living on St. Aubin's boulevard.

Argenterie	Silverware
4 sallieres et shovels.	4 salt cellars and spoons.
1 stand complet.	1 stand complete.
2 boats.	2 sauce boats.
1 grande culie a soupe.	1 large soup spoon (ladle).
1 paire de pince a thé.	1 pr. tea tongs.
1 paire mouchette.	1 pr. candle snuffers.
1 porte do. plat.	1 flat snuffer holder.
1 caftiere.	1 coffee pot.
1 grand server.	1 large tray.
2 moindre do.	2 smaller trays.
1 culie a ponche.	1 punch ladle.
1 tankard.	1 tankard.
1 branche.	1 candelabra.
1 paire de chandelliers.	1 pr. candlesticks.
2 petites mogues.	2 small mugs.
1 grand paivrie.	1 large pepper pot(?).
1 pot a thé.	1 tea pot.
1 pot a deux hanches.	1 two-handled mug.
1 grand pot a deux hanches et un couverture.	1 large two-handled mug and cover.
1 coupe.	1 mug (cup).
12 culies a soupe.	12 soup spoons.
2 poivries.	2 pepper pots.
Argent fait à la maison. £110 d'ordre.	Money in the house. £110 d'ordre.

Utensils dans la cuisine de devant

Quatre haut chandelliers neufs de cuivre.
7 autres do., moindre de cuivre.
1 petit do pour une chandelle de cire.
2 portes mouchettes de cuivre.
2 do. plats.
3 caftiere de cuivre.
1 mortier et pilons.
1 rechaut do.
1 poivrier do.
2 grand couverture a chaudiere do.
1 grand mogue do.
1 cullier a pot do.
1 cercle do.
1 scrutore de Noyer plaqué.
1 table ovalle et 2 plians de mahogany.
1 ecran.
8 chaires enfonsés de Pavis.
1 grille de fer, & garde feu, do, pallette,
    poker & pincette do.
1 stand pour des verres de mahogany.
1 table rond de sape.
4 plats chandelliers.

Utensils in the front kitchen

4 new high copper candlesticks.
7 smaller copper ones.
1 small do for wax.
2 copper snuffer holders.
2 flat do.
3 copper coffee pots.
Pestle and mortar.
Copper heating pan.
1 copper pepper pot.
2 lge. copper pan covers.
1 lge. copper mug.
1 copper cooking ladle.
1 circular do.
1 walnut veneer writing desk.
1 oval table and 2 mahogany stools.
1 screen.
8 rush-seated chairs.
Iron grate, fire guard, shovel, poker and
    pincers.
1 mahogany stand for glasses.
1 round deal table.
4 flat candlesticks.

Dans le Parloir

Un scrutore avec des glaces.
Une table de marbre avec une frême.
Une table de mahogany avec deux pliants
    et un tapis.
Neuf chaires and un fauteuil de noyer enfonsé
    de toile travaillée.
Une table ronde à thé de mahogany.
Une mirror.
Trois caises, une contenant 12 coûteaux et
    fourchets a manche d'ivoire et six
    culliers d'argent, l'autre 11 coûteaux et
    fourchets do six cullieres d'argent une
    autre contenant une douzaine coutx et
    fourchets pour déssert.
Un board pour des verres.
Deux cages.
Un grille garni de cuivre, garde feu do et deux
    petits languest do, et pallete, pincettes
    et poker.
Le tableau de Mons Thos Pipon sr.
Idem celui de Thos Pipon escr.
Cinq caises avec des fleurs sous des verres.
Deux landskips.
Une paire pistolets, barils de cuivre.
Quinze tableaux avec des verres.
Une paire de Rideaux de fenestre,
Quatre servors de mahogany.
Deux do. de bois japane.
Dans le Book case du Scrutore.

In the parlour

Mirror-fronted writing desk.
Marble table with ? frame.
A mahogany table, with two stools and a
    carpet.
9 chairs and an armchair of walnut, seated
    with petit point embroidery.
A round mahogany tea table.
A mirror.
3 cases containing 12 knives and forks with
    ivory handles and six silver spoons,
    the other 11 knives and forks do.,
    6 silver spoons and another contain-
    ing 1 doz. dessert knives and
    forks.
A shelf for glasses.
2 cages.
Grate decorated with copper, also fender,
    2 small tongs, shovel, tongs and poker,
    all copper.
Portrait of Thomas Pipon.
Same, of Thomas Pipon escr.
5 cases with flowers under glass.
2 landscape pictures.
2 pistols with copper barrels.
15 glazed pictures.
A set of window curtains.
4 mahogany trays.
2 lacqueur trays.
In the bookcase over the desk.

(Seventy-two items follow. Some represent many volumes of a work. Languages are French, English, Latin and Greek. There are four volumes of the *Tatler*. A testament and two books of common prayer had silver clasps. The only item concerning the island is 'L'Histoire de Jersey. 1 vol.' probably Falle. There are several dictionaries.)

Dans la salle de derriere

Une table carée.
Une chaire de bois.
Un step de do.
Quatre chaires enfonsée de Pavie.
Un banc de sap.
Un ecran.
Un garde feu de fer.
Une paire languest de do.
Plusieurs broches.
Deux lachefrais de blancfer.
Deux chaudieres de cuivre.
Un pot a soupe.

In the back room

A square table.
A wooden chair.
Pair wooden steps.
4 rush-seated chairs.
A deal bench.
A screen.
An iron fender.
Pair of tongs.
Several spits.
2 white metal drip pans.
2 copper saucepans.
1 soup kettle.

Dans le cabinet de bas

Un scrutore.
Une longue table de sap.
Une Harmoire pour garder des vitailles.

Small room on ground floor

A desk.
A long deal table.
A food cupboard.

Dans la laverie

Un rack pour la vessailles.
Un server de mahogany pour six verres.
3 do pour des bouteilles.
1 Dressoir garni de Fiance.

In the wash-house

A rack for vessels.
Mahogany tray for six glasses.
3 do. for bottles.
A dresser with crockery.

Dans la Blue chambre

Une paire de tirroire de Noir Bois.
10 chaire.
1 Fauteuil.
1 Grand mirror.
1 Table and 1 dress glass.
1 Harmoire de Mahogany.
1 bois de lit avec des Rideaux de damas blue.
1 Lit de plume avec les Couvertures.

In the blue room

Chest of drawers in dark wood.
10 chairs.
1 armchair.
1 large mirror.
1 dressing table and glass.
1 mahogany cupboard.
1 bedstead with blue damask hangings.
1 feather bed and covers.

Dans la Rouge Chambre

1 paire de Tirroire de mahogany.
1 landskip.
8 chaire de mahogany enfoncées de damas
    rouge.
1 Fauteuil.
1 grand mirror.
1 table and 1 dressg glass.
1 Bois de lit avec des Rideaux de d'amas
    Rouge.
1 lit de plume avec des couvertures et Blanket.
2 Rideaux de fenestre.
1 table à thé.

In the red room

A mahogany chest of drawers.
1 landscape picture,
8 mahogany chairs seated in red
    damask.
1 armchair.
1 large mirror.
1 dressing table and glass.
1 bedstead with curtains in red
    damask.
1 feather bed with covers and blanket.
2 window curtains.
1 tea table.

Dans le Fohier

Une garniture de cuivre.

In the hearth

A copper ornament.

Dans de ding Room

Une grande table ovale de mahogany.
Une table à thé de do.
1 do de marble.
1 fontaine do.
1 grand mirror sur le Fohier.
1 do.
1 grille avec sa garniture.
10 chaire et un fauteuil.
Une quantité de portraits.
Une petite table a Escrire.

In the dining room

Large mahogany oval table.
Mahogany tea table.
1 marble table.
Bowl for rinsing hands?
A large mirror above the hearth.
1 do.
A grate with its furnishings.
10 chairs and an armchair.
A number of portraits.
A small writing table.

Dans la petite chambre

1 Harmoire de chene.
6 chaire.
1 mirror et une table.
1 bois de lit et tours de lit.
Une quantité de portraits.

In the little room

An oak cupboard.
6 chairs.
A mirror and a table.
Bedstead and hangings.
A number of portraits.

Dans les Montais

Une horloge.

On the stairs

A clock.

Dans le rouge grenier ou il y a un Fohier

8 chaire de cane.
1 scrutore de chene.
1 paire de tirroir.
1 grand mirror.
1 table et Dressg glass.
1 Harmoir a Habits de sap.
1 Boit de lit avec un lit de plume, Rideaux et Couverture et Tour de Lit rouge de Sarge.

In the red attic, where there is a fireplace

8 cane-seated chairs.
An oak writing desk.
A chest of drawers.
1 large mirror.
Dressing table and glass.
A deal clothes cupboard.
A bedstead, feather bed, curtains and covers, and bed hangings in red serge.

Dans le Rouge Grenier

2 grand Baheur de Roucie.
1 petite paire de Tirroir de chene.
1 table à thé.
1 Harmoire de chene.
10 chaire enfonses de cuir.
1 Boit de lit avec un Lit de Plume, Rideaux et couvertures et Tour de Lit Rouge.

In the red attic

2 big baheurs of Russian leather.
Small oak chest of drawers.
A tea table.
An oak cupboard.
10 chairs with leather seats.
1 bedstead with feather bed, curtains and covers, and red hangings.

Dans l'autre Grenier

1 Boit de Lit avec un Lit de Plume, Rideaux et couverture et Tour de lit Jaune de Camlost.
1 Table à thé.
1 petite mirror.
L'Equipage du defunt pr la Cavallerie, Selle, et Bride.
Calle du Cavallier.
2 Selles a homme.

In the other attic

A bedstead with a feather bed, curtains and covers and bed hangings in yellow camlot.
A tea table.
A small mirror.
The deceased's cavalry equipment with saddle and bridle.
Cavalry saddle.
2 men's saddles.

Vesselle d'Estaine

7 douzne de neuve assiettes.
2 Douzne de Plus Vielles.
3 douzne de Plats de differente sorts.
2 Jute, 2 quarte et 1 pinte.
1 douzne d'assiettes a Eau.
1 Tourtiere.
2 Couleraisse.

Pewter vessels

7 doz. new plates.
2 doz. older ones.
3 doz. dishes of various sorts.
2 measures, 2 quart and 1 pint.
1 doz. soup plates?
1 pie-dish.
2 sieves.

Linge

24 paire de draps.
22 Doublies de damas et marche.
6 do de toile.
9 douzne de serviettes.
3 do Dessuimains.
6 Pce de Toile d'abord la *Nancy*.

Linen

24 pairs sheets.
22 damask and cotton table cloths.
6 linen table cloths.
9 doz. serviettes.
3 doz. kitchen cloths.
6 lengths of linen cloth from on board the *Nancy*.

China et Terriée

5½ douzne de Blanche assiettes.
1 douzne de Plats do.
2 grand Bolle de China.
1 do moyenne.
2 douzne D'assiettes de do.
7 plats de do.
6 coupe a caffé de do.
1 Harmoire contenant un quantité de china.
Une quantité de verres de plusieurs sortes.

China and Terra cotta

5½ doz. white plates.
1 doz. white dishes.
2 large china bowls.
1 medium do.
2 doz. china plates.
7 china dishes.
6 china coffee cups.
A cupboard containing a quantity of china.
A quantity of glasses of various sorts.

Le Nombre des Bêtes

Quatre vache, dont il y a une que mon cher
        Père avoit donnée a ma soeur Nancy.
Quatre chevauts.
Un chariot a cheval et une charrué complete.
Une chaise a cheval etc.

Livestock

4 cows, one of which my dear Father gave
        to my sister Nancy.
4 horses.
A horse waggon and plough complete.
A horse-drawn chair etc.

Le nombre des Futailles

3 Tonnaux.
6 Pipes.
8 Barriques.
2 barrils.
Un boucaut de chucre.
1,000lb. de fer.

Number of barrels

3 tun measures (1 c. metre).
6 casks.
8 hogsheads (large barrels).
2 barrels.
A barrel of sugar (a dry measure).
1,000lbs. of iron.

Le Nouveaux Grain

Trois Mille de Froment.
Deux mille cinq cent D'Orge.
Trois cents de Faive.

New grain

Three thousand of wheat.
2,500 of barley (? sheaves).
300 of beans (? bundles).

Compte de Bois qui est sous le Sable.

1. Un Mast longeur 18 pieds.
2. Une spare do. 57 do.
3. Une do do 38.
Un Foteaux.
1 Quintal, Ballences et poids ou Pezées.
14 Fuzils et Mousquets.
1 Sling cart.

Account of wood on the beach

A mast 18ft. long.
A spar 57ft. long.
do 38ft. long.
1 barrel.
1 weighbridge, scale and weights.
14 rifles and muskets.

Achevé le dixhuite jr de Septembre 1764.

P. Mauger. Tutr.
Ph. Lempriere.
Thos Pipon.
Ph D'Auvergne.
Gideon Villeneufve.
Elie Le Gros.   Electrs.

Ce 18me Septembre 1764 Je certifie avoir en ma possession tout le contenu du Registre cy dessus que je moblige reproduire toutes fois et quantes a qi'il appartiendra en m'en delivrant mon (nom).   Anne Pipon.

APPENDIX V

A Chart of some Baheurs

Date	Initials	Lining	Trade card	Remarks
1680	MDLC	—	—	Marguerite de la Cloche, née de Carteret. v BSJ 1934, p. 319, OJH, Vol. I, p.48.
1686	MLB	—	—	Origins unknown.
1705	IH	Yes	—	Lightly studded on ends. On loan to Museum. Origin unknown.
1738	IP	—	—	Origins unknown.
1733	MOR	—	—	Marie Orange Roy.
1751	ELB	Yes	—	Elizabeth Le Boutillier m. Jean Le Roux.
1755	—	—	Richard Lucas	Origin unknown.
1756	ELG	—	—	Sold by auction for £140 in 1974. Lining not original.
1758	ILB	Yes	Richard Lucas	In 1762 it belonged to Thomas Labey who married his cousin Jeanne. Now belongs to their great-great-granddaughter in Canada.
1763	AV	—	—	Anne Villeneuve.

Undated Examples

Date	Initials	Lining	Trade card	Remarks
	MT	—	—	Name likely to be Thoreau.
	MLH	coarse linen	—	Marie Le Hardy, b. 1672, daughter of Charles and of Marie Le Sueur. Sister of Jean Le Hardy, Jurat and married Philippe Pinel 1698, d. 1752. Date of baheur likely to be 1698.
	EMG.	—	John Clements	Origin unknown.
	IV	Yes	—	Fitted with two drawers at base. Possibly Jeanne Vibert married Jean Arthur, *c.* 1735.
	RDSX	Lined with atlas dated 1810	—	Sold by auction in 1974 for £340.
	—	Yes	Edward Smith	Trade card says 'Trunkmaker to King George II'.
	—	Yes in lid	John Selby	Date 1727 in ink in lid. Body of trunk lined with *Nouvelle Chronique*, 1884.
	—	—	—	One time owner Miss M. L. Bosdet. Now belong to Victoria and Albert (Ref. 113/1908 M640/08. They paid £10 10s. in 1908.
Of 18 recorded the totals are:				
10	14	7	5	

A GLOSSARY OF SOME LOCAL TERMINOLOGY

Abreuvoir. A watering place, mainly for farm animals.

Appairiement. A list of lands held on a certain fief, naming the holders, and stating the services and dues owed by each of them. An 'appairiement' of a Crown fief was drawn up for the purpose of distributing the burden of serving as Prévôt amongst the tenants.

Assise d'Héritage. A sitting of the Heritage Division of the Royal Court, and which certain Seigneurs attend and answer in affirmation that they owe suit of court for their fiefs. Included among them is the Lieutenant-Governor who answers for the escheated ecclesiastical fiefs which became Crown property mostly at the Suppression of the Alien Priories in 1413.

Aveux. Declarations made to the Seigneur of a fief by his tenants giving particulars of their holdings.

Bailiff (Bailli). Chief Magistrate of the Island and President of the Royal Court and States of Jersey.

Bannelais. Road-sweepings collected by the owner of the adjoining land or, in some cases, sold by the parish authorities to be used as fertiliser.

Bannie aux rabais. Sale by auction to the lowest bidder. Used in cases when it was expedient to allocate the performance of a duty to the person who would perform it for the lowest fee.

Banon. The period between harvest and seed time when the open fields were proclaimed free as pasture for all the tenants of a fief.

Bénitier. A carved stone alcove, found in some Jersey houses, over 20 examples having been recorded. Probably a piscina or holy water stoup removed from a parish church or chapel at the time of the Reformation.

Branchage. Compulsory cutting of trees and overhanging branches by the owner of any land bordering a public highway.

Champart. Part of a crop due to the Seigneur of a fief, exacted on some fields, these being 'terres champartières'.

Chefs de Charrette. Principal tenants responsible in rotation for serving as prévôt or appointing a substitute. The expense of hiring a substitute fell collectively upon the Chef and his "aides" (smaller tenants).

Chefs Plaids. The most solemn sessions of a feudal court and of the Royal Court. The Assise d'Heritage is strictly Les Chefs Plaids d'Héritage.

Clameur de Haro. Procedure by which a person can stop an alleged wrong being committed on his real property, by calling "Haro, Haro, à l'aide mon Prince, on me fait tort". This acts as an immediate injunction, and is an ancient right calling for help to the first Duke of Normandy.

Clameur de marché de bourse. The legal action instituted against a purchaser of property by a person wishing to exercise his right of "retrait", q.v.

Colombier. Dovecote belonging to the manor house of a fief.

Constable. The civic head of each parish who represents it in the States, presides over the Parish Assembly, and is head of the parish police. There is no similarity with the English word Constable. The second rank in the honorary parochial police force is the Centenier, elected to be the Constable's chief assistant, and originally in charge of 100 homesteads.

Corvée. In origin every man owed a corvée of six days' labour working on the roads. Abolished only in 1938, though for some time previously the substitution of a money payment in lieu of labour had been allowed.

Côtil. A sloping, but usually cultivable, field.

Curateur. Somone elected or appointed to manage the affairs of someone unable to do this for himself.

Dame trutice. Name given to the mother of orphan children when she was chosen to be their guardian.

Décret. Obsolete form of bankruptcy proceedings, the object of which was to dispose of the debtor's real property.

Dégrèvement. Modified form of décret, introduced in 1880, in conjunction with other changes in the law of real property, to remedy injustices in the old system.

Désastre. Bankruptcy proceedings confined to the disposal of the debtor's moveable property for the benefit of his creditors.

Dîmes. A tenth part of produce which a householder had to cede to the parish Rector. This included wheat, apples, pigs, pears, calves, colts, hemp, flax, oats, peas and beans, and sea fish.

Electeurs. A group of persons, close relatives, neighbours and friends, summoned to elect a curateur or tuteur, to whom they then act as advisers.

Extente. List of the King's revenues, parish by parish, with the amounts payable to the Crown. Extentes for 1274, 1331, 1528, 1607, 1668 and 1749 have been published.

Fief. An estate held directly, or indirectly, from the Crown on condition that certain services, which varied considerably, were rendered.

Fougère. Fern (bracken) valuable as animal bedding.

Greffier. Clerk or secretary, of the Royal Court, the States or a feudal court.

Haugard (hogard). Stack yard of a farm.

Hougue. Barrow or mound, usually of neolithic or bronze age origin, and often surviving as a place name when the actual mound has disappeared.

Jonchère. A couch, the seat being stuffed with dried fern.

Lavoir. A communal washing place. When served by a stream rather than a spring it is often called a "douet à laver".

Lieutenant-Governor. Officer appointed to represent the Crown. Until 1854 there was a Governor, usually non-resident, who was himself represented by a Lieutenant-Governor. Until recent times it was always a military appointment, carrying with it the duty of Commander-in-Chief of the garrison and the militia.

Livres, sols and deniers tournois. Money minted at Tours and current in Jersey until 1835, the livre tournois then being worth about 9¼d. or 26 to the pound sterling. The Livre d'Ordre (or "Selon l'ordre du Roi") was also in use and worth 50 per cent. more, but was not so much a coin as a fictional sum resulting from the interpretation placed on an Order in Council of 1729 which made six liards instead of four as previously, equal one sol. The commonest coin was a liard.

Livre de Quittance. A pocket book in which a man kept an account of the rentes due by him, the recipient receipting them in the book.

Messier. Officer of a feudal court responsible for collecting stray cattle and other animals, their care while impounded, and the collection of fines due when the owners claimed them.

Manor. The residence of the Seigneur of a fief, originally situated thereon, but now sometimes elsewhere.

Partage. The sharing of an estate of a deceased person amongst his heirs.

Paûte or **pouchette.** Secret hiding place constructed in the thickness of a wall, used as a family safe. It was made with a tunnel as long as a man's forearm, ending in a pottery jar.

Percage. Sanctuary path leading from a parish church to the sea, by which a criminal could escape arrest, if he then embarked and left the Island for ever.

Préciput. In its oldest and widest sense, the share of an estate to which the eldest son, "l'aîné", was entitled. Later used in the more restricted sense of land which the principal heir is entitled to choose before the remainder is divided equally between all heirs. Sometimes called "Droit d'aînesse".

Prévôt. Officer of a feudal court who served summonses and collected all dues for the Seigneur. Until 1968 when the office of Prévôt was abolished, the Prévôts du Roi (or de la Reine) made declarations at the Assise d'Heritage of all persons who had died without direct heirs. The real estate of such persons who were tenants of the Crown fiefs was enjoyed for one year (année de jouissance, or année de succession) by the Crown. The Seigneurs exercised a similar right (now abolished) in respect of their own tenants.

Procureur. A person authorised to act on behalf of another person or body. A Procureur du Bien Publique is a trustee of parish property.

Rente. In origin a kind of ground rent payable to the grantor of land by the grantee out of the produce of the land. Even when the notion of absolute ownership of land had developed, a sale of land could be regarded as a perpetual lease, the purchaser paying no cash but agreeing instead to the perpetual payment of an annual rente to the vendor and his heirs. An owner of real property could also raise money by creating a rente secured on it without parting with the ownership. In this sense it resembles a loan secured on real property. Payment was formerly in kind, usually wheat, and for a long time it continued to be calculated according to the price of wheat each year.

Retrait féodal or **seigneurial.** A Seigneur could, if he wished, buy back any land sold on his fief, for the price paid for it, and the purchaser could not refuse to cede it.

Retrait lignager. A relative could compulsorily buy back land which had been sold to someone outside the family, again for the same price, and such transactions could not be refused if the sum was produced.

Royal Court. The Court of Justice, composed of the Bailiff and 12 Jurats, who are honorary elected judges. Until 1948 they also sat in the States, but have been replaced there by Senators.

Seigneur. Lord of a manor (fief). He held rights over the land of his fief but did not necessarily own the freehold of it all.

Sénéchal. Judge, or Chairman of a feudal court, acting as assistant to the Prévôt, deputising for him in his absence, and performing executive duties.

States. The Island Parliament comprising, before 1948, Jurats, Rectors, Constables and Deputies. Since that date it is composed of 12 Senators, 12 Constables, and 29 Deputies, all elected and all unpaid.

Tenant. Anyone owning property on a given fief.

Tenant après décret; or dégrèvement. The person who takes over the real property of a debtor, as a result of a décret or dégrèvement.

Tuteur. Guardian of a minor.

Tour d'échelle. The right to place a ladder on a strip of land adjacent to a building for the purpose of repairing the said building. Also used to denote the strip of land on which the right may be exercised.

Vergée. A local land measurement of approximately 2,150 English square yards, 2 and a quarter Jersey vergées being one English acre. The vergée contains 40 perch, and the perch 484 square feet.

Verp. A cattle pound serving a fief. Unique to Jersey.

Vessels:—

   Barque. Three-masted, square-rigged on fore and mainmast, fore and aft rigged on mizzen mast.

   Barquentine. As above, but square-rigged on fore mast only.

   Brig. Two-masted, square rigged.

   Brigantine. As above on fore mast, fore and aft rigged on main mast.

   Chasse-marée. French and Channel Islands only; like a lugger, but often square-rigged topsail and fore mast.

   Cutter. Similar to Smack, q.v.

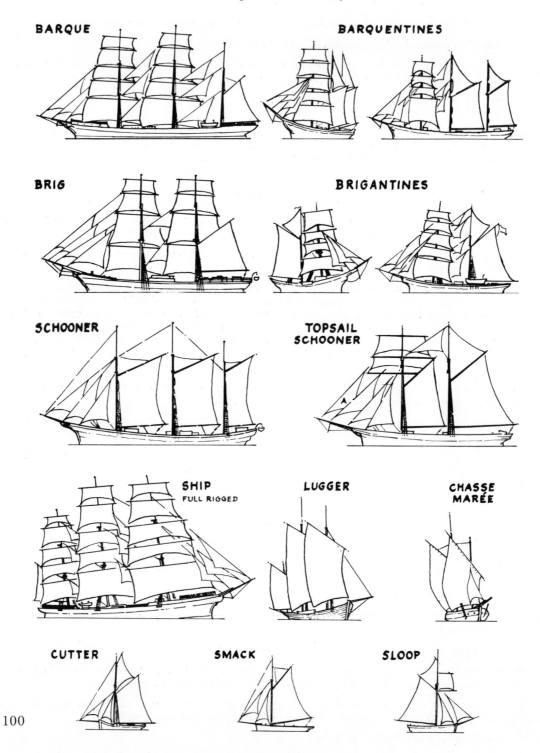

BARQUE   **BARQUENTINES**

BRIG   **BRIGANTINES**

SCHOONER   **TOPSAIL SCHOONER**

SHIP FULL RIGGED   **LUGGER**   **CHASSE MARÉE**

CUTTER   **SMACK**   **SLOOP**

100

TYPES OF VESSEL mentioned in this book:

drawn to approximate scale from descriptions and illustrations in :- Chambers', Nuttall's and the Century Dictionaries: the Observer's and Wonder Books of Ships: Bulletins of La Société Jersiaise 1963 & 1972: and Ansted's 'Channel Islands'. For clarity, rigging has largely been omitted. The flying jib mentioned in Chapter VII is marked 'A'.

C.G.S. Nov. 1978.

Lugger. Two- or three-masted quadrilateral sails slung fore and aft, but with part of sail in front of mast. Favourite vessel with smugglers.

Schooner. Two-masted, fore and aft rigged. Sometimes with more than two masts in the 19th century.

Schooner brig. See Topsail schooner.

Ship. Three-masted, square-rigged on all masts. Normally around 500 tons or more, but common at 200 tons or even less with locally-built vessels.

Sloop. Similar to Smack, q.v.

Smack. One mast, fore and aft rigged.

Snow. Two-masted, square rigged, as a Brig, but with a third mast only a foot or so away from the main mast to support a single fore and aft sail.

Topsail schooner. Two-masted, fore and aft rigged. Often more than two masts in the 19th century.

Vingtaine. A parochial division, varying between two and six per parish.

Visite Royale. Visit of the Royal Court and parish officials to inspect roads, with particular attention to encroachments or overhanging trees. Two parishes are visited each year.

Vraic. Local term for seaweed, formerly gathered in large quantities for fertiliser. "Le vraic venu" is cast up by the tide, but the more valuable type is "le vraic coupé", cut straight from the rocks.

Wheat measures. 1 quarter = 8 cabots wheat, or 12 cabots apples.; 1 cabot = 40lbs. (approximately) or 6 sixtonniers.

I am most grateful to Mr. S. W. Bisson for assistance in compiling the legal and feudal terms, and to Mr. A. Podger for the definition of types of vessel.

GLOSSARY OF SOME ARCHITECTURAL TERMS
(Vernacular architecture is that which is characteristic of a locality)

Architrave   Moulded frame surrounding a door or window.

Ashlar   Square hewn stone masonry.

Boss   Ornamental plaque at intersection of upright and horizontal parts of an architrave.

Dower wing   Section of a Jersey house, usually built on to the east or west, for retired or widowed parents. The earliest example recorded is at Le Taillis, (Mt) 1751.

Double pile   Term employed in this book to indicate a house built two rooms deep from front to back.

Gable wall   End wall of a house, usually east or west in Jersey, built very substantially, thicknesses of up to 8ft. being recorded.

Guernsey fenestration   On the ground floor, two windows on one side of the entrance door and one on the other side; fairly rare in Jersey but common in Guernsey.

Marriage stone   A stone with carved initials and usually a date and a carved motif of one or two hearts. It records a marriage which could have taken place many years before the carving of the stone, the husband's name being on the left and the wife's on the right. The names are almost always recorded syllabically. There is a great variety in such stones.

Roof   Within the period covered by this book the main types of roof were:
1. In single pile houses, double pitched.
2. In double pile houses either symmetrical or asymmetrical, double pitched.
3. Twin double pitched.
4. Hipped, with or without parapet.

Mansard roofs were rare. The parapet appeared mainly, though not entirely, in the town. The dower wing could be added to any type, and occasionally had a different type of roof from the main house.

Stairs   *Baluster.* Short post or pillar, in a series and supported by a handrail.
Flying staircase. A curving flight, not supported by any continuous newel or string, and which has no visible support except the wall into which it is built.
Newel. Central post in a winding staircase, or the upright member at the base of the stairs, or at the intersection of the flights.
Riser. Vertical surface of a step.
String. Continuous member supporting a flight of steps.
Tread. Horizontal surface of a step.
Pendant. The bottom end of the newel, taken through the ceiling of the lower flight, and carved or turned. In later examples this was merely applied, and so decorative, but not functional.

(I am indebted to Pevsner's *Dictionary of Architecture* and to my son John Stevens, A.R.I.B.A., for some of the above definitions.)

TYPES OF ROOF
(seen from the gable-end)

IN SINGLE-PILE HOUSES

DOUBLE-PITCH, *without or with Dower Annexe (which may be present with any roof type)*

IN DOUBLE-PILE HOUSES

ASYMMETRICAL DOUBLE-PITCH

SYMMETRICAL & TWIN DOUBLE-PITCH

 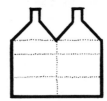

HIPPED

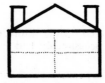 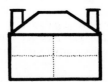

HIPPED, WITH PARAPET

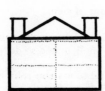 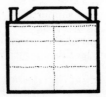

A SELECT BIBLIOGRAPHY OF RELEVANT LOCAL WORKS

Actes des Etats 1524–1800. (A.E.)

Balleine, G. R., *The Bailiwick of Jersey*, 1951, revised 1970; *A Biographical Dictionary of Jersey* (B.D.J.); *A History of Jersey*, 1950; *The Tragedy of Philippe d'Auvergne*, 1973.

Bisson, S. W., *Jersey, our Island*, 1950.

Bulletins, La Société Jersiaise, annually from 1873. (B.S.J.)

de Gruchy, G. F. B., *Medieval Land Tenures*, 1957.

de la Croix, *Jersey et ses antiquités*, 1859.

Durell, Rev. E., *A Picturesque and Historical Guide to the Island of Jersey*, 1847.

Inglis, H. D., *The Channel Islands*, 1838.

Le Couteur, Rev. François, *Traité sur le cidre*, 1806.

Le Maistre, Dr. Frank, *Dictionnaire Jersiais Français*, 1966.

Le Quesne, Charles, *A Constitutional History of Jersey*, 1856.

Lemprière, Raoul, *A Portrait of the Channel Islands*, 1970; *A History of the Channel Islands*, 1974.

Marett, R. R., *A Jerseyman at Oxford*, 1941.

Mayne, Richard, *Old Channel Islands Silver*, 1969; *Mailships of the Channel Islands*, 1971; *Jersey through the Lens* (with Joan Stevens), 1975.

Messervy, Daniel, *Le Journal de . . . 1769–72*. Published 1896.

Nicolle, E. T., *The Town of St. Helier*, 1931.

Payne, J. Bertrand, *An Armorial of Jersey*, 1859.

Plees, W., *An Account of the Island of Jersey*, 1817.

Quayle, T., *General View of the agriculture . . .*, 1815.

Stead, J., *A Picture of Jersey*, 1809.

Stevens, Joan, *Old Jersey Houses*, Vol. I, 1965; *Victorian Voices*, 1969.

Stevens, Charles, 'Jersey Place Names', 1975. (In typescript in Museum Library.)

INDEX

(*Note*: The initial in brackets after the name of a house indicates the parish in which it is situated. Persons listed in the schedule of initialled stones, Appendix I, are not included in this index. It has not always been possible to differentiate between two people of the same name.)

245

JERSEY FIEFS

A provisional map of Fiefs recorded from the 1...

Fifteen Fiefs owing Suite de Cour, in capitals: the five in bold capitals are Fiefs Nobles.

Anneville. 4D.
DES ARBRES. 6A.B.
à l'Archier. 4D. 11B.
La Fosse Astelle. 11A.
d'Audeport. 4D. 11B.
DES AUGRÈS. 7A.C.
L'Aumône, (My.) 2A.C.
L'Aumône, (C). 11c.
d'Aval. 1c.
Evêque d'Avranches. 2A.3c.

Bagot. v. Gorges.
Barbey, Wm. v. Monts.
ès Baudains. 10D.
Bekalowe. 6c.
Abbé de Bellozanne. 7c.
Besnard. 7c. 10A.
Boutvilain. 2B.
du Buisson. 10A.
Burrier. 4c.
Abbesse de Caen. 4c. 7c. 2D.3c.
ès Cambrès. 6D.
de la Carrière. 11c.
Câtelet. 2c.D.
Chapelle. 1B.
Chastel Sedeman. 7B.
Chesnel. 2B.
Chevalier. 8B.
Collette des Augrès. 10A.
du Compte. 4D. 11B.
Crapedoit. 10D.
ès Cras. 7A.

Damereine. 11c.
ès Débénaires. 7c. 10A.
DIÉLAMENT. 3D. 7A.B.
Houque Dirvaud. 6c.
Caruée ès Dirvaux. 4c. 7B.
Douze Mancelles. 1D.

Ecrivisseur. 10A.
Egon. 10D.
Elie. 1D.
Escraqueville. 1B. 2A.
Estat. (for Roi, 1651-58).
Estourny. 4c.
Caruée Everard. 4c.

ès Faisants. 10D.
Faledoit. 11A.
ès Félars. 6D.
Fello, Feslot. 3D.
Ferons. v. Ferrans.
Ferrans. 2B.
Les Fiefs. 4A.
Fière-brache. 2D.
Fille de Carteret. 4c. 10A. 11A.
ès Fondans. 5B.
à la Fornière. 2D.
La Fosse. 10A.c.
La Fosse Astelle. v. Astelle.
FRANC FIEF EN ST. BR. 5D. 6c.
Franche Mauvellerie. 7B.

Ganouaire. 2c.
Garis. v. St. Germain.
Godeaus. v. Godelière.
Godelière. 6D. 7c.
Gombrette. 2B.
Gorges, ou Bagot. 10A.B.
Grainville. 7c. 10A.
Grand Port. 11a.
Gruchetterie. 3c.D.
ès Gruchys. 3D.
au Guenetier. 10B.

LA HAGUE. 5B. 6A.
ès Hammonds, Hammonets. 5B. 7A.
Handois. v. St. Germain.

ès Hâtains. 6D.
Haulloche. 3c.
Henot. 2D. 3c.
Hérupe. 2D. 3c.
du Homet. 10D.
ÈS HORMANS. 5B.
Houque Dirvand. v. Dir.
La Hougue. 7D.
La Houguette, (S). 10A.
La Houguette, (T). 7A.
Hubert. 7A.
Pierre Hugon. 7D.

Jourdain Payn. v. Payn.

Lanchestre. 1D.
La Lande. 3c.
Lemprière. 7c. 11B.
Lecq. 1B.
Léoville. 1D.
Longueville. 10B.
LUCE DE CARTERET. 5D.
Lulague. 2B.

Malet. 11A.
Maret. 2B.
MELECHES. 2A. 6B.D.
Moissonière. 10D.
Mont Néron. 7c.
des Monts/Wm Barbey. 11c.
Morers. v. Ouville.
Morville. 1c.D. 5A.
La Motte/St. Ouen en St. Hélier. 10A.

Mottier dit ès Poing-destres. 2A.B.
Mourier. v. Lulague.
des Mouriers. v. Ouville.
La Moye. 8B.

au Neveu. 6D.
Nièmes. 5B.
Nobretez. 6A.
Noirmont. v. Prieur.

Orillande. 1D.
Orville. v. Ouville.
d'Ouville. 2A. 6A.

au Pareur. 2a.
Patier. (O). 5B.
La Ville Patier. (S). 10B.
Payn, Guille. 3D.
Payn, Jourdain. 6B.
Paynel. 6D.
ès Payns. 10A.
Petit Rozel. 3D.
Petran. 7D.
Petrivilla. v. Prieur de St. Clément.
Caruée ès Philippes. 11A.
Pierre Hugon, v. Hugon.

Pinel. v. Chesnel.
Poingdestre. 7A.
ÈS POINGDESTRES/Mottier. 2A.B.
Ponterrin. 7B.
Portinfer. 1A.
au Prieur de:-
l'Islet. 7c. 10A.
l'Islet, du Mont Cochon, ou de St. Laurent. 6D.
Noirmont. 9A.C.
St. Clément. 10D.
St. Pierre. 6A.

Quatorze Quartiers. v. St. Germain.
Quetivel. 6B.
de Quetteville. 4c.
Robeline, Robillard. 1c.
Le Roi (The Crown). passim
Rondiole. 10A.
Roszel. 7c.
ROZEL. 4A.

St. Clair. 6D.
St. GERMAIN. 2D. 6B.

St. Hilaire. 5B.
St. Jean la Hougue Boëte. 2D.
FIEF HAUBERT DE ST. OUEN 1c.D. 5B.
ST. OUEN en St. Hélier. 10A.
ST. OUEN en St. Sauveur. 7B.
SAMARÈS. 10.c.D.
au Sauteur. 11A.
Sauvalle. 5D.
Saval. 3D. 4A.
Sotel. 6A.c.
Surville. 7A. 10A.

Tapon. 10B.
Tourgis. 3A.

Triquel. 3D.
LA TRINITÉ. 3c. 7A.
ès Unfreis. 2B.
Vanesse. 3D.
Varin. 2B.
Vaugaléme. 11A.
ès Verrants. 10A.B.
au Vesque. 1D. 2c.
Vinchelez de Bas. 1A.B.
Vinchelez de Haut. 1A.B.D.
Vingt Livres. 2c. 5B.D. 6A.

FIEFS IN ... OF ST. H...

1.2. Surville
3.4.5. ès Déb...
6. Prieur de...
7. ès Payns.
8. Rondiole.
9. La Motte, ... en St. H...
10. L'Ecrivis...

UNLOCATED ...

Andruy. G. 1331.
Angot. J.L. 1309.
les Azelynes. H. 1274.
Baon et Mourant. 15... c.
ès Benests. L. 1445.
Beton. My. 1331.
Blancs Eperons. v. Ric.
les Boffoors. L. 1331.
au Borc, Bore. L. 1331.
Boule. P. 1331.
Bourgage. P.
Bradifer. P. 1274.

(map labels)

Mottier dit ès Poingdestres
d'Ouville, d'Orville, des Mouriers, Morers
ès Ferrans: M...
au Pareur: ès ...
Varin?
L'Evêque d'Avranches
Lulague dit ès Mourier
Boutvil...
Catelet
Vinchelez de Bas
Vinchelez de Haut
Portinfer
Lecq
Chapelle
Escraqueville
au Vesque
Ganouaire
Léoville
Lanchestre
Vinchelez de Haut
ST. OUEN
Orillande
STE. MARIE
LE ROI
MELEC...
Robillard
Douze Mancelles
Aval
Morville
Morville
ès Hâtains
ès Fondans
ST. OUEN
St. Hilaire
St. Hilaire
ès Hammonds
LA HAGUE
Vingt Livres
Nobretez
Sotel
d'Ouville
DES ARBRES
Nièmes
ÈS HORMANS
LA HAGUE
ST. PIERRE
Prieur de St. Pierre
LE ROI
LE R...
5
6
LUCE DE CARTERET
Sauvalle
Hougue Dirvaud
Sotel
Bekalowe
FRANC FIEF EN ST. BRÉLADE
ès Camb...
MELECHES
? ès Neve...
LE ROI
LE ROI
Fief Chevalier
La Moye
ST. BRÉLADE
Prieur de Noirmont
Prieur de Noirmont
8
9